Morality, Crime
and Social Control
in Europe 1500–1900

Morality, Crime and Social Control

in Europe 1500–1900

Edited by
OLLI MATIKAINEN &
SATU LIDMAN

FINNISH LITERATURE SOCIETY • HELSINKI

STUDIA HISTORICA 84

Finnish Historical Society has selected
peer reviewers for this content.

© Olli Matikainen, Satu Lidman and SKS

ISBN 978-952-222-572-6
ISSN 0081-6493
www.finlit.fi/kirjat
Taitto: Keski-Suomen Sivu Oy
Painotyö: Hansaprint Oy, Vantaa 2014

Contents

HISTORIES OF SOCIAL CONTROL 7
Olli Matikainen & Satu Lidman

I Rebelling Individuals 17

"THE CHILD WHO STRIKES HIS OWN FATHER OR MOTHER SHALL BE PUT TO DEATH" 19
Assault and Verbal Abuse of Parents in Swedish and Finnish Counties 1745–1754
Jonas Liliequist

NAMING PRACTISES AS A SOCIAL CONTROL 43
The Continuity and Change of Morals in Local Peasant Communities (c. 1850–1960)
Sofia Kotilainen

THE CRIME AND PUNISHMENT OF A NINETEENTH-CENTURY FINNISH SERIAL KILLER 75
Teemu Keskisarja

II Community and Discipline 85

TO REPORT OR NOT? TO PUNISH OR NOT? 87
Between Tightening Laws, Old Habits and Loyalty in Early Modern Bavaria
Satu Lidman

LEGISLATIVE AND JUDICIAL EFFECTS OF FORBIDDEN SEXUALITY ON ENGAGEMENTS AND MARRIAGES IN LATE NINETEENTH-CENTURY CENTRAL FINLAND 107
Pasi Saarimäki

IMPROVING THE CHRISTIAN COMMUNITY 127
Agents and Objects of Control in Early Modern Church Visitations
Päivi Räisänen-Schröder

AN ARROGANT ARRENDATOR AND CONFLICT IN CHURCH RENOVATIONS IN THE MID-EIGHTEENTH-CENTURY PARISH OF KOKEMÄKI 157
Ella Viitaniemi

III On the Margins of the Society 183

WAR, SOLDIERS AND CRIME IN MODERN BRITAIN 185
Issues for Research
Clive Emsley

THE CONTROL OF VAGRANTS AND THE POOR IN FINLAND 1850–1885 207
Päivi Pukero

SHE "TOOK HIM TO TEMPLE LANE, SUBSEQUENTLY HE MISSED HIS MONEY" 225
Prostitutes and Thieves in Dundee 1865–1925
Suki Haider

IV The Ultimate Power over Life and Death 257

THE POPE'S SWORD 259
Early Modern Capital Punishment, Homicide and Cultures of Suffering – Rome in the European Context
Tomás A. Mantecón

EXECUTIONS IN THE EIGHTEENTH- AND NINETEENTH-CENTURY 299
Messages, Interpretations, and Reactions
Martin Bergman

AMNESTY OR INDIVIDUAL PARDONS? 323
Presidential Pardon as a Measure to Control Those Punished as a Result of Disciplinary Proceedings in Finland in 1918
Virpi Anttonen

ABSTRACT 351

LIST OF CONTRIBUTORS 353

INDEX 357

Histories of Social Control
Olli Matikainen & Satu Lidman

This book, based on a series of papers presented at a conference entitled *Morals and Institutional Change*[1], explores key themes in European history through a variety of case studies, all falling under the much-debated concept of "social control". A wide range of regulated practices and institutions that mediate action between humans – or between humans and the supernatural – can be treated as manifestations or forces of social control: family, local courts, parish meetings, prisons, the army and the gallows (to name a few discussed in this volume). A common feature of all these institutions is the way in which they develop a set of practices and rituals, some of which are enduring and seemingly unchanging, some in a state of transition or subjected to challenges, and others "new" and in the process of formation.

Early sociologists and historians often used the term social control as a broad heuristic tool, without offering any exact definition of the concept.[2] This vagueness was criticized in the 1980s most notably by Stan-

---

1   Held at the University of Jyväskylä, 14.–15.8.2008, the Conference was funded by Academy of Finland. The editors are thankful to Richard McMahon and Liz Eastcott for their valuable comments during the publication process.
2   See, for example, Martin Innes, *Understanding Social Control: Deviance, Crime and Social Order* (Buckingham 2003); Matthieu Deflem, "The Concept of Social Control.Theories and Applications". Paper presented at the International Conference "Charities as Instruments of Social Control in 19th century Britain" (Université de Haute Bretagne, Rennes, France, November 22–23, 2007), www.mathieudeflem. net; James J. Chriss, *Social Control. An Introduction* (Oxford 2007); Lara Kuhn, *Social Control and Human Nature: What is it we are Controlling?* (Newark 2009).

ley Cohen, who called social control a "Mickey Mouse concept" covering everything from "infant socialization to public execution".[3] Cohen subscribed to a narrower definition that reserved the concept primarily for analysing planned responses to crime and deviance, which in practice emphasizes the role of state organizations. In the German research tradition the term *Sozialdisziplinierung*, "social discipline", has been used by Heinz Schilling, among others, to describe the societal reactions and efforts of authorities to root out deviance and other forms of unwanted behaviour.[4] Order and discipline have been regarded as key concepts and forces in the history of early modern Europe.

Cohen's position was critiqued by Pieter Spierenburg in the two-volume *Social Control in Europe* (2004), which rapidly became a classic in this research field. According to Spierenburg, the main methodological weakness in Cohen's position is representing society as an actor.[5] In defining social control, Spierenburg prefers to build on the legacy of Edward Ross and early American sociology, encompassing all members of society and all institutions serving social control functions. He argues cogently that attention should be drawn "to the relationships between various mechanisms inducing people to act in a way that is desirable according to a certain standard or ideal". From this perspective, analysing forms of social control as a means of dealing with conflicts has become a central idea.[6]

In the volume at hand, both the ideas of Cohen and Spierenburg are present. On the one hand, most of the contributions could fit into the narrower definition of social control by Cohen, since they put the focus on deviance and top-down or aristocratic control of crime. On the other hand, the focus on interaction and agency stressed by Spierenburg also takes a central role in the articles. In addition, some authors introduce

---

3 Stanley Cohen, *Visions of Social Control. Crime, Punishment and Classification* (Oxford 1985), pp. 1–3.
4 See, for example, the many books and edited volumes by Heinz Schilling, especially in: *Kirchenzucht und Sozialdisziplinierung im frühneuzeitlichen Europa* (Berlin1994), and more recently in: *Early modern European civilization and its political and cultural dynamism* (Lebanon 2008).
5 Pieter Spierenburg, "Social Control and History: An introduction". In: Herman Roodenburg & Pieter Spierenburg (ed.), *Social control in Europe 1500–1800* (Ohio 2004), pp. 1–10.
6 In sociology, this standpoint is often associated with Donald Black´s theoretical work: Donald Black, "Konflikthanterings elementära former". In: Malin Åkerström(ed.), *Kriminalitet, kultur, kontroll* (Stockholm 1996), pp. 55–78.

even more "counterintuitive" ideas of social control,[7] where the institution at first sight seems to fulfil functions different from control (see, for example, Kotilainen on nicknames), yet ultimately actually carries it out.

Spierenburg's commentary on Cohen is perhaps very critical, but for researchers of social control it is interesting to observe how the controversy reflects wider paradigmatic shifts in the field. Early American sociology stressed conformity and consensual understanding of social control, but later revisionist histories, like Cohen's, emphasized repression and coercion. In other words, perceptions of social control became decidedly negative. Revisionist histories drew their influence from two very different theoretical traditions. Marxism was popular, especially in the 1970s, and for decades it was almost impossible to write anything on social control without mentioning the post-structuralist philosophy of Michel Foucault.[8] Marxism and some post-structural studies were criticised for ignoring individual agency, a standpoint that has been traditionally central in historical studies. However, after the 1980s, the influence of Marxism waned and the "linguistic turn" increased interest in microsociology and the cultural meanings of social control.[9]

The "cultural turn" was perhaps anticipated by Bruce Lenman and Geoffrey Parker in 1980, when they published their influential and often cited article on state, community and criminal law in Early Modern Europe. The authors sharply rejected the quantitative methods used by some of their colleagues as "fruitless". Their emic perspective on history went perhaps to an extreme, when they argued, "contemporaries did not normally think numerically".[10] During the last decades, qualitative perspectives have dominated the field of historical social control research, and so the interest in local communities and court records is also well

---

7 Similar ideas are to be found in Matthieu Deflem, "The Concept of Social Control".
8 Stanley Cohen & Andrew Scull, "Social Control in History and Sociology" In: Stanley Cohen & Andrew Scull (ed.), *Social Control and the State* (Cambridge 1983), pp. 1–7.
9 Mayer, John A., "Notes Towards a Working Definition of Social Control in Historical Analysis". In: Cohen & Scull, *Social Control and the State*, pp. 17–21.
10 Bruce Lenman & Geoffrey Parker, "The State, the Community and the Criminal Law in Early Modern Europe". In: V. A. C. Gatrell & Bruce Lenman & Geoffrey Parker (ed.), Crime and the Law. The Social History of Crime in Western Europe since 1500 (London 1980), p. 47.

reflected in the articles of this volume (see, for example, Lidman on Bavarian practice).[11]

*

The authors of this collection offer a close reading of a wide variety of primary sources including court records, jurisprudence and legislation as well as newspapers, administrative sources and folklore, to mention only a few. Of course, analysing the discourses of narrative sources is of major importance, but the development of new methods of "bean-counting" is not overlooked either, especially when they provide a firm basis for social analysis. These influences are seen in the careful combination of both quantitative and qualitative aspects in the analysis of experienced scholars that have, over their careers, lived through various paradigmatic changes (see, for example, Liliequist on the use of court records).

Combined with morality and crime, social control is one of the key terms assisting in understanding the shared European past. Therefore, the articles in *Morality, Crime and Social Control in Europe 1500–1900* span a long time from the beginning of the early modern period up to the twentieth century, and a wide geographical spread from various places in Finland and other Nordic countries to continental Europe and the British Isles. Nonetheless, the contributions to the volume have much in common, as they all explore the applicability of the concept of social control to their area of research.

Furthermore, it is worth noting that histories of social control are typically *longue durée* histories. There is always a tension between social order and the institutions of social control, which is often reflected, for example, in inherited or out-dated laws. Historians tend naturally to study communities and time periods in which the institutions of social control are in transition, as these kinds of settings offer more

---

11 On recent research trends, see overviews in: *The Use of Court Records and Petitions as Historical Sources*. Frühneuzeit-Info. Herausgegeben vom Institut für die Erforschung der Frühen Neuzeit (Jahrgang 23: 2012): Jonas Liliequist & Martin Almbjär, "Early Modern Court Records and Supplications in Sweden" (c. 1400–1809), pp. 7–23; Anu Koskivirta, "Medieval and Early Modern Court Records in Finland" (c. 1400– 1809), pp. 24–32; Simon Sandall, "Pre-Modern Court Records in England" (c. 1400–1809), pp. 33–44.

fruitful ground for research. The problem of loosening bonds is evident in many contributions to this volume, and the various ways in which social control is perceived by the authors widens understanding of the complexity and richness of this phenomenon.

Yet, does the current interest in microsociology, meanings and discourses mean that historians have abandoned "society" as an analytical concept? This is a critical question that has often been raised lately both in history and in sociology, and is worthy of deeper consideration in the light of the articles in this volume. Furthermore, in recent research on crime and criminals it has become more common to emphasize individual factors when explaining deviant behaviour: among others Steven Pinker has discussed the new findings in biology that have contributed to this tendency.[12] Therefore, the key methodological challenge for all the authors of the volume has been to combine the actions of "real people" with perhaps not the model of "society" as an actor, but at least certain impersonal standards and ideals that could also be stated as forces of social control.

*

Unquestionably, social control is closely linked with the fact that people live in society; from birth until the end of their lives people are influenced by and connected to other individuals. At this micro-level of the human lifespan, family is the primary starting point for the socialization of every individual, and most individuals relate to society through their family and childhood experiences. The articles in this book are meant to form a kind of "life history of social control" from its exercise within the family and local communities to interventions at the highest state level. Therefore, the first section of the volume, *Rebelling individuals*, provides examples of social control from individual perspectives. It opens with Jonas Liliequist's analyses of domestic violence against parents, such as different kinds of assaults, disrespect and insults towards one's own fa-

---

12 Steven Pinker, *The Better Angels of our Nature. The Decline of Violence in History and its Causes* (New York 2011).

ther or mother in early modern Sweden and Finland. Liliequist exposes the social meanings and practices associated with the abuse of parents.

In eighteenth-century Sweden abusing one's parents was considered to be an important issue within the criminal justice system and, as such, it received public attention and called for interventions. Modernization, however, gradually led in the opposite direction, towards what Liliequist calls the "modern silence" on the issue of violence against elderly people. Another "victim" of modernization was patriarchy, a former cultural cornerstone of European societies. In the article that follows, Sofia Kotilainen argues that in traditional society, the reputation of an individual was defined linguistically, and therefore nicknames, like name-giving in general, were forms of social control. Modernization and the decline of ties with kinsfolk and the local community – seen in Finland in the latter part of the nineteenth century – did not end the use of nicknames. However, nicknames changed from their earlier meaning, and they began to function more as "humorous sobriquets" – and less as means of social control.

In his essay, Teemu Keskisarja describes an unusual fake execution of the "serial murderer" Johan Adamsson that "took place" in Finland in January 1853. In folktales Adamsson soon became known by many wholly negative nicknames, including *kerpeikkari* ("the executioner"). At the same time, his fate did not escape the notice of nineteenth-century medical specialists and other contemporary commentators, and they judged him to be a simple person, who found it difficult to distinguish between good and evil. Whatever his personal qualities might have been, the trajectory of his life seems to provide a classic example of a criminal career: from his broken family background and childhood poverty, to his involvement in petty crime and finally to serious offences. In the end, this case stemmed from power or rather the lack of it: the outrageous murders were, concludes Keskisarja, acts of "revenge" upon society.

The life story of the murderer Adamsson, as well as many of the cases analysed in the second part of this volume, *Community and discipline*, seem to document how difficult it is to return from a criminal path when crimes become routine; being labelled by the community contributes to a downward spiral into more serious criminality and violence. The microhistorical studies of Satu Lidman, Pasi Saarimäki, Päivi Räisänen-Schröder and Ella Viitaniemi also challenge the simplified dichotomies of elite versus popular cultures and formal state control versus informal control of local communities. The authors of the second part all adopt this approach in their articles, even though at first sight these studies may seem to be culturally distant from each other. In fact, practices in the southern parts of sixteenth-century Germany as well as in eighteenth- and nineteenth-century rural Finland can all be interpreted as manifestations of the similar European tradition of discipline and control emerging during the era of Reformation and counter-Reformation.

In sixteenth-century Munich, tightening control over sexuality led to a system of double standards and an unrealistic "new morality", in which the official "truth" was more intolerant than everyday practices. Late nineteenth-century Finland, a society caught in a transitional phase, faced a similar problem: inherited, outdated legislation (stemming from the early modern period) ensured that local courts in Finland were kept busy with issues such as fornication and adultery, even though "sinners" were no longer actively controlled, as they had been during the former culmination period of church discipline. In her study of sixteenth-century church visitations in Württemberg, Räisänen-Schröder uncovers common ground in the value systems of officials and local people. According to her, visitations "represent a clear institutional change that allowed new forms [...] of control." The case study by Viitaniemi, on the twists and turns of eighteenth-century church building processes, treats "the people" as active agents within the society, being rather capable of "political" action than faceless objects of social control. Yet, social control was also an element of that society, and therefore no individual could escape from it totally.

As the studies in this volume show, the overwhelming majority of persons brought before courts in different historical moments are young men. They originate from the "rougher elements of society", as Clive Emsley points out in his article on the impact of war on crime that opens the third part of this book, entitled *On the margins of the society*.

At least their crimes and verdicts have forced these men – but in a similar manner the female convicts as well – more or less to the margins of the society. They have been labelled through their position in the arena of social control. The current paradigmatic change in the history of crime and criminal justice has witnessed a change from the Marxist-influenced "societal" approach towards more individually-oriented and gendered perspectives. Methodologically this trend has been paralleled by an emphasis on qualitative methods. However, and as Emsley argues, the major social structures still need to be considered and quantitative methods have to be developed. The social problems and criminality connected with the military during and after the war appears to be a delicate and surprisingly under-studied issue in modern society.

Closed institutions, such as vagrancy and prostitution, are subjects that have traditionally been at the core of research on crime and criminal justice, and in their articles Päivi Pukero and Suki Haider address the control of crime and the poor who lived on the margins of society. Pukero analyses the classic problem of the emergence of asylums, within the context of nineteenth-century Finland. She remains doubtful that "hidden Foucauldian agendas" can be discerned in the control of vagrancy. Instead, she argues, the motives for establishing workhouses seemed to be utilitarian and, to some extent, largely economic. Interestingly, Suki Haider takes the same practical point of view in her examination of the lives of the women living on the margins of Dundee, emphasising the need to make one's living rather than "discourses" of crime. Practising prostitution or theft were not necessarily related phenomena, or connected to the same individuals, but they were still different sides of the same coin and economic cycles within local trade affected the rates of both crimes. Typically, they belonged to the core issues that contemporaries tried to solve by the means of something that has later been labelled as social control.

As shown in the last part of this volume, *The ultimate power over life and death*, the extreme instruments of social control were the gallows. In their contributions, Thomas Mantecón and Martin Bergman consider the history of the death penalty in the context of social control. Mantecón charts the decline in the number of symbolic executions in southern European cities – the turning point being the mid-seventeenth century. He links the reasons for this development to contemporary discussions about the civilization process, as well as to a certain sensitization towards violence that gradually resulted in public executions being viewed as a nuisance. He is, however, quick to point out that this development has not always been continuous or progressive. Martin Bergman compares evidence from various European countries in his analysis of the meanings and messages transmitted by public executions. Like Mantecón, he illustrates the declining relationship between church and state, and discusses the way in which the act of execution became more of an embarrassment than a sacred ritual. The volume concludes with an article by Virpi Anttonen, who examines a distant echo of absolutist power in a modern society: the ruler's power over life and death. Anttonen traces alterations in the traditional institution of the royal pardon and how these became embedded in twentieth-century Finnish legislation. Undoubtedly, her study serves as an example in demonstrating the characteristics of social control as *longue durée* history with pan-European dimensions.

Sources

LITERATURE

Black, Donald 1996: Konflikthanteringens elementära former. In *Kriminalitet, kultur, kontroll*, ed. Malin Åkerström. Carlssons, Stockholm.

Chriss, James J. 2007: *Social Control. An Introduction*. Oxford, Polity Press.

Cohen, Stanley 1985: *Visions of Social Control. Crime, Punishment and Classification*. Cambrigde, Polity Press.

Cohen, Stanley & Scull, Andrew 1983: Social Control in History and Sociology. In *Social Control and the State*, ed. Stanley Cohen & Andrew Scull. Oxford, Oxford University Press.

Deflem, Matthieu 2007: The Concept of Social Control.Theories and Applications. *Paper presented at the International Conference "Charities as Instruments of Social Control in 19th century Britain* (Université de Haute Bretagne, Rennes, France, November 22–23, 2007, www.mathieudeflem.net).

Innes, Martin 2003: *Understanding Social Control: Deviance, Crime and Social Order.* Buckingham, Open University Press.

Koskivirta, Anu 2012: Medieval and Early Modern Court Records in Finland (c. 1400–1809). In *The Use of Court Records and Petitions as Historical Sources*. Frühneuzeit-Info, ed. Institut für die Erforschung der Frühen Neuzeit, Jahrgang 23 (2012).

Kuhn, Lara 2009: *Social Control and Human Nature: What is it we are Controlling?* Newark, LFB Scholarly Publishing.

Lenman, Bruce & Parker, Geoffrey 1980: The State, the Community and the Criminal Law in Early Modern Europe. In *Crime and the Law. The Social History of Crime in Western Europe since 1500*, ed. V. A. C. Gatrell & Bruce Lenman & Geoffrey Parker. London, Europa Publishing.

Liliequist, Jonas & Almbjär, Martin 2012: Early Modern Court records and Supplications in Sweden (c. 1400–1809). In *The Use of Court Records and Petitions as Historical Sources*. Frühneuzeit-Info, ed. Institut für die Erforshung der Frühen Neuzeit, Jahrgang 23 (2012).

Mayer, John A. 1983: Notes Towards a Working Definition of Social Control in Historical Analysis. In: Cohen & Scull, *Social Control and the State*.

Pinker, Steven 2011: *The Better Angels of our Nature. The Decline of Violence in History and its Causes*. New York, Viking.

Sandall, Simon 2012: Pre-Modern Court Records in England (c. 1400–1809). In *The Use of Court Records and Petitions as Historical Sources*. Frühneuzeit-Info, ed. Institut für die Erforshung der Frühen Neuzeit, Jahrgang 23 (2012).

Schilling, Heinz (ed.) 1994, *Kirchenzucht und Sozialdisziplinierung im frühneuzeitlichen Europa*. Berlin, Duncker & Humblot.

Schilling, Heinz (ed.) 2008: *Early modern European Civilization and its Political and Cultural Dynamism*. Lebanon, University Press of New England.

Spierenburg, Pieter 2004: Social Control and History: An introduction. In *Social control in Europe 1500–1800*, ed. Herman Roodenburg & Pieter Spierenburg. Ohio, Ohio State University Press.

I
Rebelling Individuals

"The Child who strikes his own Father or Mother shall be put to Death"

Assault and Verbal Abuse of Parents in Swedish and Finnish Counties 1745–1754[1]

Jonas Liliequist

In 1751 Rikus Anders Nilsson, a 28-year-old farmer from Venjans village in Kopparberg county, was brought before the district court accused of having pushed and kicked his father and caused him bloodshed, as well as having scratched his stepmother's face. Formally capital punishment could be prescribed for "a child who strikes his own father", but Rikus Anders was in the end sentenced to forty sets of lashes, three lashes per set (that is, 120 lashes with a double whip), and ordered to make a public apology before the district court. This article presents an outline of the first of two projected cross-sectional empirical studies based on court records covering all trials for assaults, disrespect and insults towards parents that were brought before the civil courts in early modern Sweden and Finland during a selected ten-year period from the eighteenth and seventeenth centuries respectively. These studies will be further developed by the examination of other kinds of contemporary source materials (such as sermons, pamphlets, literary texts, medical

---

[1] This study has been initiated within the research program *ALC Ageing and Living Conditions* at Umeå University, Sweden.

and religious advisory books, broadsheets and satires) as part of a larger study entitled *"Honour thy Father and thy Mother": Generational conflicts and parental abuse in early modern Sweden 1600–1800*.

Aims and central questions

One of the basic research questions in contemporary research on ageing and living conditions is: what constitutes "successful ageing"? This has also been a rationale behind this study, with the aim of putting the issue into a historical perspective. Trust, safety and protection from abuse and ill-treatment would certainly count as basic preconditions for the experience of successful ageing. But how and to what extent has society addressed this problem? Has the concept and experience of abuse always been the same? Using questions like these as a starting point means that the main focus of analysis will be a long-term historical view of changes in the social meaning of notions and practices of abuse and forms of social control. It is not the intention to provide socio-economic and historical demographic explanations for individual behaviour and variations in patterns and frequencies of trials for violence and abuse. In the foreground are the meanings, definitions, excuses and explanations connected to the concrete words and acts of *abuse and violation* as well as forms of social control, degrees of public attention, kinds of legal consequences and official justifications connected to social intervention. Questions about what kinds of actions and languages have been deemed abuse and violation in various social and cultural settings will be of central concern, as will contemporary explanations, theories, sanctions and official ways of handling abuse and violence as a societal and individual problem.

The legal context

In the Swedish historical context, the assault and abuse of parents as an independent category of crime has a history of just over three hundred years, ranging from 1540 to 1868.[2] Parental assault or abuse remained an aggravating circumstance under the law for almost a hundred years more before it finally disappeared from the statutes in 1962. Modern Swedish legislation does not distinguish between violence towards parents and other forms of violence: beating or abusing one's own elderly parents is no longer regarded as a specific aggravating circumstance by the law.

During the Middle Ages, under Swedish provincial laws the unconditional death penalty could be handed out to those guilty of the murder or manslaughter of close relations, but there were no special provisions for non-fatal violence and verbal abuse directed towards parents. It was not until the Reformation (and the increased influence of the Ten Commandments and specific wording of the Decalogue in the Old Testament) that the first steps were taken towards the criminalization of such actions and words as a separate category of crime. In 1540 the first Swedish Lutheran regent, Gustav Vasa, issued a special decree according to which all forms of minor assault and verbal abuse ("curses") of parents were to be punished with a double fine and flogging in front of the church door: "because everyone has a duty to honour their father and mother, as it stands in the Ten Commandments."[3] The Decalogue of the Old Testament in fact prescribed capital punishment as a punishment for curses as well as all kinds of physical assaults. However, it was not until 1608 that the harsh spirit of the biblical penal regulations was fully introduced into the secular administration of justice. At this time, excerpts from the Pentateuch, organized according to the Ten Commandments and referred to as "God's Law", were added to Swedish national legislation.[4] According to "God's and Swedish Law" anyone who now cursed or struck his father or mother should be put to death. In this context, "father" and "mother" also referred to step-parents and parents in law.

---

2   For the history of criminalization, see Birgitta Odén, "Relationer mellan generationerna. Rättsläget 1300–1900" in Bengt Ankarloo, Leif Eliasson, Kim Salomon and Sven Tägil (ed.) *Maktpolitik och husfrid. Studier i internationell och svensk historia tillägnad Göran Rystad* (Lund 1991).

3   Statute of King Gustavus 1540 in Schmedeman, Johan, *Kongliga stadgar, förordingar, bref och resolutioner ifrån åhr 1528 in til 1701 angående justitiae och executions åhrender* (Stockholm 1706), p. 12.

4   The introduction of God's law is comprehensively treated in Sven Kjöllerström, *Guds och Sveriges lag under reformationstiden. En kyrkorättslig studie* (Lund 1957).

Thus throughout the seventeenth century, both verbal abuse and violence toward parents resulted in a formal charge of capital punishment without distinguishing between biological parents, step-parents or in-laws. Actual legal cases were however few in number and while preparing the new law, several responses to the law committee claimed that such strict punishment did not reflect the public sense of justice. As a result the death penalty for verbal abuse and violence towards in-laws, step-parents and step-in-laws was reduced to heavy fines in 1698 by royal resolutions.[5] This was later confirmed in the new 1734 penal code and extended to verbal abuse of biological parents as well. During the period under investigation, the formal punishment meted out for striking one's biological parents was *either* capital punishment *or* forty lashes of the whip for men, thirty for women, according to the circumstances. In practice however, the royal courts always reduced the death sentences. Even during the seventeenth century, executions seem to have been rare and whipping, birching and fines the most common punishments meted out to offenders. Striking one's step-parents or in-laws resulted in a 100 *daler* fine, a sizeable amount few could afford to pay, which was therefore often transmuted to corporal punishment. The verbal abuse of one's biological parents resulted in twenty-three lashes for men and eighteen for women, or twenty days in jail on a diet of bread and water. The fine was 50 *daler* if the crime was committed against step-parents or step-in-laws. In all cases the guilty party was required to make a public apology in front of the summoned court.[6] It should also be noted that criminalization and penalties concerned adults (most often middle-aged sons or daughters) or at least those who had reached the age of criminal responsibility (15 years old). Violent and disobedient minors were left to parental discipline and chastisement.

Behind the resurgence of interest in punishing violence and abuse toward parents during the seventeenth and eighteenth centuries lay both clerical and secular interests. From the Lutheran Church's perspective it was about the authority of God's "natural and clear words". From the

---

5 Royal resolution 11 May and 14 November 1698 in Schmedeman, *Kongliga stadgar*, pp. 1510, 1527.
6 Sveriges rikes lag 1734 M:14 § 2–3

perspective of the crown, it concerned legitimizing and organizing the growth of a centralized state power. Respect for the parental generation can be said to have played a strategic and important symbolic role in the patriarchal social ideology that came to be shaped by the Lutheran foundations of state rule. This foundation was built upon Scripture and the fourth commandment in particular – "Honour thy father and thy mother: that thy days may be long upon the land which the Lord thy God giveth thee". In the Lutheran reformers' interpretation of the commandment, the duty to show respect and obedience toward parents was extended to governing authorities and their public representatives, who should be regarded as superiors, on a par with the estate of one's father and mother.[7] Thus violating one's parents meant violating the social and divine order.

The statistical picture and some methodological issues

All cases of capital crimes should, under Swedish rules, have been submitted by the district courts to the Royal Courts (*kungliga hovrätter*) for examination before a final sentence was passed. It has thus been possible to establish a picture of the general statistical trends in the number and frequencies of trials for most of the seventeenth and eighteenth centuries by using the information contained in the registries and letters of resolution from the Royal Courts, at least for the Swedish parts of the country. Letters of resolution and registries from the Royal Court in Åbo, relating to the whole of Finland (which was part of the Swedish kingdom until 1809) are either totally missing or only fragmentarily preserved for most of the seventeenth and eighteenth centuries. The general trend (with reservations for Finland) saw a steady increase in the number of trials in the eighteenth and nineteenth centuries after a very low number of cases had been brought to trial during the seventeenth century. The number of trials peaked in the mid-nineteenth century and saw a sharp decline

---

[7] Kirsi Warpula, "'Honour thy father and thy mother': The formation of authority in seventeenth-century Sweden" in Anu Koskivirta & Sari Forsström (ed.) *Manslaughter, fornication and sectarianism: Normbreaking in Finland and the Baltic area from mediaeval to modern times* (Helsinki 2002), pp. 77–99.

until the introduction of a new Penal Code in 1864, under which parental abuse disappeared as an independent category of crime. The change in the letter of the law was reflected in the disappearance of the category in the official Swedish crime statistics four years later. The data also allow us to draw a picture of the geographical distributions of trials and their variations over time, which opens up the possibility for exploring comparative perspectives. The first example is shown in the map below, which depicts significant regional differences during the ten-year period from 1745 to 1754 – one of at least two periods during the seventeenth and eighteenth centuries for which it is possible to obtain a complete picture of the frequencies and geographical distribution of trials from the whole country, including the Finnish area, based on accounts registers which the Royal Courts were required to report before the Diet.[8]

The primary aim of this study is not, however, to provide specific causal explanations for historical and regional differences in the frequencies of trials. The information given by registries and resolutions is simply too thin and the frequencies too low. Any possible conclusions that could be drawn from variations in bare statistical figures of the number of trials would be too ambiguous to allow us to make any reasonable generalizations about underlying causes. Even if it were to be complemented by a more thorough analysis of the trial records from the district courts, the focus would still be on the narrative content – what was said or asked by the court, what the parties involved said and what witnesses reported – and on what could perhaps be called "quantifications of qualitative aspects" – questions, utterances, actions, relations – which could provide the basis for qualitative analyses and interpretations of the social significance and meanings of abuse as well as social policies of intervention. This could be approached both in a more heuristic way – with the aim of finding clues about possible meanings that are only fragmentary and randomly represented in isolated cases (the "detective and gold-washing method") – and in a more truly quantitative manner – through an attempt to uncover underlying themes and motifs

---

[8] Diaries of the Royal Courts submitted to the Swedish Riksdag 1745–1754; R2904, R2908, R2909, R2999, R3000, R3085, R3086, *National Archive*, Stockholm.

in how conflicts were represented. Such patterns in their turn could be expected to vary over time and perhaps also between regions: thus representing different patterns or even "cultures" of violence and abuse. Questions could then be asked about how varieties in themes, meanings and compositions (and frequencies of trials) might be connected to specific socio-economic and demographic conditions and structures. Some of these conditions and structures – such as patterns of intergenerational co-habitation and rules of inheritance – would have been explicitly mentioned by the parties involved as the primary cause of conflict.

From this perspective, registries and resolutions provide valuable information not only about the number of trials and their geographical locations, but also about qualitative aspects such as civil status and (often) the professional title of both the indicted perpetrator and their alleged victim(s), their mutual family and household connection, the character of the alleged offence (violent assault and/or verbal abuse), and the forms of legal sanctions and penalties imposed on those found guilty of perpetrating such crimes. Given this information and the opportunity to establish comprehensive statistics about all trials during certain shorter periods, it seems more appropriate to start with cross-sectional studies covering the whole country rather than a few longitudinal studies of selected counties. A further argument for this approach would be that although Sweden and Finland were a single country with one law and one judicial system, there were also distinct regional differences in language, family patterns and cultural traditions, all of which would favour comparison across regional and cultural borders during a specific period. Social meanings would also perhaps become more clearly apparent through differences and possible contrasting effects.[9] Taking all this into consideration, two periods have been selected for comparison: the first, the 1660s and the second, 1745–1754. The study of each period will also be informed by analyses of other kinds of sources representing official policy and legal, moral and popular discourses of the seventeenth and eighteenth centuries respectively. A common questionnaire and outline

---

9 See, for example, Beatrice Moring, "Family Strategies, Inheritance Systems and the Care of the Elderly in Historical Perspective: Eastern and Western Finland". *Historical Social Research* vol. 23 1998 no. 1/2, pp. 67–82.

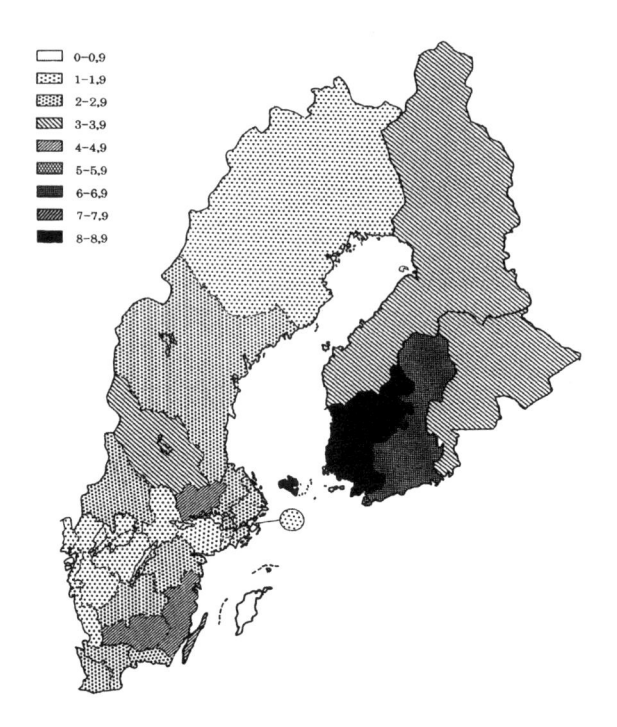

Map 1. Trials for assaults and verbal abuse of parents (including parents-in-law and step-parents) reported to Göta, Svea and Åbo Royal Courts, 1745–1754. (Mean annual figures per 100,000 inhabitants.)[10]

has been developed with basic questions and issues to be asked and considered for each case and period of investigation, under the following headings:

SITUATION

A description of basic personal and social data about the indicted perpetrator and his or her victim (such as gender, age, social class, housing and relationship both in terms of generational ties and actual household

10 Source: Diaries of the Royal Courts submitted to the Swedish Riksdag 1745–1754; R2904, R2908, R2909, R2999, R3000, R3085, R3086, *National Archive*, Stockholm. Population figures based on C. E. Quensel, Tillförlitligheten i de äldsta befintliga befolkningsdata i *Minnesskrift med anledning av den svenska befolkningsstatistikens 200-åriga bestånd* (Stockholm 1949), table 1a (1754), p.14.

26 JONAS LILIEQUIST

positions); subjects of disputes and conflicts; possible structural and underlying causes apparent from the circumstances of individual cases.

SOCIAL CONTROL

An analysis, in this context, of the degree of public attention, indignation and willingness to report found in each case. For example, questions about how and by whom the accusations of violence and abuse have been made.

SOCIAL MEANINGS

The focus will be on the actions and language of violence and abuse, as described by the parties and the witnesses. For example, what kind of remarks and actions were considered abusive or violating, and in what ways were they seen as abusive or violating?

EXPLANATIONS

Of central interest here is the way in which abusive words and actions were justified, excused or condemned by the parties involved and/or the court and the ways in which violence and abuse were explained in a more general sense.

CONSEQUENCES

Here, we are concerned with the court's judgment, penalties imposed on the perpetrator, any rituals involved and notions of shame, apology and reconciliation as central parts of what constituted the policy of social intervention.

GENDER, POWER AND AUTHORITY

Throughout the analyses consideration will be given to the ways in which actions, notions and practices relate to and intersect with gender, power and authority.

In the following section I will reflect upon some of these basic points in relation to the judicial material from the first period of investigation: 1745–1754.

SITUATIONS OF CONFLICTS AND ABUSE

Rikus Anders was not alone. During the period between 1745 and 1754 a total of 720 individuals across the whole of Finland and Sweden were brought before the courts accused of having assaulted or verbally abused one of their parents (or both), representing a total of 745 parent victims distributed over 639 trials. The figures are calculated from the registries kept by the three Royal Courts: Göta Hovrätt (covering the south of Sweden), Svea Hovrätt (the centre and north of Sweden) and Åbo Hovrätt (Finland).[11] Though scant and limited, the registry information provides some valuable information, including indications about the personal settings of the conflict and abuse situations.

PERPETRATORS AND VICTIMS

A first calculation (table 1) shows that while more than three times as many men stood accused than women, the distribution according to gender was fairly even among victims. Despite the discrepancy between the genders, compared to assault and violence in general, the female portion of accused perpetrators was still notably large. A number of these cases merely concern verbal assault, but that was the case with the accused men as well. What is important is that abuse whether verbal or physical was not the strict preserve of men, and that both men and women of the elder generation were its victims.

Tab. 1: Perpetrator and victim, absolute figures 1745–1754[12]

Court	perpetrator		victim	
	male	female	male	female
GH*	212	45	146	125
SH**	143	46	100	104
ÅH***	227	47	140	130
S:a	582	138	386	359

*GH: Göta Hovrätt (Southern Sweden) **SH: Svea Hovrätt (Northern Central Sweden) ***ÅH: Åbo Hovrätt (Finland)

11 Note 4 above.
12 Source: Diaries of the Royal Courts submitted to the Swedish Riksdag 1745–1754; R2904, R2908, R2909, R2999, R3000, R3085, R3086, *National Archive*, Stockholm.

Reversing the perspective to the victim's relationship with the perpetrator (table 2) reveals that the father appears to be the dominant victim, closely followed by the mother. In the case of Rikus Anders, an argument with his father was reported to have escalated into a fight while the stepmother seems to have been scratched in the tumult when she and another peasant tried to draw her stepson away from his father.

Tab. 2: Victim's relationship to the perpetrator (percentage) 1745–1754[13]

Court	father*	mother*	father-in-law*	mother-in-law*
GH	40	29	14	17
SH	36	30	13	21
ÅH	36	26	16	22

*including step-relations

An additional breakdown of the figures on the basis of the gender of the perpetrators (table 3 below) also suggests that the dominant abusive relationship was *son–father* in cases involving male perpetrators (table 3a) while the image becomes more blurred when concerning female perpetrators.

Tab. 3: Victim's relationship to perpetrator according to gender, ranked in decreasing order 1745–1754[14]

a) male perpetrators		
GH	SH	ÅH
father	father	father
mother	mother	mother
mother-in-law	mother-in-law	mother-in-law
father-in-law	father-in-law	father-in-law

---

13 Source: Diaries of the Royal Courts submitted to the Swedish Riksdag 1745–1754; R2904, R2908, R2909, R2999, R3000, R3085, R3086, *National Archive*, Stockholm.
14 Source: Diaries of the Royal Courts submitted to the Swedish Riksdag 1745–1754; R2904, R2908, R2909, R2999, R3000, R3085, R3086, *National Archive*, Stockholm.

b) female perpetrators		
GH	SH	ÅH
father	mother	mother-in-law
mother	mother-in-law	mother
mother-in-law	father	father
father-in-law	father-in-law	father-in-law

It is clear, however, that mothers-in-law were more often the victims of their daughters-in-law than of their sons-in- law and that fathers-in-law were least frequently victims in trials during this period (table 3b). Although step-relationships (which definitely merit further analysis) have been included in the tables, they have not been distinguished from biological relationships (Has this work been done now? It would be fascinating to know!). However, it seems that the step-relationship was not significant in the case of Rikus Anders.

Information about cohabitation and the composition of households were not normally included in the registries and resolutions, but such data can sometimes be found in the trial records and, where preserved, the examination registers kept by the priests. The court records indicate, for instance, that Rikus Anders had recently got married. The title "peasant" indicates that he had taken possession of landed property and established himself and his wife in a household of their own. However, the violence in question took place on his father's farm. The records do not provide any indication of the age of his father, Rikus Nils Andersson, but it appears that he was still working and in possession of the farm.

The question of authority

Specific disputes and conflicts often figure in the trial records as triggers for violence and abuse. One recurrent theme behind such disputes concerns *questions about authority*, not least in situations where adult children and parents lived together. In one case a son, whose retired father had been interfering with the management of the farm, mentioned the deed of gift given in front of the district court that had passed the farm into the son's possession. His father retorted: "I shit on the court and your lying papers". Statistical picture of the relationships between victims and perpetrators also suggests the idea that claims and questions of authority were important triggers of violence and insults. To a large extent sons perpetrated abuse against their fathers, daughters against their mothers and daughters-in-law against their mothers-in-law, in neat correspondence with the central male and female authority positions within households (tables 3a and 3b). The question of authority was, however, not always a simple matter, especially not in three-generational households.

Civil status and household position were not the only determiners of authority: generational belonging and age were central principles upon which authority in early modern Swedish society was based. All these factors were at work in households, sometimes overlapping and sometimes operating in tension with each other.[15] The households of landed farmers in most parts of Sweden and Finland typically included a husband and wife and their minor children, one or two servants (frequently young unmarried sons and daughters from other households) and often paternal or maternal grandparents. Depending on the stage in the family cycle, the parental generation could either be old and retired, or still in work and the head of a household that included a married son or daughter who was expected to eventually take over the running of the farm. His role as head of the household gave the master his power and authority. A husband had formal responsibility for the household and the right to dispense the household resources. As mistress, his wife was responsible for housekeeping and other female-specific chores. In their relationships with servants, both master and mistress had the same right to demand respect and obedience and, if necessary, to castigate servants who failed to show deference. The same also held true for their relationships with their own children. In her marriage, however, a wife was subordinate to her husband: he was her "head" and guardian. Until 1734 a husband had the explicit legal right to chastise his own wife. Thereafter, this right was excluded from the wording of the act in the

---

15 Anna Hansen, *Ordnade hushåll. Genus och kontroll i Jämtland under 1600-talet* (Uppsala, 2006), p. 119f.

1734 law, although such chastisement was not expressly criminalized. In the advisory literature of the seventeenth and eighteenth centuries, husbands were warned not to chastise or reprimand their wife in front of the servants, since this could undermine her authority as mistress.[16] Tensions between different hierarchal principles could be even more obvious in relationships between adult family members, particularly when adult children and parents lived in the same household. Generational cohabitation was connected to the need to secure provision and care for the older generation and the transference of the farm and landed property to the younger generation. The crucial point here was the implication of the retirement for the distribution of authority within the household. Up until 1734 the law had stipulated that the younger generation was obliged to provide and care for their elderly parents. After 1734 this requirement was removed. In its place were agreements and contracts in civil law that in principle meant that possession of the farm would be handed to a son (or son-in-law) in exchange for a promise to provide for the parents (or in-laws) in accordance with a specified contract (*sytning, födoråd*). This could mean that members of the older generation either lived in the household or, as became more common, were housed in a special cottage on the property with their own provisions (*undantag*).[17]

The precise implications of retirement for household authority have not been central issues in earlier research; neither were they specifically discussed in contemporary regulations and statutes.[18] Before 1734 (or at least during the sixteenth and seventeenth centuries) passing on the farm also meant relinquishing one's role as head of the household; however, this was not necessarily unconditional. Parents were still formally recognized as owners until their death, and contracts could specifically stipulate that they should be shown respect and obedience. After 1734 handing over property in exchange for provision and care was recognized by the law as a gift and compensation. This meant that the younger gen-

---

16 Jonas Liliequist, "Changing Discourses of Marital Violence in Sweden from the Age of Reformation to the late nineteenth century". *Gender and History* (2011:1).
17 David Gaunt, *Familjeliv i Norden* (Malmö, 1983).
18 Magnus Perlestam gives examples of how legal texts and their implications have been interpreted in different ways by historians; *Den rotfaste bonden – myt eller verklighet. Brukaransvar i Ramkvilla socken 1620–1820* (Malmö, 1998), p. 84f.

eration became the immediate owners and, as a consequence, the whole farm and property was often no longer transferred at once. The remaining part of the property would be later divided between the heirs after the death of the retired owners. However, it is not clear what implications this change had for the transference of household authority. According to the Finnish legal historian, Axel Charpentier, retired elderly persons were no longer subordinate to the new master of the household, at least not in a strictly judicial sense.[19] How arrangements worked out in practice still remains to be researched. Even if retirement meant that parents turned over the farm and their roles as heads of household in a more absolute way, adult children were still expected to show respect and be subordinate to their elders, according to the patriarchal ideology of society.

The different balance of authority in three-generational families was reflected in the trials. Before formal agreement of retirement and transfer of the farm, fathers could make use of their authority and power as masters to test their sons or sons-in-law and subsequently select whoever they thought would be best suited to running the farm (or by some other personal criteria). This was evident in the trial of Erik Eriksson, accused of having pushed and hit his father-in-law, Nils Persson. Nils had shown himself to be most unfriendly and refused to answer and co-operate with his son-in-law. During the trial, the court heard that Nils had formerly "given away" another of his daughters in marriage to a man to whom he had intended to hand over the farm, but after some time of cohabitation and much "noise" the man had been driven away. Erik suspected that Nils was employing this strategy once again, since Nils had, despite the promise given to Erik and his wife, "brought home" a third unmarried daughter.[20]

In the trial against the peasant Per Thomson and his wife Anna Matsdotter the tables seem to have been turned. Per had, according to his old father, Thomas Persson, not only assaulted his father and his wife physically, but also put him off with the words, "you have been erased from the population register: you have nothing to say, you should be quiet in

---

19 Axel Charpentier, *Om sytning* (Helsingfors, 1896), p. 65f.
20 Court record; Skedevi 4/12 1746, KLHA serie XI AI:44 1746, County of Kopparberg.

any case".[21] The wording about being erased from the population register (*mantalslängd*) – a fiscal consequence of retirement – was obviously intended to underline the loss of household authority and emphasize his father's subordinate position. A third trial provides us with an example of how withholding property could secure a certain degree of independence. According to Malin Ersdotter, her daughter Kerstin Pärsdotter and her husband, soldier Olof Giös, had been highly disrespectful to her. It was reported that during a boat-trip across Lake Liugaren Kerstin exclaimed that "it would have been just fine to throw Malin overboard". Malin complained about the harshness and neglect with which she had been treated by her daughter and son-in-law. Now in her seventies, Malin felt she had no option other than to pass her property into the hands of unrelated people who would take care of her.[22]

Claims to inheritance

Claims to inheritance constitute a second recurrent theme of generational disputes in the trial records. This was the origin of the violence in the case of Rikus Anders Nilsson and his father Rikus Nils Andersson. Rikus Anders had gone to his father's house to discuss the monetary compensation he had received instead of a lamb and a sheep, which was his maternal inheritance. Rikus Anders wanted to pay the money back and take the animals instead, as he had more need of them than of the money.

Since his father was not at home, Rikus Anders went to the neighbouring farm (owned by his uncle Jöns Andersson), where after a while he met his father. When he put forward his demand Rikus Anders (according to his own account) received not a word in reply. After they left Jöns Andersson's farm, the father and son soon ended up in a fight. Rikus Nils first picked up a cane in order to strike or, according to the witness Anders Jönsson's account, force his son away. The son disarmed

---

21 Court record; Tortuna 31/9 1746, AI:12, County of Västmanland.
22 Court record; Rättvik 30/11 1748, KLHA Serie XI AI:46b, County of Kopparberg.

his father and they both grabbed and kicked each other, during which time Rikus Anders wounded his father above the knee. When his father grabbed a new wooden pole, Rikus Anders snatched it away from him. According to the witness's account, he then pushed his father backwards and kicked out at him until his stepmother, Margareta Matsdotter, and Jöns Andersson intervened. They led Rikus Anders backwards into the stable, and during the tumult he scratched his stepmother's face. This incident and the escape of his father marked the end of the fight.

Social control

It seems from the limited number of examined trial records that few cases were brought before the court directly by the parents involved (at least not as complaints before the county sheriff). In most cases the sheriff had "received information" about what had happened from hearsay or from the parish priest (or other local church and parish officials). Parents could even show an obvious reluctance to pursue complaints, causing the court to admonish them to be sincere and not to "hide the truth". Sometimes a plaintiff would even try to withdraw his complaint. The county sheriff immediately dismissed such attempts as something that could not be decided by the offended party. Often a decision to withdraw or play down complaints would result from prior reconciliation between the parties involved. This indicates an often uncomfortable negotiation between the attitudes of common people and the logic of the judicial system. Parents wanted their adult sons and daughters to be reprimanded in some way, but they did not wish them to be subjected to the harsh and dishonouring measures (even capital punishment) that were stipulated by the law. The reasons for this were simple: elderly parents depended on their children for their care and in many cases continued to live in proximal relationships. Therefore, when parents wanted to take action they usually took their complaints to the priest or other local church official rather than to the county sheriff. In practice the Reformation had not totally abolished the church's judicial jurisdiction: in fact it was strengthened during the seventeenth and eighteenth centuries by the development of a local "parish justice" based on the principles of improvement and reconciliation rather than on deterrent punishment. Complaints about discord and abuse between family and household members could thus be investigated by the parish priest with the assistance of either a special church council (*kyrkoråd*) or the parish general meeting (*sockenstämman*). A system of escalating sanctions (from admonitions and warnings to fines and sitting in the stocks on a Sunday) could be employed before a case was handed over to the civil court as a last resort if improvement and reconciliation failed to emerge.[23]

This was probably what Rikus Nils and his wife had in mind when they visited the local church official in their village (*uppsyningsmannen*). They told him of their complaints against their son, showed him their wounds and asked that the priest be informed. In this case, however, the priest obviously found the complaints to be of such a serious nature that he decided to forward them directly to the county sheriff, who immediately detained Rikus Anders until the court sessions were summoned. Later, in court, both father and stepmother pleaded for mercy and forgiveness on behalf of their son, claiming that they had already been reconciled. So far, there has been very little research into the content and extension of local parish justice, but the initial impression is that a number of cases were dealt with at this parish level and were never brought before the civil courts.[24]

Finnish historian Beatrice Moring has emphasized that, compared to those involving non-domestic "ordinary" fighting and violence, a very few domestic cases were ever recorded in the protocols and civil courts. Given the public nature of family life in small villages, it is unlikely that these figures could hide a large number of conflicts, which suggests that violence within the family was a relatively rare phenomenon.[25] However,

---

23 For a survey of the two traditions, see K.H Johansson, *Svensk sockensjälvstyrelse 1686–1862* (Lund, 1937) p. 330ff.
24 Johansson, *Svensk sockensjälvstyrelse*, focuses on questions of local self-government. Carin Bergström, *Lantprästen. Prästens funktion i det agrara samhället 1720–1800* (Stockholm, 1991) and Björn Furuhagen, *Berusade bönder och bråkiga båtsmän. Social kontroll vid sockenstämmor och ting under 1700-talet* (Stockholm, 1996) both focus on these cases but primarily from a quantitative point of view.
25 Beatrice Moring, "Conflict or Cooperation? Old Age and Retirement in the Nordic Past", *Journal of Family History*, vol. 28 no. 2, April 2003, p. 249.

on first impression it appears that there were significant variations in the activities and efficiency of local parish justice over time, between parishes, local priests and in organization. It seems that the system of justice that involved a specifically appointed church council – who was assisted by local officials (*sexmän*) and village constables (*uppsyningsmän, byvaktare*) – established a more ambitious, far reaching and more efficient system for the control of morals than was the case when the Parish General Meeting was the principal forum. Church councils occurred most frequently in the diocese of Västerås (especially in Kopparberg), in Northern Sweden and in parts of Finland. An interesting question is whether high levels of activity within local parish justice correspond with high frequencies of trials in civil courts. Local village officials were specifically instructed to report about the lives of their neighbours, and (like priests) they could also act as informers for the civil courts. Such regional and temporal differences would imply the possibility of a substantial dark figure of violent incidents never brought before the courts, which must be taken into account.

Social meanings

How should the violent reaction of Rikus Anders's father be understood? Rikus Nils told the court that he had felt offended by his son's request and that this was the reason why he had picked up the fence pole and threatened to hit Rikus Anders. Although the record does not indicate why Rikus Nils felt so offended, the circumstances suggest some probable explanations. Once again, the tension between different hierarchal principles could be a starting point. In this case there was no question of cohabitation. Rikus Anders had recently got married and his independent position was indicated by the reference to him as a "peasant" (*bonde*) in the trial records. At the same time he was still his father's son and as such was obliged (according to the Lutheran catechism's explanation of the fourth commandment) to treat his father with reverence (*vördnad*) and to be obedient.

Perhaps Rikus Nils was offended because he felt that Anders had acted not like a son but as an independent man when he made his request in front of other people. This would explain not only why Rikus Nils became so offended, but also his initial silence: ignoring his son's remark was a way of demonstrating his authority to those who had witnessed the request. Anders had come of age (both literally and in terms of his marriage and household position) and his father no longer had the right to castigate him. However, it seems that Rikus Nils may have felt that he was justified in wishing to chastise his son: not only was he offended by the request, he also threatened to beat him. His wife's actions also suggest that she felt justified in chastising her stepson. She ran over and hit Rikus Anders in the mouth. Such a signifier of reprimand in his father's violent response might explain the strength of Rikus Anders's reaction. As someone who had recently become master of a household, he might well have been particularly sensitive to being treated as a subordinate.

There is a further possible interpretation, connected to the old tradition in Kopparberg of dividing farms between the sons. According to a statement from the middle of the eighteenth century, it was degrading for an heir in this part of the country to accept the bulk of their inheritance in cash, as this could be a sign of illegitimacy.[26] If these connotations were widespread and well known, Rikus Nils might have been offended because he thought that Rikus Anders believed that he had been treated as though he was illegitimate. By the same token, when his father refused to convert the monetary compensation Rikus Anders may have felt as though he was being treated in a way befitting an illegitimate son.

Rikus Anders's case illustrates a common dilemma faced by historians who consult narrative sources. This is even more pronounced in judicial material: a courtroom is, of course, not always the best place to search for "the truth". In Anders's case, as in many others, it is also evident that the injured parties played down compromising details, which could have further implicated the accused and led to more severe pun-

---

26 Orvar Löfgren, "Familj, släkt och hushåll" in Hellspong and Löfgren *Land och stad. Svenska samhällen och livsformer från medeltid till nutid* (Malmö, 1995), p. 233.

ishment, and even perhaps put the witnesses in a less favourably light. Thus in Rikus Anders's case, for example, all those involved were in full agreement that the quarrel and fighting had taken place after nine o'clock on Sunday evening and, as a result, the Sabbath peace had not been broken. Everyone agreed that nobody had been intoxicated. Furthermore, witnesses and the parties involved all maintained that not a single insulting word had been uttered during the entire fight and quarrel. The court really tried to press the parties and witnesses on these points, especially the lack of insults, but without any success (to the great frustration of the historian). It is here that "the detective and gold-washing method" comes in to play: in other words, reading through a great number of trial records in search of details of information from similar situations.

Explanations

The attempts of Rikus Anders's parents to play down and diminish his guilt provide some indication of how the origins of violence were understood (both within contemporary cultural stereotypes and judicial doctrines). Immediately after his first testimony, Rikus Nils Andersson requested that "forgiveness and forbearance" be shown to his son, who had apologized to and in turn been forgiven by his father. Furthermore, by his own account, Rikus Nils had provoked his son to his "thoughtless behaviour" when he (Rikus Nils) had threatened to beat him with a wooden pole. This explanation was in line with Scripture verses according to which parents not only had the right to be venerated, but also bore a responsibility "not to provoke one's children to wrath".[27] The court heard that Rikus Nils was himself known to be hot-tempered. Both father and son had acted not out of hatred and bitterness but from a sudden emotional outburst. This was also in line with prevailing judicial distinctions between violence arising from hatred and sustained hostil-

---

27 *Ephesians* 6: "And you fathers, provoke not your children to wrath; but bring them up in nurture and admonition of the Lord".

ity (*vredesmod, långan vräkt*) and that resulting from "sudden discord" (*brådan skillnad, hastigt mod*), which could be judged more leniently.[28]

References to individuals' tempers and emotional states seem to have been the most central explanatory theme rather than structural causes (such as cohabitation and problems of sustenance). Individuals were characterized as hot-headed or patient and long-suffering, filled with hatred and bitterness or humble and forbearing. In this respect a more comprehensive analysis would, of course, benefit from an exploration of prevailing notions and doctrines about emotions and emotional life and stereotypes according to gender and different life stages.

Consequences and concluding remarks

From a modern perspective the most conspicuous consequence (or perhaps lack of consequence) was that only Rikus Anders was sentenced, although he himself had been subjected to rather serious violence. During their fight his father had kicked him in the head and drawn blood. This was surely taken into consideration by the court as an extenuating circumstance, along with the fact that it was Rikus Nils who instigated the violence. However, the court never considered prosecuting Rikus Nils for kicking his son in the head and causing bloodshed. The same holds true for the blow to the mouth that Rikus Anders received from his stepmother. Even though the court had taken into consideration the general opinion that the father possessed "an angry disposition", no blame was attached to Rikus Nils. The court could in fact admonish the assaulted parent not to provoke the son or daughter, but the law text sided strongly with the parental generation, prescribing that the child who strikes his own father or mother should be put to death. However, the death penalty was rarely handed down to those convicted of such crimes, and it is often obvious that the court really tried to find reasons for not passing a capital sentence. In Rikus Anders's case the fact that he

---

28 Most explicit in cases of revenge, violation of privacy in one's home and manslaughter; Sveriges rikes lag 1734 M: 18 § 1, M: 20 § 1 § 5, M:24 § 5.

had not hit his father with his bare hands or other implement were seen as extenuating circumstances. For this and other reasons Anders was not given the death penalty; instead he was sentenced to corporal punishment, which was later confirmed by the Royal Court, Svea Hovrätt.

The case of Rikus Anders was not in any way exceptional. It seems that in many cases both sides indulged in violence and verbal insults. Cases involving systematic, serious and brutal maltreatment of elderly parents did not appear very often in the trials. Perhaps an investigation of murder and homicide cases could reveal cases of serious abuse, which had not been brought to court before the victim's death. What is revealed however, is how the complexity of paternal authority, which was thought to be the very foundation of social order, contributed to situations of ambivalence and conflict.

Sources

ARCHIVAL MATERIAL

Court records, Provincial Archive, Uppsala.
Diaries of the Royal Courts submitted to the Swedish Riksdag 1745-54; R2904, R2908, R2909, R2999, R3000, R3085, R3086, National Archive, Stockholm.

PRINTED SOURCES

Ephesians 6 http://www.biblegateway.com/.
Schmedeman, Johan 1706: *Kongl. stadgar, förordningar, bref och resolutioner, ifrån åhr 1528 in til 1701* Stockholm.
Sveriges rikes lag: gillad och antagen på riksdagen år 1734. Facsimile edition 1983. Inst. för rättshistorisk forskning, Stockholm.

LITERATURE

Bergström, Carin 1991: *Lantprästen. Prästens funktion i det agrara samhället 1720–1800.* Nordiska museet, Stockholm.
Charpentier, Axel 1896: *Om sytning.* Helsingfors universitet, Helsingfors.
Furuhagen, Björn 1996: *Berusade bönder och bråkiga båtsmän. Social kontroll vid sockenstämmor och ting under 1700-talet*: Brutus Östlings bokförlag Symposion, Stockholm.
Gaunt, David 1996: *Familjeliv i Norden.* Gidlunds, Stockholm.
Hansen, Anna 2006: *Ordnade hushåll: genus och kontroll i Jämtland under 1600-talet.* Acta Universitatis Upsaliensis, Uppsala.
Johansson, K. H 1937: *Svensk sockensjälvstyrelse 1686–1862.* Lunds universitet, Lund.

Kjöllerström, Sven 1957: *Guds och Sveriges lag under reformationstiden. En kyrkorättslig studie.* Gleerups förlag, Lund.

Liliequist, Jonas 2011: Changing Discourses of Marital Violence in Sweden from the Age of Reformation to the late nineteenth century. *Gender & History* 23 (1) April 2011, pp. 1–25.

Löfgren, Orvar 1994: Familj, släkt och hushåll. In *Land och stad. Svenska samhällen och livsformer från medeltid till nutid*, ed. Mats Hellspong and Orvar Löfgren, Gleerups förlag, Malmö.

Moring, Beatrice 1998: Family Strategies, Inheritance Systems and the Care of the Elderly in Historical Perspective: Eastern and Western Finland. *Historical Social Research* 23 (1/2) 1998, pp. 67–82.

Moring, Beatrice 2003: Conflict or cooperation? Old age and retirement in the Nordic past. *Journal of Family History* 28 (2) April 2003, pp. 231–257.

Odén, Birgitta 1991: Relationer mellan generationerna. Rättsläget 1300–1900. In *Maktpolitik och husfrid. Studier i internationell och svensk historia tillägnad Göran Rystad*, ed. Bengt Ankarloo, Leif Eliasson, Kim Salomon and Sven Tägil, Lund University Press, Lund, pp. 85–116.

Perlestam, Magnus 1998: *Den rotfaste bonden – myt eller verklighet. Brukaransvar i Ramkvilla socken 1620–1820.* Magnus Perlestam, Lund.

Quensel, C. E. 1949: Tillförlitligheten i de äldsta befintliga befolkningsdata. In *Minnesskrift med anledning av den svenska befolkningsstatistikens 200-åriga bestånd*, SCB [Statistiska centralbyrån] Stockholm, pp. 9–32.

Warpula, Kirsi 2002: "Honour thy father and thy mother": The formation of authority in seventeenth-century Sweden. In *Manslaughter, fornication and sectarianism: Norm-breaking in Finland and the Baltic area from mediaeval to modern times*, ed. Anu Koskivirta and Sari Forsström, Finnish Academy of Science and Letters, Helsinki, pp. 77–99.

Naming Practises as a Social Control
The Continuity and Change of Morals in Local Peasant Communities (c. 1850–1960)
Sofia Kotilainen

The continuity and change of morals in local peasant communities

What could better describe the mutual attitudes and respect of people living near each other than the names that individuals were given by their communities? As an aged man from Kivijärvi said when remembering earlier nicknames, "it is when a name is given to someone, so that it will follow him the rest of his life."[1] Language and speech were particularly strong social institutions within early modern communities. Personal names are usually regarded as a relatively neutral part of everyday speech. Certain names have been used to categorize other members of the community and to try to define their social positions. In this article I concentrate on one of these naming practices and explore its connection with social control in early modern life. I will analyse why name-calling was an important linguistic form of communal regulation.

---

[1] Interview H2 with a man born in Kivijärvi in the 1920s. 23/5/2001. Although nicknames changed as an individual grew older, information about earlier nicknames was still retained in the social memory.

I argue that traditional name-giving customs were appreciated in early modern societies specifically because of their controlling dimension.[2] In many ways, traditional name-giving expressed (by implication) local and perhaps otherwise unspoken norms. Different forms of unofficial social control can be discerned in the traditional name-giving practices of clans (for example, the giving of inherited forenames[3] and family names) as well as in nicknaming.

In eastern Finland women continued to use their father's surname even after they got married. In peasant families the practice of wives keeping their own family names persisted until the first decades of the twentieth century, when it became common for a woman to take her husband's name upon marriage. Among the upper estates this custom was already the norm by the end of the nineteenth century. The principal rule regarding children was that they would be given their father's surname, thus surnames formed patrilineal chains, which connected the generations. Surnames were used among eastern peasants already in the sixteenth century. They were important tools in the construction of family identity. In western Finland it was more common for the name of the house or farm in which family each time lived to be adopted as a surname-like nickname. The nickname would usually change when one moved to another farm. This is why nicknames or sobriquets were not as permanent as eastern surnames. In Kivijärvi, for example, the vast majority of inhabitants had eastern family name as consequence of the settlement history of the region.[4]

Also the church and its clergy controlled the orthography of personal

---

2   This article is based on my presentation at the international conference "Morals and institutional change", held at the University of Jyväskylä in 2008.
3   In this article I shall use the term "forename" rather than "first name", since the use of a name as a first or second (or other) forename may have had significance. The term "Christian name" (in Swedish *dopnamn* and in Finnish *ristimänimi*) is here treated as being synonymous with the term forename.
4   For details see Sofia Kotilainen, *Suvun nimissä. Nimenannon käytännöt Sisä-Suomessa 1700-luvun alusta 1950-luvulle* (Bibliotheca Historica 120. Helsinki, 2008. In English: *In the Name of the Family – Naming Practices in Central Finland from the beginning of the Eighteenth to the Mid-twentieth Century*. Helsinki: Finnish Literature Society. English summary: http://kirjat.finlit.fi/kuvat/978-952-222-048-6_3summ.pdf); Sofia Kotilainen, "An inherited name as the foundation of a person's identity. How the existence of a dead person was continued in the names of his or her descendants". *Thanatos* 1 (1) 2012, the online journal of the Finnish Death Studies Association, http://thanatosjournal.files.wordpress.com/2012/03/kotilainen_inherited-name_thanatos-20121.pdf.

names: local vicars and their chaplains registered Christian names in baptismal records. Although officials determined how a child's name should be written, the name itself would have been chosen by the child's parents and used by the local community – who could employ a fairly free variety of familiar forms. Detailed examination of the selection criteria applied in nicknaming enables us to examine the history of social control from a cultural and linguistic perspective.

I examine the choice and use of peasant nicknames with the help of micro-analysis of the local community, thus allowing me to consider the collective mentalities that lay behind these decisions. The results of this analysis may help us to understand ways of thinking and communal values of "lower" social groups, aspects that were not explicitly recorded within documents of the period. This kind of approach is needed: at least in Finnish historical research (and linguistics), this socially controlling aspect has not been considered in the depth that would be necessary to discuss differences between the sexes, for example.[5] Thus, a fresh perspective on the subject can be found by analysing the moral attitudes implicit in the naming processes. In this article I concentrate on studying forms of social control implicit in nicknames preserved in the social memory. Which ways of thinking and moral values influenced the choice of informal names that were given to individuals? Furthermore, we should consider how and why nicknaming practices changed as the agrarian community modernized and what this tells us about changes in communal moral values.

---

5   For analysis of the cultural nature of and changes in name-calling elsewhere in Europe see, for example, Anton Blok, "Nicknames as Symbolic Inversions", in id. *Honour and Violence* (Cambridge, 2001) pp. 155–172; Richard Breen, "Naming Practices in Western Ireland", *Man*, New Series 17/4 (1982) pp. 701–713; David D. Gilmore, "Some Notes on Community Nicknaming in Spain", *Man*, New Series 17/4 (1982), pp. 686–700; and Clodagh Tait, "Namesakes and Nicknames: Naming Practices in Early Modern Ireland, 1540–1700", *Continuity and Change*, 21 (2006), pp. 328–330. On the pronounced masculine Mediterranean naming culture see, for example, Gilmore, "Some Notes on Community Nicknaming in Spain", pp. 687, 692. In northern European research the connection between name-calling and gender has not, on the whole, been sufficiently problematized. For example, the differences between nicknames given to men and women has not been fully explored in a recent article collection that also charts connections between language and gender from the historical viewpoint. Cf. Britt-Louise Gunnarsson, Sonja Entzenberg and Maria Ohlsson (ed.), *Språk och kön i nutida och historiskt prespektiv. Studier presenterade vid Den sjätte nordiska konferensen om språk och kön, Uppsala 6–7 oktober 2006* [Language and Gender in Contemporary and Historical Perspective. Studies Presented at the Sixth Nordic Conference on Language and Gender, Uppsala, Sweden, October 6–7, 2006] (Skrifter utgivna av Institutionen för nordiska språk 71; Uppsala, 2007).

Language, moral values and social control

Nicknames were based on Christian names or family names and were formed through communal interaction. They changed over the course of a person's lifetime and also varied according to speaker.[6] Up until the end of the nineteenth century, official documents were written in Swedish. In this context, Finnish forms of personal names could be considered nicknames alongside different kinds of shortened forms of forenames. The official names recorded in church registers were remoulded in speech as hypocorisms or popular forms of personal names that were undoubtedly easier to pronounce. Within small communities the aim of distinguishing namesakes from one another in speech was one basic reason for assigning nicknames,[7] but such naming also had other functions. Nicknames were part of popular peasant culture, and their purpose was often to entertain others or put the person who was "named" in his or her place. Chants and refrains based on these names can even be described as popular poetry.[8]

In this article I examine mainly personal nicknames, although in the region of Kivijärvi there were also some inherited nicknames. Within the sources I have studied, very little information about nicknames related to wider family or kinship groups has survived, unless unofficial names based on place of domicile are included in this category. Along with their inherited surname parishioners were generally given a nickname that expressed their place of domicile – this connected members of the same family.

Nicknames could be pet names or terms of endearment, or they could be used to jeer at or mock an individual. However, irrespective of its specific purpose, such a name functioned as a kind of a code that contained a message about the name's meaning and an anecdote about its

---

6 Similarly during the initiation rites of different people's personal names could also change as a symbol to mark a new phase of life (such as reaching a certain age or a change in social position). For example, a ruler would been given a new name, when he was enthroned. See Arnold van Gennep, *The Rites of Passage* (Chicago, 1960) pp. 101, 105, 112.
7 On differences between these types of nicknaming, cf. Breen, "Naming Practices in Western Ireland", pp. 707–708; João de Pina-Cabral, "Nicknames and the Experience of Community", *Man* 19/1 (1984) pp. 149–150.
8 Kirsti Mäkinen, *Lollot ja kollot: Suomalaista naapurihuumoria* (Helsinki, 2007) pp. 58–61, 63–69; cf. however Matti Kuusi, *Sananlaskut ja puheenparret* (Helsinki, 1954) p. 43.

origin. When a separate name incorporated a whole story, its repetition summoned up its meaning in a straightforward way. This assisted its permanence as a part of social memory, so long as those who knew the story remembered the name.[9]

Language was a significant social institution of everyday life for peasant communities.[10] First of all, local dialects formed a common language for people living near each other. This made it possible to communicate with neighbours and also to control daily activities. The older peasant society was based more on oral tradition and social memory than on written communication, and rumours and gossip (which contained information of varying degrees of reliability) spread rapidly. During this period, when people defined the honour and dignity of their neighbours locally, language and speech could be effective instruments of control. However, at the turn of the eighteenth and nineteenth centuries complaints involving name-calling were rarely brought before the courts in northern Central Finland, at least not as a crime against someone's honour or reputation.[11]

Because names were used metaphorically[12] (in other words, the whole family or kinship community was called by a single surname or nickname, or a nickname connected to a certain incident was seen to be a more general reflection of an individual's personality) they transformed indicators of reputation. Giving nicknames expresses the continuous need to classify, define and delimit reality[13] by shaping it linguistically: a one-dimensional picture stands in place of a diverse reality. Someone who was assigned a communal "mockery name" would be remembered by society first and foremost for the feature that his or her nickname described.

9 James Fentress & Chris Wickham, *Social Memory. New perspectives on the past* (Oxford, 1992) pp. 7, 87–114; Jan Vansina, *Oral Tradition as History* (London, 1985) pp. 94, 152–154.
10 Cf. M. A. K. Halliday, *Language as social semiotic: The social interpretation of language and meaning* (London, 1992[1978]), pp. 183–184.
11 Kotilainen, *Suvun nimissä*, pp. 30–31; cf. Petri Karonen, "Talonpojat oikeutta paossa: Rikollisuudesta Keski-Suomessa 1700-luvun lopulla", in Heikki Roiko-Jokela, and Timo Pitkänen (ed.), *Sisä-Suomen tuomiokirjat tutkimuslähteinä ja elämän kuvaajina* (Jyväskylä, 1995) pp. 60–64, 66–67.
12 Cf. Paul Ricoeur, *The Rule of Metaphor: The Creation of Meaning in Language* (London and New York, 2003) pp. 26–29.
13 Cf. Breen, "Naming Practices in Western Ireland", pp. 701–703, 711–712; Ricoeur, *The Rule of Metaphor*, pp. 65. On the communal controlling function of unofficial naming cf. Pierre Bourdieu, "The Social Space and the Genesis of Groups", *Theory and Society* 14/6 (1985) pp. 732.

The stories attached to names included a certain degree of overstatement, exaggeration and perversion of the truth in order to communally justify the name choices. This fictional side of the anecdotes attached to names was connected to rumours and the exclusive nature of social memory. Seeds of truth were planted along the way, and stories were used as a way of structuring the world. Such stories were not necessarily completely true, but they still represented something of the values and opinions of those who were remembered and those who remembered.

My research is concerned with a small and remote agrarian community (the old parish of Kivijärvi in northern Central Finland) whose members were bound together by a tight network of interaction. The parish had a small population and so everybody knew each other. At the beginning of the twentieth century, following population growth in the preceding decades, the old parish of Kivijärvi was divided into three parishes: Kivijärvi, Kannonkoski and Kinnula (the latter two had originally been villages that formed part of the old Kivijärvi parish). I have used source material from the area covered by the old parish. Around four hundred people lived in the villages of Kivijärvi in the 1750s. The population grew to about one thousand in 1800, and by 1860 Kivijärvi was home to over three thousand people. In the 1910s, just before Kinnula became an independent parish, Kivijärvi had almost six thousand inhabitants. By the mid-twentieth century, Kinnula and Kivijärvi had populations of around three thousand and Kannonkoski was home to around three and a half thousand people.[14]

Agriculture provided the primary means of earning a livelihood in old Kivijärvi. The largest social groups within the community were householders, sharecroppers and cottagers. Only a few educated people or families who belonged to the upper estates lived in the parish: the most important of these were chaplains and, after the mid-nineteenth century, vicars. The end of the nineteenth century saw the beginning of an influx of shopkeepers and officials (such as schoolteachers), who moved into the parish area from elsewhere in Finland. Economic and cultural modernization took place relatively late (in the twentieth century) in this

---

14 Kotilainen, *Suvun nimissä*, pp. 363–364 (appendix 2).

small local community. Inhabitants who had been born in Kivijärvi were usually fairly closely related and had family ties common for several of them: their families had lived in the area for several centuries. Social control was strong and changed only gradually. Long-standing communality was based and depended upon patriarchal family and kinship networks.[15]

Nicknames (like all other personal names) are clues, which can provide a wealth of information about human nature and activities, even though they form a relatively small part of language.[16] I study the moral assumptions of small communities primarily in the light of local memory and oral tradition, because memory and oral tradition provide a way of examining the mentalities of social groups that are not represented in other source material. This is especially true of the lower social classes in the early modern era: Finnish-speaking agrarian people did not produce many written documents themselves. Nicknames were not widely recorded in official documents, but they can certainly be found within oral traditions. In my earlier research I have studied naming practices among rural kinship communities in the Kivijärvi region from the beginning of the eighteenth century to the middle of the twentieth century. I have used collective biographical data (of around nine thousand individuals) in order to determine the attitudes and values that lay behind name-giving practices within the families studied. I have also examined the continuities and changes that occurred when individualization and modern civic society gradually displaced the hereditary customs of traditional agrarian society and weakened local social control.[17] All

15 Kotilainen, *Suvun nimissä*, pp. 107–118, 375–377 (appendices 7–8).
16 Carlo Ginzburg, *Johtolankoja: Kirjoituksia mikrohistoriasta ja historiallisesta metodista* (Helsinki, 1996), pp. 45–50, 68–75.
17 CBD: Collective biographical data concerning the Hakkarainen and Kotilainen families, who lived in the Kivijärvi area, have been compiled mainly from documents in the archives of the parishes of Kannonkoski, Kinnula, Kivijärvi, and Viitasaari. These comprise records of baptisms, marriages and funerals; confirmation records and records of unconfirmed children; migration records and demographic statistics. The oldest archives of the parishes of Viitasaari and Kivijärvi are stored in the Provincial Archives of Jyväskylä. The research extends from c. 1730 to 1960. Compiled by Sofia Kotilainen. Kotilainen, *Suvun nimissä*; Sofia Kotilainen, "Förtroende och andra former av symboliskt kapital i fadderskapsstrategier", *Historisk Tidskrift för Finland* 97 (3) 2012; Sofia Kotilainen, "Several names, several identities? The orthography of Finnish country people's names from the 18th to 20th centuries". Ann-Catrine Edlund & Susanne Haugen (ed.), *Människor som skriver. Perspektiv på vardagligt skriftbruk och identitet.* Nordliga studier 4, Vardagligt skriftbruk 2 (Umeå, 2013); Sofia Kotilainen, "Rural people's literacy skills in the remembrance of the departed: the writing of personal names on sepulchral monuments at the turn of the nineteenth and twentieth centuries", *Mortality*, 18 (2) 2013.

nicknames that I mention in this article do not necessarily belong to the members of the two families, who compose my collective biographical database. I have also referred to other local people. However, most of those mentioned were still kin to each other. My research is therefore particularly focused on naming practices within agrarian kinship communities.

In brief, morality can be seen as the distillation of dominant communal views, appreciations and norms that determine what is good or bad, right or wrong, valuable or worthless, and approved or rejected. In this respect the concept of morality relates to social control, a concept which is a very ambiguous and much-researched phenomenon.[18] From the age of Enlightenment onwards, European gentility and learned people defined their moral philosophical principles by invoking not only religion, but also temporal authorities (such as ancient Greek or contemporary thinkers). Discussions and debates on the subject increased as the modern self-concept began to develop in an increasingly individual direction.[19]

Communal norms were constructed quite differently among the Finnish peasant population. Lutheranism and popular moral assumptions (often inherited from forefathers) were central, with the result that the local community in the early modern period was rather coherent in terms of mentality. The controlling power within peripheral rural communities greatly regulated the opportunities for individualization, the emergence of increasingly "inner" norms (i.e. self-control) and the development of individual conscience in the early modern era – something that permeated religiosity. The crumbling of the older, collective world of ideas had progressed so far by the end of the eighteenth century that individualism gradually began to determine the mentality of the rural population. The individual started to perceive his or her soul

---

18 See, for example, Olli Matikainen, *Verenperijät: Väkivalta ja yhteisön murros itäisessä Suomessa 1500–1600-luvulla* (Bibliotheca Historica 78; Helsinki, 2002); Pieter Spierenburg, "Social Control and History: An Introduction", in Herman Roodenburg and Pieter Spierenburg (ed.), *Social Control in Europe* vol. I: *1500–1800* (Columbus, 2004), pp. 1–17. On the other hand one can see that nicknames have also challenged or questioned communal morals and existing norms to some extent. Blok, *Honour and Violence*, pp. 156.

19 J. B. Schneewind, *The Invention of Autonomy: A History of Modern Moral Philosophy* (Cambridge, 1998); Adam Smith, *The Theory of Moral Sentiments*, ed. Knud Haakonssen (Cambridge Texts in the History of Philosophy; Cambridge, 2002 [1759]).

as being separate from nature and the community around him. As communal norms loosened to a more unofficial direction, the consciousness of one's own self strengthened in relation to communal force.[20] Modernization changed the situation very slowly, however. Communality in Kivijärvi, for instance, was still relatively strong at the beginning of the twentieth century.

The early modern agrarian community and its strong sense of mutual belonging did not represent an ideal state of communality, a social model in which continuous love for one's neighbour could have existed. In a situation where nobody was left alone, the community could (if it so wished) stigmatize and marginalize those members who were disliked. Name-calling was often real mockery or mischief, an attempt to draw collective attention to an individual's negative quality or qualities. At the basis of communality is the debarring of differentially treated individuals.[21] However, for the individual involved, remaining a member of their local community, despite the stigmatization, was often the only option; the traditional home district of his family and his closest kin formed a safety net without which it was difficult to manage, either socially or economically.[22]

Communal respectability and being honourable referred both to the individual's understanding of their own behaviour and to the community's perceptions that behaviour. Reputation was based on what others thought of a person and the way in which they voiced their opinions about him. In the Finnish language the idea of reputation has also been understood as subsequent criticism or after-effect: reputation was formed not only through gossip, but also by what the community (afterwards) remembered and mentioned of a person's life. The blameless-

---

20 Cf. Norbert Elias, *The Civilizing Process*, vol. I: *The History of Manners* (Oxford, 1978), pp. 252–262; Petri Karonen, *Pohjoinen suurvalta: Ruotsi ja Suomi 1521–1809* (Porvoo–Helsinki–Juva, 1999) pp. 48–53, 161–167, 334–336, 341–342; Kotilainen, *Suvun nimissä*; Sofia Kotilainen, "Namngivningspraxis och attityder: val av kungliga och kejserliga förnamn hos den finskspråkiga allmogen efter år 1809", *Folkmålsstudier* 47 (Meddelanden från Föreningen för nordisk filologi. Helsingfors, 2009); Kustaa H. J. Vilkuna, "Jumala elä rankase minua: Yksilöllisen subjektin synty", in Heikki Roiko-Jokela (ed.), *Siperiasta siirtoväkeen: Murrosaikoja ja käännekohtia Suomen historiassa* (Jyväskylä, 1996) pp. 71–73.
21 Stuart Hall, "Kulttuurisen identiteetin kysymyksiä", in Stuart Hall, *Identiteetti* ed. Mikko Lehtonen and Juha Herkman (Tampere, 1999) pp. 22, 152–154; Pirjo Markkola, "Marginaali historian keskipisteessä", in Jarmo Peltola and Pirjo Markkola (ed.), *Kuokkavieraiden pidot: Historian marginaalista marginaalihistoriaan* (Tampere, 1996) pp. 9–11.
22 Kotilainen, *Suvun nimissä*, pp. 69–70, 113–117.

ness or "badness" of a reputation was connected to having a "good or bad name" in the local community. Etymologically, in Finnish "naming" is close to "mentioning".[23] An individual's name, reputation and identity overlapped in many ways. Confidence in the individual himself and the good name of his family were of crucial importance. Honourableness, like all other human qualities, is thus relative, connected to time, place and community. Honour attached to names is a case of social capital (trust and shared communal values). However, some information about personal nicknames was not distributed to all members of the community: "And then those names of one's own nobody knew, so that it was spoken there only besides. And few knew self name of one's own."[24] This again originates from the communal function of naming: it was a way to control the community's opinion about the individual.

Different forms of controlling naming

Giving nicknames was a culturally constructed and relatively stable institution in the early modern period. The linguistic content of unofficial names often described a specific quality of an individual. However, the name itself was not always so transparent. Often in oral memory a short explanatory story is attached to a nickname, and this allows one to define its origins. Nicknames and their explanations were frequently represented in a form of dictum. In pre-literary culture, proverbs performed the essential function of maintaining experiential information. In short polished information was usually learnt by ear as part of the everyday chores of early youth. This formed the foundation of popular thoughts, and knowledge attained later in life built upon this. Proverbs were essentially compacted experiential information, and this was especially true in a community steeped in oral tradition. With the help of proverbs,

---

23 For example Christfrid Ganander, *Nytt Finskt Lexicon*, ed. Liisa Nuutinen (Helsinki, 1997 [original manuscript 1787]) p. 535; cf. Jari Eilola, "Cuca tiesi cungin mielen? Kengä kenegä sydämen? Maine ja luotettavuus uuden ajan alun pikkukaupungeissa", in Jari Eilola (ed.), *Sietämättömät ja täydellinen maailma: Kirjoituksia suvaitsemattomuudesta* (Jyväskylän Historiallinen Arkisto 6; Jyväskylä, 2003) pp. 126–131.
24 Interview H8 with a woman born in Kivijärvi in the 1920s. 3/12/2005.

old wisdom could be applied and adapted according to recent events. Using familiar dictums, members of the community could teach, thank, scold, annoy and insult others without being too outspoken. The meaning of one's words would have been clear to anyone from the same social circle.[25]

The sources I have analysed consist of archive material from the Institute for the Languages of Finland. The names have been selected to material from the name-collecting competition of 1972 (this material was recorded by local amateurs). Although the material provides information about names at very different times (extending from the end of the nineteenth century until the 1950s and beyond), it was compiled at the same point in time.[26] More complete analysis of the material would also require reciprocal comparison of a source group of a different type and from a different period.[27] Nevertheless, the mere analysis of the competition results already reveals a number of motives for particular name selections. Together with the results of my earlier research, this material indicates that changes in naming practices took place alongside the modernization of early modern communal life.

Knowledge about old nicknames may not always be available; it can be far removed from even the older generations. Those interviewed have not necessarily been able to explain some nicknames. This applies to between 7 and 9 percent of all nicknames of both sexes, a rather small proportion.[28] Often the name in question is very old and its linguistic origin has become unclear. These names also include old dialectical words that are very general, or linguistically non-transparent in other ways. Without an accurate memory of the naming process, it is impossible to explain how such words became part of an individual's nickname.

---

25 Natalie Zemon Davis, *Society and Culture in Early Modern France* (Stanford, Calif., 1977 [1975]) pp. 243–244; Outi Lauhakangas *Puheesta ihminen tunnetaan. Sananlaskujen funktiot sosiaalisessa vuorovaikutuksessa* (Suomalaisen Kirjallisuuden Seuran Toimituksia 1001; Helsinki, 2004) pp. 135–166.
26 Eeva Maria Närhi, "The Onomastic Central Archives: The Foundation of Finnish Onomastics", in Heikki Leskinen, and Eero Kiviniemi (ed.), *Finnish Onomastics: Namenkunde in Finnland* (Helsinki, 1990) pp. 15–17.
27 On the diverse sources of micro-level research into personal names, see Kotilainen, *Suvun nimissä*, pp. 26–44.
28 See tables 1 and 2.

The nicknames of my sources can be classified according to what would seem to have been the selection criteria: place of domicile, occupation or social position, physical or mental qualities, speech or special characteristics of language, and memorable incidents or occasions in a person's life.[29] In addition, I have also noted how naming practices varied according to gender and age. I have chosen to study in some detail those nicknames that can be dated with the help of other information about the individual. I have also connected the oral tradition with collective biographical data based on archive documents in order to verify the accuracy of oral memory, identify individuals who received nicknames, and examine with care the whole operational environment.[30] If one wishes to discover the whole diverse range of meanings of names, it is useful to know something more about individuals' life histories, rather than simply mere explanations of nicknames. The small quantity of collection material about nicknames from the 1950s completes the data about modern nicknames in Kinnula recorded in literature based on local oral memories.[31]

My sources include 182 nicknames from the region of old Kivijärvi. Of these, it is possible to date more accurately 119 nicknames, of which only around a fifth are women's nicknames. Men received nicknames significantly more often than women. In addition, the criteria for choosing men's and women's names were different. Men's nicknames were connected to place of domicile and occupation.[32] In this article the analy-

---

29 Earlier researchers of material relating to Finnish nicknames have drawn the same conclusions about groupings. Cf. Pekka Laaksonen, "Nätti, Tulikuuma ja Tuskanpunainen. Jätkäperinteen liikanimiä", in Hannes Sihvo (ed.), *Nimikirja*, Kalevalaseuran vuosikirja 52 (Helsinki–Porvoo, 1972) pp. 189–192; Samuli Paulaharju, "Lisä- ja haukkumanimistä", *Kotiseutu* 1912, 125–127; Urpo Vento, "Tunsitteko Jepulis-Penjamin? Liikanimistä ja roolinimistä kertomusperinteessä", in Hannes Sihvo (ed.), *Nimikirja*, Kalevalaseuran vuosikirja 52 (Helsinki–Porvoo, 1972) pp. 166–169, 175; Kustaa Vilkuna, "Ihmisten puhuttelua edessä ja takana", *Kotiseutu*. Suomen Kotiseutuliiton aikakauslehti 1958, 96–97. See also Blok, *Honour and Violence*, p. 159; Breen, "Naming Practices in Western Ireland", p. 707; Gilmore, "Some Notes on Community Nicknaming in Spain", pp. 689–691.
30 For the collective biographical method in historical research, see, for example, K. S. B. Keats-Rohan, "Biography, Identity and Names: Understanding the Pursuit of the Individual in Prosopography", in (ed.), *Prosopography Approaches and Applications. A Handbook* (Prosopographica et Genealogica 13; Oxford, 2007). Collective biographical data (CBD) relating to families and clans in Kivijärvi. Compiled by Sofia Kotilainen.
31 Kristiina Kinnunen, Piia Kinnunen, Tomi Niemonen, Mari Salonpää and Reetta Salonpää (ed.), *Ei nimi miestä pahenna: huumorilla höystettyä ruokaa Kinnulasta* (Kinnula, 2006).
32 Tables 1 and 2; CBD.

sis is concerned with only a small proportion of local nicknames: in reality, for instance, being named after a dwelling place or family member was substantially more common than the material might suggest. Without exception, every member of community would have received a nickname relating to his or her home, and most would also have been called by their parents' names since childhood.[33]

A person might have had more than one nickname. However, one or a few of these names generally became better known than the rest. This is also evident in oral memories. Attached quantitative examination of individuals shows that they could also have nicknames with dual elements, which explained the choice of name. These selection criteria have been expressed in the table so that each one forms half of a single name. One man, who lived in Kivijärvi at the turn of the nineteenth and twentieth centuries and worked as forest guard, was given a nickname that described not only his place of domicile, but also his leisure activities. He lived in Teerisuo (bog of black grouse) and was eager to tell hunting stories, in which he boasted considerably. The whole parish knew him familiarly as *Grouse-Vikke*.[34]

There were certain established practices of nickname formation, whether for an individual or a whole family. A man's occupation or his special skills compared with the rest of the community was often used as the basis for his nickname,[35] for example, *Pertti-suutar* or *Suutar-Pertti* ("Shoemaker Pertti")[36] and *Hauta-Poavo* ("Grave-Poavo") for gravedigger Paavo Nykänen.[37] Antti Hakkarainen, a small man born in Kivijärvi, worked as a tailor (at the turn of the nineteenth and twentieth century) and was especially known for making the finest women's clothes,

---

33 Cf. Kotilainen, *Suvun nimissä*, pp. 298–299. For instance in working communities of lumbermen the most common naming criteria has been outward appearance. Most workers would have come from outside the parish, their family and kin backgrounds would not have been widely known by others and the tasks performed by all members of the community would have broadly similar. Laaksonen, "Nätti, Tulikuuma ja Tuskanpunainen", p. 189.
34 Institute for the Languages of Finland (Kotus), Names Archive, nicknames, Kivijärvi, Pohjonen 1972. Vikke is popular form of the forename Vihtori (this is the Finnish equivalent of Viktor). Kustaa Vilkuna, *Etunimet*, ed. Pirjo Mikkonen. (4th edn., Helsinki, 2005 [1976]) p. 248.
35 Interview H5 with a man born in Kivijärvi in the 1910s. 28/7/2005.
36 This seems to be a Finnish shortened form of the German forename Albert or Adalbert. It may also be a shortened form of Robert, Herbert, Hubert or Engelbert. Vilkuna, *Etunimet*, p. 181.
37 Finnish Literature Society (SKS), Folklore Archives (KRA). Rautiainen Albert 2227. 1950 and 3931. 1960.

hence those who mocked him would refer to Antti as *Mamselli-Antti* ("Mademoiselle-Antti"). As a young man Yrjö Hakkarainen was known as Graduate Forester, when he said of himself when arrived to the forest working site, that the "Forest officer is coming". Lauri or Lassi Kotilainen, who had graduated from merchants' school, was called the "rejoicing shopkeeper" because he "went from feast to feast with a violin and played. The whole village knew this name."[38]

Tab. 1: Selection criteria of men's nicknames

TIME	A	B	C	D	E	F	G	H	TOTAL	TOTAL
	%	%	%	%	%	%	%	%	N	%
late 1800	35,4	22,9	12,5	4,2	4,2	8,3	8,3	4,2	24	100
early 1900	25,0	17,5	10,0	12,5	8,8	6,3	10,0	10,0	40	100
1920's–1930's	27,8	29,6	13,0	11,1	3,7	3,7	3,7	7,4	27	100
1950's	33,3	0,0	41,7	25,0	0,0	0,0	0,0	0,0	6	100
TOTAL	28,9	21,1	13,4	10,8	5,7	5,7	7,2	7,2	97	100

Explanations of the capital letters: A = place of domicile, B = occupation, C = physical qualities, D = occurences and incidents, E = linguistic anomalies, F = mental qualities, G = family member, H = inexplicable
Source: Kotus, Names Archive, nicknames, Kannonkoski, Kinnula and Kivijärvi (1972).

It was very common for individuals to be named after their dwelling places. Such nicknames consisted of the farmstead name and a Christian name.[39] Women seldom received nicknames that were known by the wider local community. For a woman to be given a name that expressed something other than her place of domicile or family background, she had to occupy a position in her local community that was somehow exceptional. Often women who were nicknamed were involved with public life or economic activity in one way or another.[40] For

---

38 Kotus, Names Archive, nicknames, Kivijärvi, Pohjonen 1972.
39 Laaksonen, "Nätti, Tulikuuma ja Tuskanpunainen"; Vento, "Tunsitteko Jepulis-Penjamin?"; Vilkuna "Ihmisten puhuttelua edessä ja takana".
40 For instance, in sixteenth-century French towns, women who had a public occupation (such as midwife or teacher) might be given a special nickname. Very old women were also typically given nicknames. Cf. Blok, *Honour and Violence*, p. 167; Davis, *Society and Culture in Early Modern France*, p. 71.

example, midwives, held in very high esteem within the local hierarchy because of their special skills, may have been given nicknames that were widely known.[41]

Tab. 2: Selection criteria of women's nicknames

	A	B	C	D	E	F	G	H	TOTA	TOTA
	%	%	%	%	%	%	%	&	N	%
Late 1800	50,0	33,3	0,0	0,0	0,0	16,7	0,0	0,0	6	100
Early 1900	55,6	16,7	0,0	5,6	22,2	0,0	0,0	0,0	9	100
1920s–1930s	14,3	14,3	35,7	21,4	0,0	14,3	0,0	0,0	7	100
1950s	0,0	0,0	0,0	0,0	0,0	0,0	0,0	0,0	0	100
TOTAL	40,0	20,0	11,1	11,1	8,9	8,9	0,0	0,0	22	100

A = family names, B = place of domicile, C = occupation, D = mental qualities, E = physical qualities, F = inexplicable, G = linguistic anomalies, H = occurrences and indicents
Source: Kotus, Names Archive, nicknames, Kannonkoski, Kinnula and Kivijärvi (1972).

Women's nicknames most often referred in some way to a family member (in 40 percent of cases). Women were frequently named after their place of domicile, but not quite as commonly as was the case among men.[42] Women who, in the eyes of their community, had quite a bad reputation or who had lost their reputation entirely were most likely given unofficial names. The receiving (and giving) of nicknames was a gendered practice. Most women were called only after their fathers, husbands or sons (in other words, the male heads of family). In a fairly typical form of nickname the genitive form of the man's (husband's) forename would be attached to the women's forename. Thus, the way in which women were named often reflected their connection to a man with a higher status than themselves in the hierarchy of the patriarchal community.[43] In this way, naming practices functioned as a means of exerting and reflecting social control over women.

41 Cf. Kotus, Names Archive, nicknames, Kivijärvi, Pohjonen 1972.
42 Tables 1 and 2.
43 Kotilainen, *Suvun nimissä*, pp. 82–84, 287.

Unusual physical and mental qualities

My source material indicates that, in addition to the more common origins of nicknames (place of domicile, occupation and family), there were also other recurrent themes among the choice of nicknames. Physical appearance and mental attributes could be combined with forenames or surnames to form a socially controlling nickname. Such nicknames were more common among men than women and they also divided to different periods of time more regularly.[44] However, in some cases a nickname that referred to a woman's physical appearance became particularly well known. Normally women occupied a lower position than men within the agrarian social hierarchy of power. For this reason, a woman who was exceptionally tall or fat was regarded as abnormal – some kind of spectacle, a wonder of nature or simply as a good joke. Large women were collectively viewed as freaks. Through naming, the community reminded them of their appearance and status. *Isohilma* ("Big Hilma"), for example, was well known because she was very fat.[45] Although there were also many overweight men, in this case a woman was even larger than the men around her. Hilma had to be shown her place through the use of an insulting name (or names).

In other ways, being fat was not necessarily perceived negatively in agrarian Finland. In fact, being able to eat so much that one gained weight (despite daily hard work) was also a sign of well-being.[46] In earlier years Kivijärvi residents sometimes said that it "can be seen from well to home, like Drying barn-Emma". The Emma in question was the big and handsome daughter of a Kivijärvi householder.[47] Sightings of her large figure were not necessarily reported in negative tones. In those days, a householder's wife (like the farm owner himself) was supposed to look strong and well fed, because this symbolized the prosperity of the farm.[48] Those working in agrarian household would eat heavy meals

---

44 Tables 1 and 2.
45 Kotus, Names Archive, place-names, Kyyjärvi, Kolhinen 1969.
46 Kotilainen, *Suvun nimissä*; cf. Anu Korhonen, *Silmän ilot: Kauneuden kulttuurihistoriaa uuden ajan alussa* (Jyväskylä, 2005) pp. 51–57, 59, 73.
47 SKS KRA. Leppänen, Jalmari 113. 1937.
48 Interview H1, with a man born in Kivijärvi in the 1910s. 26/7/2000; c.f. Korhonen 2005, 51–57, 59, 73.

(at least when farmer provided them meals), but they also burnt off a lot of energy through physical toil.[49] After the famine of 1860s one could keep as a wealthy and this way respectable such rural being, whose body caught store extra nutriment.

Names that referred to a person's physical appearance could be given at anytime, whether as a child or when old age had been etched onto the body. Some people's physical features (and the collective references to them) seem to have accompanied them from the cradle to the grave. In some cases, a person's way of life might have increased the prominence given to their features in the collective imagination. *Haukka-Ellu* ("Hawk-Ellu"),[50] for example, "resembled a kind of a hawk. Eyes, nose and mouth tight. Grabbed the hand like a hawk would have pounced on its prey. A famous fighter in his day, and had a lot of scars. When he came to a house where local people were celebrating a wedding, he had asked whether he could brawl if he would pay the damages.[51] He died in the 1920s as an old man."[52]

Quite often informal, popular nicknames – even though they might be completely neutral in their linguistic meaning – would be given to people with personalities that were viewed as unique or to those who had been deemed insane or mentally ill. Such individuals and their behaviour were considered to be in some way abnormal, and this difference from the rest of the community seems to have stuck in minds of local people. My research material suggests that these exceptional personalities came to mind more easily when informants were reminiscing about nicknames they heard and used as children and adolescents. This was true even when the nicknames themselves were not exceptional and were similar to the names given to "normal" villagers.[53]

---

49 Sofia Kotilainen (ed.), *Het pikkusevverran paljo Kivijärven Perinnepiirin tallentamaa muistitietoa* (Kivijärvi, 2001) pp. 50–52, 200–201.
50 Here, Ellu is a dialectal form of the man's name Elias.
51 *"Saako rahalla räiskää?"*
52 Kotus, Names Archive, nicknames, Kivijärvi, Takkala 1972.
53 For example, Kotus, Names Archive, nicknames, Kannonkoski, Kokkila 1972, Kinnula, Nykänen 1972.

Linguistic anomalies: repetition and expletives

It seems that nicknames could also refer to linguistic anomalies such as (largely unconscious) repetition of sounds or words. The community, perhaps bored by the meaningless interjections they heard day after day, would ease their irritation by using them as the basis of a nickname. Almost every third word used by *Tuota-Ville* was the word *tuota* ("er", or perhaps "like", would be its English equivalent).[54] *Änkkä-Lempi* ("Stammering Lempi") "got her name already as a child because of her stammering speech, and she had to keep it for the rest of her life. The village community knew her only by this name."[55] In oral culture, speech disorders became emphasized through social communication. There was greater stigma attached to such disorders was much greater than was attached to illiteracy for nineteenth- and early twentieth-century peasants.

Those who could not speak were referred to as someone who differed from other locals. The stigmatization of someone who was dumb was often expressed through a nickname.[56] Overall linguistic anomalies were the origin of less than six percent of men's nicknames, and among women these kinds of names existed not without one exception.[57] Speech defects were, after all, relatively rare. Thus, the community noticed, remembered and remarked on speech disorders when they heard them, and for this reason they could easily be mocked. Some of those who had speech defects faced their challenges fearlessly. In turn-of-the-century Kivijärvi, Jussi Kinnunen, also known as *Rappos-Jussi*, bravely used the r-phoneme despite his difficulties. He reportedly "crushed the r", when using terms and phrases that he had specifically sought out because they contained the r-phoneme. Jussi worked as a carpenter and built several cottages, all of which were sold without difficulty. When going to the building site he reportedly always said with burr: "Must go to the merry-go-round."[58]

---

54 Kotus, Names Archive, nicknames, Kannonkoski, Heino 1972.
55 Kotus, Names Archive, nicknames, Kivijärvi, Rautiainen 1972.
56 Kotus, Names Archive, nicknames, Kannonkoski, Ruhanen 1968–1969.
57 Tables 1 and 2.
58 Kotus, Names Archive, nicknames, Kivijärvi, Takkala 1972.

Accidents happen: situation comedy in names

Some men's nicknames were derived from unforgettable occasions or incidents. This was not the case for women, and it seems likely that this difference stemmed from the fact that men more frequently moved and acted in the world outside the household. Most of the remembered names of this origin in Kivijärvi date from the beginning of the twentieth century.[59] Usually it was people who repeated phrases or sayings or who consistently behaved in a certain way that received nicknames. However, in some cases the humorousness of a single incident (or its absurdity or exceptionality) resulted in a permanent name[60]. "In the nineteenth century, one man who was searching for his cottage had said that he was looking for a place for his *kölsä*[61]. This was the reason why people called him Kölsäläinen[62] and why people also spoke of Kölsä's cottage."[63] But if you don't do anything, you don't make mistakes either. "Someone could get a name that played a joke on her. If, for example, parishioners thought she, [as a] cottager woman, was too dressed up."[64] Unfortunately, common opinion was slow to change after something negative or amusing had happened. The social memory of the local community had a long reach and could extend through several generations.

At worst, name-calling could also result in communal sanctions. In Kivijärvi people started to call a man (whose family name was Kotilainen) Sibelius, "since he invented that song. Sibelius was the kind of man who constructed songs about his neighbours for the fun of it and one of the neighbours reared up and came to complain to the rural police chief. The police chief pondered how he should proceed. He told his officers to fetch that man and that the accordion should also be collected. So, in came Sibelius and his accordion, two-row accordion, on his shoulder.

---

59 Tables 1 and 2.
60 See, for example, Kinnunen et al., *Ei nimi miestä pahenna*.
61 *Kölsä* was an old dialectal form of the word *mökki*, in the sense of a dilapidated cottage, i.e. a hut or shack (*hybble* in Swedish). Cf. Ganander, *Nytt Finskt Lexicon*, p. 384.
62 In the Finnish language personal appellations are often formed from place names and other nouns signifying places combined with the derivative suffix *-lainen/ -läinen*. The suffix *-inen* has also been commonly used in eastern peasant surnames.
63 Kotus, Names Archive, nicknames, Kannonkoski, Heino 1972.
64 Cf. Kotus, Names Archive, nicknames, Kivijärvi, Pohjonen 1972.

And police chief said: 'this person here complains that you have made up a libellous song about him'. Sibelius said that yes he has made up a song, but that he has not done it to mock someone. He just made up a song.[65]

It was summertime, and there was a rowan tree there in the yard. It was there in the old cantor's house where he lived, where there was the office of the local police chief. So police chief told him 'under that rowan you go to sit and sing that song'. He listened with the policemen, the complainant was there also. And then Sibelius started to play the song with his two-row accordion. He sang the song precisely from the beginning to the end. And there were not such ribald words in the song, that one could perform it. But it was such an amusing song that the police chief said afterwards that it had really been difficult for him to keep straight-faced, but serious he had to be. And when Sibelius got to the end, the police chief said 'go to your homes, this is not a mockery song [...]'. But people then gave the name Sibelius to that man."[66]

The effect of modernization on the controlling dimension of nicknames

A prerequisite of all communal action in the early modern age was that parties involved could trust one another. Everyone depended on the everyday safety net of the local community. The reputation of names – that is, which personal features or attributes became known in the community and were attached to his names – defined an individual's public image. For early modern people honourableness meant the right to be treated as a person with his or her own value. It was a natural quality, which was manifested in the social respect he or she enjoyed.[67] Analysis of the selec-

---

65 Sofia Kotilainen (ed.), "Minä tiijän yhen tappauksen", *Viiden Kunnan Sanomat* 30 (2005) p. 21.
66 Kotilainen, "Minä tiijän yhen tappauksen", p. 21. On the communal functions of mockery songs cf. also Marjatta Rahikainen, "Yhteisöjen nurja puoli: Nimittely ja pilkkaaminen maalaispitäjässä", in Riitta Oittinen and Marjatta Rahikainen (ed.), *Keulakuvia ja peränpitäjiä: Vanhan ja uuden yhteiskunnan rajalla* (Helsinki, 2000) pp. 166–177; Kustaa H. J. Vilkuna, "Herotes oli koira: humoristinen puhe rikoksena", in Olli Matikainen (ed.), *Rikos historiassa* (Jyväskylän Historiallinen Arkisto 5; Jyväskylä, 2000) pp. 229–266.
67 Natalie Zemon Davis, *Women on the Margins: Three Seventeenth-Century Lives* (Cambridge, Mass., 1997) pp. 8, 34–35; Frank Henderson Stewart, *Honor* (Chicago and London, 1994) p. 21; *Vanhan kirjasuomen sanakirja: Toinen osa J–K* (Kotimaisten kielten tutkimuskeskuksen julkaisuja 1994; Helsinki, 1994), pp. 769–770.

tion criteria behind nicknames emphasizes how the community defined the quality of someone's honour and reputation rather than how a person himself understood his own respectability. The focus is therefore on the image of individual in the eyes of community: the community's perception of him[68], even if this was inaccurate and had been hewn by mockers.

Reputation is based on being noticed. Once someone has received recognition of some sort – whether they have been found to be more prominent or more incapable than others – it is hard for them to rid themselves of this reputation. It becomes a stigma, which a person bears with him, like a name. At the same time, this acknowledgment of deviance from others produces an individual identity, in the same way as a proper name's function is to separate him from others.[69] Being identifiable is also based on a form of trust: others can rely on the fact that the individual will display a consistent kind of behaviour in his social relations. For example, an individual will usually be responsible and keep his word, when he has made a promise.[70] The function of communal trust was to reduce randomness and unpredictability in social relations.[71]

Local name-calling practices changed from the end of the nineteenth century to the 1950s. This was not so apparent in names that referred to place of domicile or occupation, because almost everyone could have been referred to in this way (in reality such names were even more common than the quantitative study here suggests). However, the practice of incorporating a family member's name into a nickname changed significantly by the first decades of the twentieth century. Among women such names had become less common by the 1920s and 1930s. Although the local community still was patriarchal to a certain extent, naming practices were already changing. It is also likely that such names were more

---

68 An individual's reputation is formed when he acts as a part of a communal network: social relationships that extended over a wide area and high enough up the social hierarchy were usually prerequisites for achieving respect and reputation. Charles J. Fombrun, *Reputation: Realizing Value from the Corporate Image* (Boston, 1996) p. 21.
69 C.f. Fombrun, *Reputation*, pp. 10–11, 18.
70 C.f. Fombrun, *Reputation*, pp. 60–68; Anthony Giddens, *The Consequences of Modernity* (Cambridge, 1995 [1990]) pp. 32–35; Robert D. Putnam, *Bowling Alone: The Collapse and Revival of American Community* (New York, 2000) pp. 134–138; *Vanhan kirjasuomen sanakirja, toinen osa J–K* (Helsinki, 1994) pp. 773–775.
71 Barbara A. Misztal, *Trust in Modern Societies: The Search for the Bases of Social Order* (Cambridge, 1998 [1996]) pp. 12, 16–17.

common than the research material suggests, but by the mid-twentieth century women clearly started to be defined by other features, such as occupation. Women increasingly began to work or participate in the local community outside their own households. Occupational naming in twentieth-century male nicknames also increased, and at the same time "family member" male nicknames (already relatively rare among adult men) became statistically insignificant. Local occupational structures were changing radically and with modernization men, in particular, found themselves undertaking new, and increasingly non-agrarian, occupations (such as lorry driver or shop assistant, for example).[72]

Tab. 3: Comparison of the differences between women's and men's nicknames

TIME	A	A	B	B	C	C	D	D	TOTAL	TOTAL
	N	%	N	%	N	%	N	%	N	%
late 1800										
men	2	8,3	5,5	22,9	3	12,5	2	8,3	24	52,0
women	3	50,0	0	0,0	0	0,0	0	0,0	6	50,0
early 1900										
men	4	10,0	7	17,5	4	10,0	2,5	6,3	40	43,8
women	5	55,6	0	0,0	2	22,2	0,5	5,6	9	83,4
1920's–1930's										
men	1	3,7	8	29,6	3,5	13,0	1	3,7	27	50,0
women	1	14,3	2,5	35,7	0	0,0	1,5	21,4	7	71,4
1950's										
men	0	0,0	0	0,0	2,5	41,7	0	0,0	6	41,7
women	0	0,0	0	0,0	0	0,0	0	0,0	0	0
TOTAL										
men	7	7,2	20,5	21,1	13	13,4	5,5	5,7	97	47,4
women	9	40,0	2,5	11,1	2	8.9	2,5	11,1	22	71,1

Explanations of the capital letters: A = family member, B = occupation, C = physical quality, D = mental quality
Source: Kotus, Names Archive, nicknames, Kannonkoski, Kinnula and Kivijärvi (1972).

72 Tables 1, 2 and 3; Kotilainen, *Suvun nimissä*, pp. 373–374 (Appendix 6).

Male and female nicknames based on personal qualities did not change in the same ways. Names based on appearance had become more common among men by the 1950s; whereas the practice of naming women in this way had reduced. Undoubtedly the study of changes in female nicknames of this kind is complicated by the fact that the research material contains little information about physical qualities, even though these names were likely to have been more commonly used in the community. The trend for nicknames based on mental qualities has been entirely different. There was a notable increase in the number of female names based on mental qualities in the early twentieth century, but male names of a similar type decreased.[73] This shift of focus from female appearance to female mental characteristics indicates that name-givers had begun to consider women as more active communal actors, rather than just objects to be physically appraised. It seems that female speech – both what was said and how it was said – as well as thoughts and actions began to interest (predominantly male) name-givers more than had previously been the case.

In Kinnula there is a relatively old and strong tradition of giving humorous nicknames. Such nicknames characteristically develop among men as they undertake their daily chores, and in most cases only men have been given nicknames. The concept of name-smiths has been mentioned within the context of name-giving.[74] This reference to the artisan profession is interesting because it accurately reflects the relationship between name-giving and other forms of language. The name-smith skilfully connects old and new material. In this way he creates and compiles the spoken language of his community, whose insights have become part of the community's everyday communication. Fluent language and verbal expression have to primarily include in "informational capital", especially with regard to grammatical knowledge. However, at the same time rhetorical knowledge helps to make speech socially and culturally acceptable, and thus is required for language to become social capital. A gifted speaker can often convince others and bring them

---

73 Tables 1 and 2.
74 Kinnunen et al., *Ei nimi miestä pahenna*, foreword and pp. 45, 52 (Kinnula's naming tradition is still evident at the beginning of the twenty-first century and shows no sign of fading away).

to his side, which makes speech a communal action. If speech is not socially correct, the communicative function of language is not feasible. The value of linguistic capital is determined by the "markets" and social relationships within which language is used.[75]

Nicknames that have endured usually describe their subjects concisely and can serve as a verbal monument of an aspect or phase of an individual's life. The kinds of naming skills seen in Kinnula have (in the twentieth century and even earlier) resulted in inventive minds in the community assigning a humorous nickname on the basis of an individual's experiences. There is usually a juicy story behind such nicknames. In some cases they have their origins in youth, or they have been given soon after individuals moved to the parish or began to take part in communal activities. Many names stem from an individual's occupation or livelihood. Modern "name-bearers" know the histories of their names, and for many they are also a source of pride. Receiving a funny but harmless nickname from fellow villagers is also traditionally a sign of approval in Kinnula.[76] Nicknames can be used as symbols of communality, as a trademark of a group (consisting of neighbours, villagers or parishioners). When they are pejorative, however, such names are also a form of debarment from the community.

In Kinnula, like elsewhere in Kivijärvi, the need to distinguish between namesakes has been a significant function of nicknames.[77] Nicknames have been also inherited names: in Kinnula, for example, nicknames have been transferred from father to son[78] and may also have been applied to all kin as a memory of the forefather's nickname. Such nicknames may have been used to distinguish between other people with the same surname.[79] There is a long-standing tradition of nicknaming in Kinnula, particularly because these names have been used on a daily

---

75 Pierre Bourdieu, *Sosiologian kysymyksiä* (Tampere, 1985) pp. 94–95, 112–113; Pierre Bourdieu, *Language and Symbolic Power* (Cambridge, 2003 [1991]) pp. 66–76; Quentin Skinner, *Visions of Politics* vol. I: *Regarding Method* (Cambridge, 2002) pp. 82, 103–104.
76 Cf. Kinnunen et al., *Ei nimi miestä pahenna*, passim.
77 Kinnunen et al., *Ei nimi miestä pahenna*, pp. 33, 39, 60; Kotilainen, *Suvun nimissä*, p. 95.
78 And, at least in the latter half of the twentieth century, nicknames could also be passed from a father to his daughter.
79 Since the nicknames characteristic for some part of kin has also been used as enterprise names. See, for example, Kinnunen et al., *Ei nimi miestä pahenna*, p. 45.

basis. In the twentieth century at least, nicknames have been used so often that informants have sometimes found it difficult to immediately recall the official (church-registered) name of someone they have been discussing. Furthermore, by the end of the century, nicknames were also frequently used in front of the named person. Individuals are well aware of their own nicknames and may even have adjusted it. Several of those, whose nickname is extremely well known, have even received mail addressed to their nickname and giving only Kinnula as their address.[80]

Nicknames were still being given at the beginning of the twenty-first century and so it seems that the tradition is still alive in the area. Although nicknames are no longer so strongly connected to control within the local hierarchy, they still have social value. Nowadays, men are proud of their names and the stories behind them. They describe how local nicknames have become "honorary titles" (sometimes even "hereditary titles") and claim that pejorative names are no longer known.[81] However, this could be a reflection of the earlier tradition that you never tell an individual about their worst nicknames, even though you might share such information with many other members of your local community. With the modernization of society nicknames became public secrets to a greater extent than had previously been the case.[82] They were used only in unofficial situations if one really wanted to estimate an individual, but in order not to insult an individual (and by extension his family) public naming was avoided.

Nicknames as symbols of intangible capital and communal power

In agrarian communities the most important everyday types of nicknames derived from someone's place of domicile or family background.

---

[80] Interview H10 with a man born in Kivijärvi in the 1940s. 8/4/2007; Kinnunen et al., *Ei nimi miestä pahenna*, passim.

[81] Kinnunen et al., *Ei nimi miestä pahenna*, passim. Cf. also Rahikainen, "Yhteisöjen nurja puoli", pp. 165–166.

[82] Cf. Blok, *Honour and Violence*, p. 156; Gilmore, "Some Notes on Community Nicknaming in Spain", pp. 693–694.

Nicknames that referred to specific occasions were common, as were occupational nicknames for those members of an agrarian community whose livelihood was not directly based on farming. Physical or mental qualities were the basis for only a relatively small minority of nicknames, which were used largely when these qualities were significantly different from the norm. We should note the challenges that the source material presents. In competition collections of nicknames, selections have been made by the collector (and the informants). Nicknames only used by very close family or kin are not well represented, and there were hardly any examples of more negative nicknames of anyone still living at the time names were being compiled. Nevertheless, identifying various groupings of names has brought to the fore certain communal values and appreciations. In the early modern period an individual's social position – or in the case of a woman that of the head of her family – was more important than his or her personal qualities. The importance of individual attributes within naming practices began to increase in the modern era.

Giving nicknames has been particularly characteristic of "manly" culture. Personal nicknames were almost never given to women unless they had placed themselves in a central and visible position in the local community – in other words that their presence was noticed and had an impact upon men's sphere of action. A woman with an occupation outside of her household (for example, a teacher or a postmistress) had in her behaviour surpassed the norms set for "general" women. Usually a "normal" woman could be identified most easily by reference to her father or husband. This practice reflects the strength of patriarchal communality, even into the first half of the twentieth century.

More extraordinary nicknames were a common way of signalling to others the extent of someone's abnormality, if he (or she) failed to conform to strict and standardized frames of behaviour within agrarian society. However, because it was not always possible to confront the individual himself or to respond to the irritation with violence, naming was a route to canalize disagreements and solve problems in civilized manner. An individual's reputation was defined linguistically, when it wasn't resorted to violence or clearing ruined reputation in court anymore.[83] Through the use of nicknames, village people could chastise or punish someone, and put him in his place. Within a small community, name-calling was a way to clear the atmosphere. Nicknames, like proverbs, were forms of moral control within the community, and through them adults were able to teach younger people. Villagers with negative nicknames provided warning examples of ways of living that were not advisable, given the bounds of local norms.

Nicknames functioned as symbols of intangible capital and communal trust. A person might be named because he was known for his exceptional ability (or skill) or because he was capable of performing a particular duty better than others in his community. Such a name was an honourable title, by which an individual would be known across a wide area. On the other hand, nicknames could be (and according to the recorded material often were) given in order to mock the person who was named. An individual's social or physical difference from the norm was (further) stigmatized through his nickname. Such a name functioned as a form of communal discipline, which aimed to standardize the individual as a part of the community. Unless this did not succeed by derision and ridicule, the nickname became the factor that separated individual from his community, which expressed his otherness and isolation from others in the group.

One important question remains: where did a name-giver's controlling power over others come from? Some name-givers simply had excellent verbal abilities and a playful mind[84]. Most of the nicknames may have been amusing from the community's point of view, but the object of derision probably did not derive so much enjoyment from being the centre of this kind of attention. Through their actions, name-givers tried define the norms and boundaries of their community in ways that were most profitable from their perspective. Via naming used communal power was on the other hand sensible for baselines of single name-callers and aimed to carrying out their personal ambitions. In addition, a person who had become a kind of local opinion leader represented

---

83 In early modern society, which was strongly hierarchical, honour was central to maintaining one's social position. Cf. Eilola, "Cuca tiesi cungin mielen?"; Matikainen, *Verenperijät*, pp. 86–117.

84 Cf. Blok, *Honour and Violence*, pp. 155–157.

through his action – even when this took the form of name-calling and mockery – the viewpoint of the wider community.[85] Most nicknames, in fact, tell us more about collective perceptions of particular individuals than about individual ways of thinking. The selection criteria that underpinned naming had to be accepted by wider community if a given nickname was to become established in common usage.

Name-callers were the most asocial members of agrarian communities. They were unable to tolerate those whose conditions of existence were different. Although name-givers obviously had a stable position within the local hierarchy (evidenced by their ability to establish nicknames that affected the reputations of others), this did not necessarily mean that they were able to communicate or co-operate with everyone in their community. On the other hand, those who received pejorative names usually had to tolerate being an object of ridicule. In early modern peasant communities, nicknaming was indication of a strong collective morality, within which individual opinions, intentions or ideas did not gain approval easily.

The giving of nicknames is first and foremost a sign of a small and close-knit community. Its social cohesion is so strong that it will not allow great deviance, but it does reward obedient members of the flock with honorific names – especially if the rewarded actions serve the targets of co-operation as defined by the leading members of the community. However, such earthly honours are evanescent: with the onset of modernity, individuality became a more important factor than membership of the wider group, and those who were nicknamed were freed from most of the pressure of social watching. At most, the nickname became a humorous sobriquet, unencumbered by communal baggage. This kind of name might have shaped personal identity in certain relationships with friends, but it would not define the whole family and kin group in the same way as early modern nicknames, which could even function as inherited names and form the basis of family identity.

---

85 Cf. Bourdieu, "The Social Space and the Genesis of Groups", pp. 731–732.

Sources

ARCHIVAL SOURCES
Finnish Literature Society (SKS), Folklore archives (KRA)
Rautiainen Albert 2227. 1950 and 3931. 1960.
Leppänen, Jalmari 113. 1937.
Research Institute for the Languages of Finland (Kotus), Names Archive
Nicknames of Kannonkoski, Kinnula and Kivijärvi (1972).
Place-names of Kannonkoski (1968–1969) and Kyyjärvi (1969).

INTERVIEWS
H1. Man. Born in Kivijärvi in the 1910s. Interview 26/7/2000.
H2. Man. Born in Kivijärvi in the 1920s. Interview 23/5/2001.
H5. Man. Born in Kivijärvi in the 910s. Interview 28/7/2005.
H8. Woman. Born in Kivijärvi in the 1920s. Interview 3/12/2005.
H10. Man. Born in Kivijärvi in the 1940s. Interview 8/4/2007.

COLLECTIVE BIOGRAPHICAL DATA
Collective biographical data (CBD) concerning the Hakkarainen and Kotilainen families, who lived in the Kivijärvi area, have been compiled by Sofia Kotilainen mainly from documents in the archives of the parishes of Kannonkoski, Kinnula, Kivijärvi, and Viitasaari. These comprise records of baptisms, marriages and funerals; confirmation records and records of unconfirmed children; migration records and demographic statistics. The oldest archives of the parishes of Viitasaari and Kivijärvi are stored in the Provincial Archives of Jyväskylä. The research extends from c. 1730 to 1960.

LITERATURE
Blok, Anton 2001: Nicknames as Symbolic Inversions. In *Honour and Violence*, ed. Anton Blok. Polity Press, Cambridge, pp. 155–172.
Bourdieu, Pierre 1985a: The Social Space and the Genesis of Groups. *Theory and Society* 14 (6) 1985, pp. 723–744.
Bourdieu, Pierre 1985b: *Sosiologian kysymyksiä*. Vastapaino, Tampere.
Bourdieu, Pierre 1986 [1983]: The Forms of Capital. In *Handbook of Theory and Research for the Sociology of Education*, ed. J. G. Richardson. Greenwood Press, Westport, CT, pp. 241–258.
Bourdieu, Pierre 2003 [1991]: *Language and Symbolic Power*. Polity Press, Cambridge.
Breen, Richard 1982: Naming Practices in Western Ireland. *Man* 17 (4) 1982, pp. 701–713.
Davis, Natalie Zemon 1977 [1975]: *Society and Culture in Early Modern France*. Stanford University Press, Stanford, California.
Davis, Natalie Zemon 1997: *Women on the Margins: Three Seventeenth-Century Lives*. Harvard University Press, Cambridge, Mass.
Eilola, Jari 2003: "Cuca tiesi cungin mielen? Kengä kenegä sydämen?" Maine ja luotettavuus uuden ajan alun pikkukaupungeissa. In *Sietämättömät ja täydellinen maailma. Kirjoi-*

tuksia suvaitsemattomuudesta, ed. Jari Eilola. Jyväskylän Historiallinen Yhdistys ja Kopijyvä, Jyväskylä, pp. 121–158.

Elias, Norbert 1978: *The Civilizing Process. Vol 1: The History of Manners*. Basil Blackwell, Oxford.

Fentress, James & Wickham, Chris 1992: *Social Memory. New perspectives on the past*. Blackwell, Oxford.

Fombrun, Charles J. 1996: *Reputation. Realizing Value from the Corporate Image*. Harvard Business School Press, Boston.

Gennep, Arnold van 1960: *The Rites of Passage*. The University of Chicago Press, Chicago.

Ganander, Christfrid 1997: *Nytt Finskt Lexicon*. Alkuperäiskäsikirjoituksesta [vuodelta 1787] ja sen näköispainoksesta toimittanut Liisa Nuutinen. Suomalaisen Kirjallisuuden Seura ja Kotimaisten kielten tutkimuskeskus, Helsinki.

Giddens, Anthony 1995 [1990]: *The Consequenses of Modernity*. Polity Press, Cambridge.

Gilmore, David D. 1982: Some Notes on Community Nicknaming in Spain. *Man* 17 (4) 1982, pp. 686–700.

Ginzburg, Carlo 1996: *Johtolankoja. Kirjoituksia mikrohistoriasta ja historiallisesta metodista*. Gaudeamus, Helsinki.

Gunnarsson, Britt-Louise, Entzenberg, Sonja & Ohlsson, Maria (ed.) 2007: *Språk och kön i nutida och historiskt prespektiv. Studier presenterade vid Den sjätte nordiska konferensen om språk och kön, Uppsala 6–7 oktober 2006* (Language and Gender in Contemporary and Historical Perspective. Studies Presented at the Sixth Nordic Conference on Language and Gender, Uppsala, Sweden, October 6–7, 2006). Uppsala Universitet, Uppsala.

Hall, Stuart 1999: Kulttuurisen identiteetin kysymyksiä. In *Identiteetti*, ed. Stuart Hall, transl. Mikko Lehtonen and Juha Herkman. Vastapaino, Tampere, pp. 19–76.

Halliday, M. A. K. 1992 [1978]: *Language as social semiotic. The social interpretation of language and meaning*. Edward Arnold, London.

Karonen, Petri 1995: Talonpojat oikeutta paossa – Rikollisuudesta Keski-Suomessa 1700-luvun lopulla. In *Sisä-Suomen tuomiokirjat tutkimuslähteinä ja elämän kuvaajina*, ed. Heikki Roiko-Jokela and Timo Pitkänen. Jyväskylän yliopiston historian laitos, Jyväskylän maakunta-arkisto ja Jyväskylän historiallinen yhdistys, Jyväskylä, pp. 57–77.

Karonen, Petri 1999: *Pohjoinen suurvalta. Ruotsi ja Suomi 1521–1809*. WSOY, Porvoo–Helsinki–Juva.

Keats-Rohan, K. S. B. 2007: Biography, Identity and Names: Understanding the Pursuit of the Individual in Prosopography. In *Prosopography Approaches and Applications. A Handbook*, ed. K. S. B. Keats-Rohan. Unit for Prosopographical Research, Oxford, pp. 139–181.

Kinnunen, Kristiina, Kinnunen, Piia, Niemonen, Tomi, Salonpää, Mari and Salonpää, Reetta (ed.) 2006: *Ei nimi miestä pahenna – huumorilla höystettyä ruokaa Kinnulasta*. InnoWii Oy, Kinnula.

Kiviniemi, Eero, Pitkänen, Ritva Liisa & Zilliacus, Kurt (toim.) 1974: *Nimistöntutkimuksen terminologia – Terminologin inom namnforskningen*. Helsingin yliopisto, Helsinki.

Korhonen, Anu 2005: *Silmän ilot. Kauneuden kulttuurihistoriaa uuden ajan alussa*. Atena, Jyväskylä.

Kotilainen, Sofia (ed.) 2001: *Het pikkusevverran paljo Kivijärven Perinnepiirin tallentamaa muistitietoa*. Kivijärven kunta, Kivijärvi.

Kotilainen, Sofia (ed.) 2005: Minä tiijän yhen tappauksen. *Viiden Kunnan Sanomat* 30/2005, 28/7/2005, p. 21.

Kotilainen, Sofia 2008: *Suvun nimissä. Nimenannon käytännöt Sisä-Suomessa 1700-luvun alusta 1950-luvulle*. SKS, Helsinki (English summary: http://kirjat.finlit.fi/kuvat/978-952-222-048-6_3summ.pdf).

Kotilainen, Sofia, 2009: Namngivningspraxis och attityder: val av kungliga och kejserliga förnamn hos den finskspråkiga allmogen efter år 1809. *Folkmålsstudier* 47 2009, pp. 27–44.

Kotilainen, Sofia 2012: Förtroende och andra former av symboliskt kapital i fadderskapsstrategier. *Historisk Tidskrift för Finland* 97 (3) 2012, pp. 295–326.

Kotilainen, Sofia 2012: An inherited name as the foundation of a person's identity. How the existence of a dead person was continued in the names of his or her descendants. *Thanatos* 1 (1) 2012, the online journal of the Finnish Death Studies Association, http://thanatosjournal.files.wordpress.com/2012/03/kotilainen_inherited-name_thanatos-20121.pdf.

Kotilainen, Sofia 2013: Rural people's literacy skills in the remembrance of the departed: the writing of personal names on sepulchral monuments at the turn of the nineteenth and twentieth centuries. *Mortality* 18 (2) 2013, pp. 173–194.

Kotilainen, Sofia 2013: Several names, several identities? The orthography of Finnish countryry people's names from the 18th to 20th centuries. In *Människor som skriver. Perspektiv på vardagligt skriftbruk och identitet*, ed. Ann-Catrine Edlund and Susanne Haugen. Umeå universitet och Kungl. Skytteanska Samfundet, Umeå, pp. 61–74.

Kuusi, Matti 1954: *Sananlaskut ja puheenparret*. SKS, Helsinki.

Laaksonen, Pekka 1972: Nätti, Tulikuuma ja Tuskanpunainen. Jätkäperinteen liikanimiä. In *Nimikirja*, ed. Hannes Sihvo. WSOY, Helsinki–Porvoo, pp. 178–203.

Lauhakangas, Outi, 2004: *Puheesta ihminen tunnetaan. Sananlaskujen funktiot sosiaalisessa vuorovaikutuksessa*. SKS, Helsinki.

Markkola, Pirjo 1996: Marginaali historian keskipisteessä. In *Kuokkavieraiden pidot. Historian marginaalista marginaalihistoriaan*, ed. Jarmo Peltola and Pirjo Markkola. Vastapaino, Tampere, pp. 7–19.

Matikainen, Olli 2002: *Verenperijät: Väkivalta ja yhteisön murros itäisessä Suomessa 1500–1600-luvulla*. SKS, Helsinki.

Misztal, Barbara A. 1998[1996]: *Trust in Modern Societies. The Search for the Bases of Social Order*. Polity Press, Cambridge.

Mäkinen, Kirsti 2007: *Lollot ja kollot. Suomalaista naapurihuumoria*. Otava, Helsinki.

Närhi, Eeva Maria 1990: The Onomastic Central Archives – the Foundation of Finnish Onomastics. In *Finnish Onomastics. Namenkunde in Finnland*, ed. Heikki Leskinen and Eero Kiviniemi. Finnish Literature Society, Helsinki, pp. 9–25.

Paulaharju, Samuli 1912: Lisä- ja haukkumanimistä. *Kotiseutu* 1912, pp. 124–127.

Pina-Cabral, João de 1984: Nicknames and the Experience of Community. *Man* 19 (1) 1984, pp. 148–150.

Putnam, Robert D. 2000: *Bowling Alone. The Collapse and Revival of American Community*. Simon & Schuster, New York.

Rahikainen, Marjatta 2000: Yhteisöjen nurja puoli. Nimittely ja pilkkaaminen maalaispitäjässä. In *Keulakuvia ja peränpitäjiä. Vanhan ja uuden yhteiskunnan rajalla*, ed. Riitta Oittinen and Marjatta Rahikainen. Suomen Historiallinen Seura, Helsinki, pp. 163–179.

Ricoeur, Paul 2003: *The Rule of Metaphor. The creation of meaning in language*. Routledge, London and New York.

Schneewind, J. B. 1998: *The Invention of Autonomy. A History of Modern Moral Philosophy*. Cambridge University Press, Cambridge.

Skinner, Quentin 2002: *Visions of Politics. Volume I. Regarding Method*. Cambridge University Press, Cambridge.

Smith, Adam 2002 [1759]: *The Theory of Moral Sentiments*. Edited by Knud Haakonssen. Cambridge University Press, Cambridge.

Spierenburg, Pieter 2004: Social Control and History: An Introduction. In *Social Control in Europe. Volume 1, 1500–1800*, ed. Herman Roodenburg and Pieter Spierenburg. The Ohio State University Press, Columbus, pp. 1–22.

Stewart, Frank Henderson 1994: *Honor*. The University of Chicago Press, Chicago & London.

Tait, Clodagh 2006: Namesakes and nicknames: naming practices in early modern Ireland, 1540–1700. *Continuity and Change* 2/2006, pp. 313–340.

Vansina, Jan 1985: *Oral Tradition as History*. James Currey, London.

Vento, Urpo 1972: Tunsitteko Jepulis-Penjamin? Liikanimistä ja roolinimistä kertomusperinteessä. In *Nimikirja*, ed. Hannes Sihvo. WSOY, Helsinki–Porvoo, pp. 160–177.

Vilkuna, Kustaa 1958: Ihmisten puhuttelua edessä ja takana. *Kotiseutu* 1958, pp. 93–97.

Vilkuna, Kustaa 2005[1976]: *Etunimet*, ed. Pirjo Mikkonen (4th edn.), Otava, Helsinki.

Vilkuna, Kustaa H. J. 1996: Jumala elä rankase minua. Yksilöllisen subjektin synty. In *Siperiasta siirtoväkeen: murrosaikoja ja käännekohtia Suomen historiassa*, ed. Heikki Roiko-Jokela. Kopijyvä, Jyväskylä, pp. 71–93.

Vilkuna, Kustaa H. J. 2000: Herotes oli koira: humoristinen puhe rikoksena. *Rikos historiassa*, ed. Olli Matikainen. Jyväskylä, Kopijyvä, pp. 229–266.

VKS 1994: *Vanhan kirjasuomen sanakirja. Toinen osa J–K*. Kotimaisten kielten tutkimuskeskus, Painatuskeskus, Helsinki.

The Crime and Punishment of a Nineteenth-Century Finnish Serial Killer

Teemu Keskisarja

Judicial and cultural precedent

It is difficult to name any single criminal case that would have deeply affected Finnish legal history. Principal characters are lawyers or statesmen, not criminals, and turning points seldom contain individual drama. But the illiterate farmhand Johan Adamsson (1826–1854) makes an exception. In the autumn of 1849 he committed twelve homicides, more than any Finnish criminal ever has.[1] This "achievement" brought him, in addition to literary and folkloristic notoriety, a place in the history of capital punishment.

The brutal case upset the society, but horror and wrath were not the only emotions. It was the Finnish crime of the century in many ways, and Johan Adamsson became a celebrity – not in dimensions of the world-famous Jack the Ripper, but as much as it was possible in a small and undeveloped rural country like Finland. As the first Finnish criminal he interested the newspapers and authors widely, and a portrait of

---

[1] District Court of Nastola, Hollola and Asikkala 21.11.1849; Lammi 1.12.1849; Vanaja 6.5.1850; Heinola 17.2.1850; Pernaja, Myrskylä and Lapinjärvi 25.–26.2.1850, Provincial Archives of Hämeenlinna.

the murderer was painted by a respected artist. Judicial documents were published in commercial editions and sold in bookstores. The cultural phenomenon was odd and caused among other things the birth of Finnish criminal journalism.

As a legal pre-judgment Johan Adamsson affected Finnish legislation during next generations. Basis for discussion was internationally original. The autonomous Grand Duchy of Finland had given up death penalty already in 1826 as one of the first countries in the world. This radical solution, confirmed by Nicholas I in St. Petersburg, dated almost three decades before the Adamsson case. Since then the hardest possible punishment was a life sentence to forced labour in Siberia. An execution was possible only in most dramatic crimes against the state and these did not take place in the peaceful grand duchy. Mutinies and assassinations did not take place. Abolition of capital punishment seemed to succeed, but the line was tested during Adamsson's long trial and even later through his precedent.

The scale of punishments was not enough for the man who had committed twelve murders. He did not deserve life in Siberia. This one unheard crime forced Finnish judicial system to reconsider the need of capital punishment and even torture. Johan Adamsson almost became the last person ever executed in Finland (excluding wartimes of the twentieth century). He also became a central object in a very principled judicial and cultural debate.

The Finnish circuit courts and Superior Court sentenced Johan Adamsson to death. Public opinion supported execution and the judges hoped emperor of Russia to confirm the doom. Finally, the emperor Nicholas the First spared Adamsson's life, but not with a normal mercy. Public show was organized anyway, and the mercy was kept secret. Officials tricked the criminal himself and the common people. They were told that the execution will happen, but it was a fake execution. Neither Finnish penal code nor judicial tradition knew that kind of punishment.[2]

When the supposed execution took place in January 1853 an enormous crowd travelled along snowy roads and frozen lakes to the small pro-

---

2   Justice Department of Senate, Act 372/1851, National Archives of Finland.

vincial town of Heinola. The officials organized a worldly spectacle and religious ceremony, but it was all in vain. At the last moment executioner stopped his axe inches from the neck. A bailiff read the imperial orders that saved Adamsson's life. The crowd was disappointed and furious.

The last execution in Finnish legal history was cancelled, but couple of months later the officials re-enforced another old practice. Torture had been completely illegal already for a long time, since eighteenth-century enlightenment and Swedish king Gustav III. In general, nobody missed it neither as a punishment nor a method of investigation. But in this specific serial killer case the criminal was more or less officially tortured to death.

According to Russian emperor's special orders Adamsson was flogged and slowly buried alive or "masoned to death" to a tiny hole in the fortress island of Sveaborg in front of Helsinki. The circumstances were considered cruel torment even in the context of the mid-nineteenth century prison standards. The unique punishment was public, and the serial killer lived his last times like a circus animal. Passers-by could watch the monster behind the bars. He could not move an inch or even scratch his scars.[3]

Profile of an early modern serial killer

"Serial killer" is a modern word, of course, and also the concept was unknown in nineteenth-century Finland as well as in the more developed societies of the same epoch. Despite terminological anachronism, it is possible to ask, if this ancient agrarian society criminal reminded killers of urban and industrialized world or global popular culture. Evident question for the contemporaries was why he did these twelve murders? The man was not sexually pervert, did not hear voices or see ghosts (at least before killings). To put it simple, he was not particularly insane in contrast to modern cannibals or paedophiles.

---

3   The article is mostly based on the book Teemu Keskisarja, *Suomen ainoa sarjamurhaaja: Juhani Adaminpojan rikos ja rangaistus* (Jyväskylä, 2008).

Johan Adamsson's criminal career culminated during one autumn, however, he was quite versatile violent offender and not simple to profile. Among twelve victims were his mother, stepfather, half-sister and half-brother. These were seemingly impulsive crimes without a rational motive. But Adamsson committed also bloody robberies and killed accidental on-comings more or less without reason. He killed men, women, old people and also children. He murdered for money, revenge or self-defence and just for fun. Some of the murders had no evident motive, which was an incomprehensible and shocking matter to contemporaries. That is why the case was considered too shocking for the common people or Finnish-speaking farmers and the censorship tried to hide some details.

Nineteenth-century lawyers, priests and also doctors researched the mental background of Adamsson's behaviour. They concluded that he had a more or less normal intelligence, and he was judicially accountable without any doubt; not and idiot, but not emotionally balanced, of course. He lacked Christian education or any education at all. His morals and ethics were "inhuman low", one doctor said. He had no ability to understand the difference between right and wrong or feel any kind of empathy for the victims. Modern science would probably use terms like psychopath or sociopath to describe him.

Bitterness and fury seemed to be the most pronounced motives for his actions. In comparison to later examples it is not surprising that Johan Adamsson had lived an extremely traumatic childhood, which contained father's suicide and mother's public disgrace punishment for fornication. Step-father beat him mercilessly, and as youngster Adamsson earned his living by begging and working in the lowest positions of his home village. He feuded with farm owner and committed crimes against property. In a way, serial killings were a social protest crime even if the victims were not noblemen or officials. The murders were an assault against the Finnish class society, where the farmhands lived in enslaved conditions.

Still, the social aspect was somewhat unconvincing. It was easy to point out, that on similar conditions grew several thousands young men, who did not become serial killers or even criminals. Some scientists believed that the reason for Adamsson's behaviour was physical; he seemed to have wounds or congenital deformation in his skull. Finnish research results were similar to Cesare Lombroso's anthropological criminology, which came to fashion in the late nineteenth century.

Johan Adamsson was an exceptional creature, but at the same time he fits in long-term patterns and was a typical Finnish violent offender. Though relatively young – he was 23 during the murders – he was already an alcoholic. If the Finnish society or the village community were to blame, one factor was that the farmhands got part of their salary in spirits. It was easy to develop a serious drinking problem already as a youngster. Nevertheless, the alcohol culture was only a stimulant, not a fundamental reason to criminality.

Debate on death penalty in Finland

Lawyers and politicians continued debating the Adamsson case decades after the man had died, as he provided arguments both for the supporters and opponents of death penalty. Debate in the nineteenth-century Finland was timeless and not especially national. Same kind of discourse advanced in Sweden, where capital punishment was in force until 1910s in spite of the wide cultural and social protests.[4] In Finland, the basic arguments represented nothing new under the sun. For example Cesare Beccaria, the most famous abolitionist of the death penalty, had presented similar standpoints in the previous century.

In the nineteenth-century Finland practical arguments were more important than theological: Should the judicial system maintain public executions as a warning example? Or should it frighten potential criminals? Because of these aspects, different parties researched the details of Adamsson's public fake execution. At the same time Finnish intelligentsia found imposing examples in European newspapers. They read for example Charles Dickens' articles on executions in London.

---

4   For Swedish discource, see Martin Bergman, *Dödsstraffet, kyrkan och staten i Sverige från 1700-tal till 1900-tal*, Skrifter utgivna av Institutet för rättshistorisk forskning, Serien 1, Rättshistoriskt bibliotek 53 (Stockholm, 1996).

One party concluded from the all-round evidence, that public violence brutalizes the masses. And maybe they were right in this specific case. Fake execution show in Heinola January 1853 did not reach religious atmosphere. It was like a market place, not like a worthy ceremony. During the previous centuries execution was often described as a collective atonement, but the nineteenth-century observers found more negative emotions like vindictiveness and vulgar curiosity.

The settings of the show were same as in the golden era of death penalty: executioner's clothes, axe, colours and textiles in the scaffold. The priest played his role well preparing Adamsson to supposed death. But in the mid-nineteenth century people, who had not seen executions for thirty years, did not understand these symbols any more. One banal aspect was, that all the public, from old women to little boys, was drunk. This was a perpetual problem also in the past, but for some reason the officials did not remember that.

The fake execution became almost a fiasco. The Finnish authorities never tested the method again, although in Russia revolutionaries and terrorists were sometimes frightened with similar kind of tricks before sending to Siberia. According to this grotesque Finnish example, it was difficult to insist that real public executions could provide some positive mental experiences for the community.

Public death penalty was seemingly impractical but the Adamsson case sent also another message to the authorities. The crime seemed to be unknown for legislation and outside the categories of homicide. If these kinds of crimes were possible, maybe one should keep the death penalty as a last weapon, although the society would use it only once in a century?

But the next serial killer never entered Finland. The public had almost forgotten the Adamsson case, when another modern type of crime arose into discussion. Russian terrorists' assassinations against the emperor Alexander II were sensations also in the Grand Duchy of Finland. The newspapers paralleled serial killer and terrorist; neither had right to be treated as a normal criminal. Mainly because of these exceptional crimes the capital punishment remained in the statute book even if it was never put in practice.

Torture and death for a warning example?

The execution was only a fake, but the torture of Johan Adamsson happened in reality and before the public. It was a difficult solution for many reasons, even if the victim was a unique serial killer. In Swedish and Finnish judicial tradition torture had never been central. It was only occasionally used, for example in the seventeenth-century witch-hunts. Johan Adamsson was a last test. Imperial orders made sure, that his fate was as torturous as possible.

Johan Adamsson's "masoning to death" in the fortress of Sveaborg seemed to prove that torture was against the Finnish sense of justice. It was an efficient warning to potential criminals – possibly stronger than a quick, painless death in execution. But the problem was that when the first lust for revenge had passed, the public started to feel some compassion and sympathy for the poor criminal. And that was a mental effect the authorities did not hope for.

The executions had came to end already in the early nineteenth century, earlier than in almost any other country and about eighty years earlier than in Sweden, the former mother country. In international history of capital punishment's abolition Finland became a long-term practical example. It is difficult to say if this was because or regardless of the Adamsson case.

In the Finnish judicial debate Adamsson case could have been a turning point, but finally it did not bring death penalty back to practice. One domestic serial killer and few Russian terrorists were not enough. The threat was too abstract in dimensions of the whole society. At the same time the statistics seemed to prove decline or at least stability in conventional homicide rates.

Modernization meant that the penal code was reformed to moderate direction. In the late nineteenth century flogging and various religiously based disgrace punishments exited from legislation. The new system was based on deprivation of liberty and the state build modern prisons. The process was difficult in many ways. The public opinion did not cry out for scaffolds, but some remissions seemed to be too much. Compared to ancient fortresses the new and very expensive prisons looked like rest-homes. The conditions did not scare poor and hungry criminals, vice versa. On the other hand, also the Finnish criminals were shocked in era of change. For many observers long sentences to imprisonment seemed more inhuman than mechanical torture.

Violent Finns

For the nineteenth-century Finnish authorities the main question was, how the moderate penal policy affected the criminality rates. Latest half a century after the Adamsson case it was clear, that the statistics were not pleasing but horrific. Violent crime became more general. Homicide rates reached culmination in the 1920s and 1930s and were higher than ever since the Middle Ages. The ratio was about ten homicides per year and 100 000 inhabitants. Amazingly, homicide rate was in Finland even sixteen times higher than in Sweden.

Finland has for long been – and still is – the most violent country in Western Europe. The most dramatic rise in homicide rates began in late the nineteenth century, at the same time as the modern and moderate criminal policy started. Of course, the reason or result is not so simple. During the same period a socio-economic change begun. The forms of social control faded, as also Clive Emsley has pointed out.[5] Finland was one of the most agrarian countries in Europe, but it developed rapidly towards industrial and urban society. In the early twentieth century Finland was politically more unsteady than western neighbors. One factor behind the homicide rates was the alcohol policy, which failed dramatically in prohibition.[6]

---

5   For social control in general, see Clive Emsley, *Crime and Society in England 1750–1900* (London, 1987) and *Crime, Police and Penal Policy: European Experiences 1750–1940* (New York, 2007).
6   For Finnish violence in far-reaching perspective, see Anu Koskivirta, *The Enemy within: Homicide and Control in Eastern Finland in the Final years of Swedish Rule*, Studia Fennica, Historica; 5 (Helsinki, 2003); Olli Matikainen, Verenperijät: *Väkivalta ja yhteisön murros itäisessä Suomessa 1500–1600-luvulla*, Bibliotheca historica 78 (Helsinki, 2002); Heikki Ylikangas, *Knife fighters: Violent Crime in Southern Ostrobothnia 1790–1825* (Helsinki, 1998); Martti Lehti, *Väkivallan hyökyaalto: 1900-luvun alkuvuosikymmenten henkirikollisuus Suomessa ja Luoteis-Virossa* (Helsinki, 2001); Juha Rajala, *Kurittajia ja puukkosankareita: Väkivalta ja sen kontrollointi Kannaksen rajaseudulla 1885–1917* (Helsinki, 2004).

Finnish violence has a complex background. Historical criminology has searched for the roots of violence from many directions. For example genes, alcohol culture, fiery domestic policy, scattered settlement and inadequate social skills have been among explanations for long.[7] However, Finnish researchers are unanimous, that the earliest abolition of executions in Western Europe is not the root of our highest homicide numbers. But on the other hand, one could say that Finnish criminal policy has not been successful in the long run. On the grounds of limited historical evidence, it would be impossible to write a pamphlet for or against the capital punishment.

Finland is the most violent country in Western Europe, but hitherto no Finnish serial killer has appeared since Johan Adamsson. One reason for this is concrete and evident. Internationally the serial killers belong to urban societies and regions of large populations. In sparsely populated Finland no criminal could reach anonymity in crowds. Official authority and judicial apparatus was relatively well organized in the nineteenth century or already during the Swedish regime. The resources could not prevent conventional homicide, but one beast was certainly caught, when he was about to upset the whole system. These facts had an influence on the story of the only serial killer. Johan Adamsson's was caught already after six weeks of amok run.

Johan Adamsson was a celebrity, but the fame did not last for long after his death in 1854. In the late nineteenth and early twentieth century Finnish criminal journalism discovered more international monsters. Notorious criminals were imported goods like many cultural phenomena. For example, Jack the Ripper inspired in one year more Finnish columns than domestic Adamsson had inspired during almost four decades.

The Finnish popular culture never found Johan Adamsson. In the long run the public considered his character too simple and black-and-white and impossible to identify with. The only unquestionably feature in his murders was their quantity. And that was not enough for twentieth- or twentyfirst-century culture, which wanted detective stories and

---

[7] For the most traditional explanations, see Veli Verkko, *Homicides and suicides in Finland and their dependence on national character*, Scandinavian studies in sociology 3 (København, 1951).

intellectual challenge. As a judicial precedent Adamsson played his role better. The most important credit was that he forced his contemporaries to ponder the basic ethical principles of legalized violence.[8]

Sources

ARCHIVAL SOURCES

The National Archives of Finland
    Justice Department of Senate, Act 372/1851.
The Provincial Archives of Hämeenlinna
    District Court of Heinola 17.2.1850.
    Lammi 1.12.1849.
    Nastola, Hollola and Asikkala 21.11.1849.
    Pernaja, Myrskylä and Lapinjärvi 25–26.2.1850.
    Vanaja 6.5.1850.

LITERATURE

Bergman, Martin 1996: *Dödsstraffet, kyrkan och staten i Sverige från 1700-tal till 1900-tal.* Skrifter utgivna av Institutet för rättshistorisk forskning, Serien 1. Rättshistoriskt bibliotek 53, Stockholm.
Emsley, Clive 1987: *Crime and society in England 1750–1900.* London.
Emsley, Clive 2007: *Crime, police and penal policy. European experiences 1750–1940.* New York.
Keskisarja, Teemu 2008: *Suomen ainoa sarjamurhaaja. Juhani Adaminpojan rikos ja rangaistus.* Jyväskylä.
Koskivirta, Anu 2003: *The Enemy Within. Homicide and control in Eastern Finland in the final years of Swedish rule.* Studia Fennica, Historica 5. Helsinki.
Lagus, Robert 1862: Om dödstraff. Juridiskt Album 1861. Helsingfors.
Lehti, Martti 2001: *Väkivallan hyökyaalto. 1900-luvun alkuvuosikymmenten henkirikollisuus Suomessa ja Luoteis-Virossa.* Helsinki.
Lindstedt, Jukka 1999: *Kuolemaan tuomitut. Kuolemanrangaistukset Suomessa toisen maailmansodan aikana.* Suomalaisen lakimiesyhdistyksen julkaisuja, A-sarja N:o 221. Helsinki.
Matikainen, Olli 2002: *Verenperijät. Väkivalta ja yhteisön murros itäisessä Suomessa 1500–1600-luvulla.* Bibliotheca historica 78. Helsinki.
Rajala, Juha 2004: *Kurittajia ja puukkosankareita. Väkivalta ja sen kontrollointi Kannaksen rajaseudulla 1885–1917.* Helsinki.
Verkko, Veli 1951: *Homicides and suicides in Finland and their dependence on national character.* Scandinavian studies in sociology 3. København.
Ylikangas, Heikki 1998: *Knife fighters. Violent Crime in Southern Ostrobothnia 1790–1825.* Helsinki.

---

8   See, for example, Robert Lagus, "Om dödstraff". *Juridiskt Album 1861* (Helsingfors 1862); Jukka Lindstedt, *Kuolemaan tuomitut. Kuolemanrangaistukset Suomessa toisen maailmansodan aikana.* Suomalaisen lakimiesyhdistyksen julkaisuja, A-sarja N:o 221 (Helsinki 1999).

II
Community and Discipline

To report or not? To punish or not?
Between Tightening Laws, Old Habits and Loyalty in Early Modern Bavaria
Satu Lidman

The tightening of the criminal justice system – that is both jurisdiction and actual verdicts – was a phenomenon experienced in most European territories from the mid-sixteenth century onwards. The duchy of Bavaria was no exception, and in fact its contributions to the history of state-initiated social control seem to have been among the strictest.[1] The Bavarian dukes required their subjects to report all suspicious individuals to authorities, and when investigating immoral behaviour, the courts quite depended on the data they could receive from the people. Although payments could be made for such information, people were often reluctant to co-operate; changes in the minds and actions of the people took place more slowly than one might expect, given the juridical changes of the period.

This article deals with questions concerning ideological and normative changes on the one hand, and practices of reporting and punishing crimes on the other. The analysis of jurisdiction and actual shaming

---

1   "Social control" is a term that can be extended to explain many kinds of phenomena, as among others Spierenburg has pointed out (Pieter Spierenburg, "Social Control and History: An Introduction", in Herman Roodenburg and Pieter Spierenburg (ed.), Social Control in Europe 1500–1800, Vol. 1 (Ohio, 2004), pp. 1, 6, 10–16). In this article social control is mainly used to describe the aristocratic point of view; it is seen as a means of authorities to discipline their subjects.

punishments focuses on specific groups of moral offences: the control of premarital relationships (*Unzucht, Leichtfertigkeit*), often interpreted as prostitution-like activity, and policies towards women who were accused for being concubines of Catholic clergymen (*Konkubinentum*). The main sources consulted include Bavarian ducal legislation from the sixteenth and early seventeenth century and records of the Munich magistrates' court from around 1600.

Legal measures to combat moral offences

In the Middle Ages, many cases of illegal sexual relations were to some extent accepted, or at least tolerated by the people. In the confessional climate of the post-Reformation era, however, relationships between men and women were sexualized. Consequently, they were criminalized more specifically than before; a supposed sexual misconduct became one of the most important targets of aristocratic control. As sexual purity was now at the heart of the new moral politics, the number of legal charges of moral offences grew in most European countries.[2] The accents of the social control *from below* on the one hand, and actual punishment praxis on the other, changed in a slower tempo, yet the tendency was the same.

The growing attention paid to "suspicious" sexual activities did not mean, of course, that people had actually become more immoral. Instead, this phenomenon should be scrutinized within the context of tightening legislation and increasing criminalization of moral offences, as well as other changes of criminal justice system, such as the grow-

---

2   Reinhard Heydenreuter, "Der Magistrat als Befehlsempfänger – Die Disziplinierung der Stadtobrigkeit 1579 bis 1651", in Richard van Bauer (ed.), Geschichte der Stadt München (Munich, 1992) pp. 195–196; Stefan Breit, "Leichtfertigkeit" und ländliche Gesellschaft: Voreheliche Sexualität in der frühen Neuzeit (Munich, 1991), pp. 74, 78–79; Susanna Burghartz, Zeiten der Reinheit – Orte der Unzucht: Ehe und Sexualität in Basel während der Frühen Neuzeit (Paderborn, 1999), pp. 286–287. See also Wolfgang Behringer, "Mörder, Diebe, Ehebrecher: Verbrechen und Strafen in Kurbayern vom 16. bis 18. Jahrhundert", in Richard van Dülmen (ed.), Verbrechen, Strafen und soziale Kontrolle (Frankfurt am Main, 1990), p. 100; Mia Korpiola, Between Betrothal and Bedding: The Making of Marriage in Sweden, ca. 1200–1610 (Saarijärvi, 2004), pp. 266–267; Satu Lidman, "Unzüchtige Weiber und Priesterkonkubinen vor dem Münchner Rat um 1600", Oberbayerisches Archiv, 128 (Munich, 2004).

ing number of *ex officio* charges, and the pressure on local authorities to prosecute crimes. Its driving force was a confessional philosophy, through which the regulation of sexual matters was at the core of control and thus the climate of "new morality" and "total purity" that was created. These aims were, however, unrealistic and because of this, they effectively produced rather than reduced criminality.[3]

Among others statutes dealing with moral offences embodied the first signs of absolutist governing of the early modern territorial states.[4] A central theme of these disciplinary texts was the theory of God's wrath (*Zorn Gottes*). For early modern people this would explain many of the difficulties they faced; famine, wars and plagues were seen as the results and as collective payback of individual sins and immorality. As the residence of the Bavarian dukes Munich was expected to serve as a moral model for other cities of the territory; the ducal statutes were to be followed carefully in the city.[5]

The dukes saw themselves as "fathers of the nation" and in order to avoid God's wrath with its collective consequences, they felt responsible for controlling and punishing their subjects, just as a father was supposed to discipline his children. This required interference in matters that would today be seen as intimate and private, for example the sex lives of citizens. As individual immorality was believed to cause collective problems, the lawfulness of one's sexuality was a matter of concern for the whole community.[6] The prosecution and punishment of those who perpetrated moral offences became more or less everybody's concern.

---

3 A similar development took place in Scandinavia, see Eva Österberg and Dag Lindström, Crime and Social Control in Medieval and Early Modern Swedish Towns (Studia Historica Upsaliensia, 152; Uppsala, 1988), pp. 122–125.
4 Hans Schlosser, "Rechtsetzung und Gesetzgebungsverständnis im Territorialstaat Bayern im 16. Jahrhundert", Zeitschrift für bayerische Landesgeschichte, 50 (Munich, 1987), pp. 49–50.
5 Ulrike Strasser, "Vom Fall der Ehre zum Fall der Leichtfertigkeit: Geschlechtsspezifische Aspekte der Konfessionalisierung am Beispiel Münchner Eheversprechens- und Alimentationsklagen (1592–1649)", in Peer Frieß and Rolf Kießling (ed.), Konfessionalisierung und Region (Konstanz, 1999), pp. 244, 229; Heydenreuter, "Der Magistrat als Befehlsempfänger", pp. 195–196. See also BayHstA: KMS 1524/VIII/10, 1541/X/3, 1595/I/15, 1604/XII/2.
6 Satu Lidman, Zum Spektakel und Abscheu. Schand- und Ehrenstrafen als Mittel öffentlicher Disziplinierung in München um 1600 (Frankfurt am Main, 2008), pp. 76–77, 83–86.

Strasser has come to the conclusion that women were punished more often and more severely than men for moral offences, and the sources of the study in hand support this interpretation.[7] It is a great paradox of this field of social control that even though sexual relationships inevitably involved couples, or at least two persons, most of the documented cases only refer to legal processes involving female suspects. Nevertheless, this does not indicate that men would have escaped punishments entirely. In many cases sanctions for men were different from those imposed upon women, and therefore they have not been central to my research focusing on public shaming. While women were put in the pillory, men often paid a fine, and consequently, their sentences were listed in a different type of records.

Nevertheless, it seems fair to say that in many cases men were not even accused of sexual wrongdoings. This is connected to the moral expectations concerning women that were so typical for early modern culture.[8] The image of women was strongly bi-dimensional: the secular motherhood was expected to see Mary as its prototype, but Eve, sexualized through the Fall of Man, was to be its antithesis. Women and the female honour were mainly defined according to sexual categories; in practice a woman's honour could be severely damaged by even a suspicion of forbidden sexual activity. This kind of philosophy was common in both Protestant and Catholic territories.[9]

---

7   Ulrike Strasser, *State of Virginity: Gender, Religion and Politics in an Early Modern Catholic State* (Ann Arbor, 2004), p. 92; Lidman, *Zum Spektakel und Abscheu*, p. 343.
8   For the image of women in sixteenth- and seventeenth-century literature, see, for example, Aegidius Albertinus, *Haußpolicey* (Munich, 1602), 1. Teil, 1 r–4 r & 2. Teil, 58 r–59 v & 61 r–61 v; Jacob Döpler, *Theatrum poenarum, suppliciorum et executionum criminalium oder Schauplatz der Leibes- und Lebensstrafen* (Sondershausen, 1693), p. 517.
    Canon law only recognized three permitted stages of sexuality: virginity, marriage and celibacy. Sexual intercourse was only permissible between married couples. (Breit, "*Leichtfertigkeit*", pp. 75–76; Annette Lömker-Schlögell, "Prostituierte – um vermeydung willen merers übels in der christenhait", in Bernd-Ulrich Hergemöller (ed.), *Randgruppen der spätmittelalterlichen Gesellschaft: Ein Hand- und Studienbuch* (Warendorf, 1994), p. 56.)
9   R. W. Scribner, *Religion and Culture in Germany (1400–1800)* (Studies in Medieval and Reformation Thought, 81; Köln, 2001), pp. 133–138, 141–142; Klaus Schreiner and Gerd Schwerhoff (ed.), *Verletzte Ehre: Ehrenkonflikte in Gesellschaften des Mittelalters und der frühen Neuzeit* (Norm und Struktur, Studien zum sozialen Wandel in Mittelalter und früher Neuzeit, 5; Köln, 1995), p. 19; Breit, "*Leichtfertigkeit*", pp. 5–6; Susanna Burghartz, "Geschlecht – Körper – Ehre. Überlegungen zur weiblichen Ehre in der frühen Neuzeit am Beispiel der Basler Ehegerichtsprotokolle", in Klaus Schreiner and Gerd Schwerhoff (ed.), *Verletzte Ehre: Ehrenkonflikte in Gesellschaften des Mittelalters und der frühen Neuzeit* (Köln, 1995),

In the religiously coloured argumentation of the sixteenth century, the chaste statuses of virginity and honourable marriage were fundamental parts of women's social standing and legal position. Therefore, a charge of illicit premarital sexual relations severely endangered one's position in the community. However, many lower-class and poor women had long-term relationships, but they were obliged to remain unmarried because of their economic situation. These women were easily labelled with unchastity, *Leichtfertigkeit,* and viewed as sexually unclean, or even associated with prostitutes.[10] As Strasser argues:

> Whereas the prostitute began to embody the sexualized lower-class woman whose body threatened to pollute the Catholic community, the nun was destined to represent the upper-class virgin whose purity (and class) promised and symbolized the intactness of the same community and its immunity against social, sexual and spiritual pollution.[11]

Similarly, Schwerhoff emphasizes that especially lower-class women were often subjected to both sexual suspicion and abuse.[12] Although among the aristocracy there was a general belief that it was in the nature of "common people" to behave in a morally irresponsible manner,

---

pp. 214–215, 218–219, 232–234; Wolfgang Reinhard, *Ausgewählte Abhandlungen* (Berlin, 1997), p. 86.
See also Lyndal Roper, *Das Fromme Haus: Frauen und Moral in der Reformation* (Frankfurt am Main, 1999), p. 75; Gerd Schwerhoff, *Köln im Kreuzverhör: Kriminalität, Herrschaft und Gesellschaft in einer frühneuzeitlichen Stadt* (Bonn/Berlin, 1991), p. 178; Ralf-Peter Fuchs, *Um die Ehre: Westfälische Beleidigungsprozesse vor dem Reichskammergericht 1525–1805* (Paderborn, 1999), p. 231; Behringer, "Mörder, Diebe, Ehebrecher", pp. 99–102.
For further examples in the protocols, see StadtA: RP 211 (1596), Fol. 16 v & 221 r und 219 (1604), Fol. 76 r.

10 Roper, *Das Fromme Haus,* pp. 7–9, 21, 109–110; Lyndal Roper, "Ödipus und Teufel", in Andreas Blauert and Gerd Schwerhoff (ed.), *Mit den Waffen der Justiz: Zur Kriminalitätsgeschichte des späten Mittelalters und der Frühen Neuzeit* (Frankfurt am Main, 1993), pp. 38–41; Ulinka Rublack, *The Crimes of Women in Early Modern Germany* (Oxford, 1999), pp. 149–150.
For more about early modern marriage and premarital relationships, see Richard van Dülmen, "Fest der Liebe: Heirat und Ehe in der Frühen Neuzeit", in Richard van Dülmen (ed.), *Armut, Liebe, Ehre: Studien zur historischen Kulturforschung* (Frankfurt am Main, 1988), pp. 67–90.

11 Strasser, *State of Virginity,* pp. 12, 20–23, 29–30, 52–58, 173–174.

12 Schwerhoff, *Köln,* p. 376.
See also, Lömker-Schlögell, "Prostituierte", pp. 71–72, 78; Ernst Schubert, "Soziale Randgruppen und Bevölkerungsentwicklung im Mittelalter", *Saeculum: Jahrbuch für Universalgeschichte* (Freiburg/Munich, 1989), p. 338.

sexual misbehaviour was viewed as especially characteristic of lower-class women. Yet, in what ways did all this actually appear in the local legal discussions?

In 1553 the Bavarian territorial law first mentioned the crime of *Leichtfertigkeit* as a grave moral offence, but no specific sanctions were as yet inflicted.[13] In the records of the Munich magistrates' court, the term *Leichtfertigkeit* was associated with a variety of undesirable sexual behaviours, not just premarital relationships. Undoubtedly, it must have been difficult for the magistrates to differentiate between love and mutual consent on the one hand, and abuse, prostitution, sexual recklessness and other forms of immorality, on the other. In cases of moral offences it was always challenging to establish which party was at fault, but in most cases suspicion seem to fell upon the woman.

However, and as Spierenburg also notes, it was "not always clear, though, who was disciplining whom."[14] In the same manner Schilling writes about the complexity and diversity of social control, even when being scrutinized in terms of control *from above*.[15] Additionally, in the context early modern Munich, social control cannot that easily be placed between authority and people, as the authority in itself was strongly dived in two: the bourgeois magistrates and the duke with his ducal court. There were constant disagreements concerning the limits of judicial power between these two instances. The magistrates were in many ways closer to the people than the members of the duke's court, but they still wanted to emphasize their authoritative position in their relation to common men.[16] One major way to do this was, of course, to pass own statutes.

In 1596 the Munich magistrates' court set out its position on women who were found guilty of immoral sexual behaviour. A clear distinction was drawn between a first offence and recidivism, which was also a common practice when determining the appropriate sanction for other

---

13 LO 1553, Fol. 110 r–110 v.
14 Spierenburg, "Social Control and History", p. 16.
15 Heinz Schilling, "Discipline. The State and the Churches in Early Modern Europe", in Herman Roodenburg and Pieter Spierenburg (ed.), *Social Control in Europe 1500–1800*, Vol. 1 (Ohio, 2004), p. 26.
16 For these power relations and struggles in Munich see Lidman, *Zum Spektakel und Abscheu*, pp. 32–47.

types of crimes. With each offence the punishment would become more severe, more painful and more shameful. After the first two transgressions the offender was to be expelled from Munich, and with the third offence, from the whole duchy, after she had been pilloried. If a woman received a fourth sentence, her flesh would also be cut.[17]

As a permanent and visible sign of immorality, especially the last measure was to serve the purposes of social control through deterrence. Yet all of these sanctions were supposed to dishonour and stigmatize the convicted, and therefore they had to be executed in public. Only this way they could actualize their wished impact as "warning examples" and help to maintain moral standards as well as prevent further crimes. The collective honour of the society was to be restored through public shaming of individual wrongdoers.

In sixteenth-century Munich one aspect of the predominant "moral problem" was especially disturbing for the authorities, as they wanted to make the duchy an exemplary Catholic territory: the clergy's concubines. Most women who faced such charges, officially worked in priests' households as maids or cooks, but for a reason or another they may have become sexually involved with their masters. In many cases they had left their parental homes on the countryside at a young age in the hope of finding a better life in the city. The very existence of these potentially suspicious women was embarrassing and dreadful, as it did not fit into the ideal picture of Catholic priests having promised to be sexually continent. The religious "fathers" were supposed to provide a moral example for their "children" in the congregation.[18]

---

17 "so offt ein leichtfertige weibs person in fronuest der schergenstuben eingeführt würdet, so solle die selbige das erste mal zu einer wahrnung allein angeloben nit mer in die statt vnd burgfrid zekhommen. kombt eine aber zum andern mal, so solle die durch die ambtleüth ausgeführt vnd jr statt vnd burgfridt verbotten werden. were es aber die ain zum 3ten mal eingebracht wurde, so ist die selbige auf den pranger zestellen, vnd durch den züchtiger auszuführen, vnd neben betroung einer leibs straff jr das landt vnd statt zuerweigern. zum vierten mal soll man solliche auf den pranger stellen vnd ein sarten aushauwen." (StadtA: RP 211 (1596), Fol. 226 r–226 v).
See also BayHstA: KMS 1595/I/15, KMS 1598/III/13, Biii r–Biii v; StadtA: BR 60 B 14 (1598), Fol. 8, Biii r–Biii v.
For similarity to other German laws, see Abraham Sauer, *Straffbüchlein von Abraham Sauer* (Frankfurt am Main, 1579), pp. 86–89; Döpler, *Theatrum*, p. 888.
18 Lidman, *Zum Spektakel und Abscheu*, pp. 344–346. For concubines in Roman law and for expectations of Catholic priests in the community see Breit, *"Leichtfertigkeit"*, pp. 161, 249; Angelo Turchini, "Bayern und Mailand im Zeichen der konfessionellen Bürokratisierung", in Wolfgang Reinhard and Heinz

In 1553 Bavarian territorial laws prohibited the holding of concubines in priests' households, but at this time such cases were not yet vigorously pursued. In 1578 it was determined that the clergymen keeping concubines should be sent to an ecclesiastical court in Freisingen, which would then usually impose a fine or some kind of a penitence ritual.[19] Despite the moral failings of the clergy, dishonouring secular punishments could not involve the privileged, and so the female participants would be publicly disgraced in the name of collective purity. However, one also has to consider the possibility of false charges based on the eagerness of the authorities to wipe out immorality and see sexual interactions where there were none.

In the end of the sixteenth century, an ever-increasing number of concubines, however, were subjected to public shaming. The dukes regularly reminded the magistrates that they should be more efficient in this matter. In 1612, for example, duke Maximilian wrote a letter to the Munich magistrates in which he complained that the concubine Barbara Ferchtlin "had practised her life of immorality" in Munich for twenty years. In his opinion, as "the whole city knew" about the dubious life of certain priests and their maids, "something" should be done as soon as possible.[20] Practically, this meant punishments that would bring the issue into general attention in the community, and regular reporting of the current state of affairs in the ducal court.

During the early years of the seventeenth century, duke Maximilian would often bluster about "the irritating sin of that dammed obscenity" that had overrun his country and, even more shockingly, its capitol city Munich. In his view the magistrates were not doing their work as efficient as he was expecting. They should not hesitate but immediately arrest every woman suspected of concubinage, and make them

---

Schilling (ed.) *Die Katholische Konfessionalisierung* (Reformationsgeschichtliche Studien und Texte, 135; Münster, 1995), p. 403. For contemporary perceptions of celibacy see, for example, Albertinus, *Haußpolicey*, 1. Teil, 47 v & 2. Teil, 56 v–57 r.

19 LO 1578, Fol. 36 v–37 r, StadtA: BR (1606), Mandate 60 B 3, Fol. 3 r–3 v; Reinhard Heydenreuter, *Kriminalitätsgeschichte Bayerns von Anfängen bis ins 20. Jahrhundert.* (Regensburg, 2003), pp. 107–109; Michael Schattenhofer, *Das alte Rathaus: Seine bauliche Entwicklung und seine stadtgeschichtliche Bedeutung* (Munich, 1972), p. 301.

20 See, for example, StadtA: BR 62 (1578), Fol. 189 r–190 r; BayHstA: KMS 1595/I/15; StadtA: BR 62 (1601), fol. 190 r–191 v, BR 62 (1611), Fol. 184 v and BR 62 (1612), Fol. 185 r–185 v.

stand in front of the church on three consecutive Sundays, before being expelled. Recidivists were to be pilloried as well as banished from the whole duchy, and those convicted of a third offence should also be whipped.[21] Even though the duke made no mention of mutilation, Maximilian's sanctions were, by and large, more severe than those inflicted for *Leichtfertigkeit* and *Unzucht*: already a first-time offender could be dishonoured in public.

Social control and praxis

It seems that not only premarital courting, but also shared households in marriage-like unions and even the sexual relationships of priests, had earlier been quite commonplace and largely tolerated. However, in the increasingly confessional climate of the sixteenth century, such behaviour now ranked among the most severely punished forms of immorality.[22] It is worth noticing though, that the expressions and terms used in the protocols for these "wrongdoings" were creations of the judicial and moral rhetoric *from above*; those who were involved in the actual cases might have used different language when discussing sexual matters.[23] Nevertheless, even a cursory examination of sixteenth- and seventeenth-century protocols and literature reveals that sexual misconduct truly was an essential part of the contemporary moral discussion, at least among the aristocracy. And, it was inseparably linked with the objectives of social control.

Collective values were emphasized in the early modern community, and those who damaged the collective honour were to be punished. This was not only a matter of the state or the city, but to some extent other groups or individuals including families, neighbours and colleagues, possessed the power of sanctioning. Thus, in addition to judicial sanc-

---

21 StadtA: BR Mandate 60 B 3 (1604), Fol. 2 v, 60 B 8 (1607), Fol. 668 r–668 v und 60 B 2 (1617), Fol. 544 v–545 r.
22 Heydenreuter, "Der Magistrat als Befehlsempfänger", pp. 195–196; Heydenreuter, *Kriminalitätsgeschichte Bayerns*, pp. 103–04. With the label *Leichtfertigkeit* a woman lost her status as a virgin and therefore also her honour. (Breit, *"Leichtfertigkeit"*, pp. 5–6).
23 For more on interpretation of court statements, see Roper, "Ödipus und Teufel", pp. 55–57.

tions, the manifestations of a more unofficial and even spontaneous social control have to be taken into account as likely possibilities. One could also speak of a form of co-operation between the authorities and the people.[24] However, it is important to note that the sources of legal history largely force us to deal with the aristocratic point of view. In other words, in many cases of forbidden sexual relationships legal action was never taken: either nobody wanted to inform the authorities due to one's own interest, or the community simply could not accept that the "fallen" individual was as morally reprehensible as was claimed.

The reactions of the community and its willingness to report suspicions were probably closely related to the social positions of the defendants. But, who were these women accused in Munich of engaging in a forbidden relationship or acting in an otherwise immoral fashion? They were young and old; maids, craftsmen's wives or women employed in the duke's court; citizens or only residents, sometimes originated in other cities or territories. A large number of the defendants possessed "a bad reputation of being indecent women". Especially unmarried and poor women – whether guilty or not – were socially vulnerable and could quite easily become the subject of gossip. In fact, the authority-initiated social control seems to have functioned best when the defendants were brought to trial due to rumours.

From the judicial point of view, every immoral person should be punished, because his or her behaviour caused general irritation and could excite God's wrath. The idea that the forbidden sexual activity of one person could harm the whole community was widespread in both Catholic and Protestant territories.[25] This, and other religious ideas of high morals and chastity, functioned as a driving force of social control. People would have felt under pressure to observe their fellow citizens and

---

24 See Schwerhoff, *Köln*, pp. 27–29; Karl Härter, "Soziale Disziplinierung durch Strafe? Intentionen frühneuzeitlicher Policeyordnungen und staatliche Sanktionspraxis", *Zeitschrift für historische Forschung*, 26 (Berlin, 1999), p. 371; Martin Dinges, "Die Ehre als Thema der Stadtgeschichte. Eine Semantik im Übergang vom Ancien Régime zur Moderne", *Zeitschrift für historische Forschung*, 16 (Berlin, 1989), p. 430.

25 Burghartz, "Geschlecht – Körper – Ehre", p. 217; Susanna Burghartz, "Ordering Discourse and Society: Moral Politics, Marriage, and Fornication during the Reformation and the Confessionalization Process in Germany and Switzerland", in Herman Roodenburg and Pieter Spierenburg (ed.), *Social Control in Europe 1500–1800*, Vol. 1. (Ohio, 2004), pp. 78, 81–87.

strangers, out of fear that the misdeeds of others could cause collective trouble. Additionally, the ducal mandates also encouraged individuals to expose and report any suspicious behaviour. Nevertheless, it would be short-sighted to imagine that people reported everything they saw to the authorities: surely they also had sympathy for their fellow citizens and did not always see or hear life around them in the way as the authorities might have wished.

There is good reason to believe that many illicit intimate relationships went unreported. Individuals might not have wanted to take part in legal processes, not even as eyewitnesses. Besides, many pages of the protocols seem to tell the stories of young people who were quite innocently in love. It must have been difficult for people to understand why such couples should be regarded as criminals in the first place. Yet, in the confessional climate of the time, the authorities often interpreted innocent kisses, looks and gestures as indications of immoral behaviour. If something of this nature had already occurred, it was easy enough to suppose that premarital sexual intercourse or even illicit pregnancy had also taken place. However, the brevity of the reports might indicate that the magistrates were seldom familiar with the exact details of such relationships – or that they did not see the importance of discussing them.[26]

The court cases taken into account in this study are concerned with the kind of forbidden sexual behaviour that was punished by public shaming. However, for relatively similar moral offences some defendants would be sentenced to pay fines, while in other cases those found guilty would be executed.[27] In addition to the crime itself, the social position and the gender of the accused played a significant role in the severity of the sentence. Some convicts simply could not pay their fines or had been stigmatized by earlier punishments and so they were to be disgraced in public. Nevertheless, shaming punishments especially for

---

26 See for example StadtA: SG MP 866/6 (1607–1609), Fol. 272 r–277 r and RP 224 (1609), Fol. 124 v, 146 r, 151 v 6 192 r.
27 For another point of view on Bavarian criminal history, see Strasser, *State of Virginity*. For Scandinavian sanctions, see Österberg and Lindström, *Crime and Social Control*, pp. 126–27; Korpiola, *Between Betrothal and Bedding*, p. 272; Hans Eyvind Naess and Eva Österberg, "Sanctions, Agreements, Sufferings", in Eva Österberg and Solvi Sogner (ed.), *People Meet the Law: Control and Conflict-Handling in the Courts. The Nordic Countries in the Post-Reformation and Pre-Industrial Period* (Otta, 2000), pp. 140–42.

moral offences became more widespread by the end of the sixteenth century. As the public nature of these sanctions required the presence of an audience, these occasions were essential for manifestations of authority-initiated social control.

In their letters to the magistrates' court the Bavarian dukes commented on various cases of forbidden sexual behaviour they had heard about. They also gave detailed instructions of how these "reckless females" should be punished. The dukes described how, for example, certain women had been seen "going in and out in the priest's houses, sitting in their chair, eating in their table, even taken a bath or spending the night in there". Only in a few cases were there specific allegations that a woman had shared a bed with a priest. Once it had been assumed that a priest had kissed a girl, it was "easy" to suppose that something more serious had occurred.[28] However, it was never suggested that the priests involved could have prevented this "inevitable" immorality from taking place.

When a person was arrested and prosecuted for unchastity of some kind, it gave the magistrates the opportunity to find out about other possible suspects. It was common practice to ask for "more names" in the questionings. Still, and even though this kind of information could benefit the defendants, they often spoke out only after they had been tortured.[29] In his ruling concerning certain individual cases duke Maximilian also ordered the magistrates to gather evidence from the neighbourhood. The officials were advised that they could use threats of torture or even apply thumbscrews, if necessary. Under these circumstances neighbours were often willing to describe various examples of the concubines' misbehaviour, but in most cases nobody had ever really witnessed any acts of indecency. Nevertheless, several women were punished on the basis of this kind of evidence. They were expelled from the town, sometimes even banished from the whole duchy, and publicly dishonoured in different ways.[30]

---

28 Lidman, *Zum Spektakel und Abscheu*, pp. 347–50. See also StadtA: BR 62 (1613), Fol. 186 r–187 r.
29 See, for example, StadtA: SG MP 866/10 (1616/1617), Fol. 140 r–140 v, RP 233 (1618), Fol. 83 v and SG MP 866/11 (1618), Fol. 13 r–14 v & Fol. 34 r.
30 StadtA: SG MP 866/8 (1612–1614), Fol. 155 v–156, BR 62 (1613), fol. 187 r–189 r, RP 228 (1613), Fol. 58 r, 249 r & 257 v and RP 232 (1617), Fol. 147 r.

The documentation of these kinds of cases in the court records seem to support the interpretation according to which all people did not necessarily report voluntarily, but were rather forced to reveal aggravating facts concerning other members of the community. However, it only took a few loose tongues to expose somebody for serious suspicions.

When not exposed by gossip, forbidden relationships were often discovered only when a woman could no longer hide her pregnancy. As Rublack points out, this generally means that there must have been a significant amount of sexual activity that other people never knew about. If such a case was brought to trial, the man in question would often try to make the accused woman appear sexually neglectful. He would tell the judges that his partner had been both willing and experienced, and rather portray himself as victim of seduction, which made her more or less a "bad" woman. If the judges believed this account, or if there was evidence of the woman's prior sexual history, it was possible that she would be punished and her partner would escape any real sanction. Because virginity and sexual purity formed the essential criteria of a woman's virtues, a bad reputation or prior sexual experience would have had a very negative effect upon the prospects of a woman involved in the legal process.[31]

According to Roper the widespread movement against prostitution resulted in suspicion being attached to women in general. The expression "whore" no longer referred to a profession: it had become a moral category.[32] Yet occasionally, and especially in the cases of premarital relationships, there seems to have been some understanding among the Munich magistrates for the difficult positions of female defendants. For example motherhood was often used as grounds for milder punishments; pregnant women or women nursing infants were not put in the pillory, whipped or expelled during the coldest winter months. Nevertheless, one also comes across examples where this practice was

---

31 Rublack, *The Crimes of Women*, pp. 139, 235, 238–241; StadtA: RP 211 (1596), Fol. 81 r & 85 v–86 r and SG MP 866/4 (1599–1602), Fol. 33 r–33 v & 34 v.
 See also Roper, *Das Fromme Haus*, pp. 76–77, 110–111; Behringer, "Mörder, Diebe, Ehebrecher", p. 100.
32 Roper, *Das Fromme Haus*, pp. 112–113. On discrimination and marginalization of prostitutes, see Roper, *Das Fromme Haus*, pp. 88–89; Rublack, *The Crimes of Women*, pp. 8–10.

reversed.[33] An examination of the protocols largely supports the idea that the female defendants' points of view were seldom taken seriously, especially if they belonged to the less fortunate social groups.

However, the tightening legislation threatened every member of the community, not only those who were "suspicious by nature": high levels of morality and sexual decency were expected to be common virtues. Magistrates were under considerable pressure from the duke's court to implement the new moral politics and prevent further crimes through the use of exemplary punishments. Yet the court records clearly show that the sentences handed down by the magistrates remained relatively moderate. Despite the wide range of different sexual misbehaviours, most of the expelled women were not subjected to the most severe shaming rituals. In particular, whipping and the pillory were avoided, and cases involving mutilation were very rare. More severe punishments were favoured if there was reason to suspect that something like prostitution or pairing was involved. In theory the Bavarian jurisdiction allowed for the use of a number of severe shaming punishments, but mostly these were not employed.[34] This is not particularly surprising; rather, it is one example among others of the differences between norms and praxis.

Uprooting immorality – a mission impossible

The primary goal of early modern absolutist legislation was to preserve the internal peace in the society. To achieve this end, control and discipline were employed. The right to use punishments involving public shaming, if necessary, was clearly outlined in the numerous statutes published by the duke's office. The confessional ideals of the time were absorbed into this struggle against unwanted sexual behaviour, and so the political language of the period preached the necessity of high moral

---

33 StadtA: RP 215/1 (1600), Fol. 94 v, RP 215/2 (1600), Fol. 46 r & 158 r and RP 224 (1609), Fol. 6 v & 260 r, SG MP 866/7 (1610/1611), Fol. 107 r & 244 v and SG MP 866/8 (1612/1614), Fol. 193 r & 203 r–203 v.
34 Lidman, *Zum Spektakel und Abscheu*, pp. 335, 343–344. See also StadtA: RP 224 (1609), Fol. 260 r & 280 v.

standards and gave terrifying accounts of God's wrath. This led to increasing criminalization of moral offences – matters that had previously been the preserve of the Church, had only been punishable by fines or not mentioned in the laws at all.[35]

It is evident that regulations concerning chastity and moral purity became more repressive during the sixteenth century, and people who were accused of sexual misconduct most likely knew what kind of sanctions could await them. During trials the accused would sometimes beg that they would not be "treated in a dishonouring way" or "put into shame".[36] But then again, the court records also reveal the long criminal histories of certain individuals, upon whom all the harsh sentences and public shaming over the years seems to have had only a minimal effect. These recidivists probably no longer feared public shaming or other consequences of further legal actions; they were already outsiders and had no motivation to defend their reputation or honour.[37]

Many of the cases studied here provide accounts of behaviour and relationships that have long been decriminalized. However, and despite the fear of heavenly or worldly threats, early modern people can hardly be described as always loyal to the aristocratic aims. The duke's moral politics clearly was more intolerant than any attitudes and practices of everyday life. But was it in any ways efficient in its disciplining attempts to root out moral offences? By the beginning of the seventeenth century, a chain of ever-stricter legislation under several generations remained not particularly successful. In fact, it only had a limited impact on the punishment praxis and even less influence on ordinary people's behaviour.

As Schlosser points out, early modern jurisdiction is often associated with weakness, and contemporary legislation seen as symbolic.[38] The Munich court records strengthen this impression, as does the following story. In the spring of 1611 a young woman named Maria Gränzingerin, who was held to be a "common whore", was brought to court in Munich.

---

35 Lidman, *Zum Spektakel und Abscheu*, pp. 367–71. See also Burghartz, "Ordering Discourse and Society", pp. 85–90.
36 See, for example, StadtA: SG MP 866/3 (1598/1599), Fol. 27 v–28 r.
37 See, for example, StadtA: RP 224 (1609), Fol. 260 r, SG MP 866/7 (1610/1611), Fol. 107 r & 244 v and SG MP 866/8 (1612/1614), Fol. 193 r & 203 r–203 v.
38 Schlosser, "Rechtsetzung", pp. 59–60.

She had previously been incarcerated several times in the cellars of the city prison. On this occasion Gränzingerin was expelled from the city merely on the basis of poorly grounded assumptions about her moral standards: no more specific accusations were levelled against her at this time. This incident was not the only one involving Gränzingerin: we hear of her again in 1612 and 1613 when she was put in the pillory. The magistrates seem to have held firm to their perception that Gränzingerin was "hopelessly obscure" and an *"incorrigibilis pudana"*.[39]

In July 1616 Maria Gränzingerin was sentenced to public whipping. At that time, the 29-year-old woman had been subjected to (at least) the following catalogue of public punishments: five times held in chains, five times expelled, twice whipped and once burnt through her cheek. She was now threatened with the loss of her head if she ever returned.[40] Despite all the dishonouring and painful punishments, and even threats of decapitation, many criminals were once again taken into custody inside the duchy after they had been banished. However, after the summer of 1616 the protocols fall silent in the case of Maria Gränzingerin. It is particularly striking though that at the trials her actual suspected criminal actions never seemed to have been the issue: it appears that she was rather punished on the basis of her bad reputation. Therefore, she could be seen as a victim of the ducal social control.

In the case of Maria Gränzingerin and many others, it seems that the various sentences and punishments had very little effect on levels of moral offending. The dukes also used threats of fines and dismissal against the magistrates' court in order to make it more efficient in these matters. Every citizen was placed under an obligation to help the authorities in their attempts to uncover criminal activities and apprehend suspects. Members of the public were also required to provide any information they could during the course of the legal process. There was

---

39 StadtA: SG MP 866/7 (1610/1611), Fol. 244 r, 866/8 (1612–1614), Fol. 29 r–29 v and RP 228 (1613), Fol. 186 r. *Pudendus* = shameful; *pudeo* = to be ashamed of; *pudibundus* = shameful, disgraceful.
40 StadtA: RP 231 (1616), Fol. 145 r.
    See also BayHstA: KMS 1605/III/10; Hans Schlosser and Ingo Schwab, *Oberbayerisches Landrecht Kaiser Ludwigs des Bayern von 1346: Edition, Übersetzung und juristischer Kommentar* (Köln, 2000), pp. 217–18 and Oberbayerisches Landrecht Artikel 39.

a "nice reward" available in return for this kind of co-operation.[41] Yet there are only very few remarks of episodes connected to this kind of payments in the court records.

In the eyes of the dukes, the Munich magistrate was not successful in its in fight against immorality; those who were punished returned to court time and time again alongside first-time offenders. At the same time, the magistrates avoided issuing harsh sanctions and death sentences, even when this would have been a lawful verdict. Additionally, the tightening regulations and unrealistic moral demands created new criminality. The magistrates were ordered to execute the duke's orders, but they also wanted to keep the peace in the city whilst not embittering people through unnecessary severity – a position that necessitated constant balancing of punishments and pardons. By the turn of the sixteenth century, the power of the Bavarian dukes already exhibited many absolutist characteristics, but the Munich magistrates' court still tried to hold on to its traditional rights to pass its own judgements. It seems that both the bourgeois and ducal authorities found themselves facing an impossible task.

The history of the sixteenth-century Bavarian jurisdiction and criminalization of moral offences generally shows that harsh punishments could not root out unwanted behaviour but they rather had the opposite effect; this was a period of flourishing recidivism.[42] Additionally, the citizens of Munich were not particularly keen to report moral offences under any circumstances, and the magistrates were not too eager to prosecute them. The concubines, for example, were only "discovered" after the duke had written a letter or several letters about suspicious individuals. This perhaps indicates that both the magistrates and the citizens were ready to accept such relationships, at least to some extent. In other words, the ducal social control seems to have been quite powerless in reality.

---

41 BayHstA: KMS 1524/VIII/10, 1526/II/18, 1530/III/28, 1540/IV/3, 1546/V/5, 1561/IX/1, 1570/XII/16, 1570/XII/20, 1572/IX/14, 1577/VI/22, 1584/IX/18, 1584/X/13, 1589/VI/10, 1590/XII/8, 1601/XII/22, 1614/III/1; StadtA: RP 233 (1618), Fol. 61 r. See also BStB, Res. 2., Bavar. 244 (1516), ff. Ciii v–Ciiii r & Lv r–Lv v and BayHstA: KMS 1610/XII/10–2, Aiii v–Aiv r.
42 According to modern understanding this is due to the effect that shaming always causes stigmatization, which then supports alienation and therefore severely hinders attempts to cut short criminal careers.

Sources

ARCHIVAL SOURCES

Stadtarchiv München (The City Archives of Munich)
Ratssitzungsprotokolle 1596–1618 (StadtA: RP).
Malefizprotokolle des Unterrichters 1598–1618 (StadtA: SG MP 866).
Ordnungen und Mandate der Herzöge (StadtA: BR Mandate 60 A 1).
Bayerisches Hauptstaatsarchiv (The Bavarian State Archives in Munich)
Kurbayern Mandatsammlung 1500–1614 (BayHstA: KMS).
Bayerische Staatsbibliothek (The Bavarian State Library in Munich)
Bayerische Landesordnung 1553 / LO 1553 (Baystabi: ESgl/2 Bavar. 509 a).

PRINTED SOURCES

Albertinus, Aegidius 1602: *Haußpolicey,* München.
Döpler, Jakob 1693: *Theatrum poenarum, suppliciorum et executionum criminalium oder Schauplatz der Leibes- und Lebensstrafen,* Sondershausen.
Sauer, Abraham 1579: *Straffbüchlein von Abraham Sauer,* Frankfurt am Main.

LITERATURE

Behringer, Wolfgang 1990: Mörder, Diebe, Ehebrecher: Verbrechen und Strafen in Kurbayern vom 16. bis 18. Jahrhundert. In *Verbrechen, Strafen und soziale Kontrolle,* ed. Richard van Dülmen, Frankfurt am Main, pp. 85–293.
Breit, Stefan 1991: *"Leichtfertigkeit" und ländliche Gesellschaft: Voreheliche Sexualität in der frühen Neuzeit,* München.
Burghartz, Susanna 2004: Ordering Discourse and Society: Moral Politics, Marriage, and Fornication during the Reformation and the Confessionalization Process in Germany and Switzerland. In *Social Control in Europe 1500–1800,* Vol. 1, ed. Herman Roodenburg and Pieter Spierenburg, Ohio, pp. 78–98.
Burghartz, Susanna 1995: Geschlecht – Körper – Ehre: Überlegungen zur weibli-chen Ehre in der frühen Neuzeit am Beispiel der Basler Ehegerichtsprotokolle. In *Verletzte Ehre: Ehrenkonflikte in Gesellschaften des Mittelalters und der frühen Neuzeit,* ed. Klaus Schreiner and Gerd Schwerhoff, Köln, pp. 214–234.
Burghartz, Susanna 1999: *Zeiten der Reinheit – Orte der Unzucht: Ehe und Sexualität in Basel während der Frühen Neuzeit,* Paderborn.
Dinges, Martin 1989: Die Ehre als Thema der Stadtgeschichte: Eine Semantik im Übergang vom Ancien Régime zur Moderne. *Zeitschrift für historische Forschung,* 16 (1989), pp. 409–440.
Dülmen, Richard van 1988: Fest der Liebe: Heirat und Ehe in der Frühen Neuzeit, In *Armut, Liebe, Ehre: Studien zur historischen Kulturforschung,* ed. Richard van Dülmen, Frankfurt am Main, pp. 67–106.
Fuchs, Ralf-Peter 1999: *Um die Ehre: Westfälische Beleidigungsprozesse vor dem Reichskammergericht 1525-1805,* Paderborn.
Härter, Karl 1999: Soziale Disziplinierung durch Strafe? Intentionen frühneuzeitlicher

Policeyordnungen und staatliche Sanktionspraxis. *Zeitschrift für historische Forschung*, 26 (1999), pp. 365–379.

Heydenreuter, Reinhard 1992: Der Magistrat als Befehlsempfänger – Die Disziplinierung der Stadtobrigkeit 1579 bis 1651. In *Geschichte der Stadt München*, ed. Richard van Bauer, München, pp. 189–210.

Heydenreuter, Reinhard 2003: *Kriminalitätsgeschichte Bayerns von Anfängen bis ins 20. Jahrhundert*, Regensburg.

Korpiola, Mia 2004: *Between Betrothal and Bedding: The Making of Marriage in Sweden, ca. 1200–1610*, Saarijärvi.

Lidman, Satu 2008: *Zum Spektakel und Abscheu. Schand- und Ehrenstrafen als Mittel öffentlicher Disziplinierung in München um 1600*, Frankfurt am Main.

Lidman, Satu 2004: "Unzüchtige Weiber" und Priesterkonkubinen vor dem Münchner Rat um 1600. *Oberbayerisches Archiv*, 128 (2004), pp. 65–77.

Lömker-Schlögell, Annette 1994: Prostituierte – um vermeydung willen merers übels in der christenhait. In *Randgruppen der spätmittelalterlichen Gesellschaft: Ein Hand- und Studienbuch*, ed. Bernd-Ulrich Hergemöller, Warendorf, pp. 56–88.

Naess, Hans Eyvind and Österberg, Eva 2000: Sanctions, Agreements, Sufferings. In *People Meet the Law: Control and Conflict-Handling in the Courts. The Nordic Countries in the Post-Reformation and Pre-Industrial Period*, ed. Eva Österberg and Solvi Sogner, Otta, pp. 140–166.

Reinhard, Wolfgang 1997: *Ausgewählte Abhandlungen*, Berlin.

Roper, Lyndal 1999: *Das Fromme Haus: Frauen und Moral in der Reformation*, Frankfurt am Main.

Roper, Lyndal 1993: Ödipus und Teufel. In *Mit den Waffen der Justiz: Zur Kriminalitätsgeschichte des späten Mittelalters und der Frühen Neuzeit*, ed. Andreas Blauert and Gerd Schwerhoff, Frankfurt am Main, pp. 32–53.

Rublack, Ulinka 1999: *The Crimes of Women in Early Modern Germany*, Oxford.

Schilling, Heinz 2004: Discipline: The State and the Churches in Early Modern Europe. In *Social Control in Europe 1500–1800*, Vol. 1, ed. Herman Roodenburg and Pieter Spierenburg, Ohio, pp. 25–36.

Schlosser, Hans 1987: Rechtsetzung und Gesetzgebungsverständnis im Territorialstaat Bayern im 16. Jahrhundert. *Zeitschrift für bayerische Landesgeschichte*, 50 (1987), pp. 41–61.

Schlosser, Hans and Schwab, Ingo 2000: *Oberbayerisches Landrecht Kaiser Ludwigs des Bayern von 1346: Edition, Übersetzung und juristischer Kommentar*, Köln.

Schattenhofer, Michael 1972: *Das alte Rathaus: Seine bauliche Entwicklung und seine stadtgeschichtliche Bedeutung*, München.

Schubert, Ernst 1989: Soziale Randgruppen und Bevölkerungsentwicklung im Mittelalter. *Saeculum; Jarhbuch für Universalgeschichte* (1989), pp. 294–339.

Schwerhoff, Gerd 1991: *Köln im Kreuzverhör: Kriminalität, Herrschaft und Gesellschaft in einer frühneuzeitlichen Stadt*, Bonn/Berlin.

Scribner, R. W. 2001: *Religion and Culture in Germany (1400–1800)*. Studies in Medieval and Reformation Thought, 81, Köln.

Spierenburg, Pieter 2004: Social Control and History: An Introduction. In *Social Control in Europe 1500–1800*, Vol. 1, ed. Herman Roodenburg and Pieter Spierenburg, Ohio, pp. 1–24.

Strasser, Ulrike 2004: *State of Virginity: Gender, Religion and Politics in an Early Modern Catholic State*, Ann Arbor.

Strasser, Ulrike 1999: Vom Fall der Ehre zum Fall der Leichtfertigkeit: Geschlechtsspezifische Aspekte der Konfessionalisierung am Beispiel Münchner Eheversprechens- und Alimentationsklagen (1592–1649). In *Konfessionalisierung und Region*, ed. Peer Frieß and Rolf Kießling, Konstanz, pp. 227–246.

Turchini, Angelo 1995: Bayern und Mailand im Zeichen der konfessionellen Bürokratisierung. In *Die Katholische Konfessionalisierung*, ed. Wolfgang Reinhard and Heinz Schilling (Reformationsgeschichtliche Studien und Texte, 135), Münster, pp. 394–404.

Österberg, Eva and Lindström, Dag 1988: *Crime and Social Control in Medieval and Early Modern Swedish Towns*, Studia Historica Upsaliensia, 152; Uppsala.

Legislative and Judicial Effects of Forbidden Sexuality on Engagements and Marriages in Late Nineteenth-Century Central Finland

Pasi Saarimäki

The Swedish Law of the Realm (1734), supplemented by a number of new regulations and laws, was still in force in Finland in the late nineteenth century, The legislation included articles regulating sexuality, marriage and engagement which, alongside church rules and ordinances restricted people's lives, and violations of such regulations could result in punishment. In particular, sexual activity was only permissible within marriage, and ecclesiastical and secular authorities could scrutinize the actions of ordinary people.

This article examines how sexual intercourse by those who were engaged or had extramarital affairs was treated by the courts and church bodies in the closing decades of the nineteenth century. The ways in which broken engagements and adultery were treated both in legislation and by the local courts are of particular interest. I will also consider how legislation relating to sexual behaviour restricted, or made it easier, to break off an engagement or obtain a divorce and the impact this had on the lives of ordinary people.[1] In doing so, I will examine the opera-

---

1   This article is based on my dissertation, which addresses the construction of permitted and forbidden sexuality in rural Central Finland in the late nineteenth century. See Pasi Saarimäki, *Naimisen normit käytännöt ja konfliktit. Esiaviollinen ja aviollinen seksuaalisuus 1800-luvun lopun keskisuomalaisella*

tion of the courts and the legislation, as a type of social control or more precisely, as a form of "formal" social control.[2] This will be achieved through an exploration of the effect of legislation (including the Swedish Law of the Realm from 1734 and its supplements), the Church Act 1869, the new Penal Code 1889,[3] the Marriage Act 1929),[4] and the activities of the Keuruu district court, which covered three parishes – Keuruu, Multia and Pihlajavesi – in Central Finland between 1880 and 1900. Economically and socially all three parishes were still traditionally rural and agrarian, even though great structural changes were at hand.[5]

In these areas, court sessions were held twice a year: once in winter/spring and once in autumn. I have primarily considered three different types of cases that were brought before the district court: broken engagements, cases where the clergy sued an engaged couple because of an excessive delay before marriage and divorces in which adultery was cited. Additionally, I have examined some cases in which unmarried mothers applied for maintenance payments from the fathers of their children and cases of divorce involving abandonment. I have also consulted ecclesiastical sources (from 1880–1900), including records of church council meetings, details of ecclesiastical punishments from the congregation of Keuruu and rulings on broken engagements and divorce issued by

maaseudulla (The norms, practices and conflicts of sex and marriage – Premarital and marital sexual activity in rural Central Finland in the late nineteenth century). Jyväskylä Studies in Humanities 138 (Jyväskylä, University of Jyväskylä: 2010), online: http://urn.fi/URN:ISBN:978-951-39-3830-7.
2   Informal social control was instead practiced by other people: neighbors, family, relatives etc. Thomas Hylland Eriksen, *Toista maata? Johdatus antropologiaan* (Helsinki, Gaudeamus, 2004), p. 88; Marie Lindstedt Cronberg, *Synd och skam: Ogifta mödrar på svensk landsbygd 1680–1880* (Lund, Lunds Universitet, Historiska institutionen, 1997), pp. 16–17; Eva Österberg, Malin Lennartsson and Hans Eyvind Naess, "Social Control Outside or Combined with the Secular Judicial Arena", in Eva Österberg and Solvi Sogner (ed.), *People Meet the Law: Control and Conflict-Handling in the Courts. The Nordic Countries in the Post-Reformation and Pre-Industrial Period* (Oslo, Universitetsforlaget, 2000), *passim*. Esko Hartikainen, *Heränneitä ja nukahtaneita: kulttuuri, kontrolli ja herätys 1800-luvun alun Liperissä* (Helsinki, SKS, 2005), p. 29.
3   Ruotsin Waltakunnan Laki 1734, Hyväksytty ja noudatettavaksi otettu waltiopäivillä vuonna 1734 (Helsinki, SKS, 1877); Ruotsin Valtakunnan Laki 1734, Hyväksytty ja noudatettavaksi otettu valtiopäivillä vuonna 1734 (Helsinki, SKS, 1909). In these notes the Swedish Law of the Realm (1734) will henceforth be referred to as Swe 1734.
4   Marriage Act 1929, www.finlex.fi/fi/laki/alkup/1929/19290234 (accessed 11 February 2013); F. Grönvall (ed.) *Uusi avioliittolainsäädäntö selityksineen* (Helsinki, WSOY, 1936).
5   Teppo Vihola, *Keuruun ja Pihlajaveden historia 1860–1917* (Keuruu, Keuruun ja Pihlajaveden historiatoimikunta, 1983); Mauri Mönkkönen, *Multian historia 1866–1975* (Saarijärvi, Multian kunta ja seurakunta, 1983).

the Turku and Porvoo chapters.[6] In doing so, I deal with forms of formal social control that were primarily *restrictive* rather than necessarily *punitive* in nature.[7] The study is divided into four parts: first, broken engagements and their relationship to issues of sexuality are examined; next, I consider legal marriage as the final consequence of sexual activity during engagement; adultery and its judicial consequences are studied through accounts of divorce hearings in the third section; and finally, I attempt to draw these themes together in a short discussion of the nature of social control.

The legal consequences of breaking off an engagement

At the end of nineteenth century an engagement between man and woman was a mutual and legally binding contract, which was a commitment to marriage.[8] Moreover, for engaged couples, sexual intercourse had significant consequences. These were evident when couples tried to dissolve their engagements. Breaking off an engagement was possible when the parties involved unanimously announced their wish to a local chapter. However, there was one key precondition: the couple must not have participated in sexual intercourse during their engagement.[9]

6 Court records (Juridisdiction of Jyväskylä, court district of Keuruu, II Ca:92–135) and ecclesiastical research material (Archives of congregations of Keuruu and Multia) can be found in the Provincial Archives of Jyväskylä (JyMA, Jyväskylän Maakunta-arkisto).
7 Criminal sanctions for fornication and adultery – imprisonment and fines – were punitive in nature. These themes are not, however, examined in this article.
8 Swe 1734 (1909), Code of Marriage, chapter 1, § 1–5, 3, § 1–3; Church Act 1869, chapter 9, § 72–73; Ragnar Hemmer, *Suomen oikeushistorian oppikirja II: Perheoikeuden, perintöoikeuden ja testamenttioikeuden historia* (Helsinki, Lainopillisen ylioppilastiedekunnan kustannustoimikunta, 1967), pp. 13–15. For legislation concerning betrothal during the Middle Ages and pre-modern period e.g. Jyrki Knuutila, *Avioliitto oikeudellisena ja kirkollisena instituutiona Suomessa vuoteen 1629* (Helsinki, Suomen Kirkkohistoriallinen seura, 1990); Mia Korpiola, *Between Bethothal and Bedding. Marriage Formation in Sweden 1200-1600*. (Leiden, Brill, 2009); Lizzie Carlsson, *"Jag giver dig min dotter": trolovning och äktenskap i den svenska kvinnans äldre historia 1* (Stockholm, Institutet för rättshistorisk forskning, 1965); Lizzie Carlsson, *"Jag giver dig min dotter": trolovning och äktenskap i den svenska kvinnans äldre historia 2* (Stockholm, Institutet för rättshistorisk forskning, 1972).
9 Swe 1734 (1909), Code of Marriage: chapter 4, § 4; Royal charter 11.11.1747; Ragnar Hemmer, *Suomen oikeushistorian oppikirja II*, p. 14; Sami Mahkonen, *Johdatus perheoikeuden historiaan* (Helsinki, Suomen lakimiesliiton kustannus Oy, 1978), pp. 87–88, 90; Sigrid Håkanson, *"då skall han taga henne till äkta...": Oäkta födslar, äktenskapsmarknad och giftermålssystem i Östsverige och Västsverige 1750–1850* (Stockholm, University of Stockholm, Stads och kommunhistoriska institutet, 1999), p. 134–136.

Between 1881 and 1900, the Chapters of Turku and Porvoo ruled in favour of the dissolution of thirty-eight engagements within the congregations of Keuruu and Multia.[10] The chapters first announced that the couples in question had agreed to reverse their earlier promises of marriage and then that, without exception, the chapter had received reliable testimonies that the couples had not engaged in sexual intercourse. The chapter of Porvoo dissolved the engagement of vagrants Manu Manunpoika and Erika Jeremiaantytär, for instance, because both parties had agreed to dissolve their engagement and the chapter had received testimony that they had not indulged in illicit sexual behaviour.[11] The guarantee, included in the couple's application, that the relationship had been non-sexual was sufficient evidence for the chapters.[12] It was not, however, enough for the engaged couple themselves to swear that they had remained chaste: it seems that all applications were probably sent through the local vicar, who would have attested to the non-carnal nature of the relationship, based on his knowledge of the engaged couple and testimony from possible witnesses. If ecclesiastical marriage procedure had already begun and the banns of marriage had been read out in the church,[13] engaged couples had to negotiate for dissolution with the vicar.[14] After they had given their assent, the chapters would always authorize couples to undertake new engagements and marriages. Because sexual activity had not taken place, permanent legal sanctions or restrictions were not imposed.

If the couple had different opinions about their future, the court could dissolve the engagement, so long as sexual intercourse had not

---

10 For number of dissolutions concerning engagement in Finland, see Mahkonen, *Johdatus perheoikeuden historiaan*, pp. 104–107.
11 JyMA Congregation of Keuruu, decisions of divorces 1881–1900 (I Jaa:I); Congregation of Multia, decisions of judicial separations and divorces 1881–1900 (I Jaa:1); Congregation of Keuruu, decisions of divorces 1881–1900, decision of breaking of an engagement 13.11.1888 (Chapter of Porvoo).
12 Distinct announcements were no longer compulsory after 1899 in Finland (Decision of Imperial senate 10.5.1899).
13 For a form of ecclesiastical procedure see Swe 1734 (1909), code of Marriage: chapter 7, § 2; Church Act 1869, chapter 9, § 72–73.
14 JyMA Congregation of Keuruu, decisions of divorces 1881–1900; Congregation of Multia, decisions of judicial separations and divorces 1881–1900; Mahkonen, *Johdatus perheoikeuden historiaan*, p. 90. Anna-Liisa Nieminen, "Skiljobref beviljas: epäonnistuneet avioliitot Göteborgin hiippakunnassa vuosina 1774–1778" (University of Jyväskylä, Department of History and Ethnology, unpublished master's thesis, 2003), pp. 48–50.

taken place.[15] Engaged couples regularly attested to their chastity during trials. Juho Juhonpoika, a shoemaker, and Wilhelmina Samuelintytär claimed that at no time during their seven-year engagement had they had any carnal knowledge of each other. They were "quarrelsome" and did not wish to marry. Another couple, Ida Tuomaantytär and Abraham Juhonpoika, also asserted that they had never slept together.[16] If such claims were believed, and if there were no other significant prohibitive factors, the court would grant dissolution.[17] The local court never assessed these sexual matters in any detail. It seems that denials of sexual intercourse were largely a formality, regardless of what might have actually occurred. The court would only have taken further action if concrete evidence to the contrary was presented. The dissolutions would then be confirmed by the chapters.[18]

The situation was, however, sometimes more complicated where, for instance, an engaged couple had differing opinions about whether or not their engagement should be dissolved. In these cases, or where the clergy sued a couple for delaying their church wedding, the local court had to assess the situation. Moreover, breaking off an engagement became impossible if the engaged couple confessed their sexual relationship or if there was indisputable evidence of such a relationship, in other words a child. One crofter, Kaarle Juhonpoika, opposed his fiancée's appeals for dissolution and claimed that they had lain on the same bed and lived like a wedded couple. In another case, Hilta Kasperintytär had appealed for dissolution, but faced difficulties when her fiancé Albinus claimed that Hilta was pregnant by another man. Albinus also wanted to

---

15 Swe 1734 (1909), Code of Marriage: chapter 3, § 9; chapter 4, § 4, 5; Hemmer, *Suomen oikeushistorian oppikirja II*, p. 14; Malin Lennartsson, *I säng och säte: relationer mellan kvinnor och män i 1600-talets Småland* (Lund, Lund University Press, 1999), pp. 158–159.
16 JyMA winter sessions of Keuruu 18.4.1898, § 44; winter sessions of Keuruu 20.3.1882, § 32. See also Marja Taussi Sjöberg, *Skiljas: Trolovning, äktenskap och skilsmässa i Norrland på 1800-talet* (Södertälje, Författarförlaget, 1988) pp. 119, 127, 138; Nieminen, "Skiljobref bewiljas", pp. 52–54.
17 E.g. JyMA autumn sessions of Keuruu 10.10.1892, § 45.
18 There was only one case in which the chapters questioned the court's decision. JyMA Congregation of Keuruu, decisions of divorces 1881–1900; Congregation of Multia, decisions of judicial separations and divorces t 1881–1900. On actions between chapters, courts and church councils cf. Beata Losman, "Förtryct eller jämställdhet? Kvinnorna och äktenskap i Västsverige omkring 1840". *(Svensk) Historisk Tidskrift*, 102 (1982), pp. 295, 298–299, 307–309; Håkanson *"då skall han taga henne till äkta"*, pp. 134–138.

break off the engagement, but after Hilta admitted that Albinus was the father of her child, their application was rejected.[19] Sexual matters were also raised at a church council meeting during which an engaged couple had been reprimanded for delaying their church wedding. Farmhand Alpiinus Hilpunpoika confessed to a sexual relationship with his fiancé, Hilta Sofia. She denied that their relationship had been sexual, scolded Alpiinus and asked him how he could bind himself so deeply. After these declarations the reverend insisted that the couple should have a church wedding because, in his view, there were grounds for them to marry under secular law.[20]

Sometimes, however, sexual activity made it easier to break off an engagement. There were clear grounds for dissolution if someone who was engaged had a sexual relationship with a third party before or during their engagement.[21] Sexual activity outside the engagement was seen as an offence to the agreement the couple had entered into. Ida Wilhelmina Emanuelintytär described how, during their engagement, her relationship with farmhand Stefanus Abrahaminpoika had become "colder". She subsequently had a sexual relationship with another man and gave birth to an illegitimate child. Stefanus wanted to rid himself of his unfaithful fiancée. The court eventually granted a separation on the grounds of sex with a third party during the engagement.[22]

Women could, however, also fight these cases and sometimes block the court from reaching an outcome. Abraham Evanpoika had moved in with Effia Taavetintytär after the banns of marriage had been read out in church. Abraham claimed that Effia had had sexual contact with other men after this and had subsequently fallen pregnant. Effia denied that she had been unfaithful and claimed that Abraham was the father of her

---

19 JyMA autumn sessions of Keuruu 17.9.1898, § 142; winter sessions of Keuruu 23.2.1894, § 207; autumn sessions of Keuruu 11.9.1894, § 80. See also Losman, "Förtryct eller jämställdhet?", p. 295.
20 JyMA Congregation of Keuruu, records of ecclesiastical punishments, 14.11.1887 (I Hb:4).
21 Swe 1734 (1909), Code of Marriage: chapter 4, § 3; Taussi Sjöberg, *Skiljas*, p. 143. Engagements could also be dissolved if force was involved or if one party had concealed a contagious, unhealed disease that had been contracted before the engagement. Being a drunkard during an engagement or abandoning one's fiancée were also seen as aggravating factors. (Swe 1734 (1909), Code of Marriage: chapter 4, § 1–2, 7–8).
22 JyMA winter sessions of Keuruu 29.3.1888, § 232. See also Taussi Sjöberg, *Skiljas*, pp. 27–32.

child. In the end, the court was unable to rule on the dissolution of the engagement due to a lack of evidence.[23]

According to legislation, those who engaged in sexual activity with a third person whilst betrothed should have been fined. In the district court of Keuruu, however, this section of the law was never applied; it was finally abolished when the new Penal Code was introduced in 1889.[24] Sexual intercourse during an engagement had considerable and lasting consequences for those involved. This is also evident in the section of the law, which dealt with forced engagements: if someone had been forced into a betrothal, the engagement was invalid, but only if there had not yet been any sexual contact.[25] Sexuality was an important issue for chapters and the courts because sexual intercourse during an engagement could produce a lasting legal relationship between the engaged parties.

The legal consequences of sex during an engagement

From a legal point of view, a marriage was formed if the betrothed couple had engaged in intercourse. In such a case, the fiancé had an obligation to fulfil the engagement through a church wedding. Should he fail to do so, the court was bound to announce a legal, non-ecclesiastical marriage.[26] There were similar legal consequences if a man induced a woman to sleep with him through promises of marriage. Under these circumstances, he was obliged to marry the woman, if this was her wish or the wish of her parents. If the man objected to the marriage or denied that he had made any such promises, the court would have to announce a legal, non-ecclesiastical marriage.[27]

23 JyMA autumn sessions of Keuruu 19.9.1898, § 147.
24 Swe 1734 (1877), Penal Code: chapter 55, § 2; Penal Code 1889.
25 Swe 1734 (1909), Code of Marriage: chapter 4, § 1.
26 Swe 1734 (1909), Code of Marriage: chapter 3, § 9; Hemmer, *Suomen oikeushistorian oppikirja II*, p. 49; Sami Mahkonen, *Avioero: Tutkimus avioliittolain erosäännösten taustasta ja tarkoituksesta* (Helsinki, Suomalainen lakimiesyhdistys, 1980), p. 7, footnote 9; Jouko Sihvo, *Näkökulma suomalaisten moraaliin: avoliitto, avioliitto ja seksi kirkollisessa etiikassa* (Helsinki, WSOY, 1981), pp. 23, 25.
27 Swe 1734 (1909), Code of Marriage: chapter 3, § 10; Armas Nieminen, *Taistelu sukupuolimoraalista: avioliitto ja seksuaalikysymyksiä suomalaisen hengenelämän ja yhteiskunnan murroksessa säätyajoilta 1910-luvulle* (Helsinki, WSOY, 1951), pp. 72–74; Hemmer, *Suomen oikeushistorian oppikirja II*, pp. 49–50.

It is important to recognize that sexual contact during an engagement automatically created a legal relationship. However, procuring intercourse through promises of marriage only had legal consequences when women appealed to the court that these promises be honoured. The legal result in such cases was the court's declaration of an "imperfect marriage"; a legal relationship with full marital rights.[28] A "perfect marriage", it seems, was a union that had been entered into in church.

In the Keuruu district, only two cases can be found in which the court declared that an engaged couple were legally married. The decisions in these cases were unusual and stand out as there were plenty of other similar cases in which a sexual relationship had been exposed. Abraham Wähänen and his fiancé, Maria, were brought before the court because they had delayed their church wedding. Both admitted that their relationship had been sexual. However, Maria argued that because Abraham had been intimate with other women, she did not have to marry him. In the end the court ruled that Abraham and Maria should be regarded as a married couple because they had admitted their sexual relationship.[29] In 1880, Amanda Aleksanterintytär was declared the legal wife of farmhand Kalle Kustaa. During court sessions, Amanda admitted that she had borne one child before her engagement to Kalle. She had then given birth to two more of Kalle's children during their engagement. The couple's children were cited as the reason for the pronouncement of a legal marriage.[30]

Unhappy relationships could often arise, if people were obliged to marry.[31] The court's declarations had a negative impact on the lives of such couples by imposing "imperfect marriage" on them. It seems that

---

28 Hemmer, *Suomen oikeushistorian oppikirja II*, pp. 49–50; Anu Pylkkänen, "Avioliiton historiaa: Sukujen sopimuksesta kahden kauppaan", in Pia Letto-Vanamo (ed.), *Suomen oikeushistorian pääpiirteet. Sukuvallasta moderniin oikeuteen* (Helsinki, Gaudeamus, 1991), pp. 90–91; Nieminen, *Taistelu sukupuolimoraalista*, pp. 72–74.
29 JyMA winter sessions of Keuruu 2.5.1881, § 162. On announcing imperfect marriage, see also Losman, "Förtryct eller jämställdhet?" p. 295; Nieminen, "Skiljobref bewiljas", pp. 44–48.
30 JyMA autumn sessions Keuruu 26.10.1880, § 174; winter sessions of Keuruu 27.4.1881, § 75, clerical notice; autumn sessions of Keuruu 28.11.1881, § 40.
31 Jari Eilola, "Cuckoi päällä curjanakin; cana alla armaisnakin", in Piia Einonen and Petri Karonen (ed.), *Arjen valta. Suomalaisen yhteiskunnan patriarkaalisesta järjestyksestä myöhäiskeskiajalta teollistumisen kynnykselle (v.1450–1860)* (Helsinki, SKS, 2002), p. 121.

many did not take such marriages particularly seriously nor did their local communities. Abraham Wähänen and his wife did not live together; instead they both had affairs with other people for years. Their relationships annoyed the local church, and they were eventually brought before the district court to face charges of adultery. In court, Maria shared her thoughts about their "imperfect marriage". She declared that a couple that had been pronounced married against their own will was not the equivalent of a real married couple. It seems that local people did not take this kind of marriage seriously either. In the next court session, Abraham's new partner, Wilhelmiina Annaliisantytär, defended their relationship by saying that she, like everyone else in the community, had thought that Abraham was an unmarried man.[32] Both couples filed for divorce twenty years later at the end of the 1890s, but they were unsuccessful due to lack of legal grounds. An "imperfect marriage" could only be dissolved on the same grounds as those that applied to a "perfect marriage".[33] Sex during an engagement therefore had definitive, restrictive consequences.

Although many engaged couples could face legal consequences as a result of their sexual relationships, at the end of the nineteenth century the district court was not particularly eager to pass judgment on couples.[34] This can clearly be seen in cases in which unmarried mothers arrived at the district court to apply for maintenance for their illegitimate children. The women often described how sexual intercourse had taken place either as a result of promises of marriage or an actual engagement.

The court very rarely responded to these claim even when men had been found liable for maintenance[35], and thus judged to have had sexual

---

32 JyMA autumn sessions of Keuruu 26.10.1885, § 268; winter sessions of Keuruu 24.3.1886, § 88; Congregation of Keuruu, records of church council meetings 15.3.1887.
33 JyMA autumn sessions of Keuruu 15.10.1897, § 107; winter sessions of Keuruu 17.2.1899, § 164; Hemmer, *Suomen oikeushistorian oppikirja II*, p. 49. For number of divorces concerning imperfect marriages in Finland, see Mahkonen, *Johdatus perheoikeuden historiaan*, pp. 31–36, 104–107; Nieminen, "Skiljobref bewiljas", pp. 44–48.
34 See also Lindstedt Cronberg, *Synd och skam*, p. 115; Pylkkänen, "Avioliiton historiaa: Sukujen sopimuksesta kahden kauppaan", p. 91.
35 E.g. JyMA autumn sessions of Keuruu 18.9.1884, § 249; autumn sessions of Keuruu 4.11.1886, § 257; winter sessions of Keuruu 23.3.1886, § 73.

intercourse. Why did the district court ignore the confessions of these unmarried mothers? One explanation for the court's passivity might lie in the fact that mutual engagements and promises of marriage[36] were not necessarily legally binding unless they had been declared in the presence of witnesses and along with the approval of a woman's father.[37] Plaintiffs were often aware of the informality of their engagements. Kristiina Handolin, for example, told the court that she was engaged to carpenter Abraham but that the engagement had been agreed in private. Because of this, her only evidence of their engagement was his words and a ring.[38] More substantial evidence needed to be presented in the courtroom.[39]

It is also important to understand that these couples arguing about maintenance were not yet engaged in an ecclesiastical sense: their marriage banns had not yet been read out in church. This was in contrast to the situation of those couples who had been declared legally married.[40] The court was not active in cases involving unmarried mothers, because the formal ecclesiastical process had not yet begun. The significance of the ecclesiastical engagement can perhaps be seen in this interpretation of the legislation.

Another explanation for the court's passivity might be that unmarried mothers very rarely applied for a declaration of marriage from the courts.[41] Only one mother, Amalia Samuelintytär, requested that the father of her child, Wilhelm Alho, should be forced to marry her or to provide financial maintenance. Wilhelm had earlier made promises of engagement and marriage.[42] It seems clear that plaintiffs only

---

36 Promises of marriage were not clearly defined in legislation (Lindstedt Cronberg, *Synd och skam*, p. 239).
37 Swe 1734 (1909), Code of Marriage: chapter 1, § 1–5, 3, § 1–3; Saarimäki, *Naimisen normit, käytännöt ja konfliktit*, pp. 190–191.
38 JyMA Keuruun Sk 18.9.1884, § 249; Tk 11.5.1881, § 346.
39 Lindstedt Cronberg, *Synd och skam*, pp. 115, 239; Kirsi Pohjola-Vilkuna, *Eros kylässä: Maaseudun luvaton seksuaalisuus vuosisadan vaihteessa* (Helsinki, SKS, 1995), p. 67. Showing rings or other betrothal gifts in court seems to have been irrelevant (e.g. JyMA winter sessions of Keuruu 3.4.1884, § 221).
40 JyMA winter sessions of Keuruu 2.5.1881, § 162; autumn sessions of Keuruu 26.10.1885, § 268, supplement A § 268; autumn sessions of Keuruu 26.10.1880, § 174; winter sessions of Keuruu 27.4.1881, § 75, clerical notice; autumn sessions of Keuruu 28.11.1881, § 40.
41 cf. Pohjola-Vilkuna, *Eros kylässä*, p. 67.
42 JyMA winter sessions of Keuruu 12.4.1883, § 233, supplement "kannekirja, alleg 233".

wanted to receive maintenance for their children, despite the engagements and promises that were mentioned in the courtroom. In cases involving promises of marriage, the court did not even need to consider pronouncing a legal marriage, because the women involved were not requesting it. If a betrothed couple had had sex during their relationship, the court should have automatically announced a legal marriage. Even under these circumstances, the local court in Keuruu did not take action. Only in the case of Amalia and Wilhem did the court take a stand: Wilhelm was found liable for maintenance of his child, on the grounds of his confession. However, because there was no evidence that Wilhelm had obtained sex through promises of marriage, he could not be forced to marry Amalia nor could the court announce a legal marriage.[43]

It seems clear that the local court in Keuruu was passive and did not follow the letter of the law particularly strictly with regard to promises of engagement or marriage. If they had wanted the court to react, the unmarried mothers would have had to actually demand that they be declared married. It seems, therefore, that there was little desire to use the courts in a punitive manner to force the recognition of a marriage but rather the courts were used to provide a flexible and negotiated solution between the two parties.

Out-dated legislation might be the third probable explanation for the limited interest shown by the local court. As mentioned above, sexual intercourse made it difficult to dissolve an engagement. However, in neither case did the court make any assessment of the legal status of the relationships, let alone pronounce the couple married. The idea of "imperfect marriage" had its origins in the old ecclesiastical laws of Sweden. The creation of the marriage union and sanctions against illicit behaviour were connected to the clear requirement that marriage was the only permissible setting for sexuality.[44] It seems that the Swedish Law of the Realm (1734) may have been somewhat out of step with the way in which engagements were conducted in late nineteenth-century Finland.

---

43 JyMA autumn sessions of Keuruu 26.10.1883, § 103. On passiveness of the local court, see Lindstedt Cronberg, *Synd och skam*, p. 115.
44 Mahkonen, *Johdatus perheoikeuden historiaan*, pp. 15–16.

The legal consequences of adultery in the context of divorce

A marriage was a permanent relationship. Divorces were rare in Finland in the late nineteenth century,[45] and it seems to have been significantly easier to dissolve an engagement than to dissolve a marriage. If sexual activity infringed on the sanctity of marriage, it could come to play a significant role in the rulings of the court. It was possible to obtain a divorce if adultery had been committed,[46] or if the husband had abandoned his wife. It was also possible to file for divorce through the granting of a dispensation. Cases concerning physical disability, committing a serious crime, adultery during an engagement and a quarrelsome marriage, and drunkenness, for example, were ruled in the Senate of Finland. Nevertheless, adultery and abandonment were the most frequently cited grounds for divorce in Keuruu (and elsewhere) in the late nineteenth century.[47] Once the court had reached a decision, divorces would have to be confirmed by a local chapter.

---

45 Nevertheless, number of divorces began to grow in Finland in the late nineteenth and early twentieth century, and the same trend can be seen in most of Northern and Western Europe. See Erik Allardt, *Miljöbetingade differenser i skilsmässofrekvenser. Olika normsystems och andra sociala faktorers inverkan på skilsmässofrekvenserna i Finland 1891–1950* (Helsinki, Finska vetenskaps-societen, 1953), pp. 29–37; Kari Pitkänen, "Marital dissolution in Finland: Towards a Long-Term Perspective". *Yearbook of Population Research in Finland*, 14 (1986), pp. 60–71; Mahkonen, *Avioero*, pp. 1–3, 7–9, 33–149; Robert Chester, *Divorce in Europe* (Leiden, Martinus Nijhoff Social Sciences Division, 1977); William J. Goode (ed.) *World Changes in Divorce Patterns* (New Haven–London, Yale University Press, 1993), 1–182; Roderick Phillips, *Putting asunder. A history of divorce in Western society* (Cambridge, Cambridge University Press, 1988), pp. 461–467, 516–525, 553.
46 Adultery was both grounds for divorce and a crime in the late nineteenth century. Levels of punishment were dependent on marital status and recidivism. Punishments for adultery included: imprisonment, fines and, in some cases, corporal punishments – and in principle the death penalty. After the introduction of the new penal code in 1889, punishments were limited to fines and imprisonment (Swe 1734 (1909), Penal Code: chapter 55, § 1–4, chapter 56, § 1–2; Royal charter 9.6.1780; Royal statute 20.1.1779; Penal Code 1889, chapter 19, § 1–2). On adultery as a historical phenomenon in Europe e.g. Johanna Rickman, *Love, lust, and license in early modern England: illicit sex and the nobility* (Ashgate, Aldershot, Hants, England, 2008); David Turner, *Fashioning Adultery: Gender, Sex and Civility in England 1660-1740* (Cambridge University Press, United Kingdom, 2002); Randolph Trumbach, *Sex and the Gender Revolution. Volume One. Heterosexuality and The Third Gender in Enlightenment London* (University of Chicago Press, Chicago, 1998), pp. 49–67, 325–424; Anne-Marie Sohn, "The golden age of male adultery: The Third republic". *Journal of Social History*, 28 (1995).
47 Swe 1734 (1909), Code of Marriage: chapter 13, § 1, 4–8; Imperial statute 21.4.1826; Mahkonen, *Avioero*, pp. 33–53, 105–110, 224; Taussi Sjöberg, *Skiljas*, pp. 34, 47–50; Andreas Marklund, *I hans hus. Svensk manlighet i historisk belysning* (Umeå, Boréa, 2004), pp. 209–211.

A certain standard of behaviour was, however, required of those who filed for divorce on the grounds of their spouse's adultery. The innocent party was expected to refrain from having sex with their husband or wife after the adultery had been discovered. Sexual intercourse with the "offending" spouse would make divorce impossible: the relationship would become unbreakable and complete once again. According to Andreas Marklund, intercourse had a strong effect on the formation of the marriage union. Engaging in a sexual act with a guilty spouse could be understood as a sign of forgiveness.[48]

Innocent spouses who requested a divorce often assured the court that their relationships had not been sexual after the adultery was uncovered. Nikolai Fredrikinpoika, who applied for a divorce in 1900, claimed that his wife Eva Stina had openly engaged in a sexual relationship with Kaarle Kustaanpoika immediately after their wedding. Nikolai assured the court that he had not slept with his wife after he had heard of her affair. In another case, Olga Maria accused her husband Abraham Kaarlenpoika of committing adultery with two other women. Olga wanted a divorce and asserted several times that she and her husband had not had a married life after his infidelity. The final affirmative decisions reflected the court's belief that this legal requirement had been met.[49]

If the court ultimately granted a divorce on the grounds of adultery, the judgment would have significant consequences for the party who was being divorced. Remarriage was only possible after the death of the former spouse, unless they gave their permission for such a marriage to take place. In addition, separate imperial permission was required if the party who was granted a divorce was still unmarried. Any new marriage that did not meet these requirements was invalid, and the transgressor

---

48 Swe 1734 (1909), Code of Marriage: chapter 13, § 1; Lennartsson, *I säng och säte*, pp. 261, 321; Marklund, *I hans hus*, pp. 212–214. An abandoned wife was, for her part, expected to maintain "decent and honourable" behaviour around other men for a year after her case had been heard. Her husband would have been ordered to return during this time; if he failed to do so, a divorce would be granted. (Swe 1734 (1909), Code of Marriage: chapter 13, § 6).
49 JyMA autumn sessions of Keuruu 26.10.1900, § 206; winter sessions of Keuruu 7.4.1891, § 189; autumn sessions of Keuruu 12.9.1891, § 106; winter sessions of Keuruu 23.3.1888, § 193. For confessions of sexual acts, see Antero Heikkinen, *Kirveskansa ja kansakunta: Elämänrakennusta Kuhmossa 1800-luvun jälkipuolella* (Helsinki, SKS, 2000), p. 181; Hanna Kietäväinen, "Avioliiton solmiminen ja puolisoiden välinen suhde talonpoikaissäädyssä 1600-luvun Itä-Suomessa" (University of Jyväskylä, Department of History and Ethnology, unpublished master's thesis, 2006), p. 89.

would be fined.⁵⁰ This was in contrast to similar cases involving engaged couples in which sexual infidelity did not result in the prohibition of a new legal relationship.

Keuruu district court regularly denied permission to remarry. A shoemaker, Vihtori Maijanpoika, and his wife, Ida Stiinantytär, were granted a divorce on the grounds of Ida's adultery. According to the court's judgment, Ida had to cede her marital property to her husband and would not be allowed to remarry. Correspondingly, the marriage of Matti Heikinpoika and Anna Juhontytär was dissolved in 1887 because Matti had committed adultery with a maid called Ida Bernhardintytär. Matti was fined, he lost his marital property and he was denied permission to remarry.⁵¹ Only in cases of adultery was the guilty party denied permission to remarry as a punitive measure. If a divorce was granted on grounds of abandonment, for example, remarriage was permitted.⁵² Marriage was the only permissible setting for sexual activity. Although the marriage had already been dissolved, the denial of permission to remarry was a punishment for engaging in forbidden sexuality that had broken the original marriage bond. Furthermore, denying permission to remarry aimed to completely restrict the sexual behaviour of an "offending" spouse. Due to legislation on fornication, in the late nineteenth century, those who were unmarried were not allowed to have sexual relationships.⁵³ Although, fornication was rarely discussed in the Keuruu district court,⁵⁴ the legislation itself restricted the expression of sexuality, in this case the sexuality of those who had committed adultery.

Denying permission to remarry could lead to a situation in which those found guilty of adultery could live in new illegitimate relationships

---

50   Swe 1734 (1909), Code of Marriage: chapter 2, § 11, chapter 13, § 2; Royal charter 7.9.1791; Losman, "Förtryct eller jämställdhet?", p. 293; David Gaunt, *Familjeliv i Norden* (Stockholm, Gidlund, 1996(1983)), p. 41.
51   JyMA autumn sessions of Keuruu 3.11.1893, § 270; winter sessions of Keuruu 1894, § 93; winter sessions of Keuruu 17.3.1887, § 23.
52   Swe 1734 (1909), Code of Marriage: chapter 13, § 4–6. E.g. autumn sessions of Keuruu 29.10.1892, § 318.
53   Swe 1734 (1877), Penal Code: chapter 53, § 1, 3, chapter 55, 4; Royal charter 9.6.1780, 14.8.1784; Imperial statute 1866; Penal Code 1889, chapter 20, § 9, 12; Pertti Haapala, *Sosiaalihistoria: Johdatus tutkimukseen* (Helsinki, Suomen Historiallinen Seura, 1989), p. 93, footnote 18.
54   Saarimäki, *Naimisen normit, käytännöt ja konfliktit*, pp. 193–197.

for several years without the opportunity to marry. The church council of Keuruu reprimanded several couples for *vuoteus* (living in the same bed) in March 1887. In three such cases, at least one party had committed adultery and continued the adulterous relationship. The court was told that vagrant Juho Joonaanpoika and Maria Adamintytär were living together, and that they had no fewer than five illegitimate children. The relationship with Maria had been the reason for Juho's divorce. Similarly, even though the relationship between Matti Simonpoika and his companion Kaisa had caused the dissolution of their previous marriages, they had continued their relationship.[55]

It is reasonable to suppose that the reason why couples continued their illegal relationships stems from the legal denial of remarriage. It also seems likely that such couples might have wished to legalize their relationships, if this had been possible. However, in the margins of the court report on the third case, a scribe has written that "Aleksius is coming to the vicarage".[56] In this case, reluctance to marry is a more probable explanation than denial of permission to remarry.

The subtle touch of social control

According to legislation and the church, marriage was the only setting in which the expression of sexuality was acceptable in late nineteenth-century Finland. Therefore, illicit sexual activity had clear consequences for the lives of engaged and married couples. First, it was possible to dissolve a relationship if the sanctity of a marriage or engagement was offended by engaging in sexual activity with a third party. Second, legislation restricted people's sexual behaviour by stating that the legal relationship of an engaged couple could only be dissolved if there had been no sexual contact between them. Similarly, sexual continence was required in divorces in which adultery was cited: the innocent party was not allowed to have sexual contact with their spouse after the

---

55 JyMA Congregation of Keuruu, church council meeting, 15.3.1887 II (Cb:2).
56 Ibid.

adultery had been discovered. Finally, the legal consequences of illicit sexual activity could be permanent. If an engaged couple did not want to get married but their sexual relationship was verifiable, they could be pronounced legally married by the local court. This type of an "imperfect marriage" was difficult to dissolve. In the case of adultery and divorce, legislation and the local court denied the "offending" spouse permission to remarry. Fornication was entirely prohibited by legislation and thus the expression of sexuality by the "offending" spouse was completely forbidden. Consequently, it was illicit to have an affair with a new partner, and these relationships were practically impossible to legalize.

What, in the end, was the nature of social control exerted through legislation and the local courts? It is clear that this social control was subtle: people were not severely punished for their illicit sexual behaviour, but their (sexual) lives were influenced and restricted by legislation. Therefore, we can say that social control was subtle in its approach and largely effective in its aims.

This type of social control stemmed from out-dated legislation, which had its origins in sixteenth- and seventeenth-century laws from the kingdom of Sweden. The ecclesiastical laws of 1571 and 1686 had emphasized the sanctity of marriage, the significance of sexual intercourse in creating the marriage union and the outlawing of extramarital affairs.[57] The Swedish Law of the Realm (1734) had, however, become somewhat out-dated by the late nineteenth century. The district court of Keuruu rarely announced legal marriages, even when a sexual relationship could be verified. This suggests that the regulations dealing with "imperfect marriages" were already becoming obsolete in practice. Legislation was applied more exactly in relation to adultery, which was still a significant offence in the late nineteenth century.

Matrimonial law was still developing in Finland in the late nineteenth

---

57 Mahkonen, *Johdatus perheoikeuden historiaan*, pp. 15–16, 29–30; Mahkonen, Avioero, p. 2; Lennartsson, *I säng och säte*, pp. 123–26, 158–59; Marklund, *I hans hus*, pp. 170–171. On formation of the code of marriage (1734) see Anu Pylkkänen, "Giftermålsbalken i 1734 års lag" in *Statens beroenden av familjen* (Helsingfors, Helsingfors Universitet, 1996), pp. 1–31; Heikki Ylikangas, *Suomalaisen Sven Lejonmarckin osuus vuoden 1734 lain naimiskaaren laadinnassa* (Helsinki, Suomen Historiallinen Seura, 1967).

century and at the beginning of the twentieth century.[58] According to Jouko Sihvo, "imperfect marriage" was seen as too imprecise to serve as a juridical concept: its legal ramifications were extremely difficult to interpret. "Imperfect marriage" and regulations relating to sexuality during an engagement were not mentioned in the new marriage act. Thereafter, engagement was no longer judicially binding but purely an individual agreement between man and woman.[59]

Regulations relating to adultery still existed in the new marriage act but were eased. Adultery still provided important grounds for divorce, but local courts could only deny permission to remarry for a specific reason. Furthermore this prohibition could only last for a maximum of one year.[60] This meant that sexual contact was no longer completely outlawed. The punishment of fornication was finally abolished in 1926 and this marked the outcome of a subtle and gradual shift in the social control of sexuality in modern Finland – a change that had developed and been negotiated in local courts and communities for decades beforehand.[61]

Sources

ARCHIVAL SOURCES

The Provincial Archives of Jyväskylä (Jyväskylän maakunta-arkisto, JyMA)
Archives of Juridisdiction of Jyväskylä, court district of Keuruu; Court records 1879–1901. III Ca: 92–135.
Archives of Congregations of Keuruu and Multia; Church council meetings: Keuruu, 1851–1904. II Cb: 2; Multia, 1851–1932. II Cb: 1.
Details of ecclesiastical punishments: Keuruu, 1837–1886, 1887–1906. I Hb: 3, I Hb: 4.
Decisions of juridical separations and divorces, decisions of breaking engagements issued by the chapters of Turku and Porvoo: Keuruu, 1850–1944. I Jaa: 1; Multia 1802–1900. I Jaa: 1.

---

58 E.g. Anu Pylkkänen, *Trapped in equality. Women as Legal Persons in the Modernisation of Finnish Law* (Helsinki, SKS, 2006); Urpo Kangas, *Omaisuuden yhteisyydestä omaisuuden erillisyyteen* (Helsinki, Helsingin yliopisto, 1996).
59 Sihvo, *Näkökulma suomalaisten moraaliin*, pp. 24–25; Pylkkänen, "Avioliiton historiaa: Sukujen sopimuksesta kahden kauppaan", p. 91; Marriage act 1929, I: chapter 2 (engagement).
60 The Marriage act 1929, III, chapter 1, § 70; Pohjola-Vilkuna, *Eros kylässä*, p. 56.
61 Inkeri Anttila, *Alaikäisiin kohdistuneet siveellisyysrikokset ja niiden tekijät* (Helsinki, Suomalainen lakimiesyhdistys, 1956), p. 23; Kevät Nousiainen and Anu Pylkkänen, *Sukupuoli ja oikeuden yhdenvertaisuus* (Helsinki, Helsingin yliopisto, oikeustieteellinen tiedekunta, 2001), p. 186.

LEGISLATIVE SOURCES

RVL 1734 (1877). Ruotsin Waltakunnan Laki, Hyväksytty ja noudatettawaksi otettu waltiopäivillä vuonna 1734 (The Swedish Law of the Realm 1734, Swe 1734) SKS, Helsinki.

RVL 1734 (1909). Ruotsin Valtakunnan Laki, Hyväksytty ja noudatettavaksi otettu valtiopäivillä vuonna 1734, Suomen Suuriruhtinasmaassa. Voimassaolevat osat, sekä 1 päivään heinäkuuta 1909 ilmestyneet säännökset ynnä liite. 4. painos (The Swedish Law of the Realm 1734, Swe 1734) SKS, Helsinki.

Royal Charter 11.11.1747.
Royal Statute 20.1.1779.
Royal Charter 9.6.1780.
Royal Charter 14.8.1784.
Royal Charter 7.9.1791.
Imperial Statute 26.11.1866.
Kirkkolaki 1869 (Church Act 1869), WSOY, Porvoo 1908.
Rikoslaki 1889 (Penal Code 1889).
Decision of Imperial Senate 10.5.1899.
Avioliittolaki 1929 (Marriage Act 1929), www.finlex.fi/fi/laki/alkup/1929/19290234> (accessed 11 February 2013).

LITERATURE

Allardt, Erik 1953: *Miljöbetingade differenser i skilsmässofrekvenser. Olika normsystems och andra sociala faktorers inverkan på skilsmässofrekvenserna i Finland 1891–1950*. Finska vetenskaps-societen, Helsinki.

Anttila, Inkeri 1956: *Alaikäisiin kohdistuneet siveellisyysrikokset ja niiden tekijät*. Suomalainen lakimiesyhdistys, Helsinki.

Carlsson, Lizzie 1965: *"Jag giver dig min dotter": trolovning och äktenskap i den svenska kvinnans äldre historia 1*. Institutet för Rättshistorisk Forskning, Lund.

Carlsson, Lizzie 1972: *"Jag giver dig min dotter": trolovning och äktenskap i den svenska kvinnans äldre historia 2*. Institutet för Rättshistorisk Forskning, Lund.

Chester, Robert (ed.) 1977: *Divorce in Europe*. Martinus Nijhoff Social Sciences Division, Leiden.

Eilola, Jari 2002: "Cuckoi päällä curjanakin; cana alla armaisnakin". In *Arjen valta. Suomalaisen yhteiskunnan patriarkaalisesta järjestyksestä myöhäiskeskiajalta teollistumisen kynnykselle (v.1450–1860)*, ed. Piia Einonen and Petri Karonen. SKS, Helsinki, pp. 100–127.

Gaunt, David 1996: *Familjeliv i Norden*. Gudlund, Södertälje.

Goode, William J. (ed.) 1993: *World Changes in Divorce Patterns*. Yale University Press, New Haven–London.

Grönvall, F. (ed.) 1936: *Uusi avioliittolainsäädäntö selityksineen*. WSOY, Helsinki.

Haapala, Pertti 1989: *Sosiaalihistoria – Johdatus tutkimukseen*. Suomen Historiallinen Seura, Helsinki.

Hartikainen, Esko 2005: *Heränneitä ja nukahtaneita: kulttuuri, kontrolli ja herätys 1800-luvun alun Liperissä*. SKS, Helsinki.

Heikkinen, Antero 2000: *Kirveskansa ja kansakunta. Elämänrakennusta Kuhmossa 1800-luvun jälkipuolella*. SKS, Helsinki.

Hemmer, Ragnar 1967: *Suomen oikeushistorian oppikirja II: Perheoikeuden, perintöoikeuden ja testamenttioikeuden historia.* Lainopillisen ylioppilastiedekunnan kustannustoimikunta, Helsinki.

Hylland Eriksen, Thomas 2004: *Toista maata? Johdatus antropologiaan.* Gaudeamus, Helsinki.

Håkanson, Sigrid 1999: *"då skall han taga henne till äkta..." Oäkta födslar, äktenskapsmarknad och giftermålssystem i Östsverige och Västsverige 1750–1850.* Stads och kommunhistoriska institutet, Stockholm.

Kangas, Urpo 1996: *Omaisuuden yhteisyydestä omaisuuden erillisyyteen.* Helsingin yliopisto, Helsinki.

Kietäväinen, Hanna 2006: *Avioliiton solmiminen ja puolisoiden välinen suhde talonpoikaissäädyssä 1600-luvun Itä-Suomessa* (unpublished master's theses in Finnish history), University of Jyväskylä, Department of History and ethnology.

Knuutila, Jyrki 1990: *Avioliitto oikeudellisena ja kirkollisena instituutiona Suomessa vuoteen 1629.* Suomen Kirkkohistoriallinen Seura, Helsinki.

Korpiola, Mia 2009: *Between Betrothal and Bedding. Marriage Formation in Sweden 1200–1600.* Brill, Leiden.

Lennartsson, Malin 1999: *I säng och säte: relationer mellan kvinnor och män i 1600-talets Småland.* Lund University Press, Lund.

Lindstedt Cronberg, Marie 1997: *Synd och skam. Ogifta mödrar på svensk landsbygd 1680–1880.* Historiska institutionen, Lunds Universitet, Lund.

Losman, Beata 1982: Förtryct eller jämställdhet? Kvinnorna och äktenskap i Västsverige omkring 1840. *Historisk Tidskrift* (Svensk), 102 (1982), pp. 291–318.

Mahkonen, Sami 1978: *Johdatus perheoikeuden historiaan.* Suomen lakimiesliiton kustannus Oy, Helsinki.

Mahkonen, Sami 1980: *Avioero. Tutkimus avioliittolain erosäännösten taustasta ja tarkoituksesta.* Suomalainen lakimiesyhdistys, Helsinki.

Marklund, Andreas 2004: *I hans hus. Svensk manlighet i historisk belysning.* Boréa, Umeå.

Mönkkönen, Mauri 1983: *Vanhan Ruoveden historia, osa 3, 2: Multian historia 1866–1975.* Multian kunta/Multian Seurakunta, Multia.

Nieminen, Armas 1951: *Taistelu sukupuolimoraalista: avioliitto ja seksuaalikysymyksiä suomalaisen hengenelämän ja yhteiskunnan murroksessa säätyajoilta 1910-luvulle.* WSOY, Helsinki.

Nieminen, Anna-Liisa 2003: *"Skiljobref beviljas" – epäonnistuneet avioliitot Göteborgin hiippakunnassa vuosina 1774–1778* (unpublished master's theses in Finnish history), University of Jyväskylä, Department of History.

Nousiainen, Kevät and Pylkkänen, Anu 2001: *Sukupuoli ja oikeuden yhdenvertaisuus.* Helsingin yliopisto, Helsinki.

Phillips, Roderick 1988: *Putting asunder. A history of divorce in Western society.* Cambridge University Press, Cambridge.

Pitkänen, Kari 1986: Marital dissolution in Finland: Towards a Long-Term Perspective. *Yearbook of Population Research in Finland* 14 (1986), pp. 60–71.

Pohjola-Vilkuna, Kirsi 1995: *Eros kylässä – Maaseudun luvaton seksuaalisuus vuosisadan vaihteessa.* SKS, Helsinki.

Pylkkänen, Anu 1991: Avioliiton historiaa – Sukujen sopimuksesta kahden kauppaan. In

Suomen oikeushistorian pääpiirteet. Sukuvallasta moderniin oikeuteen, ed. Pia Letto-Vanamo. Gaudeamus, Helsinki.

Pylkkänen Anu 1996: Giftermålsbalken i 1734 års lag. In *Statens beroenden av familjen*. Helsingin yliopisto, Helsinki.

Pylkkänen, Anu 2006: *Trapped in equality. Women as Legal Persons in the Modernisation of Finnish Law*. SKS, Helsinki.

Rickman, Johanna 2008: *Love, lust, and license in early modern England: illicit sex and the nobility*. Ashgate, Aldershot, Hants, England.

Saarimäki, Pasi 2010: *Naimisen normit, käytännöt ja konfliktit. Esiaviollinen ja aviollinen seksuaalisuus 1800-luvun lopun keskisuomalaisella maaseudulla*. Jyväskylän yliopisto, Jyväskylä, http://urn.fi/URN:ISBN:978-951-39-3830-7.

Sihvo, Jouko 1981: *Näkökulma suomalaisten moraaliin: avoliitto, avioliitto ja seksi kirkollisessa etiikassa*. WSOY, Porvoo–Helsinki–Juva.

Sohn, Anne-Marie 1995: The golden age of male adultery: The Third republic. *Journal of Social History* 28(3) 1995, pp. 469–490.

Taussi Sjöberg, Marja 1988: *Skiljas. Trolovning, äktenskap och skilsmässa i Norrland på 1800-talet*. Författarförlaget Södertälje.

Trumbach, Randolph 1998: *Sex and the Gender Revolution. Volume One. Heterosexuality and The Third Gender in Enlightenment London*. University of Chicago Press, Chicago.

Turner, David 2002, *Fashioning Adultery: Gender, Sex and Civility in England 1660–1740*. Cambridge University Press, United Kingdom.

Vihola, Teppo 1983: *Vanhan Ruoveden historia, osa 3, 3, 1: Keuruun ja Pihlajaveden historia 1860–1917*. Keuruun ja Pihlajaveden historiatoimikunta, Keuruu.

Ylikangas, Heikki 1967: *Suomalaisen Sven Lejonmarckin osuus vuoden 1734 lain naimiskaaren laadinnassa*. Suomen Historiallinen Seura, Helsinki.

Österberg, Eva, Lennartsson, Malin and Naess, Hans Eyvind 2000. Social Control Outside or combined with the Secular Judicial Arena. In *People Meet the Law: Control and Conflicthandling in the courts. The Nordic Countries in the Post-Reformation and Pre-Industrial Period*, ed. Eva Österberg and Solvi Sogner. Universitetsforlaget, Oslo.

Improving the Christian Community
Agents and Objects of Control in Early Modern Church Visitations
Päivi Räisänen-Schröder

In 1557, a committed Protestant ruler, duke Christoph of Württemberg, in one of his numerous mandates outlined the means by which necessary order and discipline could be established and the beatific Word of God fostered. Firstly, the appointment of suitable – learned and god-fearing – ministers and a schedule of regular parish visitations would allow the religious and moral "errors and flaws" in his territory to be detected. Secondly, those trespassers and disobedient subjects singled out in the process should be "punished to advance their improvement".[1] In this article, I explore church or parish visitations as an important feature of this religious/moral improvement project and the forms of its control in post-Reformation Germany. The sources consulted here are mostly visitation protocols from the rural parishes of Schorndorf, a district some thirty kilometres east of the Württemberg capital Stuttgart.[2]

---

1 Sabine Arend (ed.), Die evangelischen Kirchenordnungen des XVI. Jahrhunderts, Bd. 16: Baden-Württemberg II, Herzogtum Württemberg (Tübingen 2004), p. 326.
2 I used these sources in my doctoral dissertation dealing with the legitimation strategies of both worldly and ecclesiastical magistrates as well as Anabaptist and local actors in 16th and 17th century church visitations in the district of Schorndorf. See Päivi Räisänen, Ketzer im Dorf: Visitationsverfahren, Täuferbekämpfung und locale Handlungsmuster im frühneuzeitlichen Württemberg (Konstanz 2011).

The subject seems all the more important because Protestant church visitations remain relatively unstudied in Germany. In scholarship, church visitations have been understood largely as effective tools of control from above. However, this only represents one half of the story.[3] Even though the use of the visitations for airing or settling local conflicts may not have been the intention of the authorities, the visitations nonetheless also provided new avenues for communication and control on a local level. As middlemen between the sometimes contradictory, sometimes overlapping interests of the authorities and local communities, parish pastors came to play an important dual role in visitations: both as agents and as objects of control. In addition to parish pastors, religious and moral dissidents who were summoned before the visitation commission will also be examined in this study.

There are two main reasons why Württemberg is especially interesting and relevant for this research. Firstly, it was one of the states in early modern Europe with an "obsession for protocols" and it created and

---

[3] In the 1960s and 1970s a large-scale project at the University of Tübingen set out to explore early modern church visitations under the supervision of Hansgeorg Molitor and Ernst Walter Zeeden. However, after this project, interest in the subject has decreased. Only recently have a studies been published that adopt a new, cultural-history approach to the subject. Many of these studies also address questions of power, including legitimation strategies and symbolic representation of power as well as the production of knowledge as a means of control. See, for example, Stefan Brakensiek, "Legitimation durch Verfahren? Visitationen, Supplikationen, Berichte und Enqueten im frühmodernen Fürstenstaat", in Barbara Stollberg-Rilinger & Andre Krischer (ed.), *Herstellung und Darstellung von Entscheidungen: Verfahren, Verwalten und Verhandeln in der Vormoderne* (Berlin 2010), pp. 365–377; Nicolás Brochhagen, "Diskursive Aspekte landesherrlicher Machtbildung am Beispiel der Visitation der Grafschaft Ravensberg 1535", *Jahresbericht des Historischen Vereins für die Grafschaft Ravensberg* 96 (2011), pp. 193–213; Katharina Frieb, *Kirchenvisitation und Kommunikation: Die Akten zu den Visitationen in der Kuroberpfalz unter Ludwig VI. (1576–1583)* (München 2006); Frank Konersmann, "Kirchenvisitation als landesherrliches Kontrollmittel und als Regulativ dörflicher Kommunikation: Das Herzogtum Pfalz-Zweibrücken im 16. und 17. Jahrhundert", in Andreas Blauert & Gerd Schwerhoff (ed.), *Kriminalitätsgeschichte: Beiträge zur Sozial- und Kulturgeschichte der Vormoderne* (Konstanz 2000), p. 606; Peter Thaddäus Lang, "Die Erforschung der frühneuzeitlichen Kirchenvisitationen: Neuere Veröffentlichungen in Deutschland", *Rottenburger Jahrbuch für Kirchengeschichte* 16 (1997), pp. 190–191; Mareike Menne, *Herrschaftsstil und Glaubenspraxis: Die bischöflichen Visitationen im Hochstift Paderborn 1654–1691* (Paderborn 2007); Mareike Menne, "Was bergen Visitationsakten? Kritische Überlegungen anhand der Visitationen im Fürstbistum Paderborn in der zweiten Hälfte des 17. Jahrhunderts", in Werner Freitag & Christian Helbich (ed.), *Bekenntnis, soziale Ordnung und rituelle Praxis. Neue Forschungen zu Reformation und Konfessionalisierung in Westfalen* (Münster 2009), pp. 175–188; Helga Schnabel-Schüle, "Kirchenvisitationen und Landesvisitationen als Mittel der Kommunikation zwischen Herrscher und Untertanen", in Heinz Duchhardt & Gert Melville (ed.), *Im Spannungsfeld von Recht und Ritual: Soziale Kommunikation in Mittelalter und früher Neuzeit* (Köln 1997), pp. 173–186.

archived immense quantities of bureaucratic texts.[4] Secondly, after its Reformation in 1534, Württemberg developed a highly centralized and widely acknowledged church system. At the same time, like some other territories in south-western Germany and Switzerland, Württemberg had a strong tradition of peasant resistance and political communalism.[5] The case of Württemberg thus offers valuable insights into a society characterized both by the strong centralizing tendencies of the emerging state and Lutheran church and by local communities with externally controlled self-administration.[6]

Church visitations were not the primary organ of moral control in Württemberg. Rather, the right to exert control over moral offences lay to a large extent in the hands of the secular authorities. The investigation of moral offences was undertaken by local courts (required to assemble every three months under the supervision of the district bailiff). All citizens were required to attend these gatherings and were obliged to report all known moral offences. To refresh their memories, a list of delicts, ranging from soothsaying and magical practices to gluttony, blasphemy, bad housekeeping and drunkenness, was to be publicly read aloud a week before the court meeting.[7] Moral control and visitations

---

4   David W. Sabean, "Soziale Distanzierungen: Ritualisierte Gestik in deutscher bürokratischer Prosa der Frühen Neuzeit", *Historische Anthropologie* 4 (1996), pp. 222–223.
5   The lack of nobility in Württemberg is another feature not necessarily found in other regions. In the absence of a local nobility, local "notables" and their families gained a strong position in Württemberg. The nobles of the Württemberg region were *Reichsritter* (direct subjects of the Emperor), whose lands formed little enclaves within or around the ducal territory. Cf. David W. Sabean, *Power in the Blood: Popular Culture and Village Discourse in Early Modern Germany* (Cambridge 1984), p. 4; Karl Wegert, *Popular Culture, Crime and Social Control in Eighteenth-Century Württemberg* (Stuttgart 1994), p. 36. This may make it difficult to generalize about the findings of this research. This is also the main criticism against the theory of a communal Reformation espoused particularly by Peter Blickle and his students. See, for example, Peter Blickle, *Gemeindereformation: Die Menschen des 16. Jahrhunderts auf dem Weg zum Heil* (München 1985); Peter Blickle & Johannes Kunisch (ed.), *Kommunalisierung und Christianisierung: Voraussetzungen und Folgen der Reformation 1400–1600* (Berlin 1989).
6   Sabean, *Power in the Blood*, pp. 13–14; Wegert, *Popular Culture*, pp. 39–40.
7   Arend, *Kirchenordnungen*, pp. 395–398; Achim Landwehr, *Policey im Alltag: Die Implementation frühneuzeitlicher Policeyordnungen in Leonberg* (Frankfurt 2000), pp. 144–145. However, in practice the local courts did not gather as regularly as was prescribed. In fact, one of the most common accusations levelled against middle-level officials was their lax adherence to mandatory court session requirements. Ulinka Rublack argues that the local courts were generally not an effective instrument of enforcement of normative values and social control from "above". Cf. Ulinka Rublack, "Frühneuzeitliche staatliche und lokale Herrschaftspraxis in Württemberg", *Zeitschrift für Historische Forschung* 2 (1997), pp. 354–358.

were nevertheless closely linked, and the actions of the local and district magistracies were inspected during church visitations.[8] Research into visitations can, therefore, offer partial insights into the different ways in which social and moral control was exercised in sixteenth- and early seventeenth-century Württemberg.[9] Visitations are particularly noteworthy because they represent a clear institutional change that allowed new forms – or media – of control, exercise of power and communication to operate alongside existing forms. By the late sixteenth century, villagers were well aware of how visitations worked and had learned to use them for their ends.[10]

Official tools of control

The church visitation was neither a new nor a specifically Protestant institution. Rather, the practice of visiting a congregation – in the sense of "going to see, to inspect, investigate, correct, and if necessary, to punish"[11] – can be traced back to apostolic times. Up until the High Middle Ages, visitations concentrated on investigations of the clergy and were highly festive events overseen by a bishop. After this time, the importance of the institution as an instrument of control within the church declined.[12] The first territory-wide Protestant visitation was undertaken

---

8   Martin Brecht, *Kirchenordnung und Kirchenzucht in Württemberg vom 16. bis zum 18. Jahrhundert* (Stuttgart 1967), p. 36; Bruce Tolley, *Pastors and Parishioners in Württemberg During the Late Reformation 1581–1621* (Stanford 1995), p. 90.

9   This is a basic problem: the only surviving protocols of sixteenth-century local courts (*Ruggerichte*) in Württemberg are from the district of Leonberg (1579–1699), and have been thoroughly analysed by Achim Landwehr in his dissertation. Cf. Landwehr, *Policey im Alltag*, especially pp. 160–161.

10 Cf. Achim Landwehr, "Policey vor Ort: Die Implementation von Policeyordnungen in der ländlichen Gesellschaft der Frühen Neuzeit", in Karl Härter (ed.), *Policey und frühneuzeitliche Gesellschaft* (Frankfurt 2000), p. 54; Rudolf Schlögl, "Bedingungen dörflicher Kommunikation: Gemeindliche Öffentlichkeit und Visitation im 16. Jahrhundert", in: Werner Rösener (ed.), *Kommunikation in der ländlichen Gesellschaft vom Mittelalter bis zur Moderne* (Göttingen 2000), pp. 243–245, 252–253.

11 Gerald Strauss, *Luther's House of Learning: Indoctrination of the Young in the German Reformation* (Baltimore & London 1978), p. 250.

12 Thomas Paul Becker, *Konfessionalisierung in Kurköln: Untersuchungen zur Durchsetzung der katholischen Reform in den Dekanaten Ahrgau und Bonn anhand von Visitationsprotokollen 1583–1761* (Bonn 1989), pp. 1–17; Frieb, *Kirchenvisitation und Kommunikation*, pp. 4–5; Peter Thaddäus Lang, "Die Kirchenvisitationsakten des 16. Jahrhunderts und ihr Quellenwert", *Rottenburger Jahrbuch für Kirchengeschichte* 6 (1987), pp. 127–139; Schnabel-Schüle, "Kirchenvisitationen", pp. 177–178.

in the Electorate of Saxony in 1527–28 and was conducted in accordance with the guidelines formulated by Luther and Melanchthon.[13] After the Reformation, visitations regained their appeal for both secular and ecclesiastical authorities. Peter Thaddäus Lang has distinguished two phases of post-Reformation visitation activities: the "dismantling of the negative" up until the early seventeenth century was followed by "building up the positive". During the first period, the main purpose of the visitations was according to Lang to root out unwanted forms of belief and behaviour, and in the second, to improve the quality of the clergy and to investigate the material conditions of the church buildings and their furnishings.[14] This study focuses on the earlier years of what Andrew Pettegree has recently described as a complex "process of persuasion".[15]

The innovativeness of the post-Reformation visitations lies especially in their systematic approach and the close links between the ecclesiastical and political interests of the rulers.[16] Increasingly administrative proceedings that included the gathering of a broad range of local information that could be turned into useful knowledge and archived for further reference, visitations were intended to be important tools of control for the authorities.[17] Regular accounts from the parishes within a territory helped the authorities to frame particular measures in order to achieve their ideal of a society founded on moral stability and Christian order. At the same time, visitations were supposed to single out deviant individuals and provide them with instruction and, if needed, punishment. Although there should be little doubt about the religious sincerity that underpinned their disciplinary actions, early modern authorities also certainly sought to strengthen the overall power of territorial rulers. Given that the duke was the highest bishop of the Lutheran Church in Württemberg, worldly and spiritual interests of the period can hardly be separated.

13 Frieb, *Kirchenvisitation und Kommunikation*, p. 5; Schnabel-Schüle, "Kirchenvisitationen", pp. 179–180; Strauss, *Luther's House of Learning*, pp. 250–252.
14 Peter Thaddäus Lang, "Reform im Wandel: Die katholischen Visitationsinterrogatorien des 16. und 17. Jahrhunderts", in Ernst Walter Zeeden & Peter Thaddäus Lang (ed.), *Kirche und Visitation: Beiträge zur Erforschung des frühneuzeitlichen Visitationswesens in Europa* (Stuttgart 1984), p. 145.
15 Andrew Pettegree, *Reformation and the Culture of Persuasion* (Cambridge 2005), p. 6.
16 Frieb, *Kirchenvisitation und Kommunikation*, pp. 318–324, 403.
17 Brakensiek, "Legitimation", p. 370–371; Brochhagen, "Diskursive Aspekte", p. 211; Frieb, *Kirchenvisitation und Kommunikation*, pp. 292–293, 297; Menne, "Was bergen", pp. 183–184.

According to Gerald Strauss, "general reform was clearly the ultimate purpose of visitations".[18] In order to achieve this aim, visitations were supposed to "commence, and then promote and protect, the improvement of religion and morality in the populace".[19] The aim was also clearly formulated in the Württemberg ordinances. This concern has to be seen against the backdrop of the contemporary notion of God's wrath and punishment as a consequence of human sins. As the Württemberg Great Church Ordinance of 1559 put it, the misbehaviour of one sheep could damage the whole flock.[20] Within this framework of a "moral universe" (Robert W. Scribner) highly dependent on the will of God, the authorities' disciplinary and educational measures were presented as a means of guaranteeing salvation as well as securing worldly order.[21] For this reason, post-Reformation visitations generally extended their inspection to the moral and religious life of parishioners.

Visitations were ideally to be undertaken on a regular basis; they were annual or biannual events in late sixteenth- and early seventeenth- century Württemberg. A visitation commission, consisting of both ecclesiastical and secular authorities, would be assigned to the task. The head of the commission was the special superintendent (*Spezialsuperintendent* or *Spezialis*), the highest-ranking clergyman in the district. The commission had to visit parishes in the district appointed to them and send a detailed report to the synod in Stuttgart. The synod then discussed the commission's findings and outlined suggested measures in response. However, the final decision about what actions should be undertaken lay with the duke and his council. The orders framed by the duke or his

---

18 Strauss, *Luther's House of Learning*, p. 255.
19 Strauss, *Luther's House of Learning*, pp. 251–252.
20 Arend, *Kirchenordnungen*, pp. 326, 385, 406, 461; Heinrich Richard Schmidt, *Dorf und Religion: Reformierte Sittenzucht in Berner Landgemeinden der Frühen Neuzeit* (Stuttgart 1995), p. 320. On the early modern argumentation with God's wrath, see Alexander Kästner & Gerd Schwerhoff, "Religiöse Devianz in alteuropäischen Stadtgemeinschaften: Eine Einführung in systematischer Absicht", in Alexander Kästner & Gerd Schwerhoff (ed.), *Göttlicher Zorn und menschliches Maß: Religiöse Abweichung in frühneuzeitlichen Stadtgemeinschaften* (Konstanz 2013), pp.16 –17.
21 Robert W. Scribner, "Police and Territorial State in Sixteenth-Century Württemberg", in E. I. Kouri & Tom Scott (ed.), *Politics and Society in Reformation Europe: Essays for Sir Geoffrey Elton on his Sixty-fifth Birthday* (Basingstoke 1987), p. 106.

ducal councillors were then sent to the district magistrates, who were responsible for putting them into practice.[22]

Visitations involved on-site investigations of parishes, during which local clergymen and magistrates were questioned (one individual or group at a time) about different issues. In theory such questioning was supposed to strictly adhere to extensive pre-formulated questionnaires. As there were too many parishioners to interrogate during the visitations, only the local magistrates as representatives of the parish and open religious dissidents were summoned to appear before the commission. The role of pastors as informants in the visitations was crucial. Yet, at the same time, pastors themselves came under scrutiny, which put them in a precarious position. The visitors showed a keen interest in the way in which pastors conducted their lives and in their clerical accomplishments. It was pastors who had to both enforce the official Lutheran norms and monitor the religious and moral lives of their congregations. At the same time, they had to serve as moral examples to their parishioners, not least in their specifically Protestant role as heads of households.[23] If numerous offences were uncovered within his parish, a pastor could find himself under pressure to explain why his work was not bearing more fruit. The commissioners made constant demands on the pastors to fulfil their assigned tasks, even if advancement in the end lay in the hands of the Almighty.

Hearing the Word of God in the church and learning the catechism were supposed to foster improvement among the parishioners.[24] If these methods of instruction failed to bring about improvement, those who repeatedly sinned were to be banished from the congregation. The authority to use this ban was the subject of much debate in mid-sixteenth-century Württemberg. Although there were some contemporary

---

22 Arend, *Kirchenordnungen*, pp. 149–156, 385–394; Martin Brecht & Hermann Ehmer, *Südwestdeutsche Reformationsgeschichte: Zur Einführung der Reformation im Herzogtum Württemberg 1534* (Stuttgart 1984), pp. 264–265, 320–323; Landwehr, *Policey im Alltag*, p. 103; Strauss, *Luther's House of Learning*, pp. 256–267.
23 Räisänen, *Ketzer im Dorf*, pp. 211–216; Luise Schorn-Schütte, "Priest, Preacher, Pastor: Research on Clerical Office in Early Modern Europe", *Central European History* 33 (2000), pp. 26–27.
24 Cf. the instructions in the *Confessio Virtembergica* of 1552, in Hauptstaatsarchiv Stuttgart (HStAS) A63/24, f. 22r–22v, 60r–61v, 63v–64r.

theologians (including Jakob Andreae) who sympathized with Zwinglian models of communal church discipline, such schemes were not realized in the duchy at this time.[25] Rather, church discipline was modelled according to the ideas of the influential south German reformer Johannes Brenz, who persistently championed a centralized system of ecclesiastical and moral control. According to Brenz, only the Stuttgart synod had the right to excommunicate notorious sinners. In his view, parish pastors should only be allowed to admonish moral offenders in a private discussion before granting absolution and thus the right to participate in the Lord's Supper. Brenz argued that, as one could not see into the hearts of other human beings, there was no way of knowing that a sinner had not repented after hearing the sermon immediately prior to the celebration of the Eucharist. For Brenz, it was more important to let these people attend communion than to make sure no sinners were present at the sacrament (more so, as he did not believe that one could know this for sure). Andreae, on the other hand, argued that the wrath and punishment of God could be prevented more effectively if local pastors were allowed to keep their congregations uncontaminated by sinners.[26]

Agents and objects of control in the parish

Local pastors were obliged to monitor, admonish and instruct sinners in their parishes, either in personal encounters or through their sermons. They were also required to report sinners to the visitation commission. Aside from these obligations, local clerics in Württemberg had no power-

---

25 Communal institutions of social control comparable to Reformed territories, where a board of parish elders was assigned to watch over the moral behaviour of the villagers, were not established in Württemberg during the sixteenth century. For Reformed church discipline in Germany and Switzerland, see, for example, Konersmann, "Kirchenvisitation", pp. 613–15; Heinz Schilling, "Sündenzucht und frühneuzeitliche Sozialdisziplinierung: Die calvinistische presbyterale Kirchenzucht in Emden vom 16. bis ins 19. Jahrhundert", in Georg Schmidt (ed.), *Stände und Gesellschaft im Alten Reich* (Wiesbaden 1989), pp. 265–302; Heinrich Richard Schmidt, "Die Christianisierung des Sozialverhaltens als permanente Reformation: Aus der Praxis reformierter Sittengerichte in der Schweiz während der frühen Neuzeit", in Blickle & Kunisch, *Kommunalisierung und Christianisierung*, pp. 113–163; Schmidt, *Religion und Dorf*.
26 Brecht, *Kirchenordnung*, pp. 40–50.

ful official means of moral control in their hands. As discussed earlier, pastors were not allowed to ban notorious sinners from their congregations.[27] This, of course, made the pastors highly dependent on their superiors in the church organization. Official forms of control in the parishes were restricted to the pastors' regular reports detailing moral offences and offenders and the admonition of these sins and sinners, the effect of which greatly relied on the personal authority of the pastor.[28]

Pastors, like the summoned parishioners, appeared in a dual role before the visitation commission. Although on the one hand their own deeds were inspected, they were also expected to inform on others. It was the local pastor who provided the visitation commission with most information about the religious and moral condition of his parish. Village magistrates also could put forth their claims fairly easily, as they were routinely questioned by the commission anyway. The wishes and complaints of the villagers were mostly either communicated through the magistrates or expressed as anonymous statements in the protocols. If a matter was pressing, the parishioners could put forward their opinions, but for the most part the commission members had to rely on the pastors and the local magistracy for their information.

This was especially true of delicate moral and religious matters, as the parishioners were only usually willing to denounce notorious offenders or unwelcome outsiders.[29] According to Heinrich Richard Schmidt, the shared fear of God's punishment made parishioners report some moral offences; thus, in the end, the communities controlled themselves by accepting or initiating the prosecution of unwanted conduct.[30] Rudolf Schlögl has argued that this was especially true in cases in which a neighbour who did not attend communion was embroiled in a dispute with the person who denounced them. In addition, visitations could also be used as a platform to air marital disputes.[31] Schlögl further claims

---

27 Brecht, *Kirchenordnung*, pp. 40–50.
28 Jay Goodale, "Pfarrer als Außenseiter: Landpfarrer und religiöses Leben in Sachsen zur Reformationszeit", *Historische Anthropologie* 7 (1999), p. 209; Schorn-Schütte, "Priest, Preacher, Pastor", p. 29.
29 Rublack, "Herrschaftspraxis in Württemberg", pp. 355–356; Konersmann, "Kirchenvisitation", pp. 607–608.
30 Schmidt, *Religion und Dorf*, p. 320.
31 Schlögl, "Bedingungen", pp. 252–253. The Schorndorf evidence does not support this claim, however.

that visitations soon became welcome instruments of internal village conflict regulation, as they allowed disputes to be settled without the antagonists losing face.[32] It was predominantly violators of local norms and those involved in conflicts who were more likely to be reported officially. In the Schorndorf district, at least, failure to comply with official religious life – the sermons and communion – was not in itself reason enough to denounce a friend, neighbour or relative. When paired with a personal grudge, however, such failures of compliance could provide suitable arguments for denouncement.

When it came to reporting unpopular pastors, villagers readily used the opportunities afforded by the visitations. Accordingly, members of the visitation commission were advised not to blindly trust anything they heard. Pastors' accounts were to be cross-checked by hearing the opinions of notable members of the community.[33] Furthermore, local rumours could be taken as a potential source of information, although their substance had to be verified at a later stage of the process.[34] Occasionally the commission officials detected that disagreements and personal quarrels lay behind the statements. While visiting the village of Aichelberg in March 1602, the *Spezialis* of Schorndorf noted that only the local mayor Jacob Gettlin had accused the pastor, Michel Engel, of drunkenness and swearing.[35] Thus, on the one hand, the methods of separate questioning and double-checking enabled the visitors to col-

---

The Württemberg marriage court, established in 1541, was able to sort out these problems sufficiently. Brecht & Ehmer, *Südwestdeutsche Reformationsgeschichte*, pp. 234–235; Tolley, *Pastors and Parishioners*, p. 100. On settling marital disputes in Württemberg, see also Robert W. Scribner, "Mobility: Voluntary or enforced? Vagrants in Württemberg in the Sixteenth Century", in Gerhard Jaritz & Albert Müller (ed.), *Migration in der Feudalgesellschaft* (Frankfurt 1988), pp. 76–78.

32 Schlögl, "Bedingungen", p. 258.
33 Arend, *Kirchenordnungen*, p. 328; Helga Schnabel-Schüle, "Kirchenleitung und Kirchenvisitation in den Territorien des deutschen Südwestens", in Ernst Walter Zeeden (ed.), *Repertorium der Kirchenvisitationsakten aus dem 16. und 17. Jahrhundert in Archiven der Bundesrepublik Deutschland: Baden-Württemberg*, Bd. 2, Teilbd. 2: *Der protestantische Südwesten* (Stuttgart 1987), pp. 71–72; Strauss, *Luther's House of Learning*, p. 254.
34 Ralf-Peter Fuchs, *Um die Ehre: westfälische Beleidigungsprozesse vor dem Reichskammergericht 1525–1805* (Paderborn 1999), pp. 312–313, Katharina Simon-Muscheid, "Täter, Opfer und Komplizinnen – Geschlechtsspezifische Strategien und Loyalitäten im Basler 'Morrthandel' von 1522", in Andreas Blauert (ed.), *Kriminalitätsgeschichte: Beiträge zur Sozial- und Kulturgschichte der Vormoderne* (Konstanz 2000), p. 660; Tolley, *Pastors and Parishioners*, pp. 94–95.
35 HStAS A281/1120, p. 54. For a similar case in Rudersberg, see Landeskirchliches Archiv Stuttgart (LKA) A1/1588 II, f. 85v–86r.

lect information that was as reliable as possible. However, on the other hand, these methods provided the opportunity for accusations – whether founded or not – to be made against the pastor or his associates, the local officials or, indeed, one's neighbour.

In the case of the pastor of Aichelberg, the *Spezialis* also recorded pastor Engel's side of the story. When questioned about the matter, Engel first denied the mayor's accusations and made reference to his parishioners, who would vouch for his character. When further pressed by the *Spezialis*, Engel was ready to admit that he "had been running extensively after the forester (*Forstmeister*) because of the firewood and been quite heated and had soon thereafter drunk good wine that had got to him as soon as he had got out in the open air". This, the pastor was very sorry for, and he further demonstrated his remorse by bursting into tears in front of the *Spezialis* and begging him not to take any further action.[36] The case of Aichelberg illustrates the various roles that the different parties involved – in this case, the visiting *Spezialis*, the charge-raising mayor, the accused pastor and the parish (cited as witnesses to the good reputation of the pastor) – could adopt in order to achieve their goals and how the visitation commission had to take this into account in its work. The case also demonstrates how those accused of an offence had some opportunity to influence the process both by framing their story in as harmless a light as possible and by showing humility and repentance – especially, if they like Michel Engel had to admit that the accusations against them were wholly or at least partially true.

During the late sixteenth century, local priests became targets of their parishioners' criticism to such an extent that some scholars speak of a second wave of anticlericalism (the first having triggered off the Reformation some decades earlier).[37] As representatives of the official church at a local level the pastors were in some ways classic middlemen, forever balancing between the interests of the head of the church and their parishioners. The pastors in Württemberg were generally outsiders in

---

36 HStAS A281/1120, pp. 54–55.
37 For such a view, see e.g. Robert W. Scribner, "Wie wird man Außenseiter? Ein- und Ausgrenzung im frühneuzeitlichen Deutschland", in Marion Kobelt-Groch & Norbert Fischer (ed.), *Außenseiter zwischen Mittelalter und Neuzeit: Festschrift für Hans-Jürgen Goertz zum 60. Geburtstag* (Leiden 1997), p. 33.

their own parishes: most were neither born nor raised in the community they served. Most had received very specific professional training at the University of Tübingen, a very different experience from that of their parishioners. More often than not pastors did not share the dialect of the locals. Furthermore, they seldom or never married within village society.[38] On the other hand, they did undoubtedly have some ties to the local community. They could act as godfathers, loan money or write supplications on behalf of their parishioners. As numerous complaints brought forward during visitations indicate, many pastors were involved in the agricultural structures of their community through their glebe lands. A pastor's wife could also play an important part in the social life of the congregation by attending festivities and taking on the role of godmother or even midwife.[39] But there were limits to the integration of pastors, and routine conflicts could leave them vulnerable. As Robert W. Scribner has observed:

> It is a common feature of many such conflicts in rural parishes that a trivial disagreement or minor complaint often let loose a deeper reservoir of resentment and set off a chain reaction of dissension and bitterness that seemed to subvert the very basis of the cure of souls.[40]

The visitation soon proved to be a suitable platform through which a parish could rid itself of an unpopular clergyman. Complaints brought forward by parishioners against their pastors were taken seriously and were almost always looked into by higher ecclesiastical officials.[41] Jay Goodale and Frank Fätkenheuer have recently emphasized that charg-

---

38 On the social background and education of Württemberg pastors, see Tolley, *Pastors and Parishioners*, pp. 5–43; Johannes Wahl, *Lebensplanung und Alltagserfahrung: Württembergische Pfarrfamilien im 17. Jahrhundert* (Mainz 2000), pp. 35–57.
39 See e.g. HStAS 398W/14, Nr. 1; LKA A1/1583 II, f. 90r; LKA A1/1584 II, f. 89v–90r; LKA A1/1586 II, f. 93v; Frank Fätkenheuer, *Lebenswelt und Religion: Mikro-historische Untersuchungen an Beispielen aus Franken um 1600* (Göttingen 2004), pp. 224–226, 243–244; Tolley, *Pastors and Parishioners*, pp. 5–6, 52–57, 62, 154–155.
40 Robert W. Scribner, "Pastoral Care and the Reformation in Germany", in idem, *Religion and Culture in Germany (1400–1800)* (Leiden & Boston & Köln 2001), p. 193.
41 Landwehr, "Policey vor Ort", p. 54.

es raised against pastors during visitations did not necessarily reflect the quality of the accused clergymen's work. Rather, such accusations should be interpreted as indicators of the marginal position of pastors within village power structures. As Fätkenheuer has pointed out:

> [E]veryday control by the parish forced [the pastor] to permanently mind not to offend their norms and values. But even if the pastor was sure of his acceptance in the parish, he could never eliminate the possibility that a member of the congregation [...] reported internal information outside the village.[42]

To put it very simply, parishioners made claims against their pastors if and when they wished. A good deal of informal negotiating and arguing would often take place before a case was brought before the visitation commission.[43] Conflicts could be pursued and control exercised both formally and informally.

Indeed, one typical domain of conflict had its origins in the scarcity of goods within villages. This made some parishioners reluctant to pay their tithes or to accept that their clergymen should be exempt from the communal contributions made to the landlord.[44] Another area of conflict could stem from a pastor's violation of local norms and traditions that were not congruent with official ideals. Yet it was exactly this "system of values confirmed by custom which regulated family, kin, and communal affairs" and, at the same time, formed the "primary-level social controls".[45] The pastor of Hegenlohe, Jeremias Sommerhart, provides a good example of such a case. When the widowed pastor married his maid in 1585 before the end of the locally normative six months' period of mourning, there was a great deal of resentment among his parishioners. During a later visitation, members of the congregation accused their pastor of hot-tempered preaching and his wife of having a quarrelsome spirit. The outcome of the official investigation of

---

42 Fätkenheuer, *Lebenswelt und Religion*, p. 243.
43 Fätkenheuer, *Lebenswelt und Religion*, pp. 190–191, 354; Goodale, "Pfarrer als Außenseiter", p. 199.
44 LKA A1/1586 II, f. 93v, 96r.
45 Wegert, *Popular Culture*, pp. 27–28.

this conflict was the scolding of the pastor by the commissioners, who themselves were concerned by the pastor's lack of interest in theological reading and the bad example his quick temper set for the parish. Previously, representatives of the congregation had assured the commission members of their satisfaction with the clergyman, even though the disputes surrounding his marriage were already underway.[46]

The persecution of Anabaptists by the pastors can be seen as a further break with the local norms (and one which seems to have been surprisingly common within the Schorndorf district). It seems that Anabaptists, although officially deemed to be harmful heretics, were not considered deviant enough to be denounced by their neighbours or relatives. Reporting Anabaptists to the higher church officials could therefore provoke enduring conflicts between pastors and parishioners.[47] Melchior Greiner, a glass-maker from Walkersbach, criticized his pastor harshly in 1577 for "leaving the Anabaptists to the devil". He therefore refused to take part in any ceremonies of the official church.[48] Furthermore, Greiner and his family – who were labelled by the authorities as strong-headed Anabaptists and followers of the similarly objectionable Spiritualist Caspar von Schwenckfeld – used their local influence to prevent Lutheran pastors from preaching in the filial parish of Walkersbach for years. In 1583 the visitation commission was told that members of the Greiner family had torn down the chapel in Walkersbach, forcing the local pastor to preach in selected private houses in front of only four or five people.[49]

---

46 LKA A1/1582, f. 75v; LKA A1/1583 I, f. 78v; LKA A1/1583 II, f. 93r; LKA A1/1584 I, f. 100v–101r; LKA A1/1586 II, f. 96r. For a similar case in Franconia, see Fätkenheuer, *Lebenswelt und Religion*, pp. 309–310. As Luise Schorn-Schütte has pointed out, local conflicts arising from pastors' marriages and family relationships were a specifically Protestant phenomenon. Cf. Luise Schorn-Schütte, *Evangelische Geistlichkeit in der Frühen Neuzeit: Deren Anteil an der Entfaltung frühmoderner Staatlichkeit und Gesellschaft, dargestellt am Beispiel des Fürstentums Braunschweig-Wolfenbüttel, der Landgrafschaft Hessen-Kassel und der Stadt Braunschweig* (Gütersloh 1996), pp. 272–273.

47 See, for example, LKA A26/466 I, f. 70v. On not reporting Anabaptists at the local level, see, for example, Claus-Peter Clasen, *Anabaptism: A Social History, 1525–1618. Switzerland, Austria, Moravia, South and Central Germany* (Ithaca & London 1972), p. 362; Roland Hofer, "Anabaptists in Seventeenth-Century Schleitheim: Popular Resistance to the Consolidation of State Power in the Early Modern Era", *Mennonite Quarterly Review* 74 (2000), p. 127; Hanspeter Jecker, *Ketzer – Rebellen – Heilige: Das Basler Täufertum von 1580–1700* (Basel 1998), p. 606; Marlies Mattern, *Leben im Abseits. Frauen und Männer im Täufertum (1525–1550): Eine Studie zur Alltagsgeschichte* (Frankfurt 1998), pp. 174–177; John S. Oyer, "Nicodemites Among Württemberg Anabaptists", *Mennonite Quarterly Review* 71 (1997), p. 494.

48 LKA A26/466 I, f. 219v.

49 LKA A1/1583 II, f. 90v.

Over-eager denunciation of offences also displeased parishioners in many other cases. For instance, when in the 1590s the pastor of Urbach, Gregor Glareanus, reported several cases of fornication and named Anabaptists known to him, he faced various forms of resistance from the villagers. His garden was vandalized, and a significant proportion of the parishioners refused to attend his sermons, visit his house or work in his fields. These expressions of antagonism might also be seen as unofficial attempts to exercise social control in response to the pastor's use of official forms of control. To make matters even more complicated for Glareanus, some villagers were upset because they felt the Anabaptists of Urbach had been treated too leniently.[50] The reactions of the villagers to their cleric's role in the visitation can be seen as informal actions of control, effective and understandable only within the boundaries of the local community and its power relations. The pastor himself was required to officially report these kinds of incidents, as Glareanus finally did. However, rather than easing the situation, informing the visitation commission about such acts of defiance could backfire on a cleric by exacerbating the conflict and making the clergyman's daily life in the community even more difficult.

Even though they lacked the authority to expel moral or religious offenders, pastors did have some unofficial or semi-official means of control at their disposal. The pastors' power lay in their key responsibilities: the homily and the confession. It was here that their position allowed them to speak without being openly contradicted. This also provided them with the opportunity to express their resentment towards certain people or practices in the parish. For those concerned, this kind of interference seems to have been an exceptionally harsh provocation.[51] Again, the case of the Hegenlohe pastor is illustrative. For at least a year (from 1586 to 1587) Jeremias Sommerhart used his sermons as an additional channel through which he upbraided his parishioners for refusing to provide him with the tithes to which he was entitled.[52] The

---

50 Because of this perceived leniency, the pastor even received anonymous threatening letters. HStAS A282/3094c, f. 83r–85r.
51 Fätkenheuer, *Lebenswelt und Religion*, pp. 237, 328; Pettegree, *Reformation*, pp. 36–37.
52 LKA A1/1586 II, f. 96r; LKA A1/1587 II, f. 87v.

last alternative open to pastors was to report the case officially during the church visitation. Although sources do not reveal the extent to which pastors might have used the threat of reporting their parishioners to the visitation, it is safe to assume that such threats might (like sermons and confessions) have provided a way of exerting pressure in the local communication networks.

Taking part in the official ceremonies of the church – most importantly the divine services and communion – was compulsory for the parishioners.[53] In Württemberg, those who for an extended period of time had failed to attend these ceremonies were usually examined by the visitation commission in person. Officially the pastor had to exhort the dissidents twice in private and the third time in the presence of two or three local magistrates. Only after these warnings should the person – if no improvement was observed – have been reported to the visitation.[54] Exceptionally serious cases, however, could also be reported outside the regular procedure. The pastor himself decided whether or not a case was exceptionally serious; thus, the power to decide whether or not to report the alleged dissidents lay in his hands.

Irrespective of whether or not the alleged offenders repented, they would be closely watched by the pastor and questions would be asked about them during the next visitation. If they still were unwilling to conform, dissidents could be punished with fines, excommunication from the sacramental union of the congregation, a period of short imprisonment or, in cases of unbending and active Anabaptism, even expelled from the duchy.[55] All of these sanctions entailed physical and/or material hardship. The Württemberg visitation protocols of the late sixteenth century that I have studied mention few sanctions that were actually imposed (as far as I can see, none were connected to the use of the ecclesiastical ban)[56] and so it is very difficult to examine the impact that such

---

53 In rural parishes, parishioners had to attend services three times a week, and the Eucharist once a month. Heinrich Richard Schmidt, *Konfessionalisierung im 16. Jahrhundert* (München 1992), p. 122; Tolley, *Pastors and Parishioners*, p. 73.
54 Arend, *Kirchenordnungen*, pp. 331–332.
55 Räisänen, *Ketzer im Dorf*, 255–257.
56 On the lack of information regarding the punishments, see also Tolley, *Pastors and Parishioners*, pp. 70–71.

sanctions might have had at a local level. But even if they were rarely implemented, the mere existence of these punishments must have been a threatening presence for parishioners living in a close-knit community in which honour and good reputation – and, even more so, their loss – largely defined one's social capital.[57]

The power of persuasion and protocolling

As has been pointed out, pastors and parishioners could both report on others and be reported upon during the visitations. However, the final decision was always in the hands of the higher clerical authorities. In order to keep track of all the cases, the administrative genre of the protocol became increasingly important.[58] Significant power lay in the pure act of protocolling. One could argue that this was perhaps the most severe form of control: accused individuals could only exert minor influence on the process.[59] Therefore it was in the interest of those who were accused to try to give the best possible presentation of their case when they were examined. Once a suspected offender was labelled a drunkard, a quarrelsome individual or a heretic in the official correspondence, it was very difficult to shed this allegation. In their general future conduct, as well as during future visitations, those who had been labelled in this way had to be very careful about their actions and statements, so as to avoid punishment or harsher sanctions than had previously been imposed. It is therefore no surprise that strategies of legitimation and self-portrayal recorded in visitation protocols resemble those found in court records from the same period: references to one's own simplicity or lack of understanding, attempts to play down evidence or evasiveness when questioned.[60]

---

57 Brecht, *Kirchenordnung*, pp. 41, 46; Fuchs, *Um die Ehre*, pp. 11–20; Rublack, "Herrschaftspraxis in Württemberg", p. 359; Wahl, *Lebensplanung*, pp. 215–216.
58 Sabean, "Soziale Distanzierungen", pp. 222–223.
59 David W. Sabean, "Peasant Voices and Bureaucratic Texts: Narrative Structure in Early Modern German Protocols", in Peter Becker & William Clark (ed.), *Little Tools of Knowledge: Historical Essays on Academic and Bureaucratic Practices* (Ann Arbor 2001), pp. 69, 86.
60 On the extensive research on early modern court protocols, see, for example, Ralf-Peter Fuchs & Winfried Schulze, "Zeugenverhöre als historische Quellen – einige Vorüberlegungen", in idem (ed.), *Wahrheit, Wissen, Erinnerung: Zeugenverhörprotokolle als Quellen für soziale Wissensbestände in der Frü-*

Many of the villagers in the Schorndorf district who were accused of dissent made use of the contemporary perception of peasants as ignorant, easily seducible and simple-minded people. Surprisingly often, this seems to have been a successful strategy: If they showed at least some willingness to compromise (especially if they made at least a vague promise to mend their ways in the future), suspects had a fair chance of postponing further investigation at least until the next visitation.[61] In 1577, Clara Greiner from Urbach asked to be given time to think over her participation in the sermons and the sacraments, because "she didn't understand the matter properly". She proposed a period of a month's grace, after which she would provide the commission with her answer. This was granted to her, even though she came from a family known for its Anabaptist tendencies.[62] Similarly, the elderly Konrad Faut from Schlechtbach succeeded in portraying himself as simple-minded and harmless when he was summoned to appear before the visitation commission in 1615. Although he refused to recant his Anabaptist views, the visitors judged the "stubborn old man" to be too dim-witted to effectively spread heretic ideas and so concluded that he posed no threat to the community.[63] As these brief examples suggest, ultimately suspects had to provide an explanation of their thought or conduct that appeared plausible to the representatives of the official church. Furthermore, the suspected offenders had to demonstrate proper repentance and obedience to the authorities.[64]

The chances of being spared punishment increased if respectable villagers were prepared to vouch for the character of the accused. This was the case in Rommelshausen, where young apprentice Joß Veysel was questioned in 1576 because he had failed to attend the Eucharist

---

hen Neuzeit (Münster 2002), p. 25; Gerd Schwerhoff, *Aktenkundig und gerichtsnotorisch: Einführung in die Historische Kriminalitätsforschung* (Tübingen 1999), p. 63; Katharina Simon-Muscheid & Christian Simon, "Zur Lektüre von Gerichtstexten: Fiktionale Realität oder Alltag in Gerichtsquellen?", in: Dorothee Rippmann & Katharina Simon-Muscheid & Christian Simon (ed.), *Arbeit – Liebe – Streit: Texte zur Geschichte des Geschlechterverhältnisses und des Alltags, 15. bis 18. Jahrhundert* (Basel 1996), pp. 17–27.
61 See e.g. LKA A1/1585 II, f. 82v; LKA A26/466 I, f. 17r, 22r, 70v–71r, 99r–99v.
62 LKA A26/466 I, f. 219r.
63 LKA A26/466 II, f. 167r, 173r.
64 HStAS A63/42, f. 31r–32v; Räisänen, *Ketzer im Dorf*, pp. 289–322; Schwerhoff, *Köln im Kreuzverhör*, p. 107.

for four years. Veysel explained his absence by claiming that he did not understand what the pastor was preaching; indeed, the *Spezialis* noted that Veysel had recited the Ten Commandments as if in a foreign language.[65] The local magistrates assured the members of the visitation commission that Veysel was a "hardworking, poor apprentice", although not quite as simple-minded as he had claimed. According to the magistrates of Rommelshausen, Veysel was capable of understanding the sermons and basic Christian teachings. The local pastor was advised to teach Veysel privately, and the effect of these lessons was to be evaluated during the following visitation.[66] This case highlights the importance of notable local individuals, who in many cases could influence the interpretations of the visiting commission one way or the other.[67] Control was therefore exercised not only by the ducal representatives, but also by the local potentates (who most likely knew the circumstances of particular cases only too well). Thus, the exercise of control was never a simple issue; it was not a top-down process, but its effects could, at least to some extent, be negotiated between the various parties both horizontally and vertically. The power of those who were investigated lay in their ability to persuade representatives of the visitation, both through their arguments and by their behaviour. Supporting statements of respectable locals could further enhance the credibility of their accounts.

Conflict, mediation and power relations

The disciplinary measures were designed by the ruling elites. However, they would not have had any significant effect without at least partial acceptance at a local level. This is an important notion to keep in mind

---

65 LKA A26/466 I, f. 164v.
66 LKA A26/466 I, f. 164v–165r.
67 This was especially true in regard to the Anabaptist: If Anabaptists were tolerated by local magistrates, it was very hard for the ducal authorities to take measures against – or even find – them. Räisänen, *Ketzer im Dorf*, pp. 232–234, 277–289. See also Claus-Peter Clasen, *Die Wiedertäufer im Herzogtum Württemberg und in benachbarten Herrschaften: Ausbreitung, Geisteswelt und Soziologie* (Stuttgart 1965), p. 158. For similar tendencies in Switzerland, cf. Jecker, *Ketzer*, pp. 606–608; Hofer, "Popular Resistance", pp. 130–131.

when talking about the differences between official and local interests. As anthropologically oriented scholarship has emphasized for some time now, a strict dichotomy between "elite" and "popular" cultures draws an overly simplified picture of pre-modern societies. The official norms may only have appealed to some villagers on a larger scale, but these parishioners were likely to have been among the relatively wealthy local elites, who in turn exerted remarkable influence over village life.[68] Karl Wegert has therefore argued that

> any state policy which promised to enhance order and stability – by holding debt-ridden cultivators up to ridicule, enforcing communion, or imposing harsh penalties against vagrants – was bound to evoke a positive reaction among important elements of village society.[69]

The crucial point for the effectiveness of state policies was that they "fulfilled certain local needs".[70] This naturally also applies to the efforts of the Lutheran Church in Württemberg. Although the members of the visitation commissions were charged with looking for deviant forms of religiosity, superstition and magical practices; avoidance of official church services; and signs of heresy and moral offences (that were imagined to be widespread in the villages), there were some beliefs and norms that were shared by both the social elites and the general populace. Many of these were basic Christian ideals – such as the love of one's neighbour – that were essential for the functioning of the community. There was also general agreement that social, economic, political and religious life had to be somehow regulated.[71]

Despite the existence of the secular courts as institutional forms of moral control, the local population was also able to use the regular church visitations in order to report cases that seemed to threaten local

---

68 Wegert, *Popular Culture*, pp. 27, 39.
69 Wegert, *Popular Culture*, p. 35. Cf. Schmidt, *Dorf und Religion*, p. 353; Tolley, *Pastors and Parishioners*, p. 87.
70 Wegert, *Popular Culture*, p. 39.
71 Landwehr, *Policey im Alltag*, p. 317.

stability or violate basic village norms.[72] Given the scarcity of goods in many rural communities, especially in the crisis-ridden late sixteenth century, securing the common good through proper housekeeping (*Haushaltung*) was a value shared by ducal authorities and at least some of the villagers. It was largely when these fundamental norms were violated that parishioners filed claims in the visitations against pastors or local magistrates. In cases of mismanagement of communal housekeeping, the mayor would usually be held responsible.[73] In this way, visitations could be used by the parishioners as a means of exerting social control over issues that were not strictly religious matters.[74] Nonetheless, the accusations had to be phrased, if not in religious language, at least in officially approved terms in order to make the reasoning seem plausible to the visitors.

That the villagers knew this and made clever use of the strategy is evident from various conflicts in Urbach during the last decade of the sixteenth century. Not only was the mayor of Urbach, Jakob Köblin, accused of drinking heavily while in office and scolding villagers when they approached him to discuss their concerns: it was also claimed that he tolerated and even supported Anabaptists in the village and that he, together with his trusted men among the magistracy, was suspected of having stolen considerable sums of money from the parish church's treasury.[75] The Urbach pastor told the commission that the mayor had already lost the last vestiges of his authority in the early 1580s, when Köblin (at that time a widower) had remained in office even after he had impregnated his maid. In the eyes of the pastor, this was the reason why "fornication will not be rightly punished in this parish".[76] When they made their claims in front of the visitation commission, the Urbach

---

72 André Holenstein, *Bauern zwischen Bauernkrieg und Dreissigjährigem Krieg* (München 1996), p. 26. However, the protocols seldom directly name the individual who reported the offence. Generally claims against villagers are referred to in the protocols only in very general terms (such as "those of the community claim..." and "it is commonly rumoured in the village...") or through the use of passive constructions.
73 Tolley, *Pastors and Parishioners*, pp. 102–104.
74 Resource conflicts among the villagers, however, were fought and settled in other mediums – usually the secular courts of the village or district. See e.g. Holenstein, *Bauern*, pp. 20–21; Räisänen, *Ketzer im Dorf*, pp. 242–246.
75 HStAS A282/3094c, Nr. 14, f. 37r–44v; HStAS A282/3094c, f. 83v.
76 LKA A1/1582, f. 74r.

people framed their complaints against Köblin in terms of Christian justice and common good. He was said to be heartless with the poor and weak, while making a fortune out of their misery. Some women stated that when they had confronted the mayor over his refusal to provide material help to the poor, he had replied that "if he won't give them anything, they will leave".[77] The general line of argument was that, as mayor, Köblin was a serious threat to both the (material) common good of the village and its moral condition. As there was unanimous testimony against him from the pastor and all of the parishioners questioned, the visitation commission and the Stuttgart synod agreed that Köblin should be removed from office. Köblin's attempts to defend himself – including his claim that the villagers were acting out of personal hatred towards him – could not overcome such opposition.[78]

Visitations may have been especially attractive to the villagers as forums for airing and settling disputes for two reasons: firstly because of the low costs incurred; secondly, because of the visitation commission's tendency to favour reconciliation rather than punishment.[79] According to Bruce Tolley, "the practice of mediation and compromise was just as important to the church's social function as the exercise of hegemony and power".[80] Attempts by the visitation commission to mediate in local conflicts are also clearly visible in the Schorndorf material.[81] For example, in March 1602 the *Spezialis* of Schorndorf contentedly reported his success in settling a dispute between pastor Michel Engel and mayor Jacob Gettlin of Aichelberg: "In the last visitation I reconciled them and they also shook hands with another."[82] The parishioners of Urbach had, in September 1586, articulated their dissatisfaction with the local pastor, who let his cattle graze on the common pastures without participating in any labour service himself. Although the visitation commission clari-

---

77 HStAS A282/3094c, Nr. 14, f. 39r–40v.
78 HStAS A282/3094c, Nr. 14, f. 40r; HStAS A282/3094c, Nr. 15, f. 19v.
79 Schmidt, *Religion und Dorf*, p. 298.
80 Tolley, *Pastors and Parishioners*, p. 112. Similar observations, albeit *en passant*, have been made by Frieb, *Kirchenvisitation und Kommunikation*, p. 171; Schmidt, *Religion und Dorf*, p. 300.
81 See e.g. LKA A1/1585 II, f. 76v, 84r; LKA A1/1586 II, f. 93v; LKA A1/1588 I, f. 89v; LKA A1/1590, f. 90r; Räisänen, *Ketzer im Dorf*, pp. 252–254.
82 HStAS A281/1120, p. 54.

fied the *immunitas ministrorum* from the service, the villagers remained adamant that this was unfair and demanded a further resolution from the synod. Even though the exemption of clerics from labour service was clearly stated in the Württemberg church ordinance of 1559, the synod nevertheless promised to find a compromise "equitable to both parties and appropriate to the case".[83]

It could therefore be concluded that an instrument designed by the authorities largely for the exercise of control also had an appeasing dimension, necessary for the protection – or, indeed, attainment – of peace and stability in a period characterized by rapid social change, famine, plague and dearth. Theologically, this was underpinned by the notions of brotherly love and patience that the church was willing to demonstrate towards even its misguided members so long as, for their part, they showed adequate repentance and obedience. The demonstration of mercy towards the "weak" in society legitimized the paternalistic reign of the authorities as both Christian and righteous.[84] Mediation through the state authorities and official control was necessary and was, therefore, at least to a certain extent sought for at a local level. Co-operation was in fact a necessity for everyone. Members of the visitation commission depended on information from the local authorities or the general populace. On the other hand, given the centralized banning system of the Württemberg church (which only allowed the Stuttgart synod to excommunicate notorious sinners) the parishioners had to co-operate with the visitors, if they wished to rid their communities of unwanted individuals.[85]

Just as Natalie Zemon Davis noted in her study of French pardon tales of the sixteenth century, the actions of the participants in the process fitted the scenery of the "larger drama" of building state power in early modern society. Everyone had a role to play and rules to follow.

---

[83] LKA A1/1586 II, f. 93v.
[84] Cf. Brakensiek, "Legitimation", p. 368; Natalie Zemon Davis, *Fiction in the Archives: Pardon Tales and their Tellers in Sixteenth-Century France* (Stanford 1987), p. 53; Rublack, "Herrschaftspraxis in Württemberg", p. 361. On early modern concepts and practices of mercy by territorial authorities, see Ulrike Ludwig, *Das Herz der Justitia: Gestaltungspotentiale territorialer Herrschaft in der Strafrechts- und Gnadenpraxis am Beispiel Kursachsens 1548–1648* (Konstanz 2008).
[85] Konersmann, "Kirchenvisitation", pp. 607–608.

The official rules were formulated by the sovereign (in France, the king; in Württemberg, the duke), and participants were wise not to break these rules in order to get what they wanted. Therefore, supplicants had to frame their stories according to the medium; they could not portray themselves as heroes of a folktale, for example, but rather as obedient (and sometimes: simple) subjects.[86] The inequality in the power relations was apparent. The hierarchy involved in visitations may have been a little more sophisticated than that between a king and his subject, but it was no less clear. In the context of a visitation, official power lay in the hands of members of the commission, who acted as representatives of both the duke and the territorial church (which were linked through the position of the duke as the highest bishop of the church). As ducal officials, members of the commission were themselves in an inferior position to their sovereign and were therefore under pressure to act in accordance with the rules so carefully laid out for them in the numerous ordinances of the period.[87]

Improving the Christian community was thus a complex process of interaction in which different actors pursued their individual and collective goals in the official framework of moral and social norms. As scholarship has by now emphatically shown, norms did not, however, determine practices and everyday encounters in any straightforward way.[88] Ideas about how to achieve a better state of affairs varied, as did the means available to the actors striving for improvement. Early modern church visitations provide one opportunity for historians to study these multifaceted relationships and processes, where a person could at the same time be both agent and object of control and improvement.

---

86 Davis, *Fiction in the Archives*, p. 57. See also Brakensiek, "Legitimation", p. 371.
87 For early modern relations between ruler and state or local officials with further references, see e.g. Stefan Brakensiek & Heide Wunder (ed.), *Ergebene Diener ihrer Herren? Herrschaftsvermittlung im alten Europa* (Köln 2005); Brakensiek, "Legitimation"; Landwehr, "Policey vor Ort".
88 See e.g. Antje Flüchter, *Der Zölibat zwischen Devianz und Norm: Kirchenpolitik und Gemeindealltag in den Herzogtümern Jülich und Berg im 16. und 17. Jahrhundert* (Köln 2006); André Holenstein, "Die Umstände der Normen – die Normen der Umstände: Policeyordnungen im kommunikativen Handeln von Verwaltung und lokaler Gesellschaft im Ancien Régime", in Karl Härter (ed.), *Policey und frühneuzeitliche Gesellschaft* (Frankfurt 2000); Achim Landwehr, "Normdurchsetzung in der Frühen Neuzeit? Kritik eines Begriffes", *Zeitschrift für Geschichtswissenschaft* 48 (2000), pp. 146–162.

Sources

ARCHIVAL SOURCES

Hauptstaatsarchiv Stuttgart (HStAS)
HStAS A63/24: *Confessio Virtembergica* (1552).
HStAS A281/1120: Kirchenvisitationsakten, Amt Schorndorf (1602).
HStAS A282/3094: Wiedertäufer im Amt Schorndorf.
HStAS 398W/14: Schorndorf. Weltliche Verwaltung.
Landeskirchliches Archiv Stuttgart (LKA)
LKA A1/1581–1590: Synodusprotokolle (1581–1590).
LKA A26/466 I: Sektarierbücher des Synodus I (1573–1578).
LKA A26/466 II: Sektarierbücher des Synodus II (1608–1620).

PRINTED SOURCES

Arend, Sabine (ed.) 2004: *Die evangelischen Kirchenordnungen des XVI. Jahrhunderts, Bd. 16: Baden-Württemberg II, Herzogtum Württemberg.* Mohr, Tübingen.

LITERATURE

Becker, Thomas Paul 1989: *Konfessionalisierung in Kurköln: Untersuchungen zur Durchsetzung der katholischen Reform in den Dekanaten Ahrgau und Bonn anhand von Visitationsprotokollen 1583–1761.* Röhrscheid, Bonn.
Blickle, Peter 1985: *Gemeindereformation: Die Menschen des 16. Jahrhunderts auf dem Weg zum Heil.* Oldenbourg, München.
Blickle, Peter, Kunisch, Johannes (ed.) 1989: *Kommunalisierung und Christianisierung: Voraussetzungen und Folgen der Reformation 1400–1600.* Duncker & Humblot, Berlin.
Brakensiek, Stefan 2010: Legitimation durch Verfahren? Visitationen, Supplikationen, Berichte und Enqueten im frühmodernen Fürstenstaat. In *Herstellung und Darstellung von Entscheidungen: Verfahren, Verwalten und Verhandeln in der Vormoderne*, ed. Barbara Stollberg-Rilinger and Andre Krischer. Duncker & Humblot, Berlin, pp. 363–377.
Brakensiek, Stefan, Wunder, Heide (ed.) 2005: *Ergebene Diener ihrer Herren? Herrschaftsvermittlung im alten Europa.* Böhlau, Köln.
Brecht, Martin 1967: *Kirchenordnung und Kirchenzucht in Württemberg vom 16. bis zum 18. Jahrhundert.* Calwer, Stuttgart.
Brecht, Martin, Ehmer, Hermann 1984: *Südwestdeutsche Reformationsgeschichte: Zur Einführung der Reformation im Herzogtum Württemberg 1534.* Calwer, Stuttgart.
Nicolás Brochhagen 2011: Diskursive Aspekte landesherrlicher Machtbildung am Beispiel der Visitation der Grafschaft Ravensberg 1535. *Jahresbericht des Historischen Vereins für die Grafschaft Ravensberg* 96, pp. 193–213.
Clasen, Claus-Peter 1965: *Die Wiedertäufer im Herzogtum Württemberg und in benachbarten Herrschaften: Ausbreitung, Geisteswelt und Soziologie.* Kohlhammer, Stuttgart.
Clasen, Claus-Peter 1972: *Anabaptism: A Social History, 1525–1618. Switzerland, Austria, Moravia, South and Central Germany.* Cornell University Press, Ithaca & London.
Davis, Natalie Zemon 1987: *Fiction in the Archives: Pardon Tales and their Tellers in Sixteenth-Century France.* Stanford University Press, Stanford.

Flüchter, Antje 2006: *Der Zölibat zwischen Devianz und Norm: Kirchenpolitik und Gemeindealltag in den Herzogtümern Jülich und Berg im 16. und 17. Jahrhundert*. Böhlau, Köln.

Frieb, Katharina 2006: *Kirchenvisitation und Kommunikation: Die Akten zu den Visitationen in der Kuroberpfalz unter Ludwig VI. (1576–1583)*. Beck, München.

Fuchs, Ralf-Peter 1999: *Um die Ehre: westfälische Beleidigungsprozesse vor dem Reichskammergericht 1525–1805*. Schöningh, Paderborn.

Fuchs, Ralf-Peter, Schulze, Winfried 2002: Zeugenverhöre als historische Quellen - einige Vorüberlegungen. In *Wahrheit, Wissen, Erinnerung: Zeugenverhörprotokolle als Quellen für soziale Wissensbestände in der Frühen Neuzeit*, ed. Ralf-Peter Fuchs and Winfried Schulze. Lit.-Verlag, Münster, pp. 7–40.

Fätkenheuer, Frank 2004: *Lebenswelt und Religion: Mikro-historische Untersuchungen an Beispielen aus Franken um 1600*. Vandenhoeck & Ruprecht, Göttingen.

Goodale, Jay 1999: Pfarrer als Außenseiter: Landpfarrer und religiöses Leben in Sachsen zur Reformationszeit. *Historische Anthropologie* 7, pp. 191–211.

Hofer, Roland 2000: Anabaptists in Seventeenth-Century Schleitheim: Popular Resistance to the Consolidation of State Power in the Early Modern Era. *Mennonite Quarterly Review* 74, pp. 123–144.

Holenstein, André 1996: *Bauern zwischen Bauernkrieg und Dreissigjährigem Krieg*. Oldenbourg, München.

Holenstein, André 2000: Die Umstände der Normen – die Normen der Umstände: Policeyordnungen im kommunikativen Handeln von Verwaltung und lokaler Gesellschaft im Ancien Régime. In *Policey und frühneuzeitliche Gesellschaft*, ed. Karl Härter. Klostermann, Frankfurt/M., pp. 1–46.

Jecker, Hanspeter 1998: *Ketzer – Rebellen – Heilige: Das Basler Täufertum von 1580–1700*. Verlag des Kantons Basel-Landschaft, Basel.

Konersmann, Frank 2000: Kirchenvisitation als landesherrliches Kontrollmittel und als Regulativ dörflicher Kommunikation: Das Herzogtum Pfalz-Zweibrücken im 16. und 17. Jahrhundert. In *Kriminalitätsgeschichte: Beiträge zur Sozial- und Kulturgeschichte der Vormoderne*, ed. Andreas Blauert and Gerd Schwerhoff. UVK, Konstanz, pp. 603–625.

Kästner, Alexander, Schwerhoff, Gerd 2013: Religiöse Devianz in alteuropäischen Stadtgemeinschaften: Eine Einführung in systematischer Absicht. In *Göttlicher Zorn und menschliches Maß: Religiöse Abweichung in frühneuzeitlichen Stadtgemeinschaften*, ed. Alexander Kästner and Gerd Schwerhoff. UVK: Konstanz, pp. 9–43.

Landwehr, Achim 2000: "Normdurchsetzung" in der Frühen Neuzeit? Kritik eines Begriffes. *Zeitschrift für Geschichtswissenschaft* 48, pp. 146–162.

Landwehr, Achim 2000: *Policey im Alltag: Die Implementation frühneuzeitlicher Policeyordnungen in Leonberg*. Klostermann, Frankfurt/M.

Landwehr, Achim 2000: Policey vor Ort: Die Implementation von Policeyordnungen in der ländlichen Gesellschaft der Frühen Neuzeit. In *Policey und frühneuzeitliche Gesellschaft*, ed. Karl Härter. Klostermann, Frankfurt/M., pp. 47–70.

Lang, Peter Thaddäus 1984: Reform im Wandel: Die katholischen Visitationsinterrogatorien des 16. und 17. Jahrhunderts. In *Kirche und Visitation: Beiträge zur Erforschung des frühneuzeitlichen Visitationswesens in Europa*, ed. Ernst Walter Zeeden and Peter Thaddäus Lang. Klett-Cotta, Stuttgart, pp. 131–190.

Lang, Peter Thaddäus 1987: Die Kirchenvisitationsakten des 16. Jahrhunderts und ihr Quellenwert. *Rottenburger Jahrbuch für Kirchengeschichte* 6, pp. 133–153.

Lang, Peter Thaddäus 1997: Die Erforschung der frühneuzeitlichen Kirchenvisitationen: Neuere Veröffentlichungen in Deutschland. *Rottenburger Jahrbuch für Kirchengeschichte* 16, pp. 185–193.

Ludwig, Ulrike 2008: *Das Herz der Justitia: Gestaltungspotentiale territorialer Herrschaft in der Strafrechts- und Gnadenpraxis am Beispiel Kursachsens 1548–1648*. UVK, Konstanz.

Mattern, Marlies 1998: *Leben im Abseits. Frauen und Männer im Täufertum (1525–1550): Eine Studie zur Alltagsgeschichte*. Peter Lang, Frankfurt/M.

Menne, Mareike 2007: *Herrschaftsstil und Glaubenspraxis: Bischöfliche Visitation und die Inszenierung von Herrschaft im Fürstbistum Paderborn 1654–1691*. Bonifatius, Paderborn.

Menne, Mareike 2009: Was bergen Visitationsakten? Kritische Überlegungen anhand der Visitationen im Fürstbistum Paderborn in der zweiten Hälfte des 17. Jahrhunderts. In *Bekenntnis, soziale Ordnung und rituelle Praxis: Neue Forschungen zu Reformation und Konfessionalisierung in Westfalen*, ed. Werner Freitag and Christian Helbich. Aschendorff, Münster, pp. 175–188.

Oyer, John S. 1997: Nicodemites Among Württemberg Anabaptists. *Mennonite Quarterly Review* 71, pp. 487–514.

Pettegree, Andrew 2005: *Reformation and the Culture of Persuasion*. Cambridge University Press, Cambridge.

Rublack, Ulinka 1997: Frühneuzeitliche staatliche und lokale Herrschaftspraxis in Württemberg. *Zeitschrift für Historische Forschung* 2, pp. 347–378.

Räisänen, Päivi 2011: *Ketzer im Dorf: Visitationsverfahren, Täuferbekämpfung und locale Handlungsmuster im frühneuzeitlichen Württemberg*. UVK, Konstanz.

Sabean, David W. 1984: *Power in the Blood: Popular Culture and Village Discourse in Early Modern Germany*. Cambridge University Press, Cambridge.

Sabean, David W. 1996: Soziale Distanzierungen: Ritualisierte Gestik in deutscher bürokratischer Prosa der Frühen Neuzeit. *Historische Anthropologie* 4, pp. 216–233.

Sabean, David W. 2001: Peasant Voices and Bureaucratic Texts: Narrative Structure in Early Modern German Protocols. In *Little Tools of Knowledge: Historical Essays on Academic and Bureaucratic Practices*, ed. Peter Becker and William Clark. University of Michigan Press, Ann Arbor, pp. 67–93.

Schilling, Heinz 1989: Sündenzucht und frühneuzeitliche Sozialdisziplinierung: Die calvinistische presbyterale Kirchenzucht in Emden vom 16. bis ins 19. Jahrhundert. In *Stände und Gesellschaft im Alten Reich*, ed. Georg Schmidt. Steiner, Wiesbaden, pp. 265–302.

Schlögl, Rudolf 2000: Bedingungen dörflicher Kommunikation: Gemeindliche Öffentlichkeit und Visitation im 16. Jahrhundert. In *Kommunikation in der ländlichen Gesellschaft vom Mittelalter bis zur Moderne*, ed. Werner Rösener. Vandenhoeck & Ruprecht, Göttingen, pp. 241–261.

Schmidt, Heinrich Richard 1989: Die Christianisierung des Sozialverhaltens als permanente Reformation: Aus der Praxis reformierter Sittengerichte in der Schweiz während der frühen Neuzeit. In *Kommunalisierung und Christianisierung: Voraussetzungen und Folgen der Reformation 1400–1600*, ed. Peter Blickle and Johannes Kunisch. Duncker & Humblot, Berlin, pp. 113–163.

Schmidt, Heinrich Richard 1992: *Konfessionalisierung im 16. Jahrhundert*. Oldenbourg, München.

Schmidt, Heinrich Richard 1995: *Dorf und Religion: Reformierte Sittenzucht in Berner Landgemeinden der Frühen Neuzeit*. Fischer, Stuttgart.

Schnabel-Schüle, Helga 1987: Kirchenleitung und Kirchenvisitation in den Territorien des deutschen Südwestens. In *Repertorium der Kirchenvisitationsakten aus dem 16. und 17. Jahrhundert in Archiven der Bundesrepublik Deutschland*, ed. Ernst Walter Zeeden. Klett-Cotta, Stuttgart, pp. 13–104.

Schnabel-Schüle, Helga 1997: Kirchenvisitationen und Landesvisitationen als Mittel der Kommunikation zwischen Herrscher und Untertanen. In *Im Spannungsfeld von Recht und Ritual: Soziale Kommunikation in Mittelalter und früher Neuzeit*, ed. Heinz Duchhardt and Gert Melville. Böhlau, Köln, pp. 173–186.

Schorn-Schütte, Luise 1996: *Evangelische Geistlichkeit in der Frühen Neuzeit: Deren Anteil an der Entfaltung frühmoderner Staatlichkeit und Gesellschaft, dargestellt am Beispiel des Fürstentums Braunschweig-Wolfenbüttel, der Landgrafschaft Hessen-Kassel und der Stadt Braunschweig*. Gütersloher Verlagshaus, Gütersloh.

Schorn-Schütte, Luise 2000: Priest, Preacher, Pastor: Research on Clerical Office in Early Modern Europe. *Central European History* 33, pp. 1–39.

Schwerhoff, Gerd 1991: *Köln im Kreuzverhör: Kriminalität, Herrschaft und Gesellschaft in einer frühneuzeitlichen Stadt*. Bouvier, Bonn.

Schwerhoff, Gerd 1999: *Aktenkundig und gerichtsnotorisch: Einführung in die Historische Kriminalitätsforschung*. Edition diskord, Tübingen.

Scribner, Robert W. 1987: Police and Territorial State in Sixteenth-Century Württemberg. In *Politics and Society in Reformation Europe*, ed. E. I. Kouri and Tom Scott. Macmillan, Basingstoke, pp. 103–120.

Scribner, Robert W. 1988: Mobility: Voluntary or enforced? Vagrants in Württemberg in the Sixteenth Century. In *Migration in der Feudalgesellschaft*, ed. Gerhard Jaritz and Albert Müller. Campus, Frankfurt/M., pp. 65–89.

Scribner, Robert W. 1997: Wie wird man Außenseiter? Ein- und Ausgrenzung im frühneuzeitlichen Deutschland. In *Aussenseiter zwischen Mittelalter und Neuzeit*, ed. Marion Kobelt-Groch and Norbert Fischer. Brill, Leiden, pp. 21–46.

Scribner, Robert W. 2001: Pastoral Care and the Reformation in Germany. In *Religion and Culture in Germany (1400–1800)*, ed. Robert W. Scribner and Lyndal Roper. Brill, Leiden, pp. 172–194.

Simon-Muscheid, Katharina 2000: Täter, Opfer und Komplizinnen – Geschlechtsspezifische Strategien und Loyalitäten im Basler "Morrthandel" von 1522. In *Kriminalitätsgeschichte: Beiträge zur Sozial- und Kulturgeschichte der Vormoderne*, ed. Andreas Blauert and Gerd Schwerhoff. UVK, Konstanz, pp. 649–667.

Simon-Muscheid, Katharina, Christian Simon 1996: Zur Lektüre von Gerichtstexten: Fiktionale Realität oder Alltag in Gerichtsquellen?. In *Arbeit – Liebe – Streit: Texte zur Geschichte des Geschlechterverhältnisses und des Alltags, 15. bis 18. Jahrhundert*, ed. Dorothee Rippmann, Katharina Simon-Muscheid and Christian Simon. Verlag des Kantons Basel-Landschaft, Basel, pp. 17–39.

Strauss, Gerald 1978: *Luther's House of Learning: Indoctrination of the Young in the German*

Reformation. Johns Hopkins University Press, Baltimore & London.
Tolley, Bruce 1995: *Pastors and Parishioners in Württemberg During the Late Reformation 1581–1621*. Stanford University Press, Stanford.
Wahl, Johannes 2000: *Lebensplanung und Alltagserfahrung: Württembergische Pfarrfamilien im 17. Jahrhundert*. Zabern, Mainz.
Wegert, Karl 1994: Popular Culture, Crime and Social Control in 18th-century Württemberg. Steiner, Stuttgart.

An Arrogant Arrendator and Conflict in Church Renovations in the Mid-Eighteenth-Century Parish of Kokemäki

Ella Viitaniemi

During the Kokemäki district court sessions of October 1746, *arrendator*[1] Simon Stengrund summoned the rural dean and vicar of Kokemäki, Nicolaus Tolpo. Stengrund was concerned that the rural dean had allowed two pews to be removed from the church choir. This had happened when Kokemäki church was undergoing construction work and new galleries were built inside the church and the pews were subsequently reorganized.[2] According to Stengrund, these removed pews had belonged to the manor of Kokemäki, the greatest manor in the parish. As the tenant of Kokemäki manor, Stengrund complained that Tolpo had let others build new benches for themselves close to the choir. Stengrund now demanded that these places be returned to him. Tolpo responded to Stengrund's accusations stating that the manor of Kokemäki had *never* owned pews in the church. To support this assertion, he presented the church pew order from 1654. However, in the new pew order, compiled on 4 October 1746,

---

1   *Arrendator* (Swedish) = the lessee of a manor (English).
2   Turun maakunta-arkisto (TMA). Turun arkkihiippakunnan tuomiokapitulin arkisto [The Archives of the Archdiocese of Turku, Provincial archives of Turku], Tuomiokapitulin kirjekirja B I: 15. The Cathedral Chapter of Turku to Rural Dean Tolpo 10.9.1746. The parish employed a building master and also engaged the services of the glazier. The church archives of Kokemäki. Laskuja sekalaisia, kirkkoa ja pappilaa varten 1835–55. Inventaario 14.4.1746.

about three weeks before the rural dean's court appearance, the manor had been allocated sixteen places, most of which were reserved for the crofters of the manor. Therefore, the manor of Kokemäki had not been left without pews.[3] It seems, however, that the new location of bench of the manor did not meet with Stengrund's approval.

This article discusses the forms of social control in church renovations in the 1750´s in Western Finland, at Kokemäki parish. The court case between *arrendator* Stengrund and rural dean Tolpo led to further disagreements about rights and responsibilities for repairing the church and the vicarage. In these conflicts, my focus is on Simon Stengrund and his activities and status in the local political community. His actions and conflicts open the possibility of closely observing the local community and the formation of its political culture. In this article I discuss social control from three aspects: pew order, church building and vicarage building. First of all, the pew order concerns local social hierarchy and status. Actually, the pew procedure itself manifested social control. Secondly, I discuss the building and the maintenance obligations of the parish. Maintaining the church and the vicarage was one of the main tasks of the parish. This brings us to the questions of the use of resources and economic obligations at the local level. There were certain mechanisms, laws and practices, which regulated and controlled church pews, renovations, and building projects. Still, Stengrund´s actions did not follow general standards or ideals.

In this article I try to gauge Simon Stengrund´s significance and the role that he played within the local community.[4] He was a transient figure in Kokemäki, but it seems that he might also have been a venturesome leader in the local political scene. He himself as a lessee of a manor did not fit to the standard of the social structure and the estate system. Hence, he challenged the basic forms of social control by

---

3 National Archives, Helsinki (KA). Vehmaan ja Ala-Satakunnan tuomiokunnan renovoidut tuomiokirjat [Transcribed court records of the Vehmaa and Ala-Satakunta jurisdiction] II KO a:55, Varsinaisten asioiden pöytäkirjat 1746–1746. The district court sessions of Kokemäki 29–31.10.1746. f. 794–794v. The exact date is not mentioned.

4 Giovanni Levi, *Aineeton perintö, Manaajapappi ja talonpoikaisyhteisö 1600-luvun Italiassa* (*L´eredità immateriale, Carriera di un esorcista nel Piemonte del Seicento*, trans. Kaisa Kinnunen and Elina Suolahti, Helsinki, 1992) p. 145.

his actions and the conflicts with the rural dean. Stengrund tested and stretched the limits of the church and consistorial discipline, community supervision and local political practices.[5] By making a closer observation of Stengrund's case, some features of the forms and limits of social control and the possibilities of local political culture could be revealed.[6]

Who was tenant Stengrund?[7]

I first became aware of this *arrendator*, a lessee of the Kokemäki manor, when reading the letters of Cathedral Chapter of Turku to governor Ehrenmalm. In them, I read that, some individuals, lessees and stewards, who did not own any real property at the Kokemäki parish, disrupted the church renovation and even encouraged others not to participate in the repair work.[8] I started to wonder, who were these men, who did not own any land in the parish, and yet had a strong influence on the local political culture. This became a clue, which I started to follow. I studied the court records and the taxation and church registers using the methods characteristic to micro history.[9]

---

5 Pieter, Spierenburg, Social Control and history: An Introduction. *Social control in Europe Volume 1, 1500–1800*, ed. Herman Roodenburg and Pieter Spierenburg (Ohio, 2004), pp.1–22.

6 Carlo Ginzburg, "Microhistory: Two or three things that I know about it." Critical Inquiry. Vol. 20. No. 1. (Autumn 1993), pp. 10–35.

7 See the appendix "The main connections of Simon Stengrund to the Kokemäki parish through the Polviander family".

8 TMA. Tuomiokapitulin kirjekirja B I: 15. The Cathedral Chapter of Turku to Governor Ehrenmalm and to Rural Dean Tolpo 19.3.1746. About the church discipline and the concept of social control, see Pieter, Spierenburg, *Social Control and history*, pp. 11–14.

9 For example, Giovanni Levi wrote a microhistorical study of the family of *Chiesa*, who gathered social networks and authority rather than land property. Giovanni Levi, *Aineeton perintö*, 1992. In Finland Matti Peltonen has lately written, on the contrary, about a grasping social climber, the parish clerk Saxberg: Matti Peltonen, *Lukkari Saxbergin rikos ja herännäispappilan etiikka, Mikrohistoriallinen tutkimus 1800-luvun puolivälin Keuruulta* (Helsinki, 2006). Kimmo Katajala has studied peasant revolts and through these studies he has also written about tenants and stewards, especially in Kimmo Katajala, *Säätyläisiä ja nousukkaita, Veronvuokraus osana Käkisalmen läänin sääty-yhteisöä vuosina 1683–1700* (Joensuu, 1990). An interesting micro historical study of a peculiar shoemaker, who was active in local political culture, even though he did not get the vote: Sami Suodenjoki, Kuriton suutari ja kiistämisen rajat. Työväenliikkeen läpimurto hämäläisessä maalaisyhteisössä 1899–1909. SKS. Bibliotheca Historica 129. Helsinki 2012 [Unruly shoemaker and the limits of contestation. Breaktrough of labour movement in a Finnis rural community, 1899–1909]. As a theoretical basis for *political culture* I largely draw upon the ideas of Nils Erik Villstrand, for example in Nils Erik Villstrand, "Från morgonstjärna till memorial: Politisk kultur i det svenska riket 1500–1800" *Sphinx*. Societas Scientiarum Fennica, Vuosikirja 2004–2005 (2005).

Who was this Stengrund, who had taken up the best seat in the chancel? Where did he come from? Simon Stengrund did not own any land, nor did he hold any offices in Kokemäki. This, along with the fact that he changed his surname, makes piecing together the details of his life somewhat challenging. He moved a number of times and so source material that mentions him is dispersed between different parishes. Still, when studying the fragile sources, the structure of complicated connections and family relations at the local community started to surface.[10] Hence, closer observation revealed his connections to the clergy and civil servants networks of the Satakunta area.

It seems that Simon Stengrund was born on 25 November 1708 in the parish of Pirkkala. His parents were Martin (Mårten) Stenius (c. 1670–1717), the parish assistant of Pirkkala, and Kristina Simonsdotter Polviander.[11] Both families, Stenius and Polviander were well represented and networked in the priesthood of Satakunta. His grandfather, Iisak Stenius had been the vicar of Pirkkala. However, his son did not enjoy a particularly glorious career. Towards the end of his life in 1713 Martin became the chaplain of Ulvila parish, during the hard period of occupation.[12] The Stenius family lived in Tuorsniemi (in Ulvila parish) at Liinaharja/Pappila farm, which was inherited from his grandmother Katarina Arctopolitanus.[13] Simon's mother, Kristina Polviander, continued to live in Tuorsniemi until 1753.[14]

Simon Stengrund studied at the Trivial School in Pori town along with his elder brother Jakob and younger brother Martin, immediately after the school re-opened following the Great Wrath of 1722.[15] Still, Simon did not ascend to academic education as his elder brother, father

---

10 Carlo Ginzburg, "Microhistory: Two or three things that I know about it", p. 33.
11 HMA. The church archives of Pirkkala. I C:1. Syntyneiden ja kastettujen luettelo 1702–1729.
12 Yrjö Kotivuori, *Ylioppilasmatrikkeli 1640–1852: Mårten Stenius*. Verkkojulkaisu 2005, www.helsinki.fi/ylioppilasmatrikkeli/henkilo.php?id=3706 (accessed 29 January 2013). Virkkala, Kopisto and Lehtinen, *Suur-Ulvilan historia I*, p. 297.
13 The Lutiska farm was attached to the office of chaplain, but the Stenius family did not live at there. With the death of Martin Stenius and the harsh conditions of occupation the Lutiska farm fell into disrepair. Ibid. pp. 334, 655.
14 TMA. Porin kaupunki- ja maaseurakunnan arkisto. I C1:3. Kaupunkiseurakunnan kuolleiden ja haudattujen luettelot 1732–1777.
15 Kaarlo Jäntere, *Porin triviaalikoulun oppilasluettelot 1722, 1733, 1737 ja oppilasmatrikkeli 1738–1842* (Helsinki, 1926), pp. 3–4.

and grandfather had done.[16] Perhaps because Kristina had been a widow since 1717, the family may not have had the resources to provide of all of her sons with an education, or perhaps Simon was simply not sufficiently interested in studying. Becoming a steward or a manorial lessee was a good choice for the son of chaplain.[17] In order to distance himself from his clergy family, Simon changed his surname from Stenius to Stengrund.[18]

Simon Stengrund became arrendator of Kokemäki manor in 1736 and he stayed in the parish until at least 1751.[19] After the death of his mother, Simon returned to the family´s farm Tuorsniemi.[20] But why did Stengrund move to Kokemäki in the first place? Stengrund was clearly drawn by the attractive opportunity to rent the Kokemäki manor, but he also had connections and relatives in the parish through his mother Kristina. Her father, Simon Marci Polviander, was a parish assistant in Kokemäki and the chaplain before he was appointed to the vicar of Ikaalinen in 1689. However, the family retained its connections with Kokemäki. Anders Polviander, Simon Stengrund's uncle, continued in

---

16 Simon Stengrund is not mentioned in the list of university students of Finland, unlike his father, grandfather, father-in-law and brothers. Helsingin yliopiston Ylioppilasmatrikkeli 1640–1852. Stengrund is referred to as *leutenant* in the church record books of the 1760s. TMA. The church archives of Kokemäki. I Aa:3. Kokemäen emäseurakunnan Rippikirja 1752–1758. However, there is no mention of Stengrund in the register of the Finnish officers. Kaarlo Wirilander, *Suomen armeijan upseeristo ja aliupseeristo 1718–1810, Virkatalonhaltijain luettelot* (Helsinki, 1953). Stengrund's brother Jakob Stenius (1704–1766) became a vicar and also a well-known economic thinker, who focused on the development of agriculture. He is known in Finnish historical writings by his nickname Korpi-Jaakko. Yrjö Kotivuori *Ylioppilasmatrikkeli 1640–1852: Jakob Stenius (sr)*. Verkkojulkaisu 2005, www.helsinki.fi/ylioppilasmatrikkeli/henkilo.php?id=5422 (accessed 29 January 2013). His son Jacob Stenius jr. (1732–1809) was also a vicar, a practical leader of the rapid-clearing projects and was later appointed a docent of the Academy of Turku. He is referred to as Koski-Jaakko. Both father and son followed the philosophy of the enlightenment. Yrjö Kotivuori, *Ylioppilasmatrikkeli 1640–1852: Jakob Stenius (jr)*. Verkkojulkaisu 2005, www.helsinki.fi/ylioppilasmatrikkeli/henkilo.php?id=10679 (accessed 29 January 2013).
17 Katajala, *Säätyläisiä ja nousukkaita*, p. 82.
18 Wirilander, *Herrasväkeä: Suomen säätyläistö 1721–1870* (Helsinki, 1974), p. 375.
19 Turun ja Porin lääninhallituksen lääninkonttorin arkisto. Tilitositteet 1736, I Gac 59: 2395. (Ala-Satakunnan henkikirja 1736) Tuula Hockman and Tapio Salminen, *Kokemäen ja Harjavallan talonhaltijat vuoteen 1900, torpat 1891–1900 sekä papisto ennen vuotta 1870*, Kokemäen ja Harjavallan historia I:2 (Jyväskylä, 2007), p. 32.
20 Yrjö Kotivuori, *Ylioppilasmatrikkeli 1640–1852: Mårten Stenius*. Verkkojulkaisu 2005, www.helsinki.fi/ylioppilasmatrikkeli/henkilo.php?id=3706 (accessed 30 January 2013). TMA, Porin kaupunki- ja maaseurakunnan arkisto, I C1:3 Syntyneiden ja kastettujen luettelo 1732–1777. Simon Stengrund and Brita Jul. Novandra had a daughter Brita Catharina on 1 March 1757 at Tuorsniemi.

his father's footsteps and was nominated as chaplain of Harjavalta (in Kokemäki parish) in 1722.[21]

However, Anders Polviander fell out with Tolpo, shortly after the latter's appointment as vicar. Problems between the two arose within the first year of Tolpo's arrival. One of their first conflicts concerned a proposal put forward by Polviander that he should be released from sermon duty every fourth Sunday or holy day. The situation had become so dire that the rural dean and an outside pastor were needed to resolve the problems between Polviander and Tolpo. At this point Polviander promised to respect and obey the vicar, and Tolpo promised to act in a spirit of friendship towards his chaplain.[22] However, it seems that this reconciliation did not last long; new conflicts erupted between these two colourful characters. In the end, Anders Polviander was removed from office in 1737, on the grounds that he had been under the influence of alcohol whilst performing official duties.[23]

The dispute between Tolpo and Polviander was in its last stages when Simon Stengrund became the tenant of the Kokemäki manor, by 1736 at the latest.[24] Therefore, Stengrund's position may have been quite challenging from the outset. Tolpo, and even his parishioners, might have been irritated that the nephew of the drunken chaplain had decided that the first place in the church was his by right in his capacity as tenant of the greatest manor. When Tolpo and Stengrund came before the district court sessions in 1746, Anders Polviander had already been dead for three years. However, this negative connection might still have had an effect on their later actions and reactions.

Further reading of the court minutes reveals other arguments not only between Stengrund and Tolpo, but also with steward Thure Belin, who had been steward (ombudsman) of the Forsby estate in Kokemäki

---

21 Another uncle, Johannes Polviander was the vicar of Kokemäki parish in 1718/22–1729 and Tolpo was his successor. Hockman and Salminen, *Kokemäen ja Harjavallan talonhaltijat...*, pp. 137, 144–146.
22 TMA. Turun arkkihiippakunnan tuomiokapitulin arkisto. E VI:1. Porin ylä- ja ala- sekä Tyrvään rovastikuntia ja niihin kuuluvia seurakuntia koskevia asiakirjoja. The Rural Dean's visit to Kokemäki 16.1.1732.
23 Hockman and Salminen, *Kokemäen ja Harjavallan talonhaltijat*, p. 146. After he promised to give up drinking, Anders Polviander was allowed to apply for other positions. In 1741 he was nominated as the vicar of Hämeenlinna, where he died in 1743.
24 Turun ja Porin lääninhallituksen lääninkonttorin arkisto. Tilitositteet 1736, I Gac 59: 2395.

since 1731.[25] Kin networks were important for tenants and stewards; such networks strengthened the positions of tenants in the community.[26] Thure (Johan) Belin and Stengrund were related by marriage: Belin's first wife, Christina Stenia, was also part of the Stenius family. Furthermore it seems that Margareta Henriksdotter Wegelius, Belin's second wife was a cousin of Stengrund and the niece of Anders Polviander.[27] Belin, who was born in 1687, was older than Stengrund and had worked and lived in Kokemäki parish for longer than the arrendator. This made him a valuable ally.[28]

Controlled church pew order

The question of pew order was extremely important at the early modern society. Actually, the pew procedure itself manifested social control. Each church had a pew order, and in principle every parishioner had to be allocated a place in the church. People were seated in churches according to their gender, estate and status. The most coveted pews were those closest to the choir and the pulpit. This was where Stengrund wished to sit. Men sat on the south side of the main aisle and women on the north side, mirroring the seat allocation, and thus the status, of their fathers or husbands. The local estate and its officers sat in the first rows in their finer pews. The servants and the stewards of estates would sit behind them. Amongst the peasantry, those farms that supplied the cavalry sat first. Behind these favoured pews, places were allocated according to village and farm. Soldiers, craftsmen and other landless people sat to the rear of the church hall or in the galleries, if there were places left. The church pew order was an excellent instrument of social control and

---

25 VA 7492:3092. Tositekirja 1731–1731. At this time, Count Sigfrid De la Gardie owned Forsby.
26 Katajala, *Säätyläisiä ja nousukkaita*, pp. 51–52, 80–81.
27 The identity of Thure Johan Belin is questioned in Genos, 1 (1943), p. 41. Because of Belin's social status and occupation, it is difficult to find exact information about his or his wives' backgrounds. Levi, *Aineeton perintö*, p. 145.
28 Thure Belin died in the Harjavalta chapel at the Simula rustholl in 1760 at the age of 73. This was the same rustholl that had previously been owned by Tolpo. TMA. The church archives of Harjavalta. I C:1. Kuolleiden luettelo 1731–1793.

expressed the status of individuals within the community.[29] Pew order made it easy, for example, to control church attendance: absence from church was clearly visible when a place remained unfilled. However, the strict allocation system could not satisfy everybody and arguments were quite common.[30]

The district court session sided with Tolpo after revision of the pew order. The court pointed out that decision-making power in this matter lay with the parish council (*Kyrckio Råd*), according to the privilege of the clergy estate (passed in 1723).[31] Before compiling the new church order, Tolpo had sought permission from the chapter. The chapter sent a proxy, one of the vicars from the area, Kristian Wellin (the vicar of Köyliö parish)[32] to oversee the reordering. In fact according to church law (1686) the order should have been updated each year and the dean and the bishop should have reviewed the changes.[33] However, the pew order was not re-written annually in Kokemäki.

Disputes about church pew order were to be settled in the first instance at parish meetings or during the dean's visits. Any cases that could not be resolved at a parish level could be brought before the district court.[34] As well as being the vicar of Kokemäki, Tolpo was also the

---

29 Annika Sandén, "Kyrkan, kvinnorna och hiearkiernas dynamik", Historiks tidskrift 4 (2006), p. 649; Pentti Laasonen, *Suomen kirkon historia 2, Vuodet 1593–1808* (Porvoo, 1991), p. 67.
30 For example Olle Larsson, *Biskopen visiterar, Den kyrkliga överhetens möte med lokalsamhället 1650–1750* (Växjö, 1999), pp. 154–160.
31 KA. Vehmaan ja Ala-Satakunnan tuomiokunnan renovoidut tuomiokirjat. II KO a:55. Varsinaisten asioiden pöytäkirjat 1746–1746. The district court sessions of Kokemäki 29–31.10.1746. f. 794v.
Within the privilege of the clergy *estate* it was mentioned that the parish meeting was a place in which matters could be raised which were punishable under the (secular) law. 16.10.1723. Privilegia för Biskoppar och samtelige Prästerkapet i Swerige och des underliggande landskaper. R.G. Modée, *Utdrag Utur alle ifrån 7. Decemb. 1718 utkomne Publique handlingar, Placater, Förordningar, Resolutioner och Publicationer, Riksens Styrseld samt inwärtes Hushållning och Författningar i gemen, jemwäl ock Stockholms Stad i synnerhet angå, I delen* (Stockholm, 1742).
32 TMA. Turun arkkihiippakunnan tuomiokapitulin arkisto. Tuomiokapitulin kirjekirja B I: 15. The Cathedral Chapter of Turku to Governor Ehrenmalm and to Rural Dean Tolpo 10.9.1746. Later in 1786, when the new stone church was built, a new pew order was also needed. Vicar Avellan asked permission for the new order from the chapter of Turku. The chapter appointed the vicar of Köyliö, Martin Tolpo, to compile the order. TMA. Turun arkkihiippakunnan tuomiokapitulin arkisto. Tuomiokapitulin kirjekirja B I: 53. The Cathedral Chapter of Turku to Vicar Avellan and to Vicar M. Tolpo 23.8.1786. TMA. Turun tuomiokapitulin pöytäkirjat A I: 18. Turun tuomiokapitulin pöytäkirja 23.8.1786.
33 *Kircko-Laki ja Ordningi 1686*. Luku XXIV § VIII:4, Näköispainos ja uudelleen ladottu laitos vuoden 1686 kirkkolain suomennoksesta, ed. Hellemaa, Jussila, Parvio (Helsinki, 1986).
34 *Kircko-Laki ja Ordningi 1686*. Luku XXIV § VIII:4. For example, during the visit the rural dean's visit on 16 January 1734 some church pew questions were raised, after they had first been dealt with in

rural dean of the area (including his own parish). Because it seemed unlikely that the conflict between Stengrund and Tolpo could be resolved, Stengrund had no option but to bring the case to the attention of the court.

Church pew order was quite an inflexible institution, resting as it did on estate distinctions. The pew procedure could not respond to changes within the community, especially the strong population growth of the late eighteenth century. Therefore changes in land ownership – such as the emergence of tenants and the increasing number of poor non-landowners during the eighteenth century – were problematic for the church. It was difficult to point out the farm or household to which these people belonged, and this problem surfaced in the church pew order. A tenant was not the equal of the real owner of the manor. He and his family could be seen as social climbers and newcomers. Hence, the arrendator could not outstrip the old land owning families of the parish.

Stengrund was a member of a new kind of gentry. During the eighteenth century, a new social group emerged between the nobility and clergy. This new middle class included individuals who did not have a noble background. Underpinning the emergence of this new gentry were population growth, the development of educational opportunities and openings within the military. The new social group included scholars, doctors, lawyers, civil servants, factory owners, and, of course, tenants. Their social and economic status was close to that of the three highest estates but they did not enjoy political rights in the Diet. Still, by the middle of the eighteenth century this new gentry had become a larger group than the nobility and clergy combined. Members of this class not only struggled with the pew order institution, which rested on the old estate system, but also faced problems when settling in society.[35] Nevertheless, at a local level these men could interact and participate in decision making if they owned or rented land, as Stengrund did.

the parish meeting. The rural dean's visit is noted in the minutes for 16 January 1732. TMA. Turun arkkihiippakunnan tuomiokapitulin arkisto. E VI:I. Porin Ylä- ja Ala sekä Tyrvään rovastikuntia ja niihin kuuluvia seurakuntia koskevia asiakirjoja.

35 Petri Karonen, *Pohjoinen suurvalta, Ruotsi ja Suomi 1521–1809* (2nd edn., Helsinki, 2001), pp. 361–362, 394–397. Pieter Spierenburg, *Social control and History*, p. 15.

The reason why the real owners of the greatest manor in Kokemäki parish had no named pews in the parish church is very simple.[36] Before Major Knorring in the 1770s no owners ever lived in the parish. Arvid Forbus, a baron and general, was owner of the manor when the first pew order was compiled. Later, the manor became the property of Axel Julius De la Gardie and his heirs.[37] As none of them had lived in the parish, there had been no need for them to be allocated permanent places in the parish church. If any of them had visited the parish, they would have temporarily been given the very best seat near the chancel.

We do not know exactly how Stengrund's case was resolved.[38] However, we do know that the problem of church pew allocation for Kokemäki manor remained more or less unresolved in the spring of 1763, when the then owner of the manor, Major Frans Henrik von Knorring, required benches for his family and his officers after their return from the War of Pommer (1757–1762).[39] Knorring had bought the Kokemäki manor in 1755, and now finally the owner of the manor lived in the parish.[40] The parish vicar at the time, Gottleben, had to admit that there were no church places available. The lack of space in the cramped church was one of the reasons why the vicar proposed the construction of a new church building. However, building work was delayed, and as a temporary solution to the problem, a new pew order was compiled in 1764. Now Knorring and his officers sat in the first rows and other parishioners were seated behind them.[41] These changes resulted in a number of complaints.

As the latest owner of Kokemäki manor, Major Knorring clearly had the leading status in the parish. Officers, civil servants and major landowners often exerted significant influence, which they used to forward

---

36 TMA. The church archives of Kokemäki. II Ba:1. Kokemäen pitäjän kirkonkirja 1630–1784. The church pew order of Kokemäki church 23.1.1652 and 1.5.1654.
37 Tuula Hockman and Tapio Salminen, *Kokemäen ja Harjavallan talonhaltijat vuoteen 1900, torpat 1891–1900 sekä papisto ennen vuotta 1870* (Kokemäen ja Harjavallan historia I:2; Jyväskylä, 2007), p. 32; Tapio Salminen, *Joki ja sen väki. Kokemäen ja Harjavallan historia jääkaudesta 1860-luvulle* (Jyväskylä, 2007), p. 288.
38 The church pew order from the year 1746 has not survived to our days.
39 Karonen, *Pohjoinen suurvalta*, p. 398.
40 Knorring bought the manor from Ebba Margaretha De la Gardie. The manor cost 20 000 *daler kopparmynt*. Johan Adolf Lindström, "Kumo socken uti historisk hänseende", *Suomi, Tidskrift i fosterländska ämnen 1860* (Helsingfors, 1862), pp. 246–247.
41 TMA. The church archives of Kokemäki. II:Ca:1. Pitäjänkokousten pöytäkirjat 1760–1805. The parish meeting minutes of Kokemäki 17.4.1763 and 24.8.1764.

various initiatives in local politics. Major Knorring, for example, signed the earliest surviving parish meeting minutes and took an active part in the church-building project.[42] Knorring was the most significant landowner in the parish and enjoyed a high social and economic status, all of which cemented his importance and influence in the local political culture and, specifically, in parish meetings.[43] However, the position of arrendator Stengrund had been very different. Stengrund seems to have had a more informal role, and although he seems to have been very active within the parish, he also clashed with the vicar.

Church building responsibilities and social control

The church pew order was not the only problem or argument that surfaced in these district court sessions. Stengrund continued to argue with Tolpo. He, together with steward (*inspektor*) Thure Belin, accused Tolpo of lodging a complaint against them with the Cathedral Chapter of Turku. Tolpo had blamed Stengrund and Belin for disrupting the church renovation and even encouraging others not to participate in the repair work.[44]

The wooden church of Kokemäki was in great need of repair in the 1750s. The church had been rebuilt circa 1640, after the original building had been destroyed in a fire. The current church had survived the Russian occupation during the Great Wrath (1714–1721), when some churches had been destroyed or pillaged; consequently many had fallen into decay. The church of Kokemäki was spared severe vandalism, but simple lack of resources had resulted in the church becoming dilapidated.[45] In 1720, towards the end of the war, Stockholm issued a resolution

---

42 TMA. The church archives of Kokemäki. II:Ca:1. Pitäjänkokousten pöytäkirjat 1760–1805. The parish meeting minutes of Kokemäki 1760–1784.
43 K. H. Johansson, *Svensk Sockensjälvstyrelse 1686–1862: Studier särkilt med hänsyn till Linköpings stift* (Lund, 1937), pp. 42, 105, 106; Pär Frohnert, *Administration i Sverige under frihetstiden in Administrasjon i Norden på 1700-talet* (Oslo, 1985), p. 239.
44 KA. Vehmaan ja Ala-Satakunnan tuomiokirjat. II KO a:55. Varsinaisten asioiden pöytäkirjat 1746–1746. The district court sessions of Kokemäki 29–31.10.1746, f. 795–796.
45 Suomen kirkot ja kirkkotaide 1, ed. Markku Haapio (Lieto, 1978), p. 59. Tapio Salminen, *Joki ja sen väki*, p. 459. The windows of the church and the floor of the sacristy were replaced in 1715 and the armoury in 1718. These repairs may have been necessary because of vandalism by the occupiers. Parishioners later described in the district court sessions how the church had fallen into disrepair during the occupation

that general collections should be made for the burned and destroyed churches, hospitals and schools. A special resolution concerning Finland was issued in 1723.[46] According to these regulations, national collections should be made available to parishes in order that existing churches could be repaired and, where necessary, new churches built. However, times had been hard since the occupation, and parishes lacked building materials and skilled workmen.[47] Furthermore, local political life had to be reorganized before the public building resolution could be implemented.[48] The parish of Kokemäki began by repairing the roof of its church. Although in 1732 Kokemäki received money to build a new church,[49] the parish was not yet ready to undertake the construction work.

The church survived a further period of occupation (1742–1743). Luckily Kokemäki parish was able to retain its building fund. After the second occupation, discussions and renewed attempts to help Finland resumed, and the process of repairing local churches began once again.[50] The parishioners of Kokemäki chose to continue to hold over the new building project. Although a new church was needed to replace the old

---

despite their attempts to maintain it. KA. Vehmaan ja Ala-Satakunnan tuomiokirjat 1732. II KO a:39. Varsinaisten asioiden pöytäkirjat 1732–1732. The district court sessions of Kokemäki 17.2.1732, f. 116–117.

46 Den 14. Jun. 1720 Resolution uppå Prästeskapets Beswär and Den 17. Sep. 1723 Resolution och förklaring öfwer samtel. Almogens i Swerige och Finland Almänne Beswär på 1723 åhr Riksdag. Modée, *Utdrag utur alle ifrån den 7. Dec. 1718 utkomne Publique*, pp. 185, 186, 371.

47 For example, it was ten years before work could begin on the Chapel Church of Renko. The construction work took at least seven years (1730–1737) to complete, even though the church was a modest and simply constructed wooden chapel. Markus Hiekkanen, *Rengon historia, Esihistoria ja Kirkon historia* (Jyväskylä, 1993), p. 97.

48 The practices of local decision making and the local political culture have been studied by many Swedish historians (among others). The late 1980s and early to mid-1990s was a particularly intensive period in which many such studies were undertaken. Harald Gustafsson, *Sockenstugans politiska kultur, Lokal självstyre på 1800-talets landsbygd* (Stockholm, 1989); Harald Gustafsson, *Political Interaction in the Old Regime: Central Power and Local Society in the Eighteenh-Century Nordic States* (Lund, 1994); Peter Aronsson, *Bönder gör politik: Det lokala självstyret som social arena i tre smålandssocknar, 1680–1850* (Lund, 1992); Alberto Tiscornia, *Statens, godsens eller böndernas socknar?: Den sockenkommunala självstyrelsens utveckling i Västerfärnebo, Stora Malm och Jäder 1800–1880* (Uppsala, 1992); Carin Bergström, *Lantprästen: Prästens funktion i det agrara samhället 1720–1800*. Oland-Frösåkers kontrakt av ärkestiftet (Stockholm, 1991). Eva Österberg has written various articles on the subject, including "Svenska lokalsamhälle i förändring ca.1550–1850", *Historisk Tidskrift*, 3 (1987), pp. 321–340; and "Bönder och centralmakt idet tidigmoderna Sverige. Konflikt – kompromiss – politisk kultur" *Scandia*, 55/1 (1989), pp. 73–95.

49 TMA. Turun arkkihiippakunnan tuomiokapitulin arkisto. EI:4. Kuninkaalliset, keisarilliset, senaatin ja valtioneuvoston kirjeet 1713–1732. King Fredrik to the Cathedral Chapter of Turku 12.6.1732. The church archives of Kokemäki. Laskuja sekalaisia, kirkkoa ja pappilaa varten 1835–1855. Inventaario 14.4.1746.

50 Salminen, *Joki ja sen väki*, pp. 537–538. Karonen, *Pohjoinen suurvalta*, p. 394–397.

and cramped existing building, it seems likely that parishioners were unwilling to invest heavily so soon after the occupation and its attendant hardships. The peasants' behaviour seems to have had its roots in understandable risk avoidance. According to Scott, the actions of peasantry were driven by the need to secure their own subsistence above all else.[51] This seems to be the case also in Kokemäki. As a result, instead of building a new church, the old church was repaired. However, even the repairs were resisted by some of the parish men and the credibility and the *honour* of the rural dean´s author was challenged.[52]

In the spring of 1746 Tolpo wrote to the Chapter of Turku. He complained that members of the congregation "who did not own any property", seemingly manorial lessees and stewards, had refused to participate in the repair work and exhorted others (peasants) not to provide the materials requested by the building master. The chapter forwarded the complaint to the governor's office, for civil servant (*krono betienten*) to take care of this matter.[53] It was all that the chapter could actually do. Nevertheless, Tolpo defended himself against Stengrund and Belin in court. Tolpo explained that he had not mentioned any names in his letters to the chapter. In Tolpo's view Stengrund and Belin's accusation was motivated by envy and malice. He also believed that they might be trying to sidestep any possible fines. He tried to convince the court that he was referring to "his own lessees" (*"arrendatorer"*) in the parish rather than to the plaintiffs.[54] In this context he may have used *arrendatorer* to refer to the *landbönder*, or tenant, who cultivated his farms within the parish. Simula cavalry estate saw a rapid turnover of farm tenants,[55] a num-

---

51 James C. Scott, *The Moral Economy of the Peasant: Rebellion and Subsistence in Southeast Asia* (Yale, 1976), pp. 4–5. About the usefulness of Scott´s ideas, see, for example, Michel J. Patric and John Walter, *Negotiating power in early modern society. Order, hierarchy and Subordination in Britain and Ireland* (Cambridge 2001), Introduction. This theory has been used in peasant studies in Scandinavia, see, for example, Nils Erik Villstrand, *Anpassining eller protest: Lokalsamhället inför utskriviningar av fotfolk till den svenska krigsmakten 1620–1676* (Åbo, 1992), pp. 7–9; Martin Linde, *Statsmakt och bondemotstånd: Allmoge och överhet under stora nordiska kriget* (Uppsala, 2000), pp. 18–19.
52 Pieter Spierenburg, *Social control and History*, p. 17.
53 TMA. Tuomiokapitulin kirjekirja B I: 15. The Cathedral Chapter of Turku to Governor Ehrenmalm and to Rural Dean Tolpo 19.3.1746.
54 KA. Vehmaan ja Ala-Satakunnan tuomiokirjat. II KO a:55. Varsinaisten asioiden pöytäkirjat 1746–1746. The district court sessions of Kokemäki 29–31.10.1746, f. 795–796.
55 Hockman and Salminen, *Kokemäen ja Harjavallan talonhaltijat*, p. 91.

ber of whom were involved in court cases during the 1740s.[56] Within the court records no farm tenants was ever referred to as an *arrendator*. They came from a peasant background and were called *landbönder*. Tolpo's defence in court is somewhat unclear.

However, the district court found nothing insulting in Tolpo's letter. It ruled that Stengrund and Belin had summoned Tolpo to no avail and out of malice; they had to pay legal costs and five *daler* in silver to the poor of Kokemäki parish. It seems that other matters, in which Tolpo was against these men, had to be involved in the case.[57] The court had already considered the church pew dispute. The district court had not ruled in favour of arrendator Stengrund, who could do nothing but abide by the judgement and accept a new place in the church.

This map from 1773 is the only surviving picture of the wooden church of Kokemäki. The vicarage is situated to the north-west of the church.[58]

---

56 For example the district court sessions of Kokemäki 27.2.1744, f. 111v.–114. Gothard Gustafson Hälli and Matts Simonsson; 16.10.1744 f. 299v.–300v., 305v–306v. and 23.10.1745 f. 222v. 224 Jacob Påhlsson and 20.2.1746 f. 88v.–90 Matts Eriksson. KA. Vehmaan ja Ala-Satakunnan tuomiokirjat. II KO a. Varsinaisten asioiden pöytäkirjat. Some of these cases concerned contracts that farm tenants had made even before they came to Harjavalta.
57 KA. Vehmaan ja Ala-Satakunnan tuomiokirjat. II KO a:55. Varsinaisten asioiden pöytäkirjat 1746–1746. The district court sessions of Kokemäki 29–31.10.1746, f. 796. Ruotsin valtakunnan vuoden 1734 laki. Oikeudenkäynti Caari 29, § 1.
58 Source: Maanmittauslaitoksen arkisto, Jyväskylä. Turun ja Porin läänin maanmittauskonttori. Jakoarkisto. Kokemäki, Kuoppalan kylän (29) isojakokartta. Photograph: Tapio Salminen.

Shortly after this incident, Tolpo accused Simon Stengrund of refusing to participate in vicarage repairs. Tolpo had reminded the *arrendator* of his duties, but Stengrund had kept himself and his men away from the construction work. The rural dean asked the court to oblige Stengrund to take part in the work. Stengrund responded by stating that neither the owner nor himself (as one entitled to the rights of the manor) were responsible for the upkeep of the vicarage. This was because of the special privileges enjoyed by the estate and the special nature of the Kokemäki manor (*säterij*). It seems that Stengrund was fully prepared to answer the accusations levelled against him and that he knew his rights as a lessee. This dispute was also resolved by the court. Stengrund was found to be exempt from the construction and maintenance of the vicarage. On this occasion Tolpo was made to pay the legal costs.[59] Once again Tolpo's honour was at stake.[60]

Tolpo's vicarage was one of the largest houses in Kokemäki. The main building consisted of hall, four rooms and the kitchen. In addition there were several outbuildings.[61] Actually Tolpo made well with his living. In addition to the residence of the vicar, Tolpo himself owned Säpilä cavalry estate in the parish. His second cavalry farm Simula, whose buildings and farmlands were also considerable, was situated close to the Harjavalta chapel. These farms were the largest in the parish: Simula (Harjavalta) was 1 *mantal* and Säpilä 1 2/3 *mantal* ("taxation value").[62]

In the large vicarage, there was always something to repair. In the previous court case Tolpo probably referred to disputes about the baking and cooking facilities in his vicarage.[63] The rebuilding of the oven and

---

59 KA. Vehmaan ja Ala-Satakunnan tuomiokirjat. II KO a:55. Varsinaisten asioiden pöytäkirjat 1746–1746. The district court sessions of Kokemäki 29.–31.10.1746, f. 800v.–801v. Ruotsin valtakunnan vuoden 1734 lain Rakennuskaari 26, § 2. "*Pappila pitä myös caickein rakendaman mantalin jälken; mutta istundo eli säterij-cartanot ja lato-cartanot, nijn myös huonettomat raja ja pijri talot, olcon sijtä wapaat.*"

60 Pieter Spierenburg, *Social control and History*, p. 17.

61 VA 7553:1830. Tositekirja 1747–1747.

62 VA 7553:1829, 1830. Tositekirja 1747–1747. Hockman & Salminen, Kokemäen ja Harjavallan talonhaltijat..., pp.67, 91.

63 KA. Vehmaan ja Ala-Satakunnan tuomiokirjat. II KO a:50. Varsinaisten asioiden pöytäkirjat 1742–1742. The district court sessions of Kokemäki 22.–24.2.1742 (no folios); Vehmaan ja Ala-Satakunnan tuomiokirjat Vehmaan ja Ala-Satakunnan tuomiokirjat. II KO a:51. Varsinaisten asioiden pöytäkirjat 1743–1743. The district court sessions of Kokemäki 2.5.1743 (no folios).

brewery house had not progressed as Tolpo wished. The parishioners of Kokemäki had earlier promised to pay Tolpo for this construction work. The dean had probably first turned to the Chapter of Turku. Still consistorial control was not enough, because in the end the governor resolved the matter of the oven. Later, the rural police chief commanded the local men in position of trust, the so-called sixmen (*sexmän*), to collect money for the oven.[64] Hence, different forms of the control were eventually used in this small dispute of vicarage maintenance. According to Spierenburg, the main forms of social control are state justice, church (consistorial) discipline and local community in early modern society. When observing more church building obligations and practises, the similar forms of social control appear at the parish of Kokemäki as in continental Europe.[65]

The estate and manors had limited responsibility for the maintenance of the vicarage, but the church building was a matter that concerned *everyone* in the parish. Obligations relating to the vicarage and the church were set out in law. Before work on the church could begin, the parish men had to gather together to discuss the matter,[66] and the chapter and the king also had to be informed.[67] Everyone who lived in the parish was obliged to participate in the construction and maintenance of the church. The legal definition of the church included "the belfry", "the wall", "the cottage of the parish" (*sockenstuga*) and "the cottage of the poor" (*fattigstuga*). All the building materials and their transportation were arranged after the assessment of the unit of land *mantal*. Still, the daily works were arranged according to the sitting/household *matlag*. Failure to undertake the day work duty cost one *daler*; neglecting the horse day work was fined at double this rate. If work had to be halted because duties had been shirked, the day's work duty had to be completed and a daily fine of three *daler* was imposed.[68] There was no exception

---

64 KA. Vehmaan ja Ala-Satakunnan tuomiokirjat. II KO a:53. Varsinaisten asioiden pöytäkirjat 1744–1744. The district court sessions of Kokemäki 16.10.1744. f. 306v.
65 Pieter Spierenburg, *Social control and History*, p. 14.
66 Ruotsin valtakunnan vuoden 1734 laki. Rakennus Caari 26, § 1.
67 Kircko-Laki ja Ordningi 1686 Luku XXVII, § 1. "*Cosca jocu tahto Kircko eli Cappelit udest raketa / pitä se ensin Meille / ja sitte Pispalle ja Consistoriumille tiettäwäx tehtämän...*"
68 Ruotsin valtakunnan vuoden 1734 laki. Rakennus Caari 26, § 1 & 6.

to participation in church repairs: tenant Stengrund and steward Belin clearly had legal obligations.

Participation in building projects was organized and controlled from within the parish and the local community. There were at least two different forms of community supervision.[69] On the one hand, local men in positions of trust had a responsibility to oversee the organization of the work. The churchwarden (Henrik Theet, in the case of Kokemäki) controlled the church finances and may have also controlled those who supplied building materials.[70] "Sixmen" gathered payments and material proportions from the villages. They could also ensure that building material was supplied from within the area over which they exerted control.[71]

On the other hand, members of the community were also able to control participation in parish building work. The parish elite, those from the estate and rich peasants, could influence participation in, and the timing of, such projects. They were expected to be charitable, to exercise cultural patronage and to give generously to the local church. In this way they illustrated their goodwill towards the community and their higher status.[72] In Kangasala parish, for example, the decision to build a new belfry immediately was taken at a parish meeting in May 1752. The parish men had probably discussed this matter earlier: it seems unlikely that they could imagine undertaking such work almost immediately without prior discussion. However, during the meeting in May, Baron and Captain Gustaf Georg Mellin (owner of the great Liuksiala estate) announced that he was not going to take part in the belfry building project. The parish men protested loudly. They threatened to bring the

---

69 Pieter Spierenburg, Social Control and History, pp. 14–15.
70 KA. Vehmaan ja Ala-Satakunnan tuomiokirjat. II KO a:55. Varsinaisten asioiden pöytäkirjat 1746–1746. The district court sessions of Kokemäki 29–31.10.1746, f. 778v.–779v.
71 I have written more about activities of churchwardens and sexmän in Ella Viitaniemi, "'Mitä pitäjän cocouxes päätetty on / kuin Kircon tarpexi tule'. Pitäjänkokous yhteisön kuvaajana 1700-luvulla", Genos, 2 (2008), pp. 73–85.
72 Jon Stobart, "Webs of Information, Bonds of Trust: The Networks of Early Eighteenth-Century Chester Merchants", in Magrit Schulte and Jörg Vögele (ed.), Spinning the Commercial Web: International Trade, Merchants, and Commercial Cities c.1640–1939 (Frankfurt 2004), p. 225; Scott, The Moral Economy of the Peasant, p. 5; E. P. Thompson, Herrojen valta ja rahvaan kulttuuri: Valta, kulttuuri ja perinnäistavat 1700 ja 1800-lukujen Englannissa (Tampere, 1996), pp. 47–50; Matti Peltonen, Lukkari Saxbergin rikos ja herännäispappilan etiikka, p. 214.

case before the next district court sessions.[73] In the case of the Kangasala belfry, the parish men did not ally with the estate, as had earlier been the case with some parish men in Kokemäki. Instead, the parish men of Kangasala, who were well aware of their legal rights and obligations, resisted the baron's arrogant declaration.

An arrogant arrendator: a troublemaker or a local political actor?

It seems that regardless of social pressure and local control, Stengrund had no desire to participate in any extraordinary activity, such as repairing the church or the vicarage. In this way, Stengrund acted arrogantly and showed that he was not committed to the common good. His temporary lessee status in Kokemäki offers a possible explanation for such behaviour.[74] He owned neither land nor property in the parish, as was clearly stated in the court records. Stengrund might well have seen himself as an outsider in the community and therefore less responsible for the common good than other permanently settled, parishioners. Nevertheless, despite his lessee status, Stengrund was an actor in the local political culture and had an impact on public construction and repair works.

Stengrund acted *arrogantly* when refusing to take part in the church repairs, but together with Belin he offered an answer to the peasants' desires. The peasantry was often less than enthusiastic about public building projects. One reason for this can be found in the tendency of the peasantry to favour risk-avoiding behaviour. I believe that when households were living close the subsistence margin, they were unwilling to take risks and use valuable resources for parish projects that were not seen as the highest priority.[75] The initiatives of Stengrund and Belin

---

73 Hämeenlinnan Maakunta-arkisto (HMA). The church archives of Kangasala. II Ca:1. Pitäjän- ja kirkonkokousten pöytäkirjat 1751–1800. The parish meeting minutes of Kangasala 3.5.1752 and 7.6.1752. Eino Jutikkala, *Längelmäveden seudun historia II, Kangasalan historia II* (Hämeenlinna, 1954), p. 98.
74 Levi, *Aineeton perintö*, pp. 144–145.
75 Scott, *The Moral Economy of the Peasant*, pp. 4–5, 17.

allowed some of the parishioners to resist their obligations and protest against their vicar and his demands.

Stengrund succeeded in combining his own advantage and the unwillingness of the peasants. His arguments with the vicar might have had a negative effect on participation in the project. Stengrund did not want to co-operate with Tolpo and it seems clear that there was no mutual trust between these two men. When Stengrund, together with Belin, succeeded in gathering at least some of the parishioners to his side, his personal protest against the vicar became even more successful.

That Stengrund should manage to secure backing from any parishioners was not a foregone conclusion. Generally the peasantry disliked "half-lords" or other social climbers.[76] However, in this case, some members of the peasantry were prepared to co-operate with a lessee and a steward. On this occasion at least, Stengrund and Belin were not seen not as annoying upstarts but as proper allies, with whom the peasantry could act against a common enemy: the vicar Tolpo. Members of the peasantry were able to act from behind the protection of Stengrund and Belin: no peasants were named in the court proceedings. Even though the peasants remained in the background of the church repair conflict in Kokemäki, since 1742 the political role of the peasantry in Sweden had begun to change. Peasant political activity increased at both the national (*Riksdag*) and the local levels. The peasantry started to take more initiatives and make more claims.[77] In this light, the events of 1746 in Kokemäki can be seen as a local foretaste of increased peasant power and changes in the political culture.

Actually, Stengrund and Belin are part of a larger phenomenon. Several similar cases can probably be found in early modern Swedish parishes. They were part of a new kind of gentry or middling sort, who tried to find the proper social place and political role in society. They could resist the system or passively adjust to social control. One solu-

---

76 Wirilander, *Herrasväkeä*, pp. 374, 378–380.
77 Kalle Bäck, *Bonde opposition och bondeinflytande under frihetstiden: Centralmakten och östgötabödernas reaktioner i näringspolitiska frågor* (Stockholm, 1984), pp. 134–135; Karin Sennefelt, *Den politiksa sjukan: Dalupropet 1743 och frihetstida politisk kultur* (Södertälje, 2001), pp. 310–311; ead., "Marching to Stockholm", in Kimmo Kataja (ed.), *Northern Revolts: Medieval and Early Modern Peasant Unrest in the Nordic Countries* (Helsinki, 2004), pp. 196–198.

tion was that they negotiated and tried to bend the rules of social control by themselves.[78] Hence, participating and taking an active role in local politics was a functional choice, like the case of Stengrund shows. Participating in the local political culture was the only formal channel for influencing and achieving political leverage. It also helped to define their social position, even though it could also cause some conflicts. By studying, these kinds of active and peculiar men, we can find out what was possible in local political culture and the limits and forms of social control.

---

78 Pieter Spierenburg, *Social control and History*, p. 17.

The main connections of Simon Stengrund to the Kokemäki parish through the Polviander family[79]

I 1.1. Michel Marcusson   + Brita Jacobsdotter
   Knuutila, Kiukainen   Askola, Kokemäki

II 2.1. Simon Polviander (d. 1711)   + Anna Barck (d. 1729 Kokemäki)
   chaplain, Kokemäki 1675–89   parents: "manor bailiff" Nils Olofson Barck
   vicar, Ikaalinen 1689–1711   and Anna Mårtensdr. Gråån, Ulvila parish

III 3.1. Kristina Simonsdotter Polviander (1680–1763)   + Mårten Stenius (ca. 1670–1717)
        3.1.1. **Simon Stengrund (b. 1708)**
        arrendator, a lessee of Kokemäki
        manor ca. 1736–51
        + 1. Elisabet Packalenius
        + 2. Brita Juliana Nordeen

    3.2. Johannes (Johan) Polviander (d. 1729)   + 2. wife Margareta Paulin
        curate, Ikaalinen,   d. 1750 in Vuoltee, Kokemäki
        curate, Kokemäki military
        preacher 1707–1709,
        prisoner 1709–1719 (?)
        vicar, Kokemäki 1718/22–1729
    3.3. **Anders Polviander (ca. 1690–1743)**
        chaplain, Kokemäki 1722–37
        vicar, Hämeenlinna 1741–43
    3.4. Nils Polviander (d. 1716, St. Petersburg)   + Agneta Paulin
        vicar, Ikaalinen 1711–1716
        (after his father) died
        in prisoner during the
        Great Wrath 1716

    3.5. Margareta Simonsdotter Polviander   + Henrik Wegelius (d. 1719)
        3.5.1. Margareta Henriksdotter Wegelius (Wigelia) (1712–61)
        + **Thure Belin** (1687–1760)
        inspector, steward in Forsby *rustholl* 1731–51, Kokemäki
        [Belin's 1. wife Christina Stenia (d. 1733)]

79 The family tree is not completed, but it describes Stengrund's explicit connections to Kokemäki parish. TMA. The church archives of Pirkkala. I C:1. Syntyneiden ja kastettujen luettelo 1702–1729. TMA. The church archives of Harjavalta. I C:1. Kuolleiden luettelo 1731–1793. Yrjö Kotivuori, *Ylioppilasmatrikkeli 1640–1852: Henrik Wegelius*. Verkkojulkaisu 2005, www.helsinki.fi/ylioppilasmatrikkeli/henkilo.php?id=4085. *Ylioppilasmatrikkeli 1640–1852: Mårten Stenius*. Verkkojulkaisu 2005, www.helsinki.fi/ylioppilasmatrikkeli/henkilo.php?id=3706 (accessed 30 January 2013). Hockman and Salminen, *Kokemäen ja Harjavallan talonhaltijat...*, pp. 6, 32, 137, 144–146.

Sources

ARCHIVAL SOURCES

National Archives, Helsinki (KA)
Transcribed court records of the Vehmaa and Ala-Satakunta jurisdiction;
Varsinaisten asioiden pöytäkirjat II KO a:39. (1732).
Varsinaisten asioiden pöytäkirjat II KO a:50. (1742).
Varsinaisten asioiden pöytäkirjat II KO a:51. (1743).
Varsinaisten asioiden pöytäkirjat II KO a:53. (1744) .
Varsinaisten asioiden pöytäkirjat II KO a:54. (1745).
Varsinaisten asioiden pöytäkirjat II KO a:55. (1746).
Provincial accounts of the Province of Turku and Pori;
VA 7492. Tositekirja 1731–1731.
VA 7553. Tositekirja 1747–1747.

Provincial archives of Hämeenlinna (HMA)
The church archives of Kangasala.
Pitäjän- ja kirkonkokousten pöytäkirjat II Ca:1. (1751–1800).
The church archives of Pirkkala.
Syntyneiden ja kastettujen luettelo I C:1. (1702–29).

Provincial archives of Turku (TMA)
The Archives of the Archdiocese of Turku.
Turun tuomiokapitulin pöytäkirjat A I: 18. (1786).
Tuomiokapitulin kirjekirja B I: 15 (1746).
Tuomiokapitulin kirjekirja B I: 53. (1786).
Kuninkaalliset, keisarilliset, senaatin ja valtioneuvoston kirjeet EI:4. (1713–1732).
Porin Ylä- ja Ala- sekä Tyrvään rovastikuntia ja niihin kuuluvia seurakuntia koskevia asiakirjoja E VI:I.
The archives of the Fiscal Department of the Provincial Government of the Turku and Pori;
Tilitositteet, I Gac 59: 2395. (1736).
The church archives of Harjavalta;
Kuolleiden luettelo I C:1. (1731–1793).
The church archives of Kokemäki;
Pää- ja rippikirjat I Aa:3. (1752–1758).
Kokemäen pitäjän kirkonkirja II Ba:1. (1630–1784).
Pitäjänkokousten pöytäkirjat II:Ca:1. 1760–1805.
The church archives of Pori;
Kaupunkiseurakunnan kuolleiden ja haudattujen luettelot I C1:3. (1732–1777).

The parish archives of Kokemäki, Kokemäki
Laskuja sekalaisia, kirkkoa ja pappilaa varten Ji:1. (1835–55).

PRINTED SOURCES

Kircko-Laki ja Ordningi 1686 [1986]: Näköispainos ja uudelleen ladottu laitos vuoden 1686 kirkkolain suomennoksesta, ed. Hellemaa, Jussila, Parvio. Helsinki.

Kotivuori, Yrjö 2005: *Ylioppilasmatrikkeli 1640–1852*, www.helsinki.fi/ylioppilasmatrikkeli/.

Modée, R.G. 1742: *Utdrag Utur alle ifrån 7. Decemb. 1718 utkomne Publique handlingar, Placater, Förordningar, Resolutioner och Publicationer, Riksens Styrseld samt inwärtes Hushållning och Författningar i gemen, jemwäl ock Stockholms Stad i synnerhet angå, I delen.* Stockholm.

Ruotsin valtakunnan vuoden 1734 laki, http://agricola.utu.fi/julkaisut/julkaisusarja/kktk/lait/1734/.

LITERATURE

Aronsson, Peter 1992: *Bönder gör politik: Det lokala självstyret som social arena i tre smålandssocknar, 1680–1850.* Lund University, Lund.

Bergström, Carin 1991: *Lantprästen: Prästens funktion i det agrara samhället 1720–1800. Oland-Frösåkers kontrakt av ärkestiftet.* Stockholm.

Braddick, Michel J. and Walter, John 2001: Introduction. Grids of power: order hierarchy and subordination in early modern society. In *Negotiating power in early modern society. Order, hierarchy and Subordination in Britain and Ireland*, ed. Michael J. Braddick and John Walter. Cambridge, pp. 1–42.

Bäck, Kalle 1984: *Bonde opposition och bondeinflytande under frihetstiden: Centralmakten och östgötabödernas reaktioner i näringspolitiska frågor.* Stockholms universitet, Stockholm.

Frohnert, Pär 1985: Administration i Sverige under frihetstiden. In *Administrasjon i Norden på 1700-talet*, ed. Yrjö Blomstedt et al., Oslo, pp. 185–286.

Ginzburg, Carlo 1993: Microhistory: Two or three things that I know about it. *Critical Inquiry*. Vol. 20 (1) 1993, pp. 10–35.

Gustafsson, Harald 1989: *Sockenstugans politiska kultur, Lokal självstyre på 1800-talets landsbygd.* Stadshistoriska Institutet, Stockholm.

Gustafsson, Harald 1994: *Political Interaction in the Old Regime: Central Power and Local Society in the Eighteenh-Century Nordic States.* Lund.

Haapio, Markku (ed.) 1978: *Suomen kirkot ja kirkkotaide 1.* Lieto.

Hiekkanen, Markus 1993: *Rengon historia, Esihistoria ja Kirkon historia.* Jyväskylä.

Hockman, Tuula and Salminen, Tapio 2007: *Kokemäen ja Harjavallan talonhaltijat vuoteen 1900, torpat 1891–1900 sekä papisto ennen vuotta 1870*, Kokemäen ja Harjavallan historia I:2. Jyväskylä.

Johansson, K. H. 1937: *Svensk Sockensjälvstyrelse 1686–1862: Studier särkilt med hänsyn till Linköpings stift.* Lund.

Jutikkala, Eino 1954: *Längelmäveden seudun historia II, Kangasalan historia II.* Hämeenlinna.

Jäntere, Kaarlo 1926: *Porin triviaalikoulun oppilasluettelot 1722, 1733, 1737 ja oppilasmatrikkeli 1738–1842.* Helsinki.

Karonen, Petri 2001: *Pohjoinen suurvalta, Ruotsi ja Suomi 1521–1809* (2nd edn.) Helsinki.

Katajala, Kimmo 1990: *Säätyläisiä ja nousukkaita, Veronvuokraus osana Käkisalmen läänin sääty-yhteisöä vuosina 1683–1700.* Publications of Karelian Institute. University of Joensuu, Joensuu.

Laasonen, Pentti 1991: *Suomen kirkon historia 2, Vuodet 1593–1808.* Porvoo.

Larsson, Olle 1999: *Biskopen visiterar, Den kyrkliga överhetens möte med lokalsamhället 1650–1750*. Växjö.

Levi, Giovanni 1992: *Aineeton perintö, Manaajapappi ja talonpoikaisyhteisö 1600-luvun Italiassa* (*L'eredità immateriale, Carriera di un esorcista nel Piemonte del Seicento*, trans. Kaisa Kinnunen and Elina Suolahti). Helsinki.

Linde, Martin 2000: *Statsmakt och bondemotstånd: Allmoge och överhet under stora nordiska kriget*. Uppsala universitet, Uppsala.

Lindström, Johan Adolf 1862: Kumo socken uti historisk hänseende. *Suomi, Tidskrift i fosterländska ämnen 1860*. Helsingfors.

Peltonen, Matti 2006: *Lukkari Saxbergin rikos ja herännäispappilan etiikka, Mikrohistoriallinen tutkimus 1800-luvun puolivälin Keuruulta*. Gaudeamus, Helsinki.

Salminen, Tapio 2007: *Joki ja sen väki. Kokemäen ja Harjavallan historia jääkaudesta 1860-luvulle*, Jyväskylä.

Sandén, Annika 2006: Kyrkan, kvinnorna och hierarkiernas dynamik. *Historiks tidskrift*, 126 (4) 2006, pp. 643–660.

Scott, James C. 1976: *The Moral Economy of the Peasant: Rebellion and Subsistence in Southeast Asia*. Yale University, Yale.

Sennefelt, Karin 2001: *Den politiksa sjukan: Daluppropet 1743 och frihetstida politisk kultur*. Södertälje.

Sennefelt, Karin 2004: Marching to Stockholm. In *Northern Revolts: Medieval and Early Modern Peasant Unrest in the Nordic Countries*, ed. Kimmo Kataja. Finnish Literature Society, Helsinki, pp. 196–198.

Spierenburg, Pieter 2004: Social Control and history: An Introduction. In *Social control in Europe Volume 1, 1500–1800*, ed. Herman Roodenburg and Pieter Spierenburg. Ohio, pp. 1–22.

Stobart, Jon 2004: Webs of Information, Bonds of Trust: The Networks of Early Eighteenth-Century Chester Merchants. In *Spinning the Commercial Web: International Trade, Merchants, and Commercial Cities c.1640–1939*, ed. Magrit Schulte and Jörg Vögele. Frankfurt.

Suodenjoki, Sami 2012: *Kuriton suutari ja kiistämisen rajat. Työväenliikkeen läpimurto hämäläisessä maalaisyhteisössä 1899-1909*. Finnish Literature Society, Helsinki.

Thompson, E. P. 1996: *Herrojen valta ja rahvaan kulttuuri: Valta, kulttuuri ja perinnäistavat 1700 ja 1800–lukujen Englannissa*. Gaudeamus, Tampere.

Tiscornia, Alberto 1992: *Statens, godsens eller böndernas socknar?: Den sockenkommunala självstyrelsens utveckling i Västerfärnebo, Stora Malm och Jäder 1800–1880*. Acta Universitatis Upsaliensis, Uppsala.

Viitaniemi, Ella 2008: "Mitä pitäjän cocouxes päätetty on / kuin Kircon tarpexi tule". Pitäjänkokous yhteisön kuvaajana 1700-luvulla. *Genos*, 2/2008, pp. 73–85.

Villstrand, Nils Erik 1992: *Anpassining eller protest: Lokalsamhället inför utskriviningar av fotfolk till den svenska krigsmakten 1620–1676*. Åbo academy, Åbo.

Villstrand, Nils Erik 2005: Från morgonstjärna till memorial: Politisk kultur i det svenska riket 1500–1800. In *Sphinx*. Societas Scientiarum Fennica, Vuosikirja 2004–2005. Helsingfors, pp. 115–128.

Virkkala, Kopisto and Lehtinen 1967: *Suur-Ulvilan historia I*. Pori.

Wirilander, Kaarlo 1953: *Suomen armeijan upseeristo ja aliupseeristo 1718–1810, Virkatalonhaltijain luettelot*. Suomen Historiallinen Seura, Helsinki.

Österberg, Eva 1987: Svenska lokalsamhälle i förändring *ca.*1550–1850. *Historisk Tidskrift*, 3/1987, pp. 321–340.
Österberg, Eva 1989: Bönder och centralmakt idet tidigmoderna Sverige. Konlikt – kompromiss – politisk kultur. *Scandia*, 55 (1) 1989, pp. 73–95.

III
On the Margins of the Society

War, Soldiers and Crime in Modern Britain
Issues for Research[1]
Clive Emsley

In July 2006 David Bradley, a veteran of the First Gulf War, took a 7.65mm handgun that he had smuggled out of Bosnia while serving with the British Army, and shot dead his uncle, his aunt and two cousins. He showered, changed his clothes, walked to the local police station, handed over a collection of weapons and said: "I have just killed four members of my family."[2] A little over two years later the National Association of Probation Officers expressed concern that one prisoner in every eleven in Britain's overcrowded prisons, about nine percent, was an armed forces veteran and the BBC broadcast a radio programme expressing deep concern about servicemen returning psychologically damaged from the wars in Iraq and Afghanistan and slipping into drink, drugs, self harm and violent crime.[3]

The flowering of social history and "history from below" that began in the 1960s has led to flourishing research in the areas of crime and crimi-

---

[1] My thanks to James Whitfield and Chris A. Williams for their generous comments and assistance with this paper. The larger results of the study have been published in Emsley, Clive: *Soldier, Sailor, Beggarman, Thief: Crime and the British Armed Services since 1914*, Oxford: Oxford University Press, 2013.
[2] *Times*, 10 April 2008, p. 21.
[3] See, for example, *Observer*, 31 August 2008, p. 11, and *Sunday Telegraph*, 31 August 2008, p. 4: BBC Radio 4, File on 4, "In Afghanistan: The Home Front", broadcast 4 November 2008. More generally, see the campaigning book by Aly Renwick, *Hidden Wounds: The Problems of Northern Ireland Veterans in Civvy Street* (London, 1999).

nal justice history as well as in what is encapsulated under the heading of "war and society" or "the new military history." Unfortunately the two areas have tended to advance in parallel. This essay, based primarily on a survey of the British experience during the twentieth century, argues that it is time for the two areas to makes some links for future research.

War, by its very nature, is violent. Violence is central to the soldier's trade. For centuries people have feared that, when the soldier's political masters have no immediate need for his violence, then he will turn it against civilians. Often there was justification for such a fear. In 1536 François I promulgated the Edict of Paris which led to the creation of the *Maréchaussée*, literally the men of the military Marshals of France and the precursor of the *Gendarmerie nationale*, whose task it was to police the king's armies at home and to protect the king's subjects from his soldiers. The brigands of continental Europe and the highwaymen of Stuart and Hanoverian Britain appear often to have drawn recruits from discharged soldiers, as well as from deserters and stragglers. The boundary was permeable in the other direction as young men that might have been tempted into criminal behaviour joined the colours; in Georgian England judges often commented on the low number of criminal offenders brought before the assizes shortly after war had broken out. Also, it is at least arguable that the fear of soldiers returning at the end of wars contributed to a greater sensibility towards crime and hence to a greater determination to report and prosecute crime.[4] Concerns about the threat from violent veterans who had lost all respect for human life were voiced with the demobilization at the end of the American Civil War. Twenty years later, at the end of the Franco-Prussian War, Wilhelm Starke, a senior figure in the Prussian Interior Ministry, made a statistical study that showed an increase in inter-personal violence in both France and Germany. Starke suggested that some of this might have been the result of the brutalising impact of war, but his principal concern was how far the increasing consumption of alcohol influenced crime rates.[5]

---

4 Peter King, *Crime, Justice and Discretion in England, 1740–1820* (Oxford, 2000), pp. 153–161.
5 Jeffrey S. Adler, "The Making of a Moral Panic in 19th-Century America: The Boston Garroting Hysteria of 1865", *Deviant Behaviour: An Interdisciplinary Journal*, 17 (1996) pp. 259–278; Wilhelm Starke, *Verbrechen und Verbrecher in Preussen, 1854–1878: Eine kulturgeschichtliche Studie* (Berlin, 1884) pp. 61 and 152.

In the early modern world it was not always possible to differentiate clearly between soldier and civilian. Some men were pressed into service for wars; and there were some professionals, sometimes mercenaries, who fought for the prince or, less commonly, the republic that paid their wages. Many men may have considered that they were fighting for their God or their King but the wars of the French Revolution and Napoleon marked a significant shift in this respect. The Decree of the *Levée en Masse* in August 1793 announced that every French citizen was involved in the war to protect the nation against its enemies:

> The young men will go to battle; the married men will make arms and transport provisions; the women will make tents and uniforms, and will serve in the hospitals; the children will make old clothes into bandages; the old men will go out into the public squares to boost the soldiers' courage and to preach the unity of the republic and the hatred of kings.[6]

The flowery rhetoric of the members of the National Convention, who were not themselves going to carry muskets, was not to the taste of everyone in France, and nor were the conscription demands of Napoleon which led to thousands of young men going into hiding, to mayors falsifying registers of births and to communities violently resisting recruiting sergeants and gendarmes.[7] But the French armies got their men and increasingly wars were seen as conflicts to be fought by mass armies of citizen-soldiers fighting for their nation state or empire. Partly as a result of this it appears that, within France, the image of the dangerous, marauding French soldier declined during the nineteenth century. The perception that the soldier and the bandit were closely linked was replaced by the idea that the soldier who went in for a bit of thieving and trickery was showing his Gallic flair through his skills of a quick wit and bravura.[8]

---

6 *Le Moniteur*, 25 August, 1793 (my translation).
7 Alan Forrest, *Conscripts and Deserters: The Army and French Society during the Revolution and Empire* (Oxford, 1989).
8 David M. Hopkin, "Military Marauders in Nineteenth-Century French Popular Culture", *War and History*, 9. 3 (2002) pp. 251–278; idem, *Soldier and Peasant in French Popular Culture, 1766–1870* (Woodbridge, 2003), pp. 236–239, 303.

Napoleon's princely opponents remained wary of the concept of the citizen soldier. Initially the notion of armies being recruited to fight for a nation or an empire in which they, as citizens, had some kind of stake appeared a threat to the old order. But as the nineteenth century progressed conscription was also seen as a means to indoctrinate young men into a commitment to their nation state or multi-national empire. The use of conscription, together with the heady concept of nationalism, meant that by the time of the world wars of the twentieth century, armies of citizen soldiers were encouraged to see themselves as fighting for "their" country or empire against alien nations and nationalities. The popular enthusiasm for war in 1914 has, almost certainly, been over-emphasised, nevertheless many appear wholeheartedly to have embraced the notion of the national, citizen army. The British, while being latecomers to the use of conscription, manifested such sentiments through the tens of thousands that volunteered for Kitchener's Army. They accepted that "their" country needed "them". The image of the British soldier as an outsider, the scum of the earth enlisted for drink, had been in decline since the close of the nineteenth century, but after the First World War it virtually disappeared.

There is an important paradox to be highlighted here. By the beginning of the First World War most European armies were composed of citizen soldiers; but those citizens, who were now required to use lethal violence as soldiers, had grown up in a world where violence was increasingly stigmatized. From the eighteenth century at least masculinity was beginning to depend less and less on physical prowess and a man's ability to overcome his rivals by physical strength. Some violent behaviour was still condoned as contributing to a respectable gentleman's honour as well as to military prowess; the duel or, particularly in Britain, certain rough sports such as boxing and rugby were examples of this. Yet violent behaviour was also associated more and more with the rougher elements of society, with children who lacked education and discipline or with primitive peoples to whom many of the European advocates of empire considered they were bringing the advantages of civilization. The nineteenth-century, it has been urged, witnessed the significant criminalization of violent men within many (perhaps most)

Western societies.[9] But then the twentieth century required ordinary citizens to be extremely violent on behalf of their nation. Joanna Bourke has explored the mixed emotions of twentieth-century men suddenly finding themselves required to kill in the service of their nation and the different strategies that they employed to cope both during and after their exposure to conflict. She suggested that the concept of the "brutalized veteran", returning home unable to lose the violence inculcated by his military training, became a popular narrative because it offered a comprehensive explanation that avoided concerns about troubled individual consciences by providing a catchall identification of war as the problem.[10] But homicide is only one form of crime, and all kinds of crime can be found during and immediately after wars.

II

Many of the wartime concerns about crime in the twentieth century focussed on women and juveniles. Both appeared to be committing more crime and this was something picked up by the contemporary press and by sociologists, criminologists and the few historians that have reflected on the conflicts. Women, especially, young women, were feared to be involved in new opportunities for prostitution. Older women, especially those now forced to take full responsibility for managing the home and brining up the children, appeared to be increasingly drawn into petty property offences particularly to feed their families. The increase in juvenile crime was attributed to fathers being at the front and mothers being involved in war work.[11] This simple cause and effect might be disputed, not least because a large number of servicemen were un-

---

9   For these arguments with respect to Britain see, Clive Emsley, *Hard Men: Violence in England since 1750* (London, 2005); Martin J. Wiener, *Men of Blood: Violence, Manliness and Criminal Justice in Victorian England* (Cambridge, 2004); John Carter Wood, *Violence and Crime in Nineteenth-Century England: The Shadow of our Refinement* (London, 2004).
10 Joanna Bourke, *An Intimate History of Killing: Face-to-Face Killing in Twentieth-Century Warfare* (London, 1999).
11 See, inter alia, Franz Exner, *Krieg und Kriminalität in Österreich* (Vienna, 1927); Moritz Liepmann, *Krieg und Kriminalität in Deutschland* (Stuttgart, 1930); Edward Smithies, *Crime in Wartime: A Social History of Crime in World War II* (London, 1982).

married or had children simply too young to be noted by the criminal justice system. Indeed, as early as 1920 a report for the British Home Office raised problems with the assumption when it concluded that the figures revealed a father to have been absent in less than 30 percent of wartime juvenile cases. The percentage, however, was "highest in 1918 and showed a rapid decline in the following year as demobilisation took place."[12]

As for the brutalized veteran, returning from the front to rape, pillage and kill at home, initial investigations into the immediate aftermath of the First World War suggests that such an individual had little existence in reality. Nevertheless, men who returned to find that their wife had been unfaithful, sometimes meted out punishment to the wife and sometimes also to her male paramour. At times the populace and even the courts looked on this with a degree of lenity; in England the term "the unwritten law" was once again brought into play. Extreme violence and murder were not condoned in England, whatever the defence claims of the newly recognised problem of shell-shock. In Belgium, however, traumatised by four years of occupation, returning soldiers who murdered wives suspected of being unfaithful were acquitted by the courts.[13]

The post-war situation varied from country to country and context to context. In Germany where soldiers returned home, with their weapons, to a bleak economic climate and political insecurity and upheaval, there was violence. In Britain there was no revolution and soldiers did not come home with their weapons. But there were worries that weapons would make their way back to the country as a result of the war. There were also concerns that members of the "criminal class" had either volunteered or been conscripted as soldiers. At the beginning of 1918, many months before the end of the war was in sight, a committee was appointed to look into the control of firearms after the war. "It must

---

12 T[he] N[ational] A[rchives], HO 45.16515, Report of the Juvenile Organisation Committee, 1920, p. 11.
13 Clive Emsley, "Violent Crime in England in 1919: Post-War Anxieties and Press Narratives", *Continuity and Change*, 21, 1 (2008) pp. 173–195; idem, "A Legacy of Conflict? The Brutalised Veteran and Violence in Europe after the Great War", in Avdela, Efi; D'Cruze, Shani and Rowbotham, Judith ed. *Problems of Crime and Violence in Europe, 1780–2000: Essays in Criminal Justice* (Edwin Mellen Press, 2010, pp. 43–64); Xavier Rousseaux and Laurence van Ypersele, ed. *La Patrie crie Vengeance! La Répression des "Inciviques" Belges au sortie de la Guerre 1914–1918* (Brussels, 2008) pp. 56–57, 179.

be borne in mind", the committee warned, "that we can hardly hope to escape on demobilization an increase in crime.... and however effective may be the measures to facilitate the return of discharged soldiers to civilian life and peaceful occupations, it would be unreasonable to expect that all these men will be ready to settle down at once to agricultural or industrial employment." As a result of these concerns, strict new controls on firearms were introduced.[14]

The traditional forms of criminal offending continued during wartime and there were habitual offenders that developed their behaviour according to the new context. In England *Supplement "A"* of the *Police Gazette* was circulated to every police force in the country every two weeks by Scotland Yard's Criminal Record Office. It contained details of known offenders, including photographs and fingerprints. A large number of these offenders travelled the country living on their wits, and the common denominator of their *modus operandi* was the way in which they took advantage of the context in which they found themselves. There were fraudsters before the First World War, but the war provided them with new opportunities. Men in army uniforms, sometimes deserters, but often not, pretended to be recruiting sergeants or claimed to have been wounded or gassed. The aim was order obtain money or other goods from the gullible. In 1916 Lawrence Andrew Deacon, claiming to have a degree from an American university, talked his way into an appointment in a military hospital. When he proved to be both intemperate and incompetent, and unable to produce any testimonials, he was dismissed. Undaunted he passed himself off to a bank manager as a major in the Royal Army Medical Corps; this enabled him to get a cheque book and to set off around the country claiming to inspect hospitals on behalf of the War Office, paying for his lodgings with his new cheques. His luck ran out before the end of the year and he was sentenced to six months imprisonment. Deacon resurfaced in the *Supplements* ten years later and during the early 1930s he was active in the West Country with convictions for passing fraudulent cheques in Bath,

---

[14] TNA RECO 1.342, *Report of Committee on the Control of Firearms* (the Blackwell Committee), p. 3; An Act to Amend the Law Relating to Firearms, 10 & 11 George V (1920).

Bristol and Devon claiming to be an electrical contractor, an ex-army officer, and the son of a clergyman.[15] Similar individuals found similar opportunities during the Second World War. Men pretended to be army officers and persuaded hotel managers to cash worthless cheques or to accept similar cheques in payment for rooms. Others posed as Dunkirk survivors, wounded heroes of glamorous commando raids, veterans of Bomber Command, torpedoed merchant seamen and anything else likely to ingratiate them with people that might be persuaded to part with money or goods.[16]

The darkness created by the night-time blackout and the chaos caused by a bombing raid provided new opportunities for other offenders who had made some sort of criminal career out of different kinds of theft before the war. But, whatever the popular assumptions about "professional criminals", the evidence suggests that most criminal offending is not the work of individuals that seek to make a career from it. The evidence also shows that most criminal behaviour is carried out by young men; and in the two world wars of the twentieth century the British government, like other combatant governments, required fit young men from all social classes for the armed services.

The military seeks to establish an *esprit de corps* among its members and to create a camaraderie that will ensure individuals obey orders and work together as a team whatever the extreme danger that threatens them. In the British army the regiment was seen as a family that provided men with a common, binding identity with the officers acting as *paterfamilias* at different levels – the junior lieutenant at the head of an infantry platoon, the lieutenant colonel at the head of a battalion. Unfortunately what is designed for efficiency and effectiveness on the battlefield can have an undesirable impact within the civilian environment. Young military personnel, bonded as a family group each looking out for the others, when on leave could drink heavily and look for girls, with inevitable confrontations between men of different military units or between military units and civilians or the civilian police. One

---

15 *Police Gazette, Supplement A*, 1917, no. 176; 1927, no. 258; 1930, no. 277 and no. 273; 1931, no. 340 and no. 583.
16 *Police Gazette, Supplement A*, 1942, nos. 91 and 258; 1943, nos. 86, 124 and 196.

Military Policeman who served with the Parachute Regiment during the Second World War recalled:

> It was something of a local joke that the boys ... could always find some excuse to have a go at the American troops, either because the Yanks didn't stand up quickly enough when the National Anthem was played in the local Dance Hall, or because of some imagined, or manufactured, insult to a local girl.[17]

Since the men were encouraged to back their comrades up, the confrontations could become large and serious. The most extreme, and possibly best-known incident, involved some 200 Canadian soldiers attacking a London Police station in 1919 to rescue two comrades who had been arrested for drunken behaviour. A Metropolitan Police sergeant was killed in the fighting.[18] Working as a team in difficult and unpleasant situations might have been the spur to men to take advantage of a situation to their own profit. Early in 1941 some 30 members of the Pioneer Corps deployed in London to clear debris left by air raids and to demolish unsafe buildings, decided to turn the situation to their personal advantage by stripping lead from the roofs of houses. The lead was then transported in army vehicles to a scrap metal dealer's yard and the money that he paid for it was pooled and divided equally.[19] Offences of such seriousness in a civilian setting went before the civilian courts but, as yet, there has been no systematic survey of such incidents.

There were also military courts that tried offences against military discipline and some of the more conventional criminal offences that were committed within the military environment or when men were serving overseas and away from the jurisdiction of their own civil courts. Many of the court martial offences underline the fact that different contexts have different offences. In civilian life having buttons undone and hands in pockets was acceptable; in the army it was not, and the offence was aggravated if the offender responded to a superior's criticism of his

---

17 Quoted in Jack Turnbull and John Hamblett, *The Pegasus Patrol* (Privately published, G.B. 1994) p. 56.
18 *Times*, 19 June 1919, p. 9 and 20 June, p. 9.
19 *Times*, 29 March 1941, p. 2.

behaviour with impertinence; small wonder that the Military Policemen – the "Redcaps" or, less politely, "Cherry Nobs" – were often unpopular with the ordinary soldiers. Leaving a position in civilian life might lead to a private reprimand or dismissal; but in the army leaving a post or leaving a unit was a serious, punishable offence. Section 40 of the Army Act of 1881 was the perfect catch-all allowing the military authorities to punish any man found guilty of what could be construed as an action or behaviour "to the prejudice of good order and military discipline".[20] The hierarchical structure of the army could also lead to men in authority who wished to breach military discipline, or even to commit a criminal offence, using their military authority to involve subordinates in their behaviour. Early in 1944, for example, a captain in the Royal Army Medical Corps used a military vehicle to pick up young women. In order to cover his tracks he ordered a lance corporal of the Royal Army Service Corps to tell a false story about the use of the vehicle. He warned the lance corporal that if he failed to tell the story, than he, the captain, would make a report that the lance corporal was hopelessly drunk. There were other instances where NCOs or officers may have used their authority to demand sexual favours from their subordinates, and this at a time when homosexual activity was illegal in civilian law.[21]

For the First World War there has been considerable research into death sentences and executions for cowardice and desertion, but there has been no systematic study of more general criminality involving soldiers both abroad and in home bases during the war. A very brief survey of the statistics of courts martial in the British Army shows an emphasis on offences specific to the military institution. The raw figures for criminal offences reveal that there was a peak in prosecutions for violent behaviour and drunkenness during the year from October 1915 to September 1916. The figures for theft continued to rise until the end of the war. But, as with all criminal statistics, these are fraught with difficulties. First, they take no account of summary field punishments that were meted out by regimental officers at the front. Secondly it is possible that

---

20　David French, *Military Identities: The Regimental System, the British Army and the British People c.1870-2000* (Oxford, 2005) pp. 181–197.
21　TNA, WO 84.70, Army Charge Book, 21 February to 12 August 1944.

the enormous wartime increase in the ratio of military police to serving soldiers in itself generated more reported offences. Finally, it has to be remembered that the British Army increased enormously over the course of the war. By the end of 1914 volunteering had brought the army to almost a million and a half men. Two years later it was approaching three million and then, following the introduction of conscription it reached just under four million – a figure at which it remained until the armistice. The rapid growth of the army makes it difficult to draw conclusions about the number of offences for every 100,000 soldiers. A very rough estimate suggests, however, that the difficulties with violence and drunkenness were at their peak in 1915, but that theft reached its peak in the last year of the war.[22]

It is possible that conscription swept up some young men who had a propensity to steal. At the beginning of the Second World War the army, which appears to have subscribed to the contemporary, positivist view that there was a professional criminal class, was sufficient concerned about the conscription of young delinquents that it established Special Training Units (STUs) to turn such men into good soldiers. As one of the training officers subsequently put it:

> One third of [the men sent to the STUs] were already manifestly delinquent, and the other two-thirds must have come from that vast fringe of potential delinquents (possibly two or three times as numerous as those convicted...) who might have been brought before the courts had the arm of the law been longer or more active.[23]

But while the STUs claimed success, crime was not eradicated from the army that returned to France in June 1944.

There seems to have been some reduction in the severity of the system during the First World War partly, perhaps, because of the new kinds of civilian soldiers resulting from the influx of patriotic volun-

---

22 Emsley, "Violent Crime in England in 1919", pp. 177–178.
23 Joseph Trenaman, *Out of Step: A study of young delinquent soldiers in wartime; their offences, their background and their treatment under an Army experiment* (London, 1952), p. 30. The book had a preface by Sir Cyril Burt then the acknowledged expert on young male delinquents.

teers and then of conscripts. A determination to restore discipline among the regular army led to an increase in the proportion of men brought before courts martial in the immediate aftermath of the war, but thereafter courts martial continued to decline.[24] An initial sampling of some of the records from the Second World War, however, suggests a similar picture of crime and criminal justice within the army to that in the First World War. Table 1 provides a breakdown of the offences listed by the Court Martial Centre of the 21 Army Group fighting in Belgium and France in December 1944. One hundred and sixty-five men were brought before the court charged with a total of 198 offences. Most of the offences related to army discipline, and more than half involved some form of absence or attempt to escape from military duties or the military life. Sean Longden's study of the British Army that fought from D Day to Lüneberg Heath has made some use of the records of the Army Provosts and of courts martial. His work provides an interesting but under-developed discussion of criminality amongst the soldiery.[25]

Theft, for example, appears to have been a common offence with both traditional and also novel motivations. First, there were enormous opportunities with large dumps of food, clothing and petrol. The charge of "stealing public property" on the list of offences in the table refers to such incidents; and it is significant that the scale of such offending in the early months of the war had led directly to the creation of the Special Investigation Branch (SIB) of the Military Police, initially staffed by volunteers from detectives in London's Metropolitan Police. Men knew that, to keep the war going, anything that was taken would be quickly replaced – so take they did. Hungry, tired soldiers thought that materiel

---

24 French, *Military Identities*, p. 184.
25 Sean Longden, *To the Victor the Spoils: D-Day to VE Day, The Reality behind the Heroism* (Moreton in Marsh, 2004); S.F. Crozier, *A History of the Corps of the Royal Military Police* (Aldershot, 1951) chapter 10; A.V. Lovell-Knight, *The Story of the Royal Military Police* (London, 1977) chapter 16. Both Crozier and Lovell-Knight were officers in the Military Police; the latter repeats, often word-for-word, the former's description of the formation of the SIB, including the assertion that, in France in 1939, "the professional thieves [in the army] soon established contact with local receivers". The best general study of the topic is John C. Spencer, *Crime and the Services* (London, 1954). Senior's book is based on his Ph.D under the supervision of Hermann Mannheim at the London School of Economics. Senior suggested that the crimonogenic influences of military life lay in the attendant circumstances of family separation, the interruption of ordinary working life and contrasting standards of living.

lying around might as well go to them; it could be sent home, or sold on with the profit then being sent home in the form of a money postal order. Some men appear to have turned in a considerable profit and to have been running illicit businesses staffed by absentees and deserters; whether as the Provosts (and Longden) state, these men were "professional" criminals is something that merits further work.

Sergeant George Gallon of the Pioneer Corps, who instigated the lead theft mentioned earlier and tried at the Central Criminal Court in 1941, was said to have had 17 previous criminal convictions. But may not many of the offenders have developed a propensity for crime because of the opportunities offered by the war rather than being "criminals" who had been conscripted? Many of those accused of stealing public property, for example, came from service units such as the Royal Ordinance or Royal Army Service Corps who spent their time shifting petrol and other valuable equipment with considerable black market value. One motivation for crime picked up by the Provosts, was the apparent desire of offenders to commit an offence – anything from theft to insubordination – and to get caught so as to avoid getting sent forward to the front line.

At the end of the war, once again, there were concerns that men trained to kill and disturbed by the brutalising experience of the battlefield, would return home, be unable to settle and slip into violent crime. The concerns focussed particularly on men from the new elite regiments of commandos and paratroops who had been trained in unarmed combat. Such individuals turned up in novels and feature films, but Sir Harold Scott, who became the Commissioner of the Metropolitan Police in 1945, dismissed the "thoughtless libel" that such training led to criminal violence after the war. So too did John C. Spencer, who set out to explore the effects of military life on "the delinquent and the non-delinquent" both during and immediately after the war. He did, however, suggest that "access to firearms and in particular revolvers [...] made it possible for a much larger number of criminals to go about armed than hitherto." Scott, for his part, suspected that habits of dishonesty learned in the forces may have been brought back into civilian life, though in this he may simply have been reflecting a suspicion present among officials in the Home Office who had been responsible for compiling the Judicial Statistics after the First World War.[26]

III

The preceding discussion has been based primarily on qualitative evidence. There is heated debate about the value of quantitative evidence and whether it can offer anything of value to understanding the pattern of crime rather than simply demonstrating the priorities of parts of the criminal justice system or the extent of funding available for prosecutions. This is not the place to embark on a rehearsal of the debate.[27] And whatever else may be the case, the statistics provide a pattern of offending that was picked up by the press, by commentators and by those responsible for policy. They can also pose questions for further research.

In general, the statistics for England and Wales for the first 60 yeas of the twentieth century give confusing images about the impact of war on violent crime. Homicide (table 2) remained fairly static at around 260 to 320 reported offences a year up to the early 1930s. There was, however, a significant drop down to 226 offences in 1917 and 204 in 1918. The numbers increased a little in the early 1930s running at between 300 and 350 a year until the late 1950s. But whereas there was a drop in the figures during the First World War, there were two peaks during the Second – 406 reported offences in 1942 and 492 in 1945. At the beginning of the century there were around 250 to 300 serious wounding and other life endangering offences each year (table 3); the

---

26 Sir Harold Scott, *Scotland Yard* (London, 1954) p. 62; Spencer, *Crime and the Services*, p. 121. For the comments about the impact of the First World War see, *Judicial Statistics for England and Wales for 1923*, Cmd. 2385 (London, 1924–25), p. 10; *Judicial Statistics for England and Wales for1924*, Cmd. 2602 (London, 1926), p. 6.
27 The principal critic of the value of the English Judicial Statistics is Howard Taylor. See, Howard Taylor, "Rationing Crime: The Political Economy of Crime Statistics since the 1850s", *Economic History Review*, 51, 3 (1998) pp. 569–590; idem, "The Politics of the Rising Crime Statistics in England and Wales, 1914–1960", *Crime, histoire et sociétés/Crime, history and Societies*, 2, 1 (1998) pp. 5–28; idem, "Forging the Job: A Crisis of 'Modernization' or Redundancy for the Police in England and Wales, 1900–1939", *British Journal of Criminology*, 39, 1 (1999) pp. 113–135. For a sustained critique of Taylor's argument see Robert M. Morris, "Lies, damned lies and criminal statistics: Reinterpreting the Criminal Statistics of England and Wales", *Crime, histoire et sociétés/Crime, history and Societies*, 5, 1 (2001) pp. 111–127.

number fell significantly during the First World War, especially in 1917 and 1918 when the number fell below 90. By the middle of the 1930s the numbers had risen again to more than 200 with an exceptional peak in 1938 (388 offences) and thereafter there was a steady increase with a new peak in 1945 (545 offences), a drop the following year but from then onwards the number continued to rise rapidly to nearly 2000 by the end of the 1950s.

From around 200 offences reported each year in the first decade of the century, rape fell steadily with a particularly marked drop below 100 in 1916 (98), 1917 (74) and 1918 (78) (table 4). There were less than 120 offences each year during the 1920s and for most of the 1930s there were less than 100. Numbers went up again during the Second World War with peaks in 1944 (416) and 1945 (377). They stabilised briefly at around 250 a year in the late 1940s but then they began to rise steadily to around 500 a year by the beginning of the 1960s, and it is extremely unlikely that the later increase can, in any way, be attributed to the fall-out of the war. The statistics of indecent assaults on women (table 5), like various other offences, fell during the First World War but, generally speaking they followed a broad upward trend throughout the entire period rising from around 700 a year in the first decade of the century to double this number by the early 1920s. There were around 2500 such offences by the beginning of the Second World War; this number had doubled by the late 1940s, and it almost doubled again to over 9000 by the late 1950s and early 1960s.

These are raw figures. It is common to reorganise crimes as incidents per 100,000 of the population; the problem is that in many instances the figures are so small that they would scarcely register in such a reorganisation. They are also raw figures for the offences committed in England and Wales, so they take no account of offences committed by servicemen subject to military law and especially those serving overseas.

IV

For a long time soldiers and war were subjects for the military historian and military historians tended not to be interested in the behaviour of troops far beyond the battlefield. The men physically disabled by war have only recently begun to be investigated by historians and the point has been made that in the inter-war years people liked to think of the disabled as remaining plucky and cheerful. Even the hospitals that cared for them avoided discussion of any violence or criminality among their charges and any such offenders were generally removed.[28] Men who returned with mental trauma that led them sometimes to turn on family members remained hidden from view, unless they inflicted violence that became the subject of a criminal investigation. The family remained the ideal social unit, people were expected keep personal problems to themselves and there were few places to go to seek help. Joy Damousi's work echoes the suggestions of Joanna Bourke and has provided some examples of the "marriage wars" fostered by the combat experiences of husbands who served in Australian armed forces during the twentieth century. Recent campaigning literature has revived the brutalized veteran thesis, reflecting especially on the impact of conflicts at the end of the British Empire and nasty little "peace-keeping" operations. The stories of others, suggest further that it is not simply that men are brutalised by the experience of combat; often their trauma is more the result of guilt about the loss of a close friend in action, especially one who had helped in a moment of need or danger.[29]

Unfortunately, but perhaps not surprisingly, research into the dark side of military behaviour can still run into serious hostility. It was all very well for historians in the west to write about the rapes by Soviet

---

28 Deborah Cohen, *The War Come Home: Disabled Veterans in Britain and Germany, 1914–1939* (Berkeley, Cal., 2001) pp. 145–146.
29 Joy Damousi, *Living with the Aftermath: Trauma, Nostalgia and Grief in Post-War Australia* (Cambridge, 2001); Renwick, *Hidden Wounds*; Andy McNab, *Seven Troop* (London, 2008). In his account of the SAS unit in which he served McNab describes the post service behaviour of Tommy Shanks, who killed his girl friend, Charles "Nish" Bruce, who attempted to murder a girl friend and later committed suicide and Frank Collins who committed suicide. Bruce and Collins could not get over the death of a friend and fellow soldier, Al Slater, shot by the IRA during an incident at which they were present.

troops as they advanced into, and occupied parts of Nazi Germany, but when Robert Lilly did a similar study about the behaviour of American troops he could not find a US publisher, and was subjected to considerable internet abuse. As one furious critic of his research expressed it on the web: "I just checked, and this guy Robert Lilly isn't a historian at all. He's a fucking sociologist." It was unclear whether this meant that he had no right to write history, or that his academic discipline itself somehow negated the validity of his research. Lilly's book first appeared in French (in 2003) and then in Italian (in 2004) before an English language edition finally appeared in 2007.[30] The snippets of work that have been done on crimes committed by British soldiers during the twentieth century are suggestive of much more that might be done. But by ignoring crime in wartime and the possible impact of war on crime, historians are missing an important trick – war is no longer the private preserve of the military historian, and it is time that historians of crime and criminal justice woke up to the fact.

---

30 J. Robert Lilly, *Taken By Force: Rape and American GIs in Europe during World War II* (London and Basingstoke, 2007); quotation at p. xxii. The classic study of the Soviet Army in Germany is Norman Naimark, *The Russians in Germany: A History of the Soviet Zone Occupation, 1945–1959* (Cambridge, Mass., 1995).

Tab. 1: Offences before the 21 Army Group Court Martial Centre, December 1944[31]

Offence	Number
Desertion	83
Absence	37
Stealing Public Property	19
Conduct Prejudicial to the Army	14
Leaving a Post	11
Stealing	9
Insubordinate or Threatening Language	8
Robbery	2
Disobeying a Lawful Command	2
Taking Currency out of the United Kingdom	2
Striking another Soldier	2
Manslaughter	1
Indecent Assault	1
Allowing Prisoners to Escape	1
Breaking Barracks	1
Offering Violence	1
Attempting to Escape	1
Making a False Statement	1
Altering a Document	1
Sleeping at Post	1

---

31 Source: The National Archives: WO 171.190.

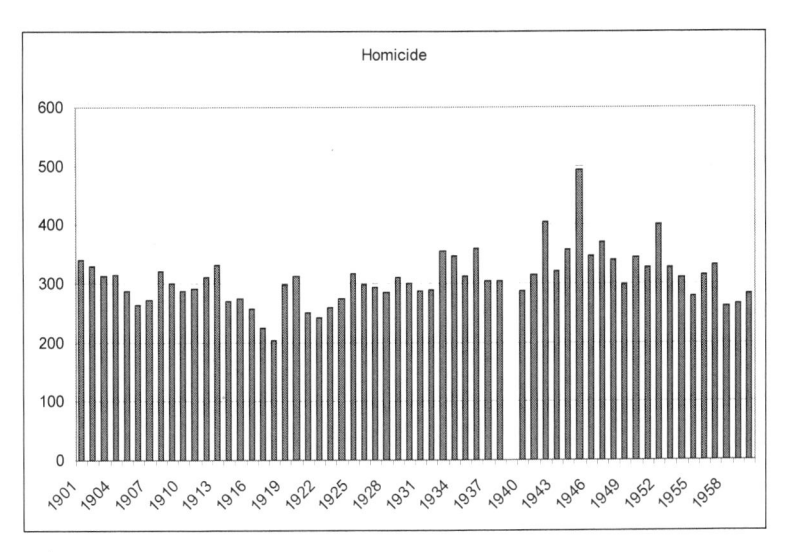

Tab. 2

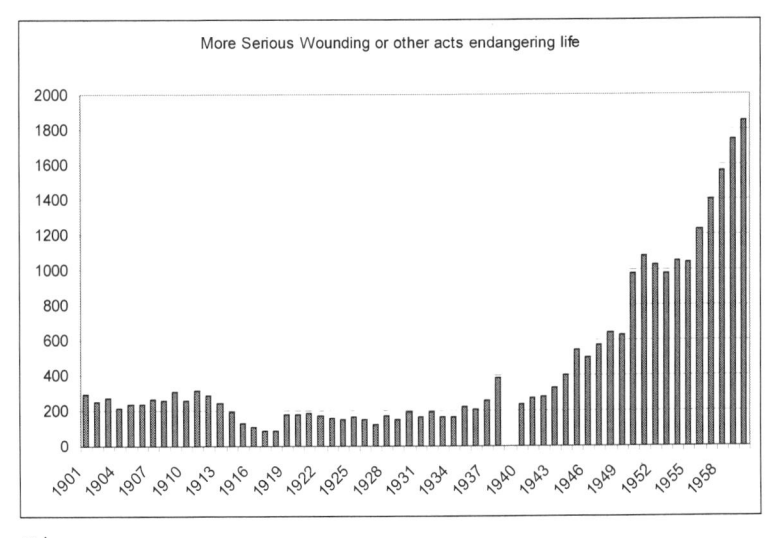

Tab. 3

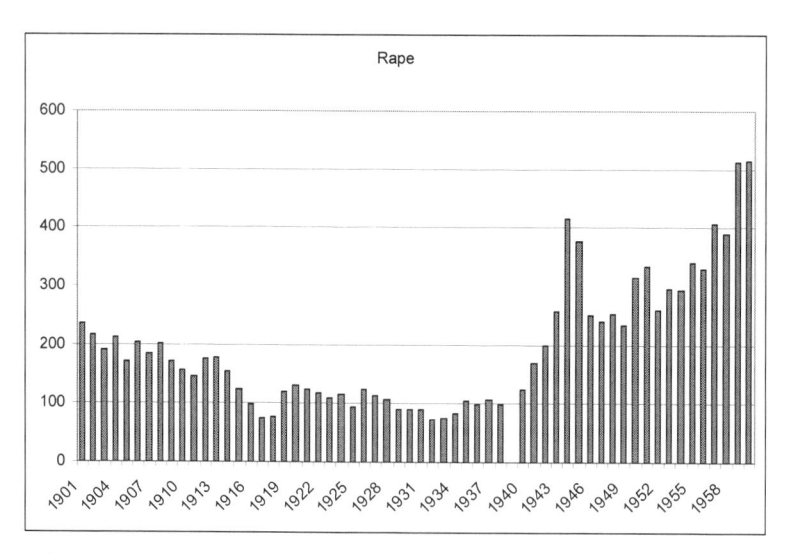

Tab. 4

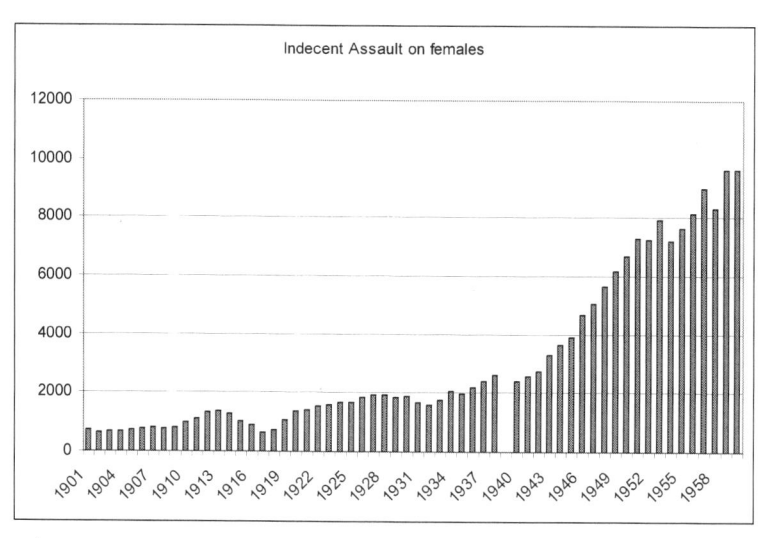

Tab. 5[32]

32 Tables 2 to 5 are based on the figures given in the annual *Judicial Statistics for England and Wales*; there are no figures for the year 1939.

Sources

ARCHIVAL SOURCES

The National Archives (TNA), Kew
  HO 45.16515, Report of the Juvenile Organisation Committee, 1920.
  RECO 1.342, Report of Committee on the Control of Firearms (the Blackwell Committee) 1918.
  WO 84.70, Army Charge Book, 21 February to 12 August 1944.
  WO 171.190, 21 Army Group Court Martial Centre, December 1944.
Printed and Media Sources
BBC Radio 4, File on 4, "In Afghanistan: The Home Front".
Judicial Statistics for England and Wales (published annually in *Parliamentary Papers*).
Le Moniteur.
Police Gazette, Supplement A.
The Observer.
The Sunday Telegraph.
The Times.

LITERATURE

Adler, Jeffrey S. 1996: The Making of a Moral Panic in 19th-Century America: The Boston Garroting Hysteria of 1865. *Deviant Behaviour: An Interdisciplinary Journal* 17 1996, pp. 259–278.
Bourke, Joanna 1999: *An Intimate History of Killing: Face-to-Face Killing in Twentieth-Century Warfare*. Granta, London.
Cohen, Deborah 2001: *The War Come Home: Disabled Veterans in Britain and Germany, 1914–1939*. University of California Press, Berkeley, Cal.
Crozier, S.F. 1951: *A History of the Corps of the Royal Military Police*. Gale and Poden, Aldershot.
Damousi, Joy 2001: *Living with the Aftermath: Trauma, Nostalgia and Grief in Post-War Australia*. Cambridge University Press, Cambridge.
Emsley, Clive 2005: Hard Men: Violence in England since 1750. Hambledon, London.
Emsley, Clive 2008: Violent Crime in England in 1919: Post-War Anxieties and Press Narratives. *Continuity and Change* 21 (1) 2008, pp. 173–195.
Emsley, Clive 2010: "A Legacy of Conflict? The Brutalised Veteran and Violence in Europe after the Great War". In *Crime, Violence and the Modern State*, ed. Efi Avdela, Shani D'Cruze and Judith Rowbotham. Edwin Mellen, Lampeter.
Exner, Franz 1927: *Krieg und Kriminalität in Österreich*. Hőlde-Pichler-Tempsky AG, Vienna.
Forrest, Alan 1989: *Conscripts and Deserters: The Army and French Society during the Revolution and Empire*. Oxford University Press, Oxford.
French, David 2005: *Military Identities: The Regimental System, the British Army and the British People c.1870-2000*. Oxford University Press, Oxford.
Hopkin, David M. 2002: Military Marauders in Nineteenth-Century French Popular Culture. *War and History* 9 (3) 2002, pp. 251–278.

Hopkin, David M. 2003: *Soldier and Peasant in French Popular Culture, 1766-1870*. Boydell Press, Woodbridge.

King, Peter 2000: *Crime, Justice and Discretion in England, 1740-1820*. Oxford University Press, Oxford.

Liepmann, Moritz 1930: *Krieg und Kriminalität in Deutschland*, Deutsche Verlag Anstalt, Stuttgart.

Lilly, J. Robert 2007: *Taken By Force: Rape and American GIs in Europe during World War II*. Palgrave, London and Basingstoke.

Longden, Sean 2004: *To the Victor the Spoils: D-Day to VE Day, The Reality behind the Heroism*. Arris, Moreton in Marsh.

Lovell-Knight, A.V. 1977: *The Story of the Royal Military Police*. Leo Cooper, London.

McNab, Andy 2008: *Seven Troop*. Bantam Press, London.

Morris, Robert M. 2001: "Lies, damned lies and criminal statistics": Reinterpreting the Criminal Statistics of England and Wales. *Crime, histoire et sociétés/Crime, history and Societies* 5 (1) 2001, pp. 111–127.

Naimark, Norman 1995: *The Russians in Germany: A History of the Soviet Zone Occupation, 1945–1959*. Harvard University Press, Cambridge, Mass.

Renwick, Aly 1999: *Hidden Wounds: The Problems of Northern Ireland Veterans in Civvy Street*. Barbed Wire, London.

Rousseaux, Xavier and Laurence van Ypersele, ed. 2008: *La Patrie crie Vengeance! La Répression des "Inciviques" Belges au sortie de la Guerre 1914–1918*, Editions Le Cri, Brussels.

Scott, Sir Harold 1954: *Scotland Yard*, Penguin Books, London.

Smithies, Edward 1982: *Crime in Wartime: A Social History of Crime in World War II*. George Allen & Unwin, London.

Spencer, John C. 1954: *Crime and the Services*. Routledge & Kegan Paul, London.

Starke, Wilhelm 1884: *Verbrechen und Verbrecher in Preussen, 1854–1878: Eine kulturgeschichtliche Studie*. Enslin, Berlin.

Taylor, Howard 1998: Rationing Crime: The Political Economy of Crime Statistics since the 1850s. *Economic History Review* 51 (3) 1998, pp. 569–590.

Taylor, Howard 1998: The Politics of the Rising Crime Statistics in England and Wales, 1914-1960: *Crime, histoire et sociétés/Crime, history and Societies* 2 (1) 1998, pp. 5–28.

Taylor, Howard 1999: Forging the Job: A Crisis of "Modernization" or Redundancy for the Police in England and Wales, 1900-1939. *British Journal of Criminology* 39 (1) 1999, pp. 113–135.

Trenaman, Joseph 1952: *Out of Step: A study of young delinquent soldiers in wartime; their offences, their background and their treatment under an Army experiment*. Methuen, London.

Turnbull, Jack and John Hamblett 1994: *The Pegasus Patrol*. John Turnbull, Privately published.

Wiener, Martin J. 2004: *Men of Blood: Violence, Manliness and Criminal Justice in Victorian England*. Cambridge University Press, Cambridge.

Wood, John Carter 2004: *Violence and Crime in Nineteenth-Century England: The Shadow of our Refinement*. Routledge, London.

The Control of Vagrants and the Poor in Finland 1850–1885

Päivi Pukero

Paul Lawrence (2004) suggests that in nineteenth-century England and France the causes of poverty and vagrancy were commonly viewed as being intrinsically linked to the failings of individuals rather than as a collective social problem. Lax personal morality, laziness and drunkenness were seen as the main causes of poverty.[1] In Finland, although vagrancy was seen as an individual problem, there was also an understanding that certain phenomena, such as crop failures, could cause unemployment and poverty. According to Lawrence, a migratory lifestyle became less acceptable within industrial economies such as England and France. Although in Finland industrialization was still undeveloped, there was also a trend towards stricter control of vagrants. The need for increased control of vagrants and the poor arose from problems within Finnish agriculture.[2]

The issue of vagrancy was the greatest social problem facing nineteenth-century Finland. It was not only a matter for the police and of

---

1 Paul Lawrence, "Policing the Poor in England and France, 1850–1900", in Clive Elmsley, Eric Johnson and Pieter Spierenburg (ed.) *Social Control in Europe Vol. 2, 1800–2000* (History of Crime and Criminal Justice Series; Ohio, 2004), pp. 211–213.
2 Arvo M. Soininen, *"Vanha maataloutemme". Maatalous ja maatalousväestö Suomessa perinnäisen maatalouden loppukaudella 1720-luvulta 1870-luvulle* (Historiallisia tutkimuksia, 96; Helsinki, 1974), pp. 388–391.

public order, but also an educational problem. Correctional treatment and prison facilities provided security for the general population, while correctional measures aimed to transform vagrants into socially useful citizens through work, education and control. Labour was an important means of correctional education; although this had traditionally been the case, the utility of work was now particularly emphasized.[3] Finnish historians agree that the desire to control vagrants was the main reason behind the huge increase in rates of imprisonment.[4] Stricter laws on vagrancy control came into operation between 1802 and 1805, and were later amended in 1852.[5] Historians also agree that the number of closed institutions, such as prisons, correction houses, alms-houses and children's homes, increased significantly in Finland during the nineteenth century.

The history of closed institutions reveals how control and authority are closely related. Closed institutions specialize in taking away the freedom of individuals for various reasons. In the 1800s, when closed institutions were established in Finland, deviants[6] (including vagrants, gypsies, disabled people and those suffering from mental illnesses) were controlled in the same way: they were placed in confinement and forced to work.[7] The increase in the number of closed institutions in eighteenth- and nineteenth-century Finland was not a unique phenomenon: in fact such an increase was a typical feature of modern societies. In this article the concept of a closed institution refers specifically to prisons,

---

3   Päivi Pukero, "'Harhaantuneiden ja eksyneiden parantaja.' Luostanlinna irtolaisten kasvatuskokeiluna 1859–1880" *Kasvatus & Aika*, 2/1 (2008), pp. 23–40.
4   Riitta Suhonen, Rikollinen nainen vai pahantapainen tyttölapsi? Kuopion lääninvankilan naisvangit ja heidän rikoksensa vuosina 1890–1910 Suomen historian lisensiaattitutkielma (Joensuu, 1994), p. 68; Veikko Virtanen, *Suomen vankeinhoito I 1808–1831* (Historiallisia tutkimuksia XXIX,1; Helsinki: SHS, 1944), pp. 111–112.
5   Toivo Nygård, *Irtolaisuus ja sen kontrolli 1800-luvun alun Suomessa* (Studia Historica Jyväskyläensia, 31; Jyväskylä, 1985), pp. 38–39; Kaarlo J. Ståhlberg, *Irtolaisuus Suomen lain mukaan* (Vankeinhoidon koulutuskeskuksen julkaisu, 4/95; Helsinki, 1995[1893]), pp. 22–27; Decree on handling vagrancy, 1852. For convenience and clarity I have translated the titles of decrees and proceedings into English. Armollinen Asetus laillisesta suojeluksesta ja kuinka suojelukseton persoonia menetettämään pitää. 14.1.1852. Kejserliga Förordningar för åren 1852.
6   According to Durkheim, no society is without its deviants: deviancy is a normal phenomenon within society. Émile Durkheim, *Sosiologian metodisäännöt* (Helsinki, 1982), pp. 14, 84–87.
7   Toivo Nygård, *Erilaisten historiaa: Marginaaliryhmät Suomessa 1800-luvulla ja 1900-luvun alussa* (Jyväskylä, 1998), pp. 139, 166.

alms-houses, mental hospitals, workhouses and houses of correction.

There is some disagreement among historians about why the historical development of social control focused on closed institutions. International debate about the system of closed institutions has tended to follow three main lines of argument. These theories can be loosely characterized as "positive", "negative" or "neutral" explanations. The first, positive, explanation is based on a belief in that a progression to humanism led to the abandonment of the death penalty. Accordingly, new punishments such as prisons and houses of correction replaced more brutal penalties. The idea of opposing the death penalty can be traced back to the Italian philosopher Cesare Beccaria.[8] Norbert Elias's theory of the civilizing process has also been extensively discussed within this context.[9]

A more negative explanation is based on Michel Foucault's (2000 [1980]) ideas about the disciplining effect of power on individuals. Prison and other facilities are seen as symbols of the disciplining of modern society.[10] Stanley Cohen (1985) and Nils Christie (1993) continued Foucault's work with a cynical tone. Their cynicism is directed toward social control and the social order itself. In contrast to Elias, Foucault, Cohen and Christie believe that social control is largely a negative category, which in itself creates deviance. In addition, they claim that social control has increased as a result of the processes of professionalization and medicalization.[11]

The third line of argument can be seen as a neutral explanation, although it takes the two other positions into account. This research tradition considers social control in a wider context. In addition it attempts to pay attention to ideological, economic, cultural and social

---

8 Cesare Beccaria, *Rikoksesta ja rangaistuksesta: Vankeinhoidon koulutuskeskuksen julkaisuja* (Helsinki, 1998), pp. 20–24.
9 David Garland, *Punishment and Welfare: A History of Penal Strategies* (Great Britain, 1985), p. 32; Hans Eyvind Naess and Eva Österberg, "Sanctions, Agreements, Sufferings", in Eva Österberg and Sølvi Bauge Sogner (ed.) *People Meet the Law: Control and Conflict-Handling in the Courts. The Nordic Countries in the Post-Reformation and Pre-Industrial Period* (Oslo, 2000), pp. 140–166.
10 Michel Foucault, *Tarkkailla ja rangaista* (Keuruu, 2000 [1980]), pp. 401–424.
11 Nils Christie *Kohti vankileirien saaristoa? Rikollisuuden kontrolli teollisuutena länsimaissa* (Helsinki, 1993), p. 11; Stanley Cohen, *Visions of Social Control: Crime, Punishment and Classification* (Cambridge, 1985), pp. 13–39; Nygård, *Erilaisten historiaa*, pp. 191–192.

elements of informal control.[12] In my article I will lean towards this later research tradition. Research into social control has, rightly, been accused of treating the poor, vagrants and prisoners as objects; marginal citizens have been viewed from above as part of the surveillance necessary for their control. Although, in this article I attempt to consider the issue from below, a macro-historical perspective cannot be avoided. The majority of earlier research and available references approach the subject from the perspective of the controller rather than the controlled.[13]

There is a lack of research about vagrancy, which focuses on the policing of deviancy. In addition there is a need for research and theories that attempt to define the national features of closed institutions. The purpose of this article is to address the absence of such research within Finland. I will consider the way in which vagrants and the poor were policed as well as examine the foundation of closed institutions in Finland. This essay presents a new hypothesis and draws on the idea of the Finnish institution system in an international context.

Researching deviancy

The study employs micro-historical and qualitative methods, its theoretical background being grounded in social history. This article is based on research of my doctoral thesis. The main purpose of my article is to examine how deviance and vagrancy was regulated in Finland during the nineteenth century. I pay special attention to the administrative decisions taken by the governor of Kuopio province and the establishment of closed institutions in Finland. In my research I use theme-analysis to present the main points of the descriptions of deviance. I outline de-

---

12 Antti Häkkinen, Panu Pulma and Miika Tervonen, *Vieraat kulkijat – tutut talot: näkökulmia etnisyyden ja köyhyyden historiaan Suomessa* (Historiallinen arkisto, 120; Helsinki, 2005); Pieter Spierenburg, "Social Control and History: An Introduction", in Herman Roodenburg and Pieter Spierenburg (ed.) *Social Control in Europe Vol. 1, 1500–1800* (History of Crime and Criminal Justice Series; Ohio, 2004), pp. 1–22.
13 Jütte faced the same problem in his research of poverty and deviance in Europe. Robert Jütte, *Poverty and Deviance in Early Modern Europe* (Cambridge, 1994), p. 3.

scriptions of themes and aggregates. The highlighted themes are tools for my analysis.[14]

I agree with Lawrence when he claims that "there is no doubt that vagrants were the most unpopular element of poorer classes".[15] In nineteenth-century Finland vagrancy and poverty were controlled by local officers such as priests, rural police chiefs and special district-officers (*kaitsijamiehet*) who were chosen to control the poor.[16] People without work or legal protection were brought before the governor. Any suspicion of drunkenness, sexual aberration or laziness was often reason enough to send someone to prison.[17] In my research I found that in fact the governor not only policed vagrancy but also dealt with all kinds of deviant behaviour.[18] Interestingly, those who were judged to be deviants were sent to a variety of different facilities.

This article is based on national and local sources. I have examined the administrative decisions taken by the governor of Kuopio province. In this article, analysis is based primarily on sources that relate to practice within institutions. Sources from Luostanlinna penal colony (in Kuopio province) are located in the Joensuu province archives. The Kuopio county prison official papers include notes and reports from Luostanlinna. Casebooks, annual reports and letters have proved to be particularly useful source materials. Although a fire at Luostanlinna in 1875 destroyed casebooks and reports from the previous ten years, it is still possible to describe the establishment of the penal colony without them.

Sources from Kylliälä children's home can be found in the Lenoblogosarchiv in Vyborg. Documents in the social welfare administration and judicial administration archives include Kylliälä regulations, a student register, incoming and outgoing correspondence and board proceedings. Material relating to Harjula alms-house is most problematic, largely because

14　Jari Eskola and Juha Suoranta, *Johdatus laadulliseen tutkimukseen* (Tampere, 1998), p. 14.
15　Lawrence, "Policing the Poor in England and France, 1850–1900", p. 213.
16　Decree on poor relief, 1852. Armollinen asetus yhteisestä vaivaisholhouksesta Suomen Isoruhtinaanmaassa. 22.3.1852. Kejserliga Förordningar för åren 1852.
17　Decree on handling vagrancy, 1852.
18　Proceedings of the governor's hearings, 1855–1860, 1861–1868, 1865–1876, 1877–1880 and 1884–1885. County Administrative Board. Joensuun maakunta-arkisto [Joensuu Province Archives].

very little of it has survived. Only a few documents from the first years of the alms-house's existence (1873–1879) can be found. The proceedings of the poor relief board offer some insight into the foundation of the institution, but it is not possible to reconstruct practice at Harjula before 1880. Source material relating to Harjula is located in the Kuopio city archives.

The national view of vagrancy, the poor and the foundation of closed institutions is based on Senate committee reports, as well as laws and acts relating to correctional treatment, the vagrancy issue and poor relief. One problem with all administrative sources is that practices within the institutions are always looked at from above, from the perspective of the controller. Another issue is that most of the documents are largely concerned with economic facts. Individuals appear as names or numbers in documents, and actual people or the details of everyday life are hidden behind the register lists. Furthermore, it is very difficult to ascertain how the objectives of institutions were followed. For these reasons, I have used newspaper reports and articles as supplementary material. The work of other historians, especially those from England and Sweden, has provided useful comparative material.

Policing deviance in the province of Kuopio

Vagrants who were brought before the governor were sieved out by authorities at a local level. Most were adults without legal protection or permanent work, but children, the sick and the elderly were also among their number. At the end of the research period, there was an increase in the number of individuals who had been apprehended for "bad manners" or their vagabond lifestyle. Time spent in prison awaiting one's hearing and the hearing itself could last anywhere from a few days to a couple of months. Lying or the use of delaying tactics was very common in these circumstances. Time spent in prison depended on the willingness of the authorities and vagrants to co-operate and settle the matter. Only 15 percent of those investigated were sentenced to work in the house of correction. It seems that local control of deviants was stricter than the control eventually exerted at the governor's hearings. It is, therefore, not wholly surprising that complaints about the governor's resolutions were rarely raised.

As a result of theme-analysis, I identified six different types of deviants defined by the governor of Kuopio province: children, the poor and crippled, bad-mannered vagrants, the Roma, those suffering from a venereal disease and the mentally ill. These individuals were sent to different kinds of facilities or closed institutions. Practice in institutions was reconstructed through the example of the penal colony of Kuopio province, Luostanlinna (founded 1859); the Kylliälä children's home in Vyborg (1829); and the Harjula alms-house in Kuopio (1873).

The first category of deviants was made up of children, including orphans, who came under the remit of poor relief. Women and children – like others who were apprehended – were housed in prison while they waited for their cases to be heard. In the case of orphans, the governor would usually try to find a parent or foster parents. The children of investigated women would be sent with their mother to the alms-house or the prison. There were only a few children's homes in Finland in the mid-1800s, and none of them were in the province of Kuopio. Children from the Kuopio province were sent to Harjula alms-house or workhouse, where, like adults, they had to work in exchange for food and shelter. Later the alms-house offered half-day schooling for children. Only a few underage boys who the governor found to be ill-mannered were sentenced to imprisonment in the penal colony.

The second group I identified from the hearings was the poor including those who were crippled or elderly. They differed from vagrants because they were sick or unable to work. The governor sent them to the host of the parish or to Harjula. Harjula was founded on the principle that "idle hands work for the devil" and thus implemented a regime of forced labour in the form of handicrafts or household work. All inmates were required to take part in the daily work or provide labour for the farm. Many poor families who were identified as homeless were sent to Harjula. Parents, usually fathers, had to work in exchange for their family's upkeep.[19]

---

19 Proceedings of the poor relief board of Kuopio, 1873–1885. Kuopion kaupungin arkisto [Kuopio City Archive].

The reputation of these kinds of alms-houses was terrible. M. A. Crowther described English workhouses as filthy, unplanned and unsupervised.[20] In Finland, popular writings and newspaper reports of the period described almshouses in terms of pity and fear. The almshouse was seen as an institution for the aged, poor and helpless and its living conditions were the subject of a great deal of criticism. Minna Canth's short story about the inmates of Harjula (written in 1886) was widely discussed in the press and by the administration.[21] (My research has shown that Canth's description of conditions was largely accurate. The annual mortality rate in Harjula was around 20 percent. Only six members of staff were responsible for nearly two hundred inmates; of these workers three were officers and none was a nurse. Furthermore the almshouse was cold and confined.) Crowther uses the term "workhouse myth" to describe rumours relating to almshouses and describes beliefs in England:

> [T]hat the guardians would be able to refuse all relief, that the bread which was taking the place of money doles for the outdoor poor was poisoned, that the children of the poor would be forcibly taken away from them. Of the workhouses even more terrifying rumours circulated, of floggings, starvation, cruel separation of mothers and infants, and dying men torn from their relations [...] that the dead did not have decent burial.[22]

Bad-mannered vagrants made up the third type of deviants brought before the governor's hearings. Many legal vagrants were given a warning and then set free. They were given three weeks to secure a job or legal protection.[23] The concept of legal protection was important in nineteenth-century Finland. Work, marriage, the parish or the alms-house could provide an individual with legal protection.[24] Par-

---

20 M. A. Crowther, *The Workhouse System 1834–1929: The History of an English Social Institution* (London, 1983), p. 29.
21 Minna Canth, *Köyhää kansaa* (Hämeenlinna, 1983[1886]), pp. 48–58.
22 Crowther, *The Workhouse System 1834–1929*, p. 31.
23 Proceedings of the governor's hearings, 1855–1885.
24 Decree on handling vagrancy, 1852/1865. Armollinen Asetus joutolaisista ja niiden kanssa menettelemisestä 23.1.1865. Finlands Författnings-Samling 1865 n:o 1.

ishes and alms-houses gave legal protection only to those who were unable to work.

Another important concept used in the decrees on handling vagrancy and by the governor, was the idea of bad-mannered individuals. In the hearings and proceedings the label "bad-mannered" was applied differently according to gender. Men were ascribed qualities that related to their temper or ability to work; they would be described as lazy, impudent and disobedient. By contrast bad-mannered females were attributed sexual characteristics such as debauchery, unchaste behaviour or immorality. In spite of these sexual descriptions, which suggested that proscribed behaviour had taken place, only a few females were sentenced for prostitution.

All illegal and bad-mannered vagrants were sentenced to forced labour; in the province of Kuopio, such vagrants were sent to Luostanlinna penal colony. The colony pursued an educational goal: vagrants were to receive vocational training and religious instruction. The aim of this educational programme was to rehabilitate lazy vagrants and transform them into useful, working citizens.[25]

Roma people made up the fourth group of deviants. The decree on handling vagrancy (1852) defined "gypsies" as vagrants, like all other vagabonds without papers. According to the decree all gypsies were to be held in the house of correction until the director of the facility decided to set them free.[26] In Kuopio province "gypsies" were categorized by their ethnic background. Within Finland the Roma were often feared and there was a great deal of mythology associated with them.[27] Roma people were viewed as lazy, criminal and sinful: they were said to bury their dead without a funeral and were believed to practise witchcraft and quackery. Although, in the province of Kuopio "gypsies" were in fact treated more leniently than the decree intended, the Roma were nevertheless subjected to extensive control and were often hospitalized.

---

25 Regulation for Kuopio Province penal colony 206/1858. Reglor för Kuopio Läns Arbetskompani. Kenraalikuvernöörin kanslia. KKK. Kansallisarkisto (KA) [Finnish National Archives], Helsinki
26 Decree on handling vagrancy, 1852.
27 Miika Tervonen, "Gypsies", "travellers" and "peasants": A Study on Ethnic Boundary Drawing in Finland and Sweden, C.1860-1925. (European University Institute 2010), p. 64–72.

The fifth and sixth groups were those infected with a venereal disease and "lunatics" respectively. Both groups were usually treated in the province hospital. If the governor suspected that someone had a venereal disease, the individual in question would be sent to hospital immediately. The governor took decisions for these individuals largely for economic reasons and he decided who was responsible for the cost of treatment: the parish, the state, the town or the individual him or herself.[28]

Mentally ill individuals were brought before the governor, even though he himself had no medical knowledge. The definition and diagnosis of mental illness was unsophisticated at that time. Only those who were viewed as a potential threat to the general population were sent to the hospital. The province hospital provided a kind of test treatment for two months. Those patients who were deemed to be incurable were transferred to the Seili hospital, near Turku, where they would remain for the rest of their lives.[29] Isolating these patients from healthy citizens was seen as more important than treating them. In nineteenth-century Finland diagnosis and treatment were poorly developed: sick people were frequently mistreated and the medical treatment itself was often painful and ineffective. If an individual was neither a danger to others nor incurable, the governor would send him or her to Harjula. Interestingly, cases involving mental health differed from others in one respect: those brought before the governor came from all social groups, not just the lower class.[30]

In conclusion it seems the governor actually defined "deviance" in the province of Kuopio: he decided who was "normal" and who was "deviant". Those deemed to be deviant were sent to a variety of facilities. Isolation was one of the main goals of all the institutions. Here, we can see the basic element of the system based on total closed institutions. Later, I shall consider whether there was a connection between closed institutions and measures directed at deviant individuals.

---

28 Proceedings of the governor's hearings, 1855–1885.
29 Decree on handling mentally ill persons, 1840. Hans Kejserliga Majestäts Rådiga Förordning, angående sinnessjukte personers wård och förbättrade anstalter till deras botande 4.2.1840. Kejserliga Förordningar för åren 1840.
30 Proceedings of the governor's hearings, 1855–1885.

Establishing closed institutions

There are a number of similarities between the foundation of, and subsequent practices at, Luostanlinna, Harjula and Kyllilä children's home. How does the example of these three institutions fit into earlier attempts to explain how and why closed institutions were founded? The emergence of closed institutions in Finland has usually been explained from idealistic, social or economic perspectives.[31]

Finnish social and criminal policy followed principles adopted from Sweden, Germany and the United States: isolation within closed institutions, on-going control and education. Furthermore, the emergence of closed institutions in Finland followed an international schedule. Prisons, workhouses and alms-houses have primarily been viewed as reforms that improved the treatment of prisoners, poor people and vagrants.[32] I argue that the emergence of closed institutions in Finland was based more on economic and social demands than on humanistic principles. Moreover, closed institutions in Finland did not seem to be an arena for scientific experiment, as was the case elsewhere (in Sweden, for example).[33]

Luostanlinna was founded in Rautavaara in 1859. The main reason for the establishment of this institution was to set sentenced vagrants to useful work. Luostanlinna was a pilot project and the first "bog-prison" in Finland, where new educational, social and criminal ideas were on trial. Luostanlinna was founded on primarily utilitarian principles. First, the institution was expected to gain financially by draining the bog and preparing the drained land for harvest. Furthermore, handicraft products and household work carried out by prisoners reduced the institution's expenses. Second, the rehabilitation of prisoners had its uses: immoral or lazy workers and those who drank were transformed into decent members of society. Third, internal exile and isolation played

---

[31] Jukka Kekkonen and Heikki Ylikangas, *Vapausrangaistuksen valtakausi: Nykyisen seuraamusjärjestelmän historiallinen tausta* (Helsinki, 1982), pp. 16–19.
[32] Veikko Kylä-Marttila, *Kysymys kuolemanrangaistuksesta autonomian ajan valtiopäivillä vuosina 1863–1888* (Vankeinhoidon historiaprojektin julkaisu, 13; Helsinki, 1986), p. 5.
[33] Roddy Nilsson, *En välbyggd maskin, en mardröm för själen: Det svenska fängelsesystemet under 1800-talet* (Bibliotheca Historica Lundensis, 93; Lund, 1999), p. 454.

an important role in Luostanlinna. "Bad-mannered" individuals were isolated from normal people, as were actual criminals. In other words, the safety of society was improved by isolating deviancy. Like Siberia, Luostanlinna was an exile site, but it was located within Finland, which was now able to benefit from work undertaken by Finnish prisoners.[34]

Luostalinna had been designed to accommodate 80 prisoners: however, the numbers at the penal colony in fact increased from 24 to 200. A typical prisoner would have been a single man in his twenties who had been found guilty of vagrancy. Re-education did not prove successful for all inmates: one in three returned to Luostanlinna after serving their sentence. The colony was closed in 1880, because its original purpose had partly failed. Although the bog draining was a successful enterprise, the education programme floundered and prisoners were subsequently moved to the workhouse in Lappeenranta. Thus, even the closure of Luostanlinna tells us something about the importance of utilitarian goals.[35]

It is important to ask why social control was extended over a larger group of individuals. What forces played the most significant role in disciplining citizens and in exercising social control? Who or what determined how different individuals or abnormal people should be treated? Where did the idea of closed institutions for deviant people come from? In earlier times disabled and mentally ill individuals had lived with their families, but in the 1800s various kinds of institutions were founded for "abnormal" people. New sites for deviants included special schools, houses of work and correction, mental hospitals and prisons.

As Crowther (1983) claims, although in England the decades between 1860 and the Great War saw a massive expansion of closed institutions, the British, on the whole, had been relatively slow to establish such facilities.[36] Crowther argues that closed institutions first expanded in countries in which the government's authority was relatively centralized or the religious establishment more hierarchical. English parish autonomy survived into the nineteenth century and this kept the con-

---

34 Regulation for Kuopio Province penal colony 206/1858.
35 Pukero, "Harhaantuneiden ja eksyneiden parantaja", pp. 25–36.
36 Crowther, *The Workhouse System 1834–1929*, pp. 58, 64.

struction of public institutions in check.[37] In Finland the development of alms-houses began when administration of the poor was separated from parishes in 1879.[38]

Harjula alms-house was founded in 1873 on the initiative of the board of the then-vacant Harjula manor. The parish of Kuopio decided to contract out its poor relief to the board. The motives behind the foundation of the alms-house were largely economic: the board needed a tenant for the manor and they pledged to care of the poor for only 30 percent of previous costs. Inmates at Harjula had to undertake household work, farming and nursing; they were also responsible for taking care of the children and teaching them to read. Perhaps this explains why it was possible to lower costs so dramatically. This contract was later ruled to be illegal and was cancelled after only nine months, at which time the parish of Kuopio and its poor relief board took responsibility for Harjula.[39] Other than this, practices at Harjula remained unchanged. Jeremy Bentham first raised the idea of a self-supporting alms-house in his plan for the great Panopticon (utilitarianism as a specific school of thought is generally accredited to Bentham). In England hopes for profitable poor relief were already waning by the beginning of the nineteenth century, whereas in Finland utilitarian expectations persisted until the end of the century.[40]

Kyllilälä children's home was founded in Vyborg in 1829. In its aims and name one can see the legacy of Johan Pestalozzi. The name of the institution was *Uppfostrings anstalten i Nygård* (in Finnish *Uudenkartanon kasvatuslaitos*): a new children's farm. Pestalozzi's first children's home was Neuhof (new farm) where he established a school.[41] Pestalozzi (1933) argued that instead of dealing with words, children should learn through activities and objects.[42] He emphasized the importance of vocational education and admired the peasant way of life. Youngsters

---

37 Crowther, *The Workhouse System 1834–1929*, p. 65.
38 Åke Sandholm, *Kyrkan och hospitalshjonen: En undersökning rörande omsorgen om de sjuka och fattiga i välfärdanstalterna i Finland* (Suomen kirkkohistoriallisen seuran toimituksia, 88; Helsinki, 1973), p. 45.
39 Proceedings of the poor relief board of Kuopio 1873–1885.
40 Crowther, *The Workhouse System 1834–1929*, pp. 27–28.
41 Sulo Salmensaari, *Kasvatus pahantapaisuuden ehkäisijänä* (Porvoo, 1915), p. 100.
42 Johan Pestalozzi, *Joutsenlaulu* (Helsinki, 1933).

learnt about farming, gardening and culture: traditional school subjects were a less significant part of the educational programme.[43] The education children received was healthy, but strict. In Kylliälä the ideas of Pestalozzi were put into practice: the aim was to use education to create useful members of society who would no longer require poor relief or maintenance from others.

Orphans at Kylliälä were taught to read and write and were trained in gardening and other skills required for farm or service work. Education made it more possible for children to manage in adult life and find permanent work. The primary goal was that the children should be able to support themselves in the future. Kylliälä also tried to provide children with the opportunity to change their position or status within society.[44] This idea was ahead of its time, although the concept of "work education" was itself very traditional.

All of the closed institutions examined were founded on utilitarian principles. In addition, Finnish political liberalism favoured goals of poor relief and purposeful punishment. Belief in severe punishments waned and made room for the idea of religious education. Freedom of occupation was also extended. Delinquency and poverty were expected to decrease if all citizens had an opportunity to participate in work.[45] European debates about social questions spread to Finland, particularly the idea of philanthropy. Mid-nineteenth-century institutional care was influenced by the need for moral education and religious work.[46] Divine Services, Sunday schools and Bible study groups were incorporated into the everyday routines of closed institutions.

I discovered a number of similarities between Luostanlinna, Harjula and Kyllilä children's home. First, the institutions were economic solutions to the problem of treating or containing deviants. Economic goals were more important than treatment itself and consequently living conditions in the institutions were often inhumane. Next, the isolation of

---

[43] Paul Natorp, *Johan Heinrich Pestalozzi: Hänen elämänvaiheensa ja elämäntyönsä* (Porvoo, 1926), pp. 59–77.
[44] Casebooks, annual reports and letters of Kylliälä 1861–1891. Leningradskij Oblastnyj Gosudarstvennyj Arhiv v gorode Vyborga (LOGAV) [Vyborg Province Archives].
[45] Jussi Pajuoja, *Katsaus rangaistuksen historiaan* (Vankeinhoidon koulutuskeskus, 3; Helsinki, 1986), p 25.
[46] Nygård, *Erilaisten historiaa*, p. 172.

deviants was a fundamental issue. Because of the belief that isolation could reduce deviancy, bad-mannered or unfortunate individuals were sent to institutions in order to separate them from "the normal people". Lastly, in Finland there was a strong belief in the power of education. Nationalism and the ideal of the "Finnish worker" influenced the educational aims of closed institutions. Religion, work and discipline were the most important features of educational programmes within such facilities.

Alms-houses and children's homes differed from criminal institutions in one important respect: their localism. While all criminal institutions were state-run, Harjula alms-house and Kylliälä children's home were run by a local poor relief board or organization. However, all of the institutions lacked well-educated employees. Luostanlinna was staffed by working men from the neighbouring villages. Harjula and Kylliälä employed only two workers – usually a couple of farmhands who kept house for the residents – besides the director and a teacher. Only the directors of these facilities were highly educated. The goals and activities of all these institutions were in many ways very similar: there were few local features in terms of views or practices.

Conclusions

Vagrancy and poverty were the greatest problems facing nineteenth-century Finnish society. The same themes are repeated in the ways in which social control was exerted over prisoners, vagrants, children, the poor and the disabled. The re-education of deviants followed principles adopted from western Europe and the United States. In addition, ideas of nationalism and liberalism also informed educational programmes.

Deviants who were brought before the governor of Kuopio province were sieved out by authorities at a local level. The hearing process and time spent in prison awaiting trial could last anywhere from a few days to a couple of months. Only 15 percent of those who were investigated were sentenced to work in the house of correction; the rest were released, institutionalized or hospitalized. Through theme-analysis I was able to identify six different types of deviants, as defined by the governor: children, the poor and disabled, bad-mannered vagrants, members of the Roma community, those who had contracted venereal disease and mentally ill individuals.

I was able to analyse the foundation of and practice at closed institutions using evidence relating to Luostanlinna, the Kylliälä children's home in Vyborg, and the Harjula alms-house in Kuopio. Although I examined sources relating to social control in a wider context, my research illustrates that utilitarian motives underpinned the establishment of these closed institutions. First, policymakers and officers tried to ensure that institutions were economically beneficial. This was to be achieved through work, improvements to the security of society and reduced costs of criminality and poor relief. Second, institutions were expected to provide social benefits. All institutions had educational goals whose purpose was rehabilitation. Subsequent improvements in the social status of inmates were also expected to result in economic benefits.

Moreover, during the period studied the education of vagrants was considered more important than programmes for children or the poor. I argue that this stems from the harm that vagrants could inflict on society. There was growing awareness in the late nineteenth century that children from a "bad" background were more likely to fall into a vagrant lifestyle. Subsequently, the treatment and education of children in institutions gradually improved.

In my research I did not discover any Foucauldian hidden agendas in the control of vagrancy or poor relief. All aims and purposes can be found in the Poor Relief Laws 1852/1879 and vagrancy legislation as outlined in the regulation of institutions. On the other hand, institutions did produce some unwelcome results including recidivism and "criminal careers", suffering and mistreatment of inmates. As Crowther says, the history of an institution such as the workhouse or a prison is history without heroes.[47]

---

47 Crowther, *The Workhouse System 1834–1929*, p. 2.

Sources

ARCHIVAL MATERIAL

Proceedings of the governor's hearings, 1855–1860, 1861–1868, 1865–1876, 1877–1880 and 1884–1885. County Administrative Board. Joensuun maakunta-arkisto [Joensuu Province Archives].

Proceedings of the poor relief board of Kuopio, 1873–1885. Kuopion kaupungin arkisto [Kuopio City Archive].

Regulation for Kuopio Province penal colony 206/1858. Reglor för Kuopio Läns Arbetskompani. Kenraalikuvernöörin kanslia. KKK. Kansallisarkisto (KA) [Finnish National Archives], Helsinki

Casebooks, annual reports and letters of Kylliälä 1861–1891. Leningradskij Oblastnyj Gosudarstvennyj Arhiv v gorode Vyborga (LOGAV) [Vyborg Province Archives].

DECREES

Decree on handling mentally ill persons, 1840. Hans Kejserliga Majeståts Rådiga Förordning, angående sinnessjukte personers wård och förbättrade anstalter till deras botande 4.2.1840. Kejserliga Förordningar för åren 1840.

Decree on handling vagrancy, 1852. Armollinen Asetus laillisesta suojeluksesta ja kuinka suojeluksettomia persoonia menetettämän pitää. 14.1.1852. Kejserliga Förordningar för åren 1852.

Decree on poor relief, 1852. Armollinen asetus yhteisestä vaivaisholhouksesta Suomen Isoruhtinaanmaassa. 22.3.1852. Kejserliga Förordningar för åren 1852.

Decree on handling vagrancy, 1852/1865. Armollinen Asetus joutolaisista ja niiden kanssa menettelemisestä 23.1.1865. Finlands Författnings-Samling 1865 n:o 1.

LITERATURE

Beccaria, Cesare 1998: *Rikoksesta ja rangaistuksesta: Vankeinhoidon koulutuskeskuksen julkaisuja.* Helsinki.

Canth, Minna 1983 [1886]: *Köyhää kansaa.* Hämeenlinna.

Christie Nils 1993: *Kohti vankileirien saaristoa? Rikollisuuden kontrolli teollisuutena länsimaissa.* Helsinki.

Cohen Stanley 1985: *Visions of Social Control: Crime, Punishment and Classification.* Cambridge.

Crowther M. A. 1983: *The Workhouse System 1834–1929: The History of an English Social Institution.* London.

Durkheim, Émile 1982: *Sosiologian metodisäännöt.* Helsinki.

Eskola, Jari and Suoranta, Juha 1998: *Johdatus laadulliseen tutkimukseen.* Tampere.

Foucault Michel 2000 [1980]: *Tarkkailla ja rangaista.* Keuruu.

Garland, David 1985: *Punishment and Welfare: A History of Penal Strategies.* Great Britain.

Häkkinen, Antti, Pulma, Panu and Tervonen, Miika 2005: *Vieraat kulkijat – tutut talot: näkökulmia etnisyyden ja köyhyyden historiaan Suomessa.* Historiallinen arkisto, Helsinki.

Jütte, Robert 1994: *Poverty and Deviance in Early Modern Europe.* Cambridge.

Kekkonen, Jukka and Ylikangas, Heikki 1982: *Vapausrangaistuksen valtakausi: Nykyisen seuraamusjärjestelmän historiallinen tausta.* Helsinki.

Kylä-Marttila, Veikko 1986: *Kysymys kuolemanrangaistuksesta autonomian ajan valtiopäivillä vuosina 1863–1888.* Vankeinhoidon historiaprojektin julkaisu, Helsinki.

Lawrence, Paul 2004: Policing the Poor in England and France, 1850–1900. In *Social Control in Europe Vol. 2, 1800–2000,* ed. Clive Elmsley, Eric Johnson and Pieter Spierenburg. History of Crime and Criminal Justice Series; Ohio, pp. 211–213.

Mantila, Harri 2005: Kielikäsityksestä kielenhuollon uusiin periaatteisiin. *Kielikello 2/2005,* pp. 4–9.

Naess, Hans Eyvind and Österberg, Eva 2000: Sanctions, Agreements, Sufferings.In *People Meet the Law: Control and Conflict-Handling in the Courts. The Nordic Countries in the Post-Reformation and Pre-Industrial Period,* ed. Eva Österberg and Sølvi Bauge Sogner. Oslo, pp. 140–166.

Natorp, Paul 1926: *Johan Heinrich Pestalozzi: Hänen elämänvaiheensa ja elämäntyönsä.* Porvoo.

Nilsson, Roddy 1999: *En välbyggd maskin, en mardröm för själen: Det svenska fängelsesystemet under 1800-talet.* Bibliotheca Historica Lundensis, Lund.

Nygård, Toivo 1985: *Irtolaisuus ja sen kontrolli 1800-luvun alun Suomessa.* Studia Historica Jyväskyläensia, Jyväskylä.

Nygård, Toivo 1998: *Erilaisten historiaa: Marginaaliryhmät Suomessa 1800-luvulla ja 1900-luvun alussa.* Jyväskylä.

Pajuoja, Jussi 1986: *Katsaus rangaistuksen historiaan.* Vankeinhoidon koulutuskeskus, Helsinki.

Pestalozzi, Johan 1933: *Joutsenlaulu.* Helsinki.

Piispa, Leena 1997: Taylorismi naisten teollisuustyön sukupuolistumisen historiassa. *Sosiologia* 32(1) 1997, pp. 39–52.

Pukero, Päivi 2008: "Harhaantuneiden ja eksyneiden parantaja." Luostanlinna irtolaisten kasvatuskokeiluna 1859–1880. *Kasvatus & Aika,* 2/1 (2008), pp. 23–40.

Salmensaari, Sulo 1915: *Kasvatus pahantapaisuuden ehkäisijänä.* Porvoo.

Sandholm, Åke 1973: *Kyrkan och hospitalshjonen: En undersökning rörande omsorgen om de sjuka och fattiga i välfärdsanstalterna i Finland.* Suomen kirkkohistoriallisen seuran toimituksia, Helsinki.

Soininen, Arvo M. 1974: *"Vanha maataloutemme". Maatalous ja maatalousväestö Suomessa perinnäisen maatalouden loppukaudella 1720-luvulta 1870-luvulle.* Historiallisia tutkimuksia, Helsinki.

Spierenburg, Pieter 2004: Social Control and History: An Introduction. In *Social Control in Europe Vol. 1, 1500–1800,* ed. Herman Roodenburg and Pieter Spierenburg. History of Crime and Criminal Justice Series. Ohio, pp. 1–22.

Ståhlberg, Kaarlo J. 1893: *Irtolaisuus Suomen lain mukaan.* Vankeinhoidon koulutuskeskuksen julkaisu, 4/95, Helsinki.

Suhonen, Riitta 1994: *Rikollinen nainen vai pahantapainen tyttölapsi? Kuopion lääninvankilan naisvangit ja heidän rikoksensa vuosina 1890–1910* (unpublished licentiate theses in Finnish History), University of Joensuu.

Tervonen, Miika 2010: *"Gypsies", "travellers" and "peasants": A Study on Ethnic Boundary Drawing in Finland and Sweden, c.1860–1925.* European University Institute.

Virtanen, Veikko 1944: *Suomen vankeinhoito I 1808–1831.* Historiallisia tutkimuksia, SHS, Helsinki.

She "took him to temple lane, subsequently he missed his money"

Prostitutes and Thieves in Dundee 1865–1925[1]

Suki Haider

> [The sailor] is scarcely clear of his ship [...] when he finds himself surrounded by men and women, who, knowing that he has money and money's worth upon him, and also how easily he can be induced to part with or deprived of these, are clamouring for the possession of him [...] by one or other of these harpies he is carried off. His fate is almost certain; being persuaded to drink, he is soon stupefied either with spirits or drugs, and his money is filched from him. He is then compelled to dispose of his clothes, bedding, and whatsoever he may possess, the proceeds too often sharing the same fate.[2]

In 1872 a series of meetings were held in Dundee with the purpose of establishing a sailors' home, which it was believed, would protect seafarers from the "long list of temptations" in the city. The neces-

---

[1] I would like to thank Richard Mc Mahon, Clive Koerner, David Allan and Susan Grace, as well as the anonymous reviewers of this collection, for their comments on earlier drafts of this article. Also to the AHRC and University of St Andrews for funding my research of female criminality in Dundee.

[2] *Report of the Society for Establishing Sailors' Homes*. Dundee Local History Centre, Lamb Collection (hereafter DLHC), 244(12), *Dundee's Sailors' Home*. I am grateful to the archivists Deirdre Sweeney and Eileen Moran for their valuable assistance.

sity for sailors' homes was recognised in almost all of Britain's shipping ports, and, according to the *Advertiser*, the description provided in the Society's report presented "no overdrawn picture" of the situation in Dundee.[3] As was confirmed by scores of eyewitnesses, the fate of the sailor was to be found naked and destitute in the street the morning after his arrival in the city, and some seafarers were relieved of their clothes and wages, at the hands of "crimps and their associates", within hours of being onshore.[4] Although a sailor's home was duly built opposite the city's harbour, the risks continued. In 1881, "an old seaman" published a pamphlet warning sailors about Dundee. In it, he advised they have their wages sent on after them to avoid losing their money and gaining a disease in the bargain during their short stay.[5] The warning was often ignored, and in 1887 Dundee's *Weekly News* reported that sailors, "flush with cash", were apt to fall prey to the shoal of "land pirates both male and female that soar about the vicinity of the Harbour".[6] "Land pirates" and "crimps", contemporaries acknowledged in only the discreetest of terms, referred to a class of rogues that included prostitutes and pimps.[7]

Historians have not sufficiently considered the profile of the female thief and this is especially true in the Scottish context.[8] Elsewhere, although prostitutes have been associated with theft for centuries,[9] both historians of prostitution and scholars of crime have often overlooked their criminality.[10] This article will discuss the relationship between

---

3 *The Dundee Advertiser* (hereafter *DA*), 29 June 1872.
4 *The People's Journal* (hereafter *PJ*), 13 July 1872.
5 Anonymous, *Good Advice to Seamen by an Old Sailor* (Dundee: Leng & Co, 1881).
6 *The Dundee Weekly News* (hereafter *WN*), 4 March 1887.
7 Landladies who charged sailors exorbitant rates for accommodation, and tailors who over-charged sailors for new clothes were also called "crimps".
8 According to The Boydell Press, Scottish criminal justice history is "almost nonexistent", www.boydell.co.uk (accessed 9 January 2009). This is no longer true. In 2009 the Crime and Policing in Scottish Society Conference generated discussion on many aspects of crime and policing in Scottish society. Nonetheless, the Scottish thief remains a neglected actor.
9 For a discussion of the link between prostitutes and theft in the eighteenth century, see David Fleming, "Public attitudes to prostitution in eighteenth-century Ireland", *Irish Economic and Social History*, XXXII (2005), 4; Tony Henderson, *Disorderly Women in Eighteenth-Century London: Prostitution and Control in the Metropolis 1730–1830* (London: Longman, 1999), p. 53.
10 As was highlighted over a decade ago, see Susan E. Grace, "*Female Criminality in York and Hull*" (unpublished doctoral thesis, University of York, 1998). *PJ*, 13 July 1872.

prostitution and theft in Dundee between 1865 and 1925, a period, when 4000 sailors were paid annually at the city's docks, and "[e]xtreme poverty" was "the lot of a large proportion of the [female] population".[11]

Contemporaries throughout Scotland were convinced of the strong link between prostitution and theft, but for the historian determining the association between the two is invariably complex, since direct references to the prostitute offender appear infrequently in the crime records. As Part I will illustrate, Dundee's High Court papers provide the clearest evidence that prostitutes stole pocket-watches and purses from drunken sailors and commercial travellers in disreputable back streets, and that prostitute-thieves accounted for a striking proportion of defendants at the high court. As the high court dealt with only Dundee's most serious offenders, to determine the extent to which prostitutes were responsible for female property crime, it is also necessary to analyse the lower court records. It is a serious impediment, therefore, that these have only survived in newspaper trial reports. Part II explains that building a picture of prostitute offending in Dundee is made doubly challenging by the inhibited style of reporting adopted by the city's press with regard to all matters connected with vice. Nevertheless, despite the refusal of contemporaries to discuss prostitution candidly, on the basis of a close examination of a variety of fragmentary sources, the evidence suggests that prostitutes were ubiquitous thieves. Part III tackles a theme of the collection: social control, and the key question: to what extent were Dundee's criminal justice practitioners responsible for the prominence of prostitutes in the city's crime records? It will be shown that the available records suggest the disproportion of prostitute-thieves does not appear to be linked to factors of social control. We will begin by setting the scene for the investigation of prostitution and theft in Dundee.

This study takes up the story of Dundee in 1865, when the major industrial port town on the east coast of Scotland was enjoying a short spell as the unchallenged jute manufacturing capital of the world. Officially recognised as a city in 1889, Dundee was unique for her depend-

---

11 Reverend Henry Williamson, founder of the Jute Operatives Union, *PJ*, 28 October 1922.

ence on jute: textile manufacture employed nearly nine-tenths of the workforce.[12] Dundee was unusual for its reliance on cheap female labour. The reason why *The Weekly News* reported, in 1888, that there was not "another town in the kingdom where the labour of women played so important a part" was because two-thirds of Dundee's jute workforce were women.[13] Well into the twentieth century, in the absence of a marriage bar in industry, more married women worked in Dundee than in any other city.[14]

In 1901, 85 percent of females aged between 15 and 24 years were textile workers.[15] As they had suffered short-time and unemployment regularly since the late 1870s we might expect considerable numbers of young women to have turned to prostitution, at least on a part-time basis, in order to avoid destitution. Nonetheless, in addition to factors that would tend to increase the number of prostitutes, there were also forces pulling in the opposite direction. The downturn in the jute trade coincided with a reduction in the prostitute's potential clients.[16] That is, at the time women's work in the mills and factories became increasingly uncertain, the number of ships bringing both fresh supplies of raw jute and fresh supplies of newly-paid sailors also declined. Furthermore, as the period progressed, Dundee suffered even more from its dependence on jute. The new century brought fewer orders for the engineering firms that manufactured the spinning and weaving looms, and they too employed fewer and fewer men, aggravating the city's demographic and economic imbalance. To add to this sorry mix, Dundee's whaling industry had already collapsed and its mariners, along with its ship builders, had left for other ports never to return. Although there was an army

---

12 W. J. Knox, *Industrial Nation: Work Culture and Society in Scotland: 1800–Present* (Edinburgh, 1999), p. 87. No other major British industry, not even the extensive Lancashire cotton industry was concentrated in such a small area: Norman Watson, *Dundee: A Short History* (Edinburgh, 2006), pp. 118–119.

13 *WN*, 22 September 1888, similar statements are found *PJ*, 21 May 1881; *WN*, 4 January 1902. There were other female occupations in Dundee: in jam making, and fish selling but they did not impact greatly on social set up and only 8% were employed as domestics compared to 22% and 26% in Glasgow and Aberdeen respectively: Susan Kingsley Kent, *Gender and Power in Britain 1640–1990* (London, 1999), p. 183.

14 Watson, *Dundee*, pp. 118–119.

15 The calculation is based on figures from the Dundee Census 1901.

16 On the importance of considering the number of potential clients: Ann Laite, "Prostitution in London, 1885–1930" (unpublished doctoral thesis, University of Cambridge, 2008), p. 43.

camp in nearby Angus, unlike Welsh Carmarthen – where the number of prostitutes in the town increased whenever the militia were stationed – there is no evidence that in Dundee the number of prostitutes corresponded with troop movements.[17] Thus, during the regular periods of economic downturn during the years of this study, at the time when we would suppose that increasing numbers of women would have sought to make ends meet by prostituting themselves, there would have been reduced opportunities to earn money by selling sex, and as a corollary fewer opportunities for robbing clients.

This is not to say that during the long years of economic stagnation Dundonian women were not on the game. We will learn of "deplorable revelations" heard by magistrates in 1913, concerning the harbour, and anecdotal evidence indicates that until the building of the Tay Road Bridge, in 1963, it remained notorious as a red-light district. An anonymous commentator, whom *The Courier* believed knew the subject well, said there were "more than 2000 fallen women" in Dundee in 1893.[18] *The People's Journal* indicated that between 1865 and 1925 approximately 3 percent of Dundee's female population, or approximately 2,500 women, were at any one time engaged in prostitution on a regular basis.[19] This evidence is hopelessly weak, but it is only by having an approximation of the numbers of prostitutes in the city that the extent of their criminality can be understood.

This article is concerned with ordinary prostitutes, the "streetwalkers", not the women who serviced the upper classes. As it is impossible to distinguish between the prostitutes who were thieves, the thieves who pretended to be prostitutes, and the prostitutes who worked with thieves, the term "prostitute-thief" and "prostitute-offender" is used to refer to this cohort of female criminals.[20]

---

17 Russell Davies, *Secret Sins: Sex, Violence and Society in Carmarthenshire 1870–1920* (Cardiff, 1996), p. 163.
18 *The Dundee Courier* (herafter *C*), 23 September 1893.
19 *PJ*, 28 October 1922; 13 July 1872.
20 Prostitute-thieves were known as "badgers" in the United States, see Anne Enright, "Book Review of The Story of Chicago May by Nuala O'Faolain", *The Sunday Times*, 1 January 2006, http://entertainment.timesonline.co.uk (accessed 2 January 2009). The term was not, however, used in Britain.

The loss of pocket watches and purses – prostitute-thieves in Dundee's court records

Reverend J. W. Horsley observed of London, in 1913, that "vice is to be found in the streets, if you search for it and know where to search".[21] Nevertheless, and despite knowing where to look, historians find prostitution a difficult area to study. Poor women bound to socially unacceptable activities typically leave few records,[22] and many of the accounts that were written are suffused with exaggeration, muddle and prejudice.[23] Dundee's High Court case papers, however, preserve the voices of some of the city's prostitutes, and it is their testimonies that provide the clearest extant picture of the relationship between prostitution and theft in Dundee.

Janet Thompson in 1882, for example, "met a man in Union Street"; they went to a public house, and afterwards "walked down the shore". It was here, she told the procurator fiscal, "I allowed him to have a connection with me". She was convicted for stealing the man's tiepin, which she was wearing at the time of her arrest. Although historians note that prostitutes were, on occasion, cheated out of their money,[24] and victims may have taken advantage of the bad reputation of a brothel to claim they had suffered a theft,[25] Dundee's High Court judges were unconvinced by the recidivist's claim that the pin was the man's pledge to return to pay what he owed.[26] Neither did they believe the defendant who told the procurator fiscal that the jacket and vest she was charged with stealing had been given to her by the soldier in exchange "for being in my company".[27]

---

21 Cited by Stefan Petrow, *Policing Morals: The Metropolitan Police and the Home Office 1870–1914* (Oxford, 1994), p. 146.
22 David McCreery, "'This Life of Misery and Shame': Female Prostitution in Guatemala City, 1880–1920", *Journal of Latin American Studies*, 18 (1986), p. 348.
23 For an important discussion of the difficulties see Timothy J. Gilfoyle, *City of Eros: New York City, Prostitution and the Commercialization of Sex, 1790–1920* (London, 1992), p. 138; Jerry White, *London in the Nineteenth Century: A Human Awful Wonder of God* (London, 2008), p. 297; Stefan Slater, "Prostitutes and Popular History: Notes on the 'Underworld', 1918–1939", *Crime, History and Societies*, 13 (2009), p. 28.
24 Donald Thomas, *The Victorian Underworld* (London, 1998), p. 96; Elizabeth Alice Clement, *Love for Sale: Courting, Treating and Prostitution in New York City, 1900–1945* (North Carolina, 2006), pp. 91, 96.
25 Heather Shore, 'The Reckoning': Disorderly Women, Informing Constables and the Westminster Justices, 1727–33", *Social History*, 34 (2009), p. 413.
26 National Archives of Scotland (hereafter NAS) JC26/1882/69.
27 NAS JC26/1876/65. Some prostitutes would make arrangements to live with a sailor and when his money ran out they would move on. For similar evidence: Michael Macilwee, *The Liverpool Underworld: Crime in the City 1750–1900* (Liverpool, 2011), p. 259.

Other prisoners unsuccessfully declared that when their accusers "had got what [they had] wanted" they had tried to recover their purses.[28]

Since at least the eighteenth century, when prostitutes were found with the personal possessions clients had reported stolen, it was usual for them to insist the items had been honestly obtained.[29] An exchange of money or property, a meeting at the harbour, a drunken sailor or commercial traveller, the loss of pocket-watches, purses and clothes during assignations in dark stairways, cramped rooms, and the most disreputable streets of the city, are in fact recurring themes in the trials of the habitual and violent female thieves tried at Dundee's High Court.[30] These themes have also been identified in European, North American and African studies of women working in prostitution.[31] As we shall see shortly, the patterns identified in Dundee's High Court archive provide the key framework for identifying prostitute-offenders tried at the city's police court.

In twenty-six of the eighty-one high court cases analysed in detail for this study, that is in 32 percent of the sample, the defendant appears to have been a prostitute-thief.[32] Since forty-one of the trials, in the high

---

28 NAS JC26/1870/60, JC26/1875/17, JC26/1870/6, JC26/1885/31.
29 Mary Clayton, "The Life and Crimes of Charlotte Walker, Prostitute and Pickpocket", *The London Journal*, 33 (2008), p. 13.
30 A selection includes NAS JC 26/1870/64, JC26/1895/9, JC26/1885/31, JC26/1865/101.
31 Gregory Durston, *Victims and Viragos: Metropolitan Women, Crime and the Eighteenth-Century Criminal Justice System* (Suffolk, 2007), p. 199; Frances Finnegan, *Poverty and Prostitution: A Study of Victorian Prostitutes in York* (Cambridge, 1979); Judith R. Walkowitz, *Prostitution and Victorian Society: Women, Class and the State* (Cambridge, 1980); David, J. V. Jones, *Crime in Nineteenth-Century Wales* (Cardiff, 1992); Clayton, "The Life and Crimes of Charlotte Walker", p. 134; Deirdre Palk, *Gender, Crime and Judicial Discretion 1780–1830* (Suffolk, 2006); James Walvin, *Leisure and Society 1830–1950* (London, 1978), p. 44; Constance Backhouse, *Petticoats and Prejudice: Women and Law in Nineteenth Century Canada* (Ontario, 1991), p. 231; Thomas, *Victorian Underworld*, p. 99; Ann M. Butler, *Daughters of Joy, Sisters of Mercy: Prostitutes in the American West 1865–90* (Chicago,1987),p. 57–58; Maria Luddy, *Prostitution and Irish Society 1800–1940* (Cambridge, 2007), pp. 46, 53; Catherine Theresa Lee, "Regulating Prostitution in Nineteenth-Century Kent: Beyond the Contagious Diseases Acts" (unpublished doctoral thesis, Open University, 2008), p. 95; Jill Harsin, *Prostitution in Nineteenth-Century Paris* (Princeton, 1985), p. 169; Hallie Rubenhold, *The Convent Garden Ladies: Pimp General Jack and the Extraordinary Story of Harris's List* (Stroud, 2005), p. 291; Susan Parnell, "Race, Power and Urban Control: Johannesburg's Inner City Slum-Yards, 1910–1923", *Journal of Southern Africa Studies*, 29 (2003), pp. 615–637.
32 The High Court records include a copy of the indictment (setting out the charges against the accused), witness accounts, confessions and other information about the accused and their alleged crime. Some case papers contain the "declaration" given by the accused to the procurator fiscal (usually Dundee's chief constable or a judge from the sheriff court). The procurator fiscal gathered the pre-trial evidence, concerning the crime to send to the Lord Advocates' Department where it was used to decide whether a prosecution should be brought and, if so, in which court. All serious offences were likely to be tried at the high court. For information see www.nas.gov.uk and Anne M. Crowther, "The Criminal

court sample, concerned women who had a string of convictions for the larceny of domestic items, it appears streetwalkers were not the primary culprits for property crime (figure 1). Yet prostitute-thieves may have been more prevalent offenders than the statistics suggest, for in fourteen of the cases studied (17 percent), the women refused to make a declaration to the procurator fiscal; denying the historian an account of the circumstances of the theft for which they were imprisoned.[33] As at least three of these cases involved the theft of watches and purses from men, it is reasonable to suppose that at least 35 percent, or one third, of thefts tried at Dundee's High Court may have involved vice.[34]

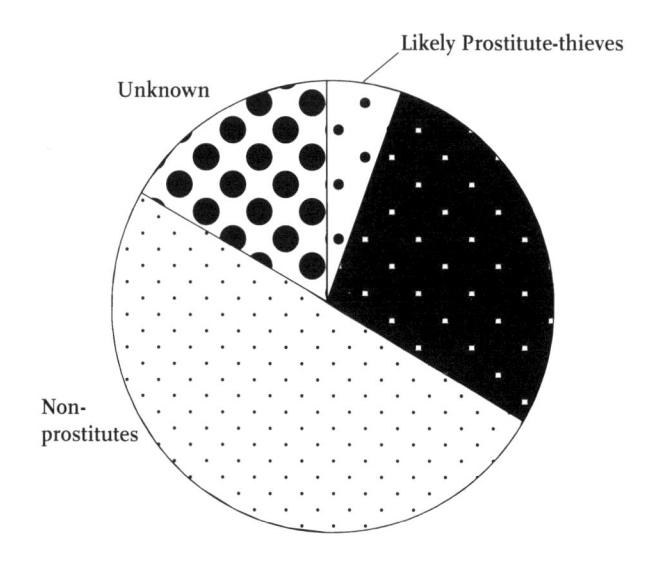

Figure 1: Proportion of prostitute-thieves in a sample of Dundee's High Court Papers 1865–1908[35]

Precognitions and their Value for the Historian", *Scottish Archives*, 1 (1995), pp. 75–92; Ian Donnachie, "Profiling Criminal Offences: The Evidence of the Lord Advocate's Papers During the First Half of the Nineteenth Century in Scotland", *Scottish Archives*, 1 (1995), pp. 85–92.

33 Defendants variously claimed they had "no recollection" of what happened, "knew nothing", or pleaded "not guilty" and so no account of the background circumstances is provided. For example, NAS JC26/1866/60, JC26/1882/12, JC26/1874/6.
34 The indictments reveal the theft of watches and purses from men in NAS JC 26/1876/1, JC 26/1874/19, JC26/1874/9.
35 Source: JC26 1865–1908: out of 81 cases it seems that there were 26 prostitute-thieves, 41 domestic thieves and of the 14 non-declarations 3 probably involved prostitute-thieves.

In view of the fact that the high court dealt only with the very small proportion of crime that was deemed serious, to get a broader picture of prostitute crime in Dundee in the period of this study, it is necessary to analyse the annual police returns.

Between 1869 and 1877, Dundee's Chief Constable McKay published details of the occupation of all the offenders cited and apprehended for crimes in the city, and "prostitute" was listed in the returns as a female trade.[36] This short run provides the only surviving official figures concerning the relationship between prostitution and theft in Dundee; fortuitously it spans the era when the city's dominant jute trade was at its peak, and the port, and presumably its prostitutes were at their busiest. As figure 2 records, according to the published police reports prostitutes committed 21 percent of known female property offences. But inevitably there are problems with this finding given the well-known problems with interpreting crime statistics.[37]

Figure 2: Females apprehended or cited for property crimes in Dundee 1869–1877[38]

1869	Prostitutes	Total Female
Theft (simple)	39	94
Theft by housebreaking	2	5
Reset of theft	2	2
Robbery and assault	2	2
1871	Prostitutes	Total Female
Theft (simple)	12	89
Theft by housebreaking	3	12
Reset of theft	0	0
Robbery and assault	0	0
1873	Prostitutes	Total Female
Theft (simple)	32	162

---

36 DLHC, *Burgh of Dundee Return of Crimes and Offences Reported to the Police ... year ending 31st* December 1869–1877 (hereafter *Return of Crimes*).
37 For an important introduction, see Clive Emsley, *Crime and Society in England, 1750–1900* (Harlow, Pearson Longman, 2005), pp. 24, 30, 95–96.
38 Source: Burgh of Dundee Return of Crimes and Offences Reported to the Police ... year ending 31st December 1869–1877.

Theft by housebreaking	1	13
Reset of theft	0	3
Robbery and assault	2	7
1875	Prostitutes	Total Female
Theft (simple)	26	183
Theft by housebreaking	1	9
Reset of theft	0	1
Robbery and assault	0	0
1877	Prostitutes	Total Female
Theft (simple)	55	256
Theft by housebreaking	1	11
Reset of theft	1	5
Robbery and assault	0	0
Total prostitutes apprehended		179
Total women apprehended		854
percent of prostitutes apprehended		20.96 percent

The first problem with the evidence, provided in figure 2, is that there is no guidance as to how the local police gathered the information, and as there is no distinction between the casual thief and the recidivist, the evidence may over-represent the number of prostitute-thieves at work in Dundee. On the other hand, and this is more likely to be the primary flaw, the police figures may seriously underestimate the number of prostitute-thieves. A prisoner would confess to being a prostitute if her defence to the charge was that the items were not stolen, but had been given to her in exchange for sex. Otherwise it is doubtful that any woman would admit to selling sex as readily as she would claim to be earning a respectable living in the city's textile trade.[39] Indeed, the historian Susan Grace suggests that where women were able to supply an occupation their prostitution may have remained hidden.[40] Thus, it

---

39 For example, only 1 in 10 women admitted into Glasgow's Lock Hospital in the 1870s gave prostitute as occupation, cited in Linda Mahood, *The Magdalenes: Prostitution in the Nineteenth Century* (London, Routledge, 1990), p. 127.
40 Grace, "Female Criminality in York and Hull", 197.

seems the Dundonian police did not categorise Sarah Brown and Catherine Grant, the women convicted of assault and robbery, as prostitutes, since both claimed to be textile workers and, according to their criminal records, neither had previous convictions for soliciting.[41] Alternatively, the information in figure 2 may have been supplied by policemen, for as an ex-chief of the Metropolitan vice squad claimed "[e]very policeman on his beat knows, by sight and name, the habitual prostitutes."[42] If this was the case the statistics will again under record the number of streetwalkers apprehended; for in Scotland, unlike England, it was only after police surveillance and several formal cautions that a woman was labelled a prostitute.[43] The effect of this policy of social control is revealed by Dundee's 1875 occupation returns, since a "millworker" was cited for "importuning" along with "prostitute[s]".[44] Because streetwalking was a transient activity for the majority of women, we should assume that some of the offenders the authorities enumerated as non-prostitutes will have sold sex unbeknownst to the police.[45]

Nevertheless, even the (probable) underestimate of prostitute offending captured in the official statistics suggests that there was a strong relationship between prostitution and theft in Dundee. By applying the finding that 21 percent of females in the 1869–1877 police occupation returns were prostitutes, to the guesstimate that there were 2,500 prostitutes in the city, we discover that this cohort may have been around seven times more likely to be cited for theft than their position in the city's female population statistics would predict. This discrepancy is illustrated in figures 3 and 4.

The finding that Dundee's prostitutes may have had a disproportionately large representation in the crime records, is in line with studies elsewhere. Jones, for example, found that between 30 and 50 percent of

---

41 WN, 16 September 1865.
42 Cited by Pamela Cox, *Gender, Justice and Welfare: Bad Girls in Britain* (Basingstoke, Palgrave Macmillan, 2003), p. 58.
43 Roger Davidson and Gayle Davis, "'A festering sore on the body of society': the Wolfenden Committee and female prostitution in mid-twentieth-century Scotland", *Journal of Scottish Historical Studies*, 24 (2004), pp. 82–83.
44 DLHC, *Return of Crimes*, 1875.
45 Clayton, "The Life and Crimes of Charlotte Walker", 9; Davies, *Secret Sins*, p. 162.

all females taken into custody in Victorian Manchester were described as prostitutes and, having trawled the Irish records from the decades before the First World War, Boyle concludes that prostitutes constituted the majority of the female prison population.[46] More recently Newby observed that, in nineteenth-century Britain, prostitutes were the largest group of female criminals.[47] To discover more about the strength of the relationship between prostitution and theft in Dundee, it is necessary to turn directly to the police and sheriff court archives.

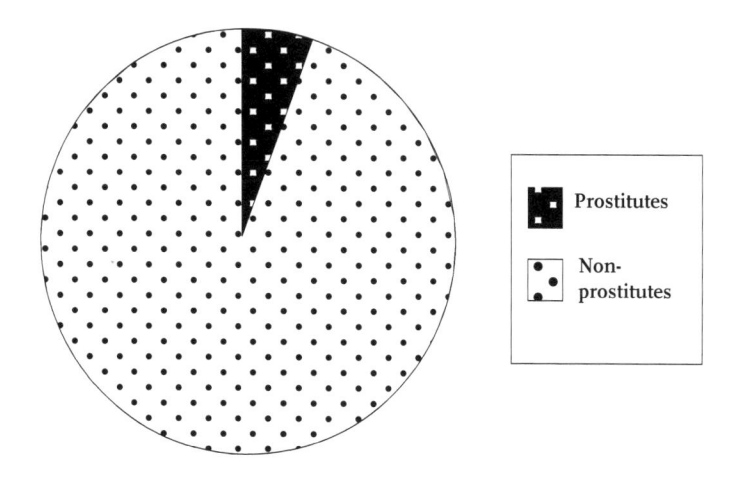

Figure 3: Estimated proportion of prostitutes in Dundee's female population 1869–1877[48]

---

46 David Jones, *Crime, Protest, Community and Police in Nineteenth-Century Britain* (London, 1982), 165; Michael D. Boyle, "Women and Crime in Belfast, 1900–1913" (unpublished doctoral thesis, Queen's University Belfast, 1997), pp. 184, 206.
47 Jennifer Newby, *Women's Lives: Researching Women's Social History 1800–1939* (Barnsley, 2011), p. 139.
48 Source: Burgh of Dundee Return of Crimes and Offences Reported to the Police ... year ending 31st December 1869–1877.

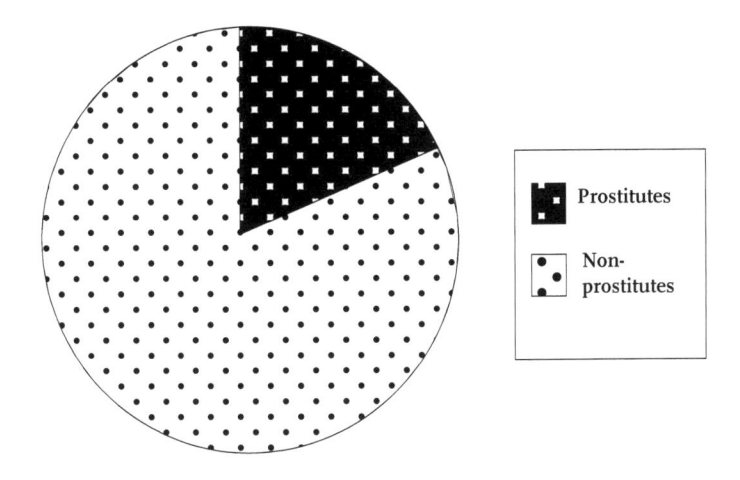

Figure 4: Proportion of female thieves known to the police to be prostitutes in Dundee's police returns, 1869–1877[49]

"Land Pirates" – prostitute-thieves in Dundee's press

In Scotland few records were made pertaining to the petty crimes dealt with summarily at the sheriff court, or by magistrates at the police court. In Dundee the records that were made concerning casual offenders and minor recidivists have not survived. Nonetheless, as elsewhere in Britain, details of local trials were published in the city's press and this is where we must pursue Dundee's prostitute-offenders. We can catch sight of them by looking for the themes we have identified in the high court archives: the theft from a sailor or commercial traveller, the loss of pocket watches, purses and clothing in Dundee's most disreputable streets, and circumstances involving drink. We also learn to recognise prostitute-offenders, in the descriptions provided by local journalists, by studying the context provided in the detailed York and Kentish prostitution reports. Our strategy is to become conversant with the language of euphemism employed by Dundee's popular press. Once we know how

---

49 Source: Burgh of Dundee Return of Crimes and Offences Reported to the Police ... year ending 31st December 1869–1877.

to recognise the archetype prostitute-offender, our eye can find the repetitive patterns in the Dundonian newspaper court columns. Given the gaps in the local sources this seems the only way to gain an impression of prostitute-offenders active in the city.

In her study of prostitution in Victorian York, Finnegan uses newspaper reports of crime as the main source of evidence of prostitutes stealing from their clients. Readers, she observes, were left in no doubt as to the defendants' occupation, particularly as many of the offences were described as occurring in brothels. York journalists were hugely interested in recounting the details of sexually-related offences. Consequently, Finnegan notes, prostitute-related crimes were "religiously reported", with sometimes as many as fifteen to twenty streetwalkers listed per week. The women were described as "unfortunates", "fallen", "abandoned", and "of ill repute"; adjectives commonly applied to prostitutes in Britain since the eighteenth century.[50]

Analysing Dundee's press from 1875–1905, when court reporting was at its height, is problematic. As for the Edwardian era, the column inches allocated to the coverage of crime shrank dramatically, as the space Dundee's newspapers devoted to advertising increased.[51] What the study of several hundred Victorian headlines has revealed is that a mere handful are similar to those regularly printed in nineteenth-century York: "A ploughman relieved of his watch by a Dundee nymph" in 1887, for example, and "A light-fingered nymph", published seven years earlier.[52] It is telling that the dexterous Catherine Cleary or Donnelly stole one pound notes and eight half sovereigns "on Wednesday night or Thursday morning", as the press provides neither details of her victim, nor the location of her crime. "Nymph", of course, has a sexual connotation, and elsewhere prostitutes were referred to as "nymphs of the pave".[53]

---

50 Finnegan, *Poverty and Prostitution*, pp. 118, 27, 213, 12. Similarly Fleming, "Public Attitudes to Prostitution in Eighteenth-Century Ireland", p. 2.
51 While the most sensational cases from around the Empire were reported in great detail, local miscreants and stories of sexual scandal were largely absent from its pages.
52 *WN*, 26 July 1887, 7 February 1880; *C*, 13 September 1892, 11 November 1892.
53 Finnegan, *Poverty and Prostitution*, pp. 89, 118. "Nymph" was in fact used in Georgian Britain to refer to a prostitute: Rubenhold, *The Convent Garden Ladies*, p.15.

The analysis of Dundee's Victorian Police and Sheriff Court reports clearly illustrates that there is no consistent relationship between crime news in newspapers and local crime rates.[54] As we saw at the start, contemporaries were well aware that prostitute-thieves were active around Dundee's harbour. We can interpret the urgent demands for a sailors' home is an indicator of the proclivity of prostitutes and pimps to rob sailors of all they possessed.[55] But notwithstanding the newsworthiness of stories concerning naked sailors at the docks, in which journalists elsewhere would have surely revelled, journalists in Dundee acknowledged in only the discreetest of terms that prostitutes and pimps had formed the sailors' welcoming party.[56] The crucial difference between Dundee's High-Court declarations and the trials reported in the city's press is that the former recorded private conversations between the female defendant and the procurator fiscal, while the latter was intended for public consumption. As Foyster and Snell emphasise, newspapers were professional businesses, and editors needed to be alert to their readership's sensitivities.[57]

It seems that, unlike their English counterparts, Dundee's editors were squeamish about making direct references to loose women. George M. Dale, in 1911, wrote of American attitudes towards prostitution: "[w]hen the social evil is mentioned society stops its ears or runs away from the issue altogether".[58] This seems to have been the gen-

---

54 Esther Snell has recently argued, in a different context, the weakness of newspapers as barometers of crime: "Discourses of criminality in the eighteenth-century press: the presentation of crime in *The Kentish Post, 1717–1768*", *Continuity and Change*, 22 (2007), p. 27.
55 *DA*, 29 June 1872.
56 York has already been discussed. For the tendency of the press to overemphasize crimes of indecency and violence: Jason Ditton and James Duffy, "Bias in the Newspaper Reporting of Crime News", *British Journal of Criminology*, 23 (1983), p. 159.
57 Elizabeth Foyster, "Introduction: Newspaper Reporting of Crime and Justice", *Continuity and Change*, 22 (2007), p. 11; Snell, "Discourses of criminality", p. 17. In Canada too, crime reports provided a "slanted" version of the female defendant's stories fashioned for respectable readers: Joan Sangster, "'Pardon Tales' from Magistrate's Court: Women, Crime and the Court in Peterborough County 1920–50", *Canadian Historical Review*, 2 (1993), p. 162.
58 George P. Dale, "Moral Prophylaxis: Prostitutes and Prostitution", *The American Journal of Nursing*, 13 (1919), p. 22. Jacqueline Baker Barnhart suggests that Americans did not want to recognize its existence by reading about it in the press: *The Fair but Frail: Prostitution in San Francisco 1849–1900* (Reno, 1986), p. 1.
For the prostitution taboo in Britain: Trevor Fisher, *Prostitution and the Victorians* (Gloucestershire, 1997), viii; Cox, *Gender, Justice and Welfare*, p. 38; Davies, *Secret Sins*, p. 156. Shani D'Cruze found a

eral Dundonian response. Reporting on the proceedings of the Sailors' Home Society, Dundee's press cited the witnesses who spoke of the "misery and sin", the "dens of infamy" and the "haunts of vice" in the lower parts of the city, but there is a noticed omission when it comes to descriptions of the sailors' assailants.[59] Equally the press did not specify the content of the "deplorable revelations", heard by magistrates in 1913, concerning prostitution around the harbour, which would have surely provided another statement on the active nature of Dundee's vice trade.[60] In fact, other than the infrequent allusion in the police court columns to women "loitering in the street", the annual mention of the accounts of Dundee's prostitute refuge and the sole appearance of a lady missionary who laboured at night, "among fallen women in Dundee" (she was a witness in a police court trial), the city's newspapers rarely refer to streetwalkers, dishonest or otherwise.[61] The articles that apply the euphemisms prevalent in the records of the prostitute refuge, "fallen girl" and "immoral life", are equally rare.[62] Certainly the language associated with streetwalkers in Yorkshire is to be found: "unfortunate" is widely used, but an absence of innuendo usually characterized its appearance in Dundee's press.

In contrast to the frankness of the *York Gazette*, it seems Dundee's journalists preferred to write in code. *The Weekly News*, for example, reported in 1897 that the "character" of a young woman, charged with thieving from a man in circumstances hugely suggestive of prostitution, "was not quite up to the mark."[63] In 1902 the paper ambiguously recounted the trial of Mary Ann Murphy: she had taken her victim "to Temple Lane. Subsequently he missed his money". As we learn from

---

"remarkable silence" on prostitution in Lancashire court papers but does not say if this was due to reluctance to face the subject: *Crimes of Outrage: Sex, Violence and Victorian Working Women* (London, 1998), p. 2. Geraldin Curtin found that Irish newspapers rarely made direct references to matters of a sexual nature in the same period: "Female Prisoners in Galway Gaol in the Late Nineteenth Century", *Journal of the Galway Archaeological and Historical Society*, 54 (2002), p. 180.

59 DLCH Lamb 244(12).
60 *The Scotsman* (herafter *S'man*), 14 May 1913.
61 *WN*, 19 October 1872, 20 July 1872, 6 September 1890.
62 Matron's Diary, Dundee and District Female Rescue Home, 1878–1880 (hereafter *Matron's Diary*), Dundee City Archives: GD/X406/2/1. I would like to thank archivists Ian Flett and Richard Cullen for alerting me to the source.
63 *WN*, 19 July 1879.

a witness that the defendant had accosted her victim, a drunken Russian sailor, outside a public house, it is likely that "subsequently" was a euphemism for commercial sex.[64] A similar subtext is evident from the description of the circumstances that led to Catherine Coleman's conviction. The recidivist and her victim went to a house where, the court heard, "[d]rink [...] was procured, and the man stayed for some time [...] [b]efore leaving, he missed the money".[65] We will meet Coleman again later, when the evidence against her is less obscure.

Despite the apparent fruitfulness of reading between the lines of Dundee's press, the vast majority of crime reports are typically devoid of insinuation or irony, and it is usually the details of the theft that provide the only clue that prostitutes appeared at the bar. While contemporary readers may have needed no more information to deduce the circumstances of the trial, it is important for the historian to be sure their suspicions are justified, and for that we must look again to the circumstances of the theft.[66] When a man was "carousing in a house [...] [with] some [drunken] young women", the use of "carousing" suggests they were prostitutes.[67] Mrs McKay was brought up for stealing £32 "from a man in a house [...] on Friday night or Saturday morning". The timing of the theft and the vast sum indicates that she was a streetwalker and that her victim was a recently paid sailor or commercial traveller. Similarly, in all likelihood Helen Kane Higgins, who stole a watch from a drunken man, and Jessie Stewart, who stole "15s from the person of a man while on a stair [...] on Saturday night", were prostitute-thieves given the context provided in the newspaper report strongly hints at a sexual foray.[68]

But there are limits to how far the context can take us. Journalists, inspired by the need for brevity, often removed the vital clues linking thefts with furtive encounters, and in doing so greatly added to the dis-

---

64 *WN*, 4 January 1902.
65 *WN*, 13 May 1893; *PJ*, 11 June 1881. It was not unusual for discharged sailors to have in the region of £75 on them.
66 Louise Jackson also believes that the press would not have used coded expressions and euphemisms unless the terms were popularly understood: *Child Sexual Abuse in Victorian England* (England, 2000), p. 55.
67 *WN*, 15 March 1890.
68 *WN*, 13, 27 March 1880.

torted picture of vice crime in Dundee.[69] The distortion of the reporting explains why, out of a sample of approximately 2,000 individual female crime reports, taken from the period when both court reporting was at its most detailed and up to 130 sailors, paid off after the long voyage to India, arrived *daily* in the city, less than five percent record prostitute or pimp involvement.[70]

Notwithstanding the obfuscatory journalism, however, there is enough evidence to suggest that there was an under reporting of the prostitute-offenders tried at Dundee's police court. The only way to recognise it, though, is with a keen and patient eye. In 1900, a judicial aside highlighted that prostitute-thieves perpetrated a significant volume of thefts. The case concerned a prostitute convicted of stealing £12 from the person of a soldier, and it prompted the magistrate to observe that this was one of *"the usual cases* of a man the worse for drink being taken to a house and pillaged".[71] My italics cordon off the crucial clue that there were more prostitute-thieves than a reading of the newspapers suggests. The inordinate discrepancy between the level of vice crime contemporaries *said occurred* around the harbour, and the amount of coverage given to issues concerning prostitution in the press, is another indication that Dundee's court correspondents were highly selective when choosing which cases to report and that they frequently neglected vice crimes. In fact, the acknowledgment from *The People's Journal* in 1872, that the public only got *"occasional glimpses"* of the crimes committed against sailors, seems to confirm that the published accounts represent only a fraction of the trials heard against prostitutes (my italics).[72]

All of the surviving evidence regarding prostitute-thieves relates to thefts *known* to the police. Scholars agree that only a small proportion of crimes were reported, and the difference between the so-called dark figure and reported criminal incidents is likely to be huge in circumstances of vice. There are several reasons, other than editorial policy, why this should be. Firstly, as Glasgow's police complained in the 1870s,

---

69 See Foyster, "Introduction: Newspaper Reporting of Crime and Justice", 11.
70 DLHC Lamb 244(12). The reference here is to cases clearly indicative of a prostitute-thief.
71 *WN*, 7 July 1900.
72 *PJ*, 6 July 1872.

men were often too embarrassed to report they had been robbed by a prostitute, and where the police had learnt of violent robberies, victims were often unwilling to co-operate with the authorities.[73] In his defence, one Dundonian man, charged with contempt of court for lying about the circumstances of the theft, said he did not want it to be known that he had been in a brothel.[74] As previous historians suggest, a victim may have preferred to shrug off the whole sorry incident.[75] Since Dundee was an import harbour, and the seamen discharged from their vessels stayed "no longer than three or four days at most", this was perhaps especially apt of sailor-victims.[76] Similarly, where the loss was small, and physical injuries had not been inflicted, a client's fury would probably be outweighed by feelings of humiliation. Victims were also intimidated by threats from pimps,[77] while married men would be deterred from raising the alarm by the knowledge that any court proceedings would be reported in their home press.

The most powerful disincentive, though, for making a complaint was probably the difficulty of proving a theft had occurred during assignations with a prostitute, when there was no other witness apart from the victim.[78] Prostitute-thieves were rarely caught red-handed. In the Temple Lane case, neither the Russian sailor's purse, nor the accomplice who ran off with it, were traced.[79] Mrs Hamilton, who was charged with stealing £12 from a soldier, when asked what she had done with the money, told the court that "she supposed she had drunk it".[80] It is relevant that

---

73 Mahood, *The Magdalenes*, p. 148. Glasgow's Chief Constable Boyle was clearly referring to prostitute-thieves when he observed, in 1890, that the majority of thefts from the person were "committed under circumstances which afforded few opportunities to the police either to detect or prevent": cited by Alistair Lindsay Goldsmith, "The Development of the City of Glasgow Police c1800–1939" (unpublished doctoral thesis, University of Strathclyde, 2002), p. 206.
74 *The Dundee Chronicle*, 29 August 1835: cited by Helen Nugent, "Poverty and Prostitution in Dundee from 1835–45" (unpublished MA dissertation, University of Dundee, 1996), p. 25. Clearly prostitution was referred to openly in these years, by our period the *Dundee Chronicle* was no longer in existence
75 Joseph O'Neill, *Crime City: Manchester's Victorian Underworld* (Berkshire, 2008), p. 135; Thomas, *Victorian Underworld*, p. 104; Marion S. Goldman, *Gold Diggers and Silver Miners: Prostitution and Social Life on the Comstock Lode* (Michigan, 1981), p. 115.
76 *PJ*, 13 July 1872.
77 A. M. Kilday, Women and Violent Crime in Enlightenment Scotland (Woodbridge, 2007), p.166.
78 Clayton, "The Life and Crimes of Charlotte Walker", p. 8.
79 *WN*, 4 January 1902.
80 *WN*, 7 July 1900.

the historian Mary Clayton demonstrates that the reason why Charlotte Walker, one of London's eighteenth-century prostitute-thieves, got away with thieving for twenty-four years was largely because of the difficulty of proving the charges against her.[81] The men who had removed, or opened their clothing, or were drunk or sleeping when their possessions were apparently stolen, were all deemed unreliable plaintiffs.[82] As Heather Shore suggests, prostitutes took advantage of unreliable evidence,[83] and presumably prostitutes at Dundee's High Court drew attention to the fact that their accusers were "guy [very] drunk" during the time of the alleged theft in order to highlight the weakness of the evidence against them.[84] The testimony of men who had been in the company of a number of women in the hours before they noticed their loss was equally distrusted, and so it is pertinent that Dundee's harbour master submitted that drunken sailors were seen being led away from the shore by up to four prostitutes.[85]

It is likely that legal proceedings will have been dropped where it was difficult to prove that the sailor had been deprived of money against his will. The Dundonian press observed the "simple-mindedness" with which "the sailor *allowed* himself to be fleeced is well known" [my italics].[86] In one example, replicated in the Thames Police Court, a sailor complained he had lost £14 while under the influence of drink; it transpired he had "forgotten" to whom he had given the money.[87] Indeed, according to the Dundonian evidence the recklessness of "Jack" while on shore was proverbial: he earned his money "like a horse" and spent it "like an ass".[88] As will be highlighted again later, the local courts and constabulary viewed the strangers who admitted they had gone to the harbour, "to get a woman", as deserving of all they experienced there.[89]

---

81 Clayton, "The Life and Crimes of Charlotte Walker", pp. 3, 6.
82 Ibid., p. 8.
83 Shore, "The Reckoning", 425.
84 For instance, NAS JC26/1885/31, JC26/1874/16, JC26/1885/32, JC26/1882/68, JC26/1870/64.
85 DLCH Lamb 244(12).
86 Ibid.
87 *PJ*, 13 July 1872; *The Times* 17 September 1866.
88 DLCH Lamb 244(12).
89 NAS JC26/1870/64, Newby, *Women's Lives*, p. 141. Similarly Butler, *Daughters of Joy*, pp. 57–58, and proceedings against prostitute-robbers were frequently dropped in North America: L. M. Dodge, "*Whores and Thieves of the Very Worst Kind": A Study of Women Crime and Prisons 1835–2000* (Illinois, 2002), p. 94.

As the number of prostitute-thieves apprehended by the police depended on the willingness of victims to report their loss, as well as the weight of the evidence, it is not unreasonable to suppose that the majority of thefts committed by Dundee's prostitutes did not result in a police charge, and consequently that the majority of these crimes have been lost to the historian. Still, as we shall see now, enough charges were brought, and enough evidence has survived to suggest that there was a strong relationship between prostitution and theft in the period of this study.

The high court sample, discussed earlier, shows that Dundee's female robbers were frequently prostitutes.[90] The women who masqueraded as streetwalkers, simply to lure men into dark alleys in order to rob them, were obviously thieves first and foremost, and certainly some of Dundee's prostitutes who worked with accomplices did so to steal. For example, Helen Robertson or Henderson "enticed" her victim into a side street and stole his watch; a passing policeman, on hearing a scuffle, arrived just in time to witness her assistants "coming out to help her".[91] As streetwalkers earned pitiful sums selling sex we should perhaps not be surprised that the evidence from this study, as well as from previous work, intimates that they routinely stole from clients.[92] Indeed, it is doubtful that once a prostitute had made more money robbing a client than she had from selling sex alone that she would desist from the more profitable activity.

As has been found elsewhere, many Dundonian prostitute-thieves seem to have taken every available opportunity to steal.[93] Ann Parkhill was an all-round offender with convictions for assaulting and robbing men, uttering base coin (false money), and receiving stolen goods, as

---

90 NAS JC26/1865/14, JC26/1874/75, JC26/1894/13, JC26/1882/15, JC26/1894/8, JC26/1895/9. Similarly, Dodge, "Whores and Thieves", p. 94.
91 WN, 20 August 1887 and similarly DA, 4 April 1876. There is no shortage of examples from elsewhere of the tricks prostitutes used – alone and with accomplices – to entice men into a deserted place to be robbed: Macilwee, The Liverpool Underworld, 162.
92 See footnote 32. Butler suggests it was also an opportunity for a prostitute to take revenge on their customers: Daughters of Joy, 58.
93 For instance JC26/1882/68, JC26/1885/32, JC26/1868/64, JC 26/1885/32. For similar O'Neill, Crime City, p. 136.

well as for a string of domestic thefts.[94] Parkhill, in common with several prostitute-thieves tried at the high court, had convictions in both Dundee and other Scottish cities. Janet Thomson – "the tiepin thief" – had previously stolen two pigs, gold earrings as well as low-value items of domestic clothing. Catherine Cleary or Donnelly, the "light-fingered nymph", whom we also met earlier with her booty of pound notes and half sovereigns, served time for stealing pennies from a child, and Mary Reed, a seventeen-year-old streetwalker admitted into Dundee's prostitute refuge, had been imprisoned for stealing a petticoat. [95]

Throughout Victorian Europe and North America streetwalkers were strongly associated with theft. For example, in Paris, in the first half of the nineteenth century, prostitutes and thieves were regarded as "virtually one and the same",[96] and in America some whores, it was said, felt it "against their religion" to let a man away with money still in his pocket.[97] O'Neill found "[n]early all" of the prostitutes known to the Manchester police, in 1868, "combined theft with selling their bodies".[98] And it was submitted by Glasgow's Chief Constable that prostitutes practised "their blandishments merely as a decoy and cloak for the purposes of robbery".[99] There is also reason to believe that some prostitutes identified more with thieving than soliciting. A Salford thief admitted "[n]one of the girls" thought "much of prostitution but it furnishes opportunities for robbing men."[100]

On this basis of the local evidence, as well as the studies from elsewhere, and considering the size of the dark figure, it is reasonable to suspect that the majority of Dundee's prostitutes supplemented the money they made selling sex with what they stole. Certainly this would explain why streetwalkers may have been around seven times more like-

---

94 For a discussion of counterfeiting as a popular choice for female criminals: Newby, *Women's Lives*, pp. 147–148.
95 *Matron's Diary*, WN, 13 February 1886; NAS JC26/1882/69.
96 Harsin, *Prostitution in Nineteenth-Century Paris*, pp. 150–151.
97 Mary Murphy, "The Private Lives of Public Women: Prostitution in Butte, Montana, 1878–1917", *Frontiers: A Journal of Women Studies*, 7 (1984), p. 34. Also see Butler, *Daughters of Joy*, p. 50.
98 O'Neill, *Crime City*, p. 127.
99 Cited in Mahood, *The Magdalenes*, p. 143.
100 Cited in O'Neill, *Crime City*, p. 136. Similarly in Clayton, "The Life and Crimes of Charlotte Walker", p. 15; Macilwee, *The Liverpool Underworld*, p. 160.

ly to be cited for theft than their position in Dundee's female population statistics would predict. On the other hand, a policy of social control may account for the disproportion of prostitute-thieves in the city's crime records. It is to the evidence of police and judicial discrimination that we turn in the final section, to verify the nature of relationship between prostitution and theft in Dundee.

"More sinned against than sinning" – prostitutes and social control

A war on streetwalkers is an obvious explanation for the disproportionate position of prostitutes in Dundee's police records. Indeed, for many contemporary criminologists it was inevitable that promiscuous women stole.[101] That said, not all Victorians pathologized prostitutes. For some prostitution was no more criminal "than an orange girls [sic] crying oranges on Sunday morning",[102] and it is important to recognise that relations between the police and prostitutes varied enormously throughout the period. As for the policing of prostitution in Scotland's third city, since prostitution was viewed as a form of vagrancy, the loitering statistics give a proxy of trivial arrests and hence the police harassment of prostitutes.[103] It is pertinent therefore, given that it was earlier estimated that there were annually 2,500 streetwalkers in the city, that, from 1876–1904, on average less than two hundred soliciting arrests were made per year.[104] Other evidence too suggests that in Dundee, as in nineteenth-century Stockholm, the authorities tolerated prostitution.[105] For example, both Chief Constable Dewar and Chief Constable Carmichael often sent

---

101 This is seen in Havelock Ellis, *The Criminal* (London: Walter Scott, 1890), p. 218.
102 Cited *S'man*, 7 July 1858.
103 For an important discussion of the law see William Cornish, William, J. Stuart Anderson, Keith Smith, et al, *The Oxford History of the Laws of England, 1820–1914, Volume XIII: Fields of Development* (Oxford 2010), p. 355.
104 Apprehensions and Convictions for Prostitution in Dundee 1878–1904, Statistics from the police returns cited in David Lennox *Working Class Life in Dundee for Twenty-Five Years: 1878–1903*, Table 103 (unpublished doctoral theses, St Andrews University, no date, approximately 1906), St Andrews University Archive: MSDA890 D8L2.
105 Yvonne Svanström, Policing Public Women: The Regulation of Prostitution in Stockholm, 1812–1880 (Stockholm, 2000).

streetwalkers to the city's rescue home rather than the police court.[106] And in Dewar's opinion, prostitutes were "perfectly entitled to go into [...] a public-house and get served".[107] Constable Dunn, writing about the city's brothels, in 1884, observed there was "a growing tendency to look leniently on this evil".[108] Sympathetic social commentators may have also limited the extent to which the police could discriminate. Chief Constable Carmichael reported, in 1913, that "[i]f the police were to interfere" with young prostitutes at the harbour, "they would be severely taken to task".[109]

Pictures of policing elsewhere equally challenge the idea that criminal justice authorities waged a war against prostitutes. In 1915, Chief Constable Ross of Edinburgh declared that prostitutes were "in many instances more sinned against than sinning", and, in his view, their male clients should be prosecuted.[110] Contradicting a previous analysis of social control in Victorian Glasgow, Goldsmith finds that perceptions of a "bigoted police are difficult to substantiate".[111] Of London, Julia Laite observes that the Metropolitan police were not keen in their role as the repressors of street prostitution,[112] similarly, Stefan Slater observes, in the interwar period, they were "the least of [the prostitutes'] worries".[113] Indeed, throughout Britain, America and Canada there were complaints that the police were too lax in their regulation of prostitutes.[114]

As prostitutes were the very antithesis of the Victorian model of femininity it is reasonable to suspect that that they would be the most

---

106 *Matron's Diary*.
107 *PJ*, 14 April 1905.
108 DLHC Lamb 237(5), John Dunn, *Dundee Burgh Police – Essay on "what alterations and improvements on the present method of dealing with crime and criminals in Scotland would be most likely to tend to the prevention of Crime and the Detection and Reclamations of Criminals?"* (Dundee, 1884), p. 7.
109 *S'man*, 14 May 1913.
110 *S'man*, 16 March 1915, Ross' was not a lone voice, see: John P. S. Maclaren, "Chasing the social evil: moral fervour and the evolution of Canada's prostitution laws 1867–1917, *Canadian Journal of Law and Sociology*, 125 (1986), p. 139.
111 Goldsmith, "The Development of the City of Glasgow Police", pp. 370–371. Mahood, on the other hand, argues that there was a suppressive approach in Glasgow: *The Magdalenes*, pp. 124–125, 143.
112 Laite, "Prostitution in London, 1885–1930", p. 173.
113 Slater, "Prostitutes and Popular History Notes on the Underworld 1918–1939", p. 41.
114 For a discussion see: Maclaren, "Chasing the social evil", p. 149; Clare V. McKanna, Jr., "Prostitutes, progressives, and police: the viability of vice in San Diego 1900–1930", *The Journal of San Diego History*, 35 (1989), www.sandiegohistory.org/journal/89winter/prostitutes.htm (accessed 2 October 2009), in addition Paula Bartley and Barbara Gwinnett, "Prostitution", in Ina Zweiniger-Bargielowska (ed.), *Women in Twentieth-Century Britain* (Harlow: Pearson, 2001), p. 217.

heavily punished of all female offenders.[115] In fact, the Scottish judiciary did not impose harsh sentences on women charged with soliciting. In Govan, for example, prostitutes convicted of their first offence of loitering were admonished, illustrating that the occasion was not used to enforce traditional sex-role expectations.[116] Equally, in Edinburgh, Chief Constable Angus claimed that the offence of importuning was not treated very severely, although he added that it all depended on the magistrate sitting.[117] Contrary to "staged dramas" at the police court, that the historian of prostitution Judith Walkowitz predicts would have occurred when streetwalkers were brought to trial, Dundee's magistrates frequently threw out charges of importuning, presumably because there was insufficient evidence to justify a conviction.[118] The Dundonian evidence reveals judges often allowed women the benefit of the doubt. For example, in 1904 the police brought 135 charges for soliciting, but the magistrates only made 77 convictions, and the situation was similar the year before.[119] In Dundee prostitutes were regularly treated compassionately in the hope they would reform. Provost Yeaman said he imposed "a lenient sentence", on Jane Brown, in the hope that she "would betake herself to respectable employment".[120] Demonstrating concerns remarkably similar to today's Scottish prison commissioners, they were also disinclined to send prostitute-recidivists – who did not pose a risk of harm to the public – to prison, when it was apparent that ratepayers' money could be better spent.[121] The Dundonian judges were not alone in their inclination to be lenient. Officers in the Met, Petrow observes of this period, were deterred from arresting

---

115 Shani D'Cruze and Louise A. Jackson, *Women, Crime and Justice in England Since 1660* (Basingstoke, 2009), p.8.
116 HMSO, *Report from the Departmental Committee on Habitual Offenders, Vagrants, Beggars, Inebriates, and Juvenile Delinquents* (Edinburgh, 1895), 8904.
117 Ibid., 8976.
118 Judith R. Walkowitz, "Review of 'Poverty and Prostitution: A Study of Victorian Prostitutes in York', by Frances Finnegan and 'Prostitution and Victorian Social Reform', by Paul McHugh," *Journal of Social History*, 16 (1983), p. 146. But elsewhere she identifies that the police were reluctant agents of moral reform: *Prostitution and Victorian Society*, p. 42.
119 Lennox, Working Class Life in Dundee for Twenty-Five Years: 1878–1903.
120 *WN*, 19 October 1872.
121 Smith, *Oxford History of Laws*, pp. 83–115, *Report of the Commission on Women Offenders* (Scotland, 2012), p.3.

prostitutes by the knowledge that "capricious" magistrates would not convict on their witness testimony alone.[122]

The Dundonian evidence does not support D'Cruze and Jackson's view that when prostitutes committed theft the Victorian criminal justice system was more ready to assume guilt.[123] A culture of judicial leniency was apparent at Catherine Coleman's trial. The recidivist, who we met earlier, on this occasion was sentenced to four days' imprisonment for stealing "a purse, 17s 4d in money, five railway tickets and a brass ring", from a clerk in circumstances strongly suggestive of prostitution. As she had several times previously been convicted of theft, "under similar circumstances", she might reasonably have expected more, and in fact the sheriff warned her that unless she reformed, she would find herself in penal servitude.[124] Similarly, in the trial of Elizabeth Anderson, the judge found the charge of theft not proven, despite knowing that Anderson had been seen drinking and walking arm-in-arm with her accuser and, deciphering the press report, when he rejected her advances had "dived her hand" into his trouser pocket and stolen 14s.[125] All in all, prostitute-larcenists do not appear to have been regarded by the local magistrates as any greater nuisance than the chaste thieves who stole shirts and shawls from washing lines and washhouses.[126] Rather it seems that Dundee's judges often had little sympathy for plaintiffs who had lost their possessions in liaisons with prostitutes – even when the proceedings concerned robbery.[127] This finding, taken together with the evidence discussed above, that magistrates frequently discharged women the police had charged with soliciting, indicates that Dundee's legal system was not punishing prostitutes unfairly.

In light of the evidence that prostitution was tolerated in the port-city, it seems reasonable to conclude that a disproportionately large number of the Dundee's streetwalkers were cited for property crime, in the police

---

122 Petrow, *Policing Morals*, pp. 220, 136.
123 D'Cruze and Jackson, *Women, Crime and Justice in England*, pp. 66, 49.
124 *WN*, 13 May 1893.
125 *WN*, 19 July 1879.
126 For comparative cases of prostitute and non-prostitute thieves see, for example, *WN*, 19 March 1870, 27 October 1866.
127 NAS JC26/1870/64.

and high court records, because many amongst them had a taste for robbery and petty theft.

Conclusions

There is a traditional Dundonian song that tells of a stranger who was plied with drink by one of the city's women, and how he was robbed. It ends by warning other men of the dangers of women and drink in Dundee.[128] As this study has found that it seems likely that the proclivity of prostitutes to steal, rather than policies of social control, explains their prominent position in the crime records, the song is apt testimony to the relationship between prostitution and theft in Victorian and Edwardian Dundee. The picture of prostitute-crime has emerged in layers since, in striking contrast to previous studies of York and Kent, reports of thefts perpetrated by prostitutes are largely absent from the pages of the Dundonian press. The difference is probably due to Dundee's culture of editorial prudery, reflecting a general social assumption that prostitution was not to be discussed directly. While inhibited reporting may be indicative of a distinctive Scottish editorial policy towards vice, the importance of the so-called dark figure to all studies of prostitute-crime cannot be overstated. As the number of prostitute-thieves apprehended by the police depended on the willingness of victims to report their loss, as well as the weight of the evidence, it is not unreasonable to suppose that the majority of thefts committed by Dundee's prostitutes did not result in a police charge, and consequently that the majority of these crimes have been lost to the historian. Nevertheless, because the local police statistics and the high court papers record that a disproportionately large number of streetwalkers were cited for property crime, it is argued that Dundee's prostitutes were ubiquitous thieves.

What is clear from the study is that the relationship between prostitution and theft in Dundee echoed patterns identified in the previous re-

---

128 The opening line of the traditional folk song *The Overgate*, "Now as I gaed up the Overgate I met a bonnie wee lass", for the complete lyrics see http://sniff.numachi.com/pages/tiOVERGATE;ttOVERGATE.html (accessed 3 January 2009).

search of Europe and North America, indicating that parallels may have existed between the most alienated women for centuries. Moreover, we have seen it is dangerous to view the discourses impacting on the female offender narrowly. A surveyor of female criminality, at the turn of the century, was, it seems, justified to observe that it was "a fact" that the authorities were often "very indulgent" of the women of the street.[129]

Sources

ARCHIVAL SOURCES

British Library
 Adam, Hargrave L, *Women and Crime* (T Werner Laurie: London, 1914).
 Dale, George P, "Moral Prophylaxis: Prostitutes and Prostitution", *The American Journal of Nursing*, 13 (1919), pp. 22–26.
 Ellis, Havelock, *The Criminal* (Walter Scott: London, 1890).

Dundee City Archives
 Women's Mission to Women, Female Rescue Home, Milnbank. Dundee and Arbroath Rescue Home, Dundee and District Female Rescue Home, Matron's Diary 1878–1880 (GD/X406/2/1).

Dundee Local History Centre Lamb's Collection
 Burgh of Dundee Return of Crimes and Offences Reported to the Police ... year ending 31st December 1869–1877 (43).
 Dundee's Sailors' Home 244(12).
 Dunn, John, Officer of the Dundee Police Force, Dundee Burgh Police – Essay on "*What Alterations and Improvements on the Present Method of Dealing with Crime and Criminals in Scotland Would be Most Likely to Tend to the Prevention of Crime and the Detection and Reclamations of Criminals?*" (Dundee, 1876) (237(5)).
 Good Advice to Seamen by an Old Sailor 1881 (25(19)).
 The Dundee Advertiser.
 The Dundee Weekly News.
 The People's Journal.
 The Scotsman.

National Archives of Scotland
 High Court records for Dundee JC26.

---

129 Hargrave L. Adam, *Woman and Crime* (London, T.Werner Laurie, 1914), p. 34.

National Library of Scotland
HMSO, *Report from the Departmental Committee on Habitual Offenders, Vagrants, Beggars, Inebriates, and Juvenile Delinquents* (Edinburgh, 1895).

University of St Andrews Library and Archives
Lennox, David, *Working Class Life in Dundee for Twenty-Five Years: 1878–1903* (unpublished dissertation, St. Andrews University, no date, approximately 1906). (MSDA890 D8L2).

LITERATURE

Backhouse, Constance 1991: *Petticoats and Prejudice: Women and Law in Nineteenth Century Canada*, Ontario.

Barnhart, Jacqueline Baker 1986: *The Fair but Frail: Prostitution in San Francisco 1849–1900*, Reno.

Bartley, Paula and Barbara Gwinnett 2001: Prostitution. In *Women in Twentieth-Century Britain*, ed. Ina Zweiniger-Bargielowska. Harlow: Pearson.

Boyle, Michael D. 1997: *Women and Crime in Belfast, 1900–1913* (unpublished doctoral thesis), Queen's University Belfast.

Butler, Ann M. 1987: *Daughters of Joy, Sisters of Mercy: Prostitutes in the American West 1865–90*. Chicago.

Clayton, Mary 2008: The Life and Crimes of Charlotte Walker, Prostitute and Pickpocket. *The London Journal*, 33 (2008), pp. 3–19.

Cornish, William, J. Stuart Anderson, Keith Smith, et al. 2010: *The Oxford History of the Laws of England, 1820–1914, Volume XIII: Fields of Development*. Oxford.

Crowther, Anne M. 1995: The Criminal Precognitions and their Value for the Historian. *Scottish Archives*, 1 (1995), pp. 75–92.

Curtin, Geraldin 2002: Female Prisoners in Galway Gaol in the Late Nineteenth Century. *Journal of the Galway Archaeological and Historical Society*, 54 (2002).

Davidson, Roger and Gayle Davis 2004: "A Festering Sore on the Body of Society": The Wolfenden Committee and Female Prostitution in Mid-Twentieth-Century Scotland. *Journal of Scottish Historical Studies*, 24 (2004), pp. 80–98.

Davies, Russell 1996: *Secret Sins: Sex, Violence and Society in Carmarthenshire 1870–1920*, Cardiff.

Ditton, Jason and James Duffy 1983: Bias in the Newspaper Reporting of Crime News. *British Journal of Criminology*, 23 (1983), pp. 159–165.

Dodge, L. M. 2002: *"Whores and Thieves of the Very Worst Kind": A Study of Women Crime and Prisons 1835–2000*, Illinois.

Donnachie, Ian 1995: Profiling Criminal Offences: The Evidence of the Lord Advocate's Papers During the First Half of the Nineteenth Century in Scotland. *Scottish Archives*, 1 (1995), pp. 85–92.

Durston, Gregory 2007: *Victims and Viragos: Metropolitan Women, Crime and the Eighteenth-Century Criminal Justice System*, Suffolk.

D'Cruze, Shani 1998: *Crimes of Outrage: Sex, Violence and Victorian Working Women*, London.

D'Cruze, Shani and Louise A. Jackson 2009: *Women, Crime and Justice in England Since 1660*, Basingstoke.

Emsley, Clive 2010 (4th edn.): *Crime and Society in England, 1750–1900*, Harlow.

Finnegan, Frances 1979: *Poverty and Prostitution: A Study of Victorian Prostitutes in York*, Cambridge.

Fisher, Trevor 1997: *Prostitution and the Victorians*, Gloucestershire.

Fleming, David 2005: Public attitudes to prostitution in eighteenth-century Ireland. *Irish Economic and Social History*, XXXII (2005).

Foyster, Elizabeth 2007: Introduction: Newspaper Reporting of Crime and Justice. *Continuity and Change*, 22 (2007), pp. 9–12.

Jill Harsin 1986: *The American Historical Review*, 91 (1986), pp. 677–678.

Gilfoyle, Timothy J. 1992: *City of Eros: New York City, Prostitution and the Commercialization of Sex, 1790–1920*, London.

Goldman, Marion S. 1981: *Gold Diggers and Silver Miners: Prostitution and Social Life on the Comstock Lode*, Michigan.

Goldsmith, Alistair Lindsay 2002: *The Development of the City of Glasgow Police c 1800–1939* (unpublished doctoral thesis), University of Strathclyde.

Grace, Susan E. 1998: *Female Criminality in York and Hull, 1830–1870* (unpublished doctoral thesis), University of York.

Henderson, Tony 1999: *Disorderly Women in Eighteenth-Century London: Prostitution and Control in the Metropolis 1830–1830*, London.

Jackson, Louise A. 1982: *Child Sexual Abuse in Victorian England*, London.

Jones, David J. V. 1992: *Crime in Nineteenth-Century Wales*, Cardiff.

Kilday, A. M. 1998: *Women and Crime in South-West Scotland: A Study of the Justiciary Court Records 1750–1815* (unpublished doctoral thesis), University of Strathclyde.

Kilday, A. M. 2007: *Women and Violent Crime in Enlightenment Scotland*, Woodbridge.

Kingsley Kent, Susan 1999: *Gender and Power in Britain 1640–1990*, London.

Knox, W. J. 1999: *Industrial Nation: Work Culture and Society in Scotland: 1800 – Present*, Edinburgh.

Laite, Julia Ann 2008: *Prostitution in London, 1885–1930* (unpublished doctoral thesis), University of Cambridge.

Lee, Catherine Theresa 2008: *Regulating Prostitution in Nineteenth-Century Kent: Beyond the Contagious Diseases Acts* (unpublished doctoral thesis), Open University.

Luddy, Maria 2007: *Prostitution and Irish Society 1800–1940*, Cambridge.

Macilwee, Michael 2011: *The Liverpool Underworld: Crime in the City 1750–1900*, Liverpool.

Mahood, Linda 1990: *The Magdalenes: Prostitution in the Nineteenth Century*, London.

McCreery, David 1986: "The Life of Misery and Shame": Female Prostitution in Guatemala City 1880–1920. *Journal of Latin American Studies*, 18 (1986), pp. 333–353.

Mckanna, Clare V. jnr. 1989: Prostitutes, Progressives, and the Police: The Viability of Vice in San Diego 1900–1930. *The Journal of San Diego History*, 35 (1989), pp. 1–14, www.sandiegohistory.org/journal/89winter/prostitutes.htm (accessed 2 October 2009).

Maclaren, John P. S. 1986: Chasing the Social Evil: Moral Fervour and the Evolution of Canada's Prostitution Laws 1867–1917. *Canadian Journal of Law and Sociology*, 125 (1986), pp. 125–165.

Murphy, Mary 1984: The Private Lives of Public Women: Prostitution in Butte, Montana, 1878–1917. *Frontiers: A Journal of Women Studies*, 7 (1984), pp. 30–35.

Newby, Jennifer 2011: *Women's Lives: Researching Women's Social History 1800–1939*, Barnsley.

O'Neill, Joseph 2008: *Crime City: Manchester's Victorian Underworld*, Berkshire.

Palk, Deirdre 2006: *Gender, Crime and Judicial Discretion 1780–1830*, Suffolk.

Parnell, Susan 2003: Race, Power and Urban Control: Johannesburg's Inner City Slum-Yards, 1910–1923. *Journal of Southern Africa Studies*, 29 (2003), pp. 615–637.

Petrow, Stefan 1994: *Policing Morals: The Metropolitan Police and the Home Office 1870–1914*, Oxford.

Rubenhold, Hallie 2005: *The Covent-Garden Ladies: Pimp General Jack and the Extraordinary Story of Harris's List*, Stroud.

Sangster, Joan 1993: Pardon Tales' from Magistrate's Court: Women, Crime and the Court in Peterborough County 1920–50. *Canadian Historical Review*, 2 (1993), pp. 161–197.

Shore, Heather 2009: The Reckoning': Disorderly Women, Informing Constables and the Westminster Justices, 1727–33. *Social History*, 34 (2009), pp. 409–427.

Slater, Stefan 2009: Prostitutes and Popular History: Notes on the "Underworld", 1918–1939. *Crime, History and Societies*, 13 (2009), pp. 25–49.

Svanström, Yvonne 2000: *Policing Public Women: The Regulation of Prostitution in Stockholm, 1812–1880*, Stockholm.

Thomas, Donald 1998: *The Victorian Underworld*, London.

Walkowitz, Judith R, 1980: *Prostitution and Victorian Society: Women, Class and the State*, Cambridge.

Walkowitz, Judith R. 1983: Review of "Poverty and Prostitution: A Study of Victorian Prostitutes in York", by Frances Finnegan and "Prostitution and Victorian Social Reform", by Paul McHugh. *Journal of Social History*, 16 (1983), pp. 145–147.

Walvin, James 1978: *Leisure and Society 1830–1950*, London.

White, Jerry 2008: *London in the Nineteenth Century: A Human Awful Wonder of God*, London.

IV
The Ultimate Power over Life and Death

The Pope's Sword

Early Modern Capital Punishment, Homicide and Cultures of Suffering – Rome in the European Context[1]

Tomás A. Mantecón

Whipped, beheaded, hanged, quartered, burned at the stake (whether before or after being hung or beheaded)... These and similar descriptions help us to build our archetype of early modern justice as arbitrary, cruel and brutal in the way that it acted upon the bodies of criminals. In summary, it appears as a sort of barbarous apparatus that criminalized all instances of opposition to, or even dissension from, the projects of the political authorities and, in the end, administrative systematic machinery that used corporal punishment to discipline criminals. The public nature and precise dramatization of early modern justice was supposed both to deter potential delinquents and to prevent any subversive action against the existing order, which was based on the superior authority of the prince, for the common good of the political body (*res publica*)).

---

[1] I thank Olli Matikainen and Satu Lidman for their comments and suggestions. I also thank Liz Eastcott and Sergio Mantecón for dealing with the translation of this chapter. The statistics for the tables and graphics in this paper come from ASR (State Rome Archive) book 285. In table 1, I have also made use of data from Pieter Spierenburg, *The Broken Spell: a Cultural & Anthropological History of Preindustrial Europe* (New Brunswick 1991), p. 229; James A. Sharpe, "Last Dying Speeches: Religion, Ideology and Public Execution in seventeenth-century England". *Past and Present* 107 (1985), pp. 144–167; Peter Linebaugh, *The London Hanged: Crime and Civil Society in the Eighteenth Century* (Cambridge 1993); Maria R. Boes, "Public Appearance and Criminal Judicial Practices in Early Modern Germany". *Social Science History*: 20(1996), pp. 259–279; *Public executions*, W.Carse Printer, 127, Trongate (Glasgow, 1820).

Certainly, this archetype of justice offers an explanation of an important part of what occurred regularly in early modern European cities. Words like "whipped", "beheaded", "hanged", "quartered" and "burnt out" were used to describe corporal punishment in early modern penal sentences. As part of the punitive discourse created by the official, repressive culture, these sentences would be read – or cried – out in public whilst the condemned criminals were escorted to the execution site. However, justice was also described in other ways than these very physical and dramatic expressions. Labels, such as "contrite", "well disposed", "edified" and "a good example to others", were also part of the punitive lexicon. Here, the focus was on the criminals' own attitudes towards punishment and referred to the values that formed part of early modern cultures of suffering. Redemption and comforting discourses were preached by some of the religious individuals who accompanied prisoners in their procession to the execution site. This was clearly evident in Catholic Europe[2]. Such discourses also lay behind the dissemination of "last dying speeches" and the publication of "crime stories" in Britain, although the arguments and meanings employed in Britain varied considerably from those that were put forward in France, Italy and Spain.[3] Despite some similar religious connections, the metaphorical interpretation of the punishment culture of suffering nearly in terms of a martyrdom – a viewpoint stressed by McKenzie (2007) – many cases from the eighteenth-century London highlight the discrepancies in this argument, as James Sharpe (2008) has recently pointed out.[4]

2   On Italy, see Vinzenzo Paglia, "La pietà dei carcerati". *Confraternite e società a Roma nei secoli XVI–XVIII*. Ed. di Storia e Letteratura (Rome 1980); "La morte confortata". *Riti della paura e mentalità religiosa a Roma nell'età moderna*, ed. di Storia e Letteratura (Rome 1982); Giovanni Romeo, *Aspettando il boia. Condannati a morte, confortatori e inquisitori nella Napoli della Controriforma* (Rome 1993), whose publications deal with Rome and Naples respectively. On Spain, see my own writings Tomás A. Mantecón, "La economía del castigo e indulto en la Castilla de Cervantes". *Revista de Historia Económica* (24: 2006, pp. 69–97); "Récits de punition et de pardon dans la Castille moderne". In: Benoît Garnot (ed.), *Normes juridiques et pratiques judiciaires du Moyen Âge à l'époque contemporaine* (Éditions Universitaires de Dijon 2007), pp. 377–384; "La justicia y el castigo del cuerpo en la Castilla moderna". In: Marta Bonaudo, Andrea Reguera & Orieta Zeberio (ed.), *Las escalas de la historia comparada*. Tomo 1: Dinámicas sociales, poderes políticos y sistemas jurídicos, ed. Miño y Dávila Editores (Buenos Aires 2008), pp. 207–228.
3   Sharpe, "Last dying speeches".
4   Andrea McKenzie, *Tyburn's Martyrs: execution in England, 1675–1775* (London 2007); James A. Sharpe, Review of Tyburn's Martyrs: execution in England, 1675–1775, Andrea McKenzie (review n° 677, 2008), www.history.ac.uk/reviews/paper/sharpe.html (accessed 2 January 2009).

In the end, it is generally accepted that the brutality of the legal and judicial official punishment was supposed to preserve the common peace and public order. The criminal's acceptance of his or her punishment was both an essential part of a ceremonial display that furthered this aim and a demonstration of the paternal, prudent and balanced version of institutional justice, which, though not egalitarian, was at least equitable and fair according to distributive principles – in a single word: *just*. In Catholic cultural tradition, the resignation and acceptance of suffering of the condemned was an expression of contrition. This attitude was in favour of the eternal salvation of the convict's soul.

Justice, corporal public punishment and urban space

The political use of prisoners' suffering (as an instrument of social control) required the public expression of a brutal and infallible punishment. This aspect is stressed in Foucault's schematic depictions of early modern justice, as characterized by the execution in 1757 of Robert Damiens.[5] Damiens's living body was subjected to an anachronistic set of physical punitive actions on his living body. The anachronistic nature of this form of execution, which had its origins in medieval punishment of the crime of lese-majesty, was proved by changes to public punishments in Spain and eighteenth-century debates on torture.[6] However, in the end, the punishment meted out to Damiens was a just expression of *one of the versions* of early modern justice: a focus on the punishment of the body and the elimination of the delinquent – and, by extension, the elimination of his or her criminal behaviour and harmful example to others. According to the Foucauldian scheme, the transition between the eighteenth and nineteenth centuries saw a change in the aims of justice: the regulation of criminal activities became the focus replacing the punishment of his or her body. Regulation was supposed to be an effective instrument for securing "docile bodies" – people who would be

---

5   Michel Foucault, *Surveiller et punir. Naissance de la prison* (Paris 1975).
6   Tomás A. Mantecón, "Récits de punition".

ductile and useful to the political authority's social control projects, as well as providing the labour required by the market.

In the end, what was a concern in Foucault's reflection was the definition of justice in liberal systems by a contrast with what he thought that was the archetype of preliberal justice. In his scheme, while the last was focused on the physical and material punishment of the bodies, perhaps even the elimination of the criminals' bodies, the former prefers to make use of the criminals' bodies and minds by controlling and shaping their full activities. Foucault's schemes give very much to think of about present days and even preliberal justice and varieties of discipline, but at going deeply with the analysis of Old Regime penal systems and their expressions in terms of public punishments allows the outburst of many other meanings to explain. Quite different to Foucault's perceptions of early modern justice can be found in the lexicon used to describe prisoners' attitudes towards their own physical punishment and torture; in the comfort provided by religious confessors and missionaries (who accompanied criminals to the execution site); and, finally, in the reactions of justice officials – and the public – to the circumstances of each execution. Early modern justice encompassed a broader range of ideas than simply the elimination of the criminal through the application of physical punishment and torture or the instruction of the social body represented by the spectators at execution ceremonies and suffering rituals.

The expression of regret, resignation and consent to punishment by prisoners not only offered instructive discipline to others, but also primarily demonstrated a preoccupation with the salvation of the soul. From a Catholic perspective, physical punishment and criminal suffering were considered instruments of penitence that enabled the condemned to attempt to atone for his or her offences both to others and, principally, to God. Suffering before dying was thought as an opportunity to reduce the Purgatory pains. The reduction of early modern justice to the features highlighted by Foucault fails to provide a realistic and comprehensive view of the topic. In fact, Foucault's provocative scheme was more a call to debate than a clear empirical assertion. Justice in the early modern period was not an unchanging monolithic phenomenon that can be reduced to a simple archetype. Instead, it can be thought of as a sort of *realities in mutation*. In addition to the *realities* discussed above (including disciplinary instruction), the need for retribution (both for the damage done to the community and to the victim) was also a feature of early modern justice. The principle of recompense for the injured party was largely rooted in traditional private forms of justice, including *vendetta* or *faida, blood feud* or *pendença*, which acted as a sort of customary justice in quite different Old Regime European societies and contexts.[7] Apart from the need to give compensations to the victim party to avoid vengeance by justice, for the political community, every criminal case also provoked the need to exact official retribution in order to satisfy *vindicta publica* and restore the common good and peace.

Official justice, in the end, aspired to address both spheres – private and public – of retribution. On the one hand, the penal official system – in its own development – tried to incorporate most aspects of *private justice* within legal proceedings and *institutional justice*. On the other hand, the elites, as part of the state-building process, wished to shift away potential juridical capacity from society towards the state spheres, in order to improve institutional social control and their monopoly of licit violence. To this effect, there had to be social recognition of the *superiority* of the official authority of the prince (*princeps*), royal government and justice (and, by extension, that of the royal representatives) over society (all individuals and social groups). This superiority should allow the prince, his representatives and institutions to arbitrate in civil and penal conflicts and to keep the peace according to law, customs and traditions. In this way, official justice tried to present itself as *the only* legitimate body that could use violence to punish criminals, in the name of achieving order and maintaining the *common peace*.

Because early modern regions and states underwent their own processes of institution-building and political development, the transition to the one hegemonic and public model of justice to the next also varied according to geographical location and the historical and social context. These

---

7   Tomás A. Mantecón, *Conflictividad y disciplinamiento social en la Cantabria rural del Antiguo Régimen* (Univ. Cantabria, Santander 1997); Osvaldo Raggio, *Faide e parentele. Lo Stato genovese visto dalla Fontanabuona* (Torino 1990); Jenny Wormald, "The Blood Feud in Early Modern Scotland". In: John Bossy, *Disputes and Settlements: Law and Human Relations in the West* (Cambridge 1983), pp. 101–144.

processes described an official and institutional imposition of a version of justice that aspired to assert *hegemony* over other expressions of justice (diverse forms of *customary justice*).[8] In spite of this aspiration, to date this process has not yet been completed. The result has ever been the historical production of diverse configurations of *hybrid justice*: official justice and customary justice have operated in varied versions, proportions, combinations and interactions according to each specific historical period and context.[9] This was, in the end, the most authentic expression of real *justice*.

In early modern times two versions of justice – customary and remunerative justice and official, legal and institutional justice – coexisted in different ways and combinations. However, notwithstanding its failure to achieve absolute imposition, in a long historical process, we can see the general and slow superposition of the latter version upon the former. This last, sometimes played an important role within the sphere of custom and was very often incorporated within the legal and judicial proceedings[10]. Even during the century of the Enlightenment, examples of customary and remunerative justice were common across great Euro-

---

8   Mario Sbriccoli, Crimen laesae maistatis: il problema del reato politico alle soglie della scienza penalistica moderna (Universidade Nova de Lisboa, Milan 1974).
9   Mantecón, *Conflictividad y disciplinamiento;* "Meaning and Social Context of Crime in Preindustrial Times: Rural Society in the North of Spain, XVII and XVIII centuries". Crime, History and Societies 1 (1998), pp. 49–73.
10 I have explained these points in different publications. Tomás A. Mantecón, "La capacidad del clero secular para apaciguar las disputas entre los campesinos montañeses del siglo XVIII". In: Enrique Martínez & Vicente Suárez (ed.), *Iglesia y sociedad*. I. III Reunión Científica de la A.E.H.M. (Univ. Las Palmas de Gran Canaria 1995), pp.149–156;*Conflictividad y disciplinamiento;* "Territorio, poderes y actitudes hacia el crimen en la Moderna Cantabria rural". In: Pablo Fernández Albaladejo (ed.), *Monarquía, Imperio y pueblos en la España Moderna*. IV Reunión Científica de la Asociación Española de Historia Moderna (Univ. Alicante 1997), pp. 757–770; "Meaning and Social Context of Crime", pp. 49–73; La muerte de Antonia Isabel Sánchez. Tiranía y escándalo en una comunidad rural del Norte de España (Centro de Estudios Cervantinos, Alcalá de Henares 1998), pp. 49–73; "El peso de la infrajudicialidad en el control del crimen durante la Edad Moderna". *Estudis* (2002), 43–75; "El control de la moralidad a través de la fiesta: flagelantes y cencerradas en la España Cantábrica del Antiguo Régimen". *Ludica. Annali di storia e civiltà del gioco* 8 (2002), pp. 141–159; "El mal uso de la justicia en la Castilla del siglo XVII. In Furor et rabies". In: José I. Fortea, Juan E. Gelabert & Tomás A. Mantecón (ed.), *Violencia, conflicto y marginación en la Edad Moderna* (Univ. Cantabria, Santander 2002), pp. 69–98; "Popular culture and arbitration of disputes in the Northern Spanish 18th century". In: Louis A. Knafla (ed.), *Crimes, punishment and Reform in Europe*. Criminal Justice History 18 (2003), pp. 39–55; "Social Control from Below: Popular Arbitration of Disputes in the Spanish Old Regime". In: Pieter Spierenburg & Herman Roodenburg (ed.), *History of Social Control*. Vol. 1. 1500–1800. (Ohio 2004,) pp. 267–287; "Les demons de Martin: folie et erreur judiciaire dans la Castille du XVIIe siècle". In: Benoît Garnot (ed.), *L'erreur judiciaire. De Jeanne d'Arc à Roland Agret*. (París 2004), pp. 61–84.

pean rural regions – from Scotland and Ostrobothnia in Finland to the Spanish regions of Cantabria and Galicia.[11] An example of this version of justice can also be seen in the procedure for the supplication of pardon in early modern Spain. In such a case the king could not exert his power of pardon unless the criminal had already received a private pardon from the injured party. This was also the case in early modern Italy.

The development of public corporal punishment was legitimated by the existence of an arbitral authority able to decide on this, making use of its recognised *superiority* over every individual, social group, estate and corporation. Through his Divine Right, the king (or equivalent representative of a superior authority, including, of course, the Pope) could justify his own *hegemony* and capacity to punish within his own power sphere and territory. In order to understand how these aims of social control were pursued, we need to consider how this form of punishment developed and how regularly it was exercised in everyday urban life. The frequency and evolution of the use of public torture can also provide insight into the values that underpinned public corporal punishment. Analysis of the reasons why an individual came to be punished corporally in public (in extreme cases, to the point of death) can provide us with information about the types of crime that were considered absolutely intolerable across each historical society.

Although, in this chapter, my own reflections on these subjects are rooted in the experiences of early modern Rome,[12] this specific case is considered within a wider, comparative European context. I have closely analysed documents from the religious confraternity of San Giovanni Decollato, also known as *La Misericordia*, which had been charged with ministering to all criminals condemned to death in Rome ever since the founding of the confraternity by Pope Innocent VIII on 9 May 1488. My

---

11 Wormald, "The Bloodfeud in Early Modern Scotland"; Mantecón, *Conflictividad y disciplinamiento*; "Meaning and Social Context of Crime in Preindustrial Times", pp. 49–73; Heikki Ylikangas, Major Fluctuations in Crimes of Violence in Finland: A Historical Analysis. *Scandinavian Journal of History* 1 (1976), pp. 81–103; "What Happened to Violence? An Analysis of the Development of Violence from Medieval Times to the Early Modern Era Based on Finnish Source Material". In: Petri Karonen, Martti Lehti, & Heikki Ylikangas (ed.), Five Centuries of Violence in Finland and the Baltic area (Helsinki), pp. 1–84; Raquel Iglesias, *Crimen, criminales y reos. La delincuencia y su represión en la antigua provincia de Santiago entre 1700 y 1834* (Gijón 2007).
12 Where torture was legally abolished in 1816.

study essentially deals with an analysis of legal violence and its effectiveness as means of repressing illegal or criminal behaviour. Through this analysis I hope to provide some understanding of the complex nature of early modern justice and its chronological changes.

Early modern European cities eventually became the stages upon which the most extreme rigour and violence that could be implemented by legal justice were performed, in the name of preserving the public peace. In early modern times, the bodies of bandits hit with arrows by members of the Spanish *Santa Hermandad* were left in the most visible locations along the main roads and city entry points. Heads and other mutilated body parts were displayed at the most important entrances of cities, as in Seville and Amsterdam in the sixteenth and seventeenth centuries[13], or in crowded urban squares, as was the case for those considered rebels against Spanish colonial interests in the Mexican region of Nueva Vizcaya in the second half of the eighteenth century.[14] Despite this, no European city or justice needed to apply the most extreme rigour and harshness at its disposal to all those criminals who, under the law, could have been subjected to capital punishment. Kings and urban magistrates only needed to publically demonstrate that they were able to develop these most extreme types of punishment and executions in order to deter potential criminals and prevent crime.

The public nature of punishments, executions and the exhibition of corporal remains should have provided sufficient evidence to show that this end was a real risk for every criminal. There also was a need to regulate the dramatization of the punishment and to promote the easy identification of the specific urban spaces as execution sites. As sites of judicial punishment, the square of San Francisco in Seville; the *dam* of Amsterdam; the squares of La Greve of Paris or Rossio in Lisbon; the Plaza Mayor of Madrid; and the Campo de' Fiori, Sant'Angelo, Piazza del Popolo in

---

13 Tomás A Mantecón, "Las culturas criminales portuarias en las ciudades atlánticas: Sevilla y Ámsterdam en su edad dorada". In: José I. Fortea & Juan E. Gelabert (ed.), *La ciudad portuaria atlántica en la historia: siglos XVI–XIX* (Univ. Cantabria, Santander 2006), pp. 159–194; Pieter Spierenburg, *The Spectacle of Suffering. Executions and the Evolution of Repression: from a Preindustrial Metropolis to the European Experience* (Cambridge 1984); Pieter Spierenburg, *The Broken Spell*.
14 Sara Ortelli, *Trama de una guerra conveniente: Nueva Vizcaya y la sombra de los apaches 1748–1790* (El Colegio de México 2007).

Rome all presented an image of a full urban political community governed by a form of legitimate justice (grounded in law and superior authority of the political rulers) that sought to preserve public order and promote the *common good*. This was presented and expressed by the authorities in contrast to some forms of customary justice that operated in the private sphere and provided justification for outbursts of vengeance, blood feuds, *vendetta* and *faida*; in short, as an alternative to overcome revenge.

Some figures relating to public executions are enough to give us a general idea of the phenomenon. Statistics from sixteenth-century Seville and Rome indicate that about 25 prisoners were executed each year (29 in Rome and 21 in Seville, with more than 60 and 20 per 100,000 inhabitants respectively). After this time, both cities saw a decrease in the proportional execution rate. By the early seventeenth century, the rate of executions in Rome was about 18 both per year and per 100,000 inhabitants. The annual proportional rate in Amsterdam between 1650 and 1750 was 1.5 executions per 100,000 inhabitants. This was considerably lower than was the case in the seventeenth-century London (14 cases). Glasgow and Rome had rates of between three and four executions per year and per 100,000 inhabitants in the second half of the eighteenth century and the starting nineteenth, when their urban populations reached averages in between 150,000 and 170,000 inhabitants.

Tab. 1: Criminals executed in public in six great early modern European cities 1551–1830

Years	Cities	Executed per year	Executed per year and 100,000 inhabitants
1551–1600	Rome	39–40	87,70
1588–1620	Seville	24–25	21,00
1562–1696	Frankfurt	2–3	15,00
1600–1650	Rome	18–19	18,70
1650–1750	Amsterdam	3–4	1,5
1703–1772	London	c. 70	14,00
1765–1820	Glasgow	1–2	3,5
1750–1800	Rome	6	3,8
1800–1830	Rome	6	3,9

Much more comparative analysis would clearly be required in order to obtain more precise – and at the same time wider – evidence of this phenomenon. However, at the moment, all the known information indicates that public executions declined in early modern Western Europe and that this process began at some point during the seventeenth century and accelerated in the eighteenth century. In the greatest cities this decline was somewhat delayed, perhaps in part because they were the places where justice could be most clearly expressed and ritualized. Large cities were also great centres of attraction for young immigrants, who could be drawn into criminal networks and urban underworlds when their expectations of urban employment were not realized. The development of diverse forms of organized crime connected to activities such as prostitution, distribution of illegal and stolen objects, smuggling and money laundering offered these young people other options, albeit by earning their living outside the law and thus running the evident risk of penal proceedings and capital punishment. This was true in the cases of Jack Sheppard, Jonathan Wild and Moll Cutpurse, all of whom were tried in London during the 1720s and 1730s.[15] Despite the specific connotations that characterized criminal informal networks in urban areas of the Dutch Republic, many young people in Amsterdam and other great cities in Western Europe were also drawn into a life of crime.[16]

The great European cities had not solved these problems of public order by the transition from the seventeenth to the eighteenth century.[17] Perhaps, because of this and in order to combat urban crime with a demonstration of a harsh version of justice, when handing down sentences some London judges included, as an additional shaming punishment, that the executed prisoner's body should be dissected for the benefit of anatomical and medical progress. There was strong social resentment of this practice in the eighteenth and, occasionally, nineteenth centuries. In some Italian cities, however, these practices had

---

15 Linebaugh, *The London Hanged*; Lucy Moore, *The Thieves' Opera: The Remarkable Lives and Deaths of Jonathan. Wild, Thief-Taker and Jack Shepherd House-Breaker* (London 1997).
16 Florike Egmond, *Underworlds. Organized crime in The Netherlands, 1650–1800* (Cambridge 1993).
17 Despite the lucid arguments of Defoe, Mandeville and even Hogarth.

also been known and implemented without any important social and cultural resistance from at least the time of the Renaissance. Perhaps in this last example, the information about what was done with the bodies of the criminals did not get so clearly the public opinion as it was the case in the end of the eighteenth century and, therefore, due to this fact, a possible opposition to this practices was not developed.

The main cities of Western Europe also saw a clear reduction in homicide rates, a decline with a historical rhythm similar to that by which public executions declined. However, there is not a simple relationship between the nearly parallel historical progressions of these two trends. It could be thought that perhaps the cruellest forms of legal punishment were part of an expression of great environmental tolerance to violence. The reduction in the homicide rate could also be explained as a cause of the decline in public and physical punishments, because homicide was the cause of capital punishment in most of the cases. However, we can, without risk, view the highest rates of homicide and the strongest presence of public physical and capital punishment as expressions of a society with a fairly robust tolerance of violence in whatever form, be it legal or illegal, licit or illicit. Therefore, it seems safe to argue that the highest rates of homicide and cruel punishment indicate the presence of an intensely *brutalized* society.

In spite of all these factors, some cities with relatively moderate rates of homicide and brutal punishment, such as Amsterdam circa 1700, had also seen social criticism of the cruel spectacle of public physical punishment. In Amsterdam during and after the 1660s, some members of the local elites and members of the foreign diplomacy who were residents of the *dam* areas began to complain about the disturbance that accompanied the public corporal executions. They spoke of the cries of the whipped prisoners, the scandal of crowds attending the brutal spectacle and the dirt produced in the square by the multitude. Some also argued that public executions were ineffective in achieving their aim of increasing social control through the spectacle of suffering and death.[18] This reaction to *spectacles of suffering* reflected both the

---

18 Spierenburg, *The Spectacle of Suffering*; Spierenburg, *The Broken Spell*.

sensitization of an elite to the human pain of prisoners and opposition to the dramatization of public punishments. At that time and earlier, however, there was a need to express urban justice publicly, because this provided material proof of the real practice of legal justice by a superior authority – the version of justice that was supposed to supersede *customary justice*. This explains why every year, even after the second half of the seventeenth century, prisoners continued to be executed in public in the main cities of early modern Western Europe.

In Rome, the decline in numbers of public executions was clearly apparent by the mid-seventeenth century and continued during the following century, although there was eventually a new increase at the beginning of the nineteenth century. This seems to follow quite a similar pattern to that experienced in Amsterdam and possibly those found in cities such as Seville and Madrid. However, the situation in London was perhaps somewhat different.[19]

Tab. 2: Criminals executed in Rome 1501–1830

Years	Executed (total)	Executed per year (average)	Executed per year and per 100,000 inhabitants
1501–1550	889	17,8	39,5
1551–1600	1,976	39,5	87,7
1601–1650	932	18,7	18,7
1651–1700	343	6,9	5,6
1701–1750	165	3,3	2,4
1751–1800	295	5,9	3,8
1801–1830	173	5,8	3,9

During the first half of the sixteenth century on average one or two individuals were executed in Rome every month. The number of executions increased to an average of three or four around 1600; during the following half a century the number of executions fell back to the proportional rate of the sixteenth century. This was the period in which official justice

19 Spierenburg, The *Spectacle of Suffering*; Mantecón, "Las culturas criminales portuarias en las ciudades atlánticas"; "Récits de punition et de pardon"; "La justicia y el castigo del cuerpo en la Castilla moderna"; Linebaugh, *The London Hanged*; McKenzie, *Tyburn's Martyrs*; Sharpe, "Review of Tyburn's Martyrs".

had the greatest presence in the city streets and squares. By the mid-seventeenth century, the number of public executions in Rome had decreased to an average of one individual executed every two months. The eighteenth century saw the continuation of this decline, with an average of one execution taking place every three or four months. Then, the brutal presence of justice on the streets became more regular than before, although it lacked the intensity of the preceding periods. At the end of the eighteenth century and in the beginning of the nineteenth, during the years of the Roman Republic and the French invasion, the numbers of public executions began to grow once again. During this time, the principles of public order were defined and redefined several times by new governments on various bases. In this context, the result was a revival of brutal and cruel punishment in public sites across Rome with the intention of preventing possible political dissent and, perhaps, sedition.

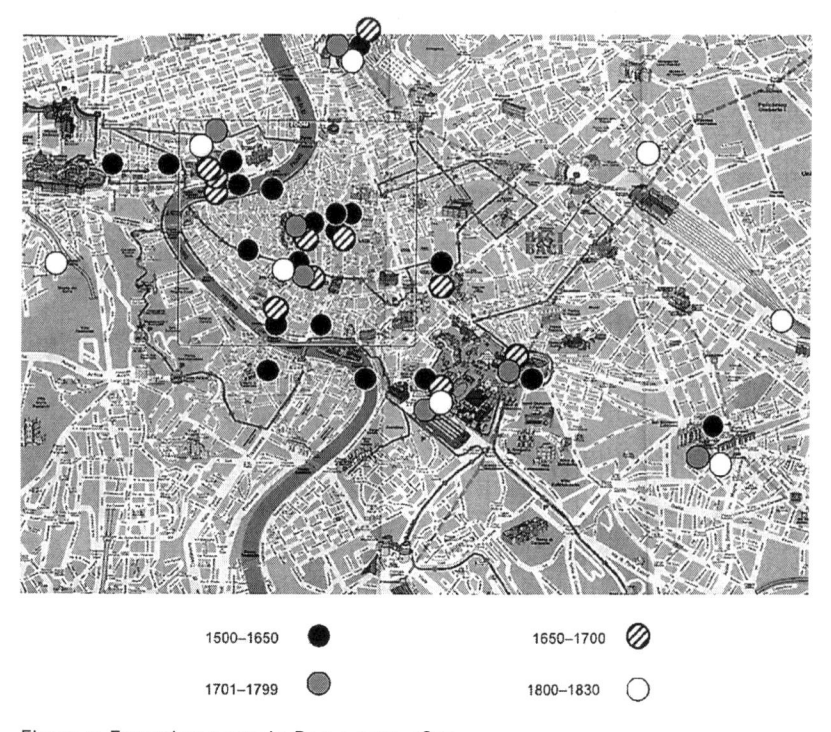

Figure 1: Execution posts in Rome 1500–1830

In the early modern period, Rome presented itself as a space where the papal justice was projected disciplinarily upon the whole urban society. The whole city was projected as a *holy city* and a model of well-ruled territory for the Christianity. Perhaps for this reason, and in a different way to the majority of the Western early modern European cities, there was not a single appointed location where ceremonies of public punishments took place, nor were there even specific sites for those convicted of different types of crimes (heresy, sodomy, homicide and monetary fraud, for example). Pope's justice should be shown in every corner of the city. In spite of this, there were some standards. The windows of the Corte Savella and Tor di Nona prisons were the main sites where condemned criminals were hanged during the early modern period. If, however, a popular commotion was considered likely, perhaps because of the social condition of the prisoner or due to their popularity or social charisma, the prison courtyard and night-time execution provided other options for the execution. Moreover, in these cases, a less dishonourable punishment, such as beheading or throat cutting, could be used rather than hanging.

During the sixteenth and part of the seventeenth centuries, public ceremonials of punishment were largely evident in all the central areas of the city: from San Pietro up to San Giovanni Laterano; from Colosseo, Montevaccino e Boca della Verità to Ripa and Santa Maria in Trastevere. After this period and even during the eighteenth century, most activity centred on the Castel Sant'Angelo, the Piazza del Popolo, the Piazza Navona, the Campo de' Fiori and the area around Bocca della Verità. Although most of these central urban locations were also suitable execution sites, public executions were largely undertaken only in the vicinity of Castel Sant'Angelo, Popolo, Navona, Campo de' Fiori and Bocca della Verità. From the end of the eighteenth century (up until the 1830s), executions were moved from city centre sites to the urban peripheries and nearby areas: from Bocca della Verità, Termini, Poggio San Lorenzo up to Viterbo, Monte Rossi and more distant places. Urban justice was slowly moving away from the city centre to the periphery. Furthermore, those executions that did take place in the city centre were increasingly carried out behind the walls of the prison or in the inner courtyard of Castel Sant'Angelo rather than in public squares or on bridges. The decline and displacement of public executions were developments experienced in combination with other changes after the middle of the seventeenth century and were even more apparent in the eighteenth.

The road to the scaffold: torture and executions

Although hanging was the most common form of execution, from 1600 the relative importance of the gallows in Rome decreased slightly, in favour of other methods of capital punishment. At the end of the eighteenth and the first half of the nineteenth centuries, the number of prisoners executed using the guillotine and firearms clearly outstripped those who were hanged. From a long-term perspective, we can see that further changes were also produced. During the first half of the seventeenth century use of the stake and the practice of stoning were declining; by about 1700 these disciplinary penal acts were practically obsolete. By the middle of the seventeenth century, the process of execution underwent many changes. Prudence, discretion and surgical cleanliness were the new principles and values that underpinned the emergent forms of capital punishment. There was no a real need for great dramatization of the most brutal penal practices. By the outset of the nineteenth century, this process had led to the hegemony of the guillotine and shooting as methods of execution. Only one form of execution that involved torture continued despite this shift: quartered death.

It had only been after 1600 that this punitive practice had been clearly declining. Although it seemed to have become a punitive anachronism, the early nineteenth century saw the revival of the practice of quartering in exceptional cases involving political crime. In the long-run historical perspective, quartering was developed in combination with other types of punishment, particularly hanging. Before 1650 prisoners could often be seen shuffling through the city streets to the execution site, where they would either be hanged before being quartered or quartered to death (while still alive). Sometimes an execution of the type described above was preceded by torment of the criminal as he or she was conducted to the execution site. Such torture was usually produced with the help of an incandescent pair of red-hot pliers or could even take the form of ritual corporal mutilations, such as the cutting of a hand, ear or eye. The removal of a hand was often employed in cases of *treason*: placing or conspiring to place the life of one's master, father and husband or king at risk[20]. In Rome, prosecutions for the political version of this crime increased, particularly during the French invasion. The political exceptionality of this historical context provoked intense reflection on the meaning of *sedition, insurrection* and, in general, *political crime*. Then, the revival of torture punishments was the counterpoint to *political dissidence*.

Graph 1: Evolution and types of execution in Rome 1501–1830

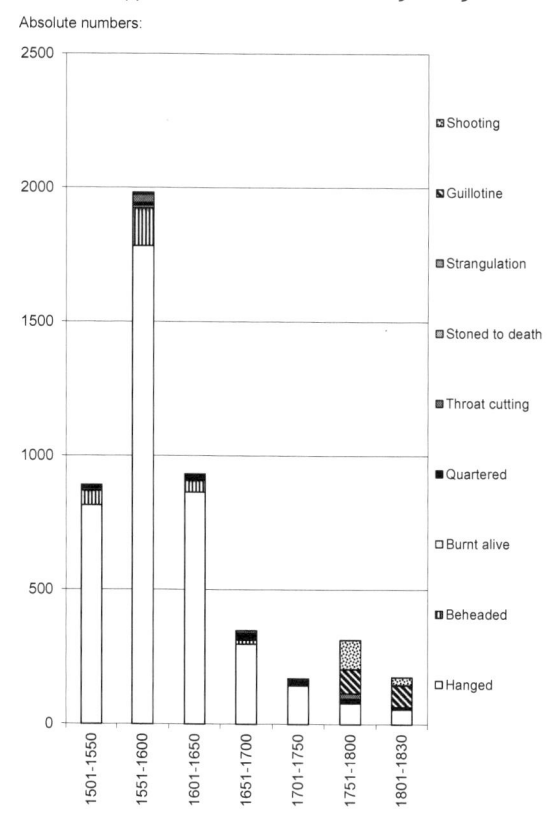

---

20 This punishment was common in cases like these across the whole of Europe: Mantecón, "Récits de punition".

Average (%):

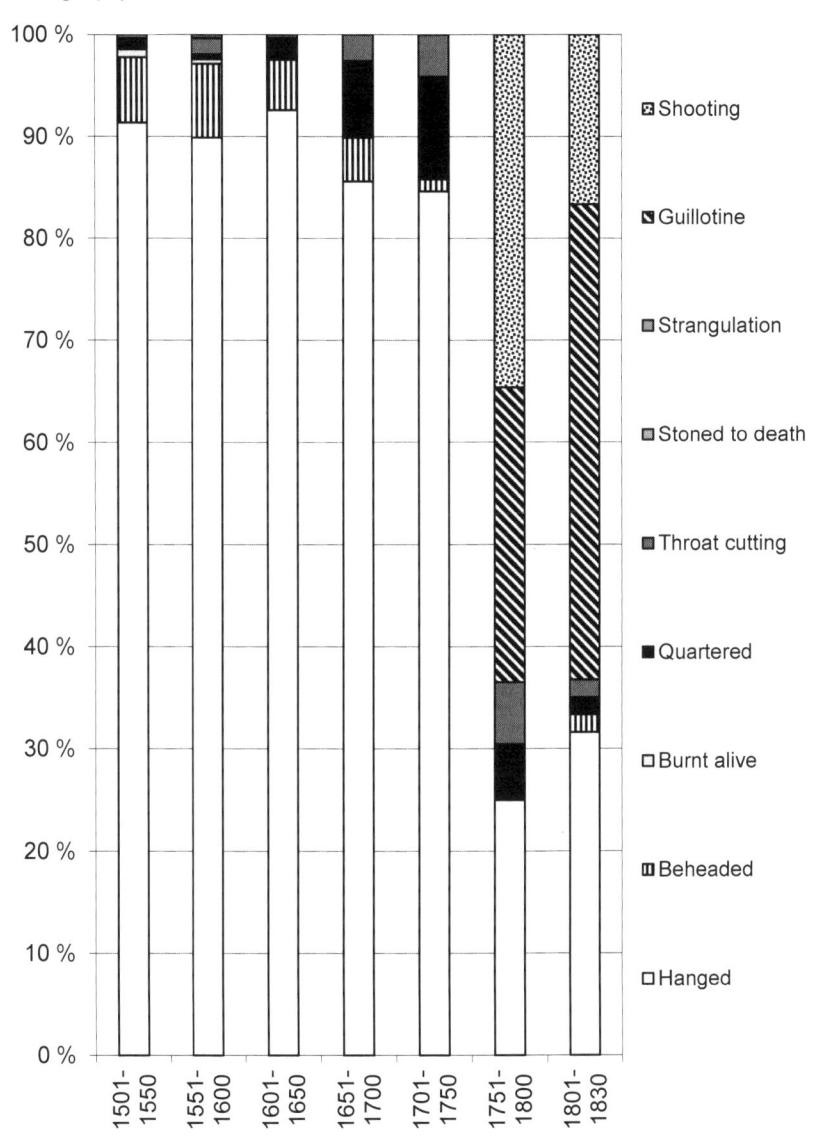

▨	Shooting
▧	Guillotine
▦	Strangulation
▥	Stoned to death
▤	Throat cutting
■	Quartered
□	Burnt alive
▥	Beheaded
□	Hanged

THE POPE'S SWORD 275

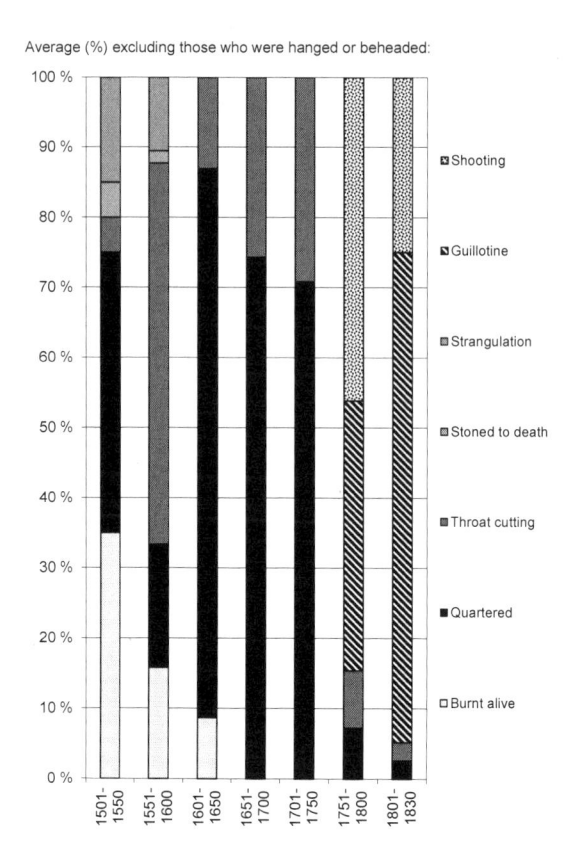

Average (%) excluding those who were hanged or beheaded:

[Chart showing distribution of execution methods across time periods 1501-1550 through 1801-1830, with categories: Shooting, Guillotine, Strangulation, Stoned to death, Throat cutting, Quartered, Burnt alive]

An examination of both the type of crime committed by those who received the death penalty and the prevailing social conditions can help to explain why some punishments that involved torture (such as quartering) persisted so much. Hired murderers (*assassini di strada* or *grassatori*) were many of those who were condemned to death by quartering. Such criminals were usually young men, often rural immigrants with few opportunities of earning money in the city. Sometimes this punishment was also to execute convicted condemned due to the commission of violent assaults, counterfeiting, piracy (*ladro di mare*), sedition or kidnapping. Until the first decades of the seventeenth century, the high persistence of this punitive practice of quartering was connected to the increased judicial attempts to repress the struggle between factions of the urban social elite which sometimes had articulated crimes committed by hired killers. Competition between notable families and powerful groups within the urban political arena meant that each urban social faction needed to use all the methods at their disposal to gain an advantage over the other groups: from political struggle within local institutions up to the action of bandits connected with kinship groups and social factions that protected them.

These tensions and struggles between social factions provoked the development of a harsh penal law during the papal reign of Sixtus V (1585–1590) and even military repression under Clement VIII (1592–1605), when the crime of lese-majesty was also associated with counterfeiters, hired assassins and bandits.[21] Papal justice not only reacted against the most violent criminals and those who committed fraud against the interests of the urban community and government: it also sought to prevent crime by pointing out the bad example set by urban criminals. However, these aims were not fully realized. The urban government did not clearly direct its legal action towards the heads of the elite social factions but rather against their subordinates and "creatures". It also failed to channel the struggles of social factions into a more civilized process of competitions and negotiations as opposed to the violence of the *grassatori* or hired killers. Despite this, the number of convicted murderers condemned to death decreased very clearly during the seventeenth century. This decline could also be one reason why quartering clear decreasing of the second half of this century, a trend that continued sharply in the eighteenth century. In spite of this decline, the harsh urban policy created a negative shape of the Pope street guards (so-called *sbirri*) that still was alive in the last decades of the eighteenth century[22].

---

21 The reigns of Urban VII (1590) and Gregory XIV (1590–1591) were too brief to allow clear actions to be taken against these sorts of conflict and crime: Fosi, Irene, 'Il governo della giustizia. In: Giorgio Ciucci (ed.), *Roma moderna* (Rome/Bari 2002), pp. 116–117.
22 Steven Hughes, "Fear and loathing in Bologna and Rome". The Papal Police in Perspective. *Journal of Social History* 21:1 (Autumn 1987), pp. 97–116.

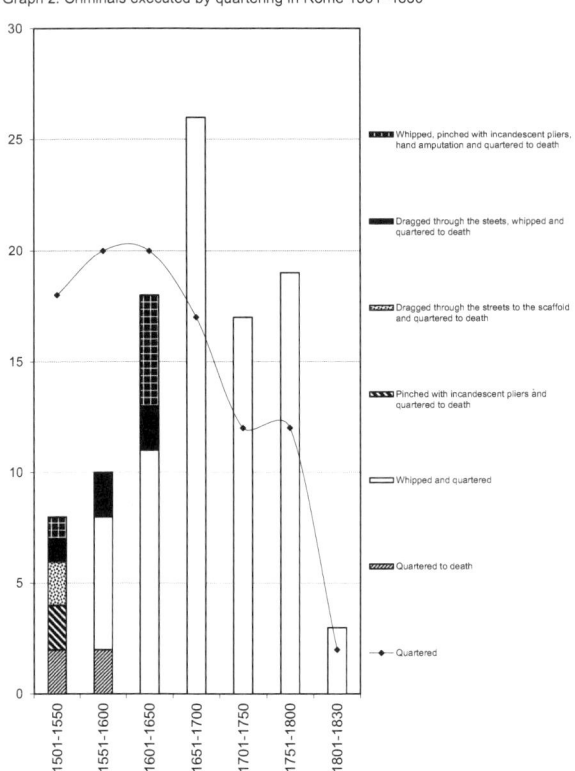

Graph 2: Criminals executed by quartering in Rome 1501–1830

Graph 2: Criminals executed by quartering in Rome 1501–1830

Legend:
- Whipped, pinched with incandescent pliers, hand amputation and quartered to death
- Dragged through the steets, whipped and quartered to death
- Dragged through the streets to the scaffold and quartered to death
- Pinched with incandescent pliers and quartered to death
- Whipped and quartered
- Quartered to death
- Quartered

Note: The bars represent the annual average numbers and the curve represents the annual rate of cases per every 100,000 inhabitants.

The analysis of capital punishment here also refers to all actions exerted upon a prisoner's body before and after his or her death. Particularly worthy of examination are those cases in which criminals were subjected to corporal damage as part of a ceremonial in which legal violence was administered. All instances of torture of the criminal body constituted a *penal culture of suffering*, a disciplinary instrument wielded by early modern official justice. The secular decline of this culture was perhaps connected to other social or cultural phenomena, such as popular interpretation of this ceremonials of punishment – sometimes very different from that expected by official authorities, as was the case in England – or the progressive weakening of the *culture of suffering by penitence*, which sought to repair the sin committed against God's law.[23]

Within this scheme, suffering before death created a spiritual climate that could ease the salvation of the soul. Physical punishment and the sinner repentance were to be proportional to the damage inflicted and the sin committed in order to make reparation. From this viewpoint, the *spectacle of suffering* created an atmosphere that not only provided a moral example for the public, but also eased the salvation of the prisoner. The sinner's resignation to and acceptance of physical torture were reparations for the sin that had been committed and, in this sense, helped to alleviate the pain that would be suffered in Purgatory.

Every specific torment applied on the body of the offender should help the graduation of physical pain that was a need to restore the soul health. The combination of different physical torturous operations practiced on the body of the criminal was expected to be enough to get the sinner salvation. Due to these cultural factors, torture was present in many versions in the most of the death penalty ceremonials. In case of heresy –whichever its forms and expressions – the application of fire as a central element of the punitive ceremonial was not only the symbol of what expected every sinner in Hell, but it also had the aim of fixing in the spectators' memory the harsh extreme of human and divine justice and the purifying function of flames. The decline of the sentence of being burnt at the stake in the seventeenth century, sharply in the second half of this period, is related to the process of overcoming the age of confessional struggles in Europe. Torturous punishment whichever its version also declined very intensively in the second half of the seventeenth and in the eighteenth centuries.

---

23 Thomas W. Laqueur, "Crowds, Carnival and the State in English Executions, 1604–1868". In: A. L. Beier, David Cannadine & James M. Rosenheim (ed.), The First Modern Society: Essays in Honour of Lawrence Stone (Cambridge 1989), pp. 305–356.

Graph 3: Hangings involving torture in Rome 1501–1830

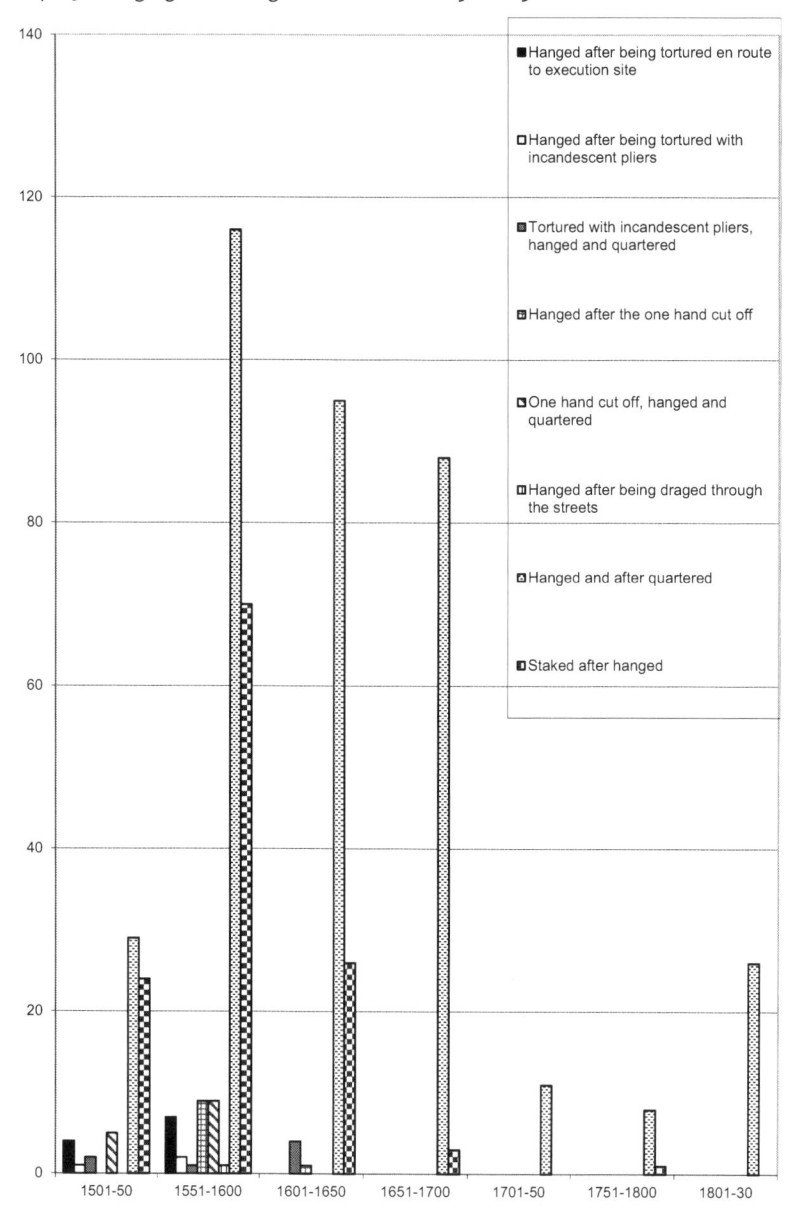

- Hanged after being tortured en route to execution site
- Hanged after being tortured with incandescent pliers
- Tortured with incandescent pliers, hanged and quartered
- Hanged after the one hand cut off
- One hand cut off, hanged and quartered
- Hanged after being draged through the streets
- Hanged and after quartered
- Staked after hanged

Graph 4: Criminals burnt at the stake in Rome 1501–1830

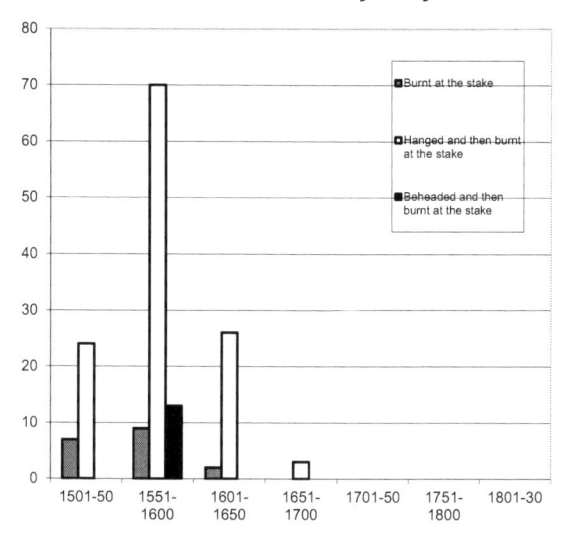

- Burnt at the stake
- Hanged and then burnt at the stake
- Beheaded and then burnt at the stake

In order to achieve the aim of the condemned contrition and acceptance of corporal punishment and death penalty, specialized officials would assist and comfort prisoners before their deaths. Missionaries or members of religious confraternities would comfort a prisoner, both whilst he or she was tortured according to the instructions of the penal sentence and afterwards at the very moment of execution.

Cultures of suffering, public executions and governance

Vinzenzo Paglia has provided an extensive account of the ways in which the confraternity of *La Misericordia* provided comfort to condemned prisoners in early modern Rome.[24] Similar institutions undertook such duties not only in other Italian cities such as Naples and Venice, but also

24 Vincenco Paglia, *La morte confortata*.

in other Italian cities and Catholic societies across the Mediterranean.[25] In Spain, confraternities dedicated to the devotion of Christ's Blood (metaphorically referring to the Passion and death of Christ) provided this religious service to the criminals condemned to death during their final hours.[26] Despite some metaphorical analogies, the situation seems to have been slightly different in some Northern European social and religious contexts, even though the pious framing and public dramatization of the event were retained on a regular basis until the end of the eighteenth or even the beginning of the nineteenth centuries.[27]

In England, for example, the "language of martyrology", so evident in the *Accounts* of the Ordinary of Newgate (the clergyman responsible for ministering to the prisoners), provided an ideal image of a "good death", which could be interpreted as both a political and a metaphysical statement. Even the final speeches of dying prisoners could somehow contain meaning that could offer informal redemption through laic and spontaneous confession. In spite of this, in the British case – as was sometimes also the case in early modern Spain – these different expressions of *suffering cultures of penitence* were not the only ways in which prisoners responded to their imminent deaths.[28] Many died without any simple expression of conformity, resignation or penitence associated with the internalization or spiritualization of their punishment. Some died "like real men" and called for the public to drink for them or pay their tavern debts. Sometimes they would even cry cursing the hangman, other justice officials or the urban authorities. Such prisoners could, socially, politically and morally, be considered *renegades* against

---

25 Giovanni Romeo, *Aspettando il boia. Condannati a morte, confortatori e inquisitori nella Napoli della Controriforma* (Sansoni Ed., Rome 1993); ChiaraTraverso, *La scuola di San Fantin o dei "Picai". Caritá e giustizia a Venezia* (Venice 2000); Fabiana Veronese, "'L'orrore del sacrilegio': abusi di sacramenti, pratiche magiche e condanne a morte a Venezia nel primo ventennio del settecento". *Studi Veneziani* LII, (2006), pp. 265–342.

26 Lourdes Amigo, "Del patíbulo al cielo. La labor asistencial de la Cofradía de la Pasión en el Valladolid del Antiguo Régimen". *La Iglesia Española y las Instituciones de Caridad. Actas del Simposium 1/4-IX-2006* (Instituto Escurialense de Investigaciones Históricas y Artísticas, San Lorenzo del Escorial 2006), pp. 511–542; José Luis Gómez Urdáñez, *La Hermandad de la Sangre de Cristo de Zaragoza: caridad y ritual religioso en la ejecución de la pena de muerte* (Asociación para el Estudio de la Semana Santa, Zaragoza 1981).

27 Martin Bergman, Execution and Liturgy. A Perspective from Sweden with the 18th and 19th centuries in Focus. Revue d'Histoire Ecclésistique 106 (2008), pp. 97–167.

28 MacKenzie, *Tyburn's Martyrs*; Sharpe, "Review of Tyburn's Martyrs".

human and sometimes even against divine law; perhaps also against popular tolerance.

Chronological analysis of changes in public executions and the historical evolution of the physical punishment of those condemned to death can also help us to consider the meaning of these punitive ceremonials and the loss of certain values from a long-term perspective. Under the *Ancient Régime* in Rome, hanging and beheading were the principal types of capital execution, for plebeian and patrician people respectively. In these cases, the bodies of some executed prisoners would be quartered and exhibited in public areas. The body parts were later collected and buried by members of a local religious confraternity. The use of public quartering as a form of execution waned in the seventeenth century and by about 1750 it had decreased sharply the historical previous numbers. Other forms of execution were also in decline. The combination of first hanging a prisoner and then burning his or her body at the stake, specifically associated with cases of heresy, was discontinued for patricians around 1600 and during the first part of the seventeenth century for common prisoners.

After 1700 no-one was burnt at the stake whilst he or she was still alive; nevertheless, from about 1650 until the beginning of the eighteenth century the stake was used to burn the bodies of some executed prisoners. Then, burning at the stake became an anachronistic practice. This was the reverse of the earlier context of confessional religious fever – the so-called *confessionalization* – that had sought to control heterodoxy and heresy, particularly during the second half of the sixteenth and the first of the seventeenth century. The official dogmatism of this earlier historical period had provided the opportunity to implement the full battery of disciplinary and punitive actions in an attempt to force people into orthodoxy.

Already in 1542, during the reign of Paulus III, Cardinal Carafa (who was later to become Paulus IV) was charged by the Pope with ensuring the efficiency of the Inquisition as an instrument to combat heresy. The second half of the sixteenth century, principally during the transition from the sixteenth to the seventeenth century, was a period of great confessional control throughout this specific court. In this context, the confessional repression was also connected to papal projects for the pacification of the urban nobility factions. Rome sought to present itself to European eyes as a pious city, an example of morality, legal justice and order. However, the reality of urban life was more challenging. The Inquisitorial tribunal, the court of the vicar-general and that of the urban magistrate, were essentially institutions through which urban society was disciplined. The censorship of books, the prosecution of superstitious practices, the fight against sodomy and polygamy, and the criminalization of prostitution were just some of the fields in which direct disciplinary actions were taken by these judicial courts.

There is still a great deal of work to be done in order to explain the effects and efficiency of all the ways in which institutional social control was projected. In the second half of the sixteenth century (under the reigns of Paulus IV and Pius IV and, later, particularly under that of Sixtus V and from Clement VIII up to Pius V), the papal office displayed a determination to improve urban social discipline and control. Under the government of Pius V, vagabonds could be subjected to mutilation or other forms of corporal punishment,[29] as was also the case at the time in other European cities, including Hamburg and Bourdeaux.[30] However, although public executions involving torture took place, they were retained only for those types of crime that involved particularly aggravating circumstances. Such executions were more likely in cases of crimes committed by outsiders or commoners and took place more frequently before 1650. In Rome, on average only two percent of those whose execution involved torture were members of urban patrician families connected to the struggle between the city's social factions or convicted of conspiracy.

In general terms, the most relevant variety of capital punishment with torture in early modern Rome was quartering to death (either with or without further punitive options). Up until 1650 there are records of cases of condemned criminals who had been physically punished whilst conducted through the city streets before being quartered to

---

29 Fosi, "Il governo della giustizia", p. 138.
30 Robert Jütte, *Poverty and Deviance in Early Modern Europe* (Cambridge 1995).

death. Some of them were even burnt at the stake after they had been quartered. By imposing such cruel punishments, judges really wanted to display the most extreme judicial harshness, rather than simply inflict a ritual mutilation to punish or brand the body of the prisoner, as was the case every time a judicial sentence condemned a criminal to the loss of an eye or part of an ear.

These last forms of ritual mutilations were frequently meted out to those convicted of theft in Rome or Venice, as well as in other Italian and early modern Castilian cities. Prostitutes could face the prospect of their nose and hair or eyebrows being cut. Against heresy there were issued more symbolic amputations. The heretic's tongue, for instance, could also be cut out publicly, as it happened quite often in many European early modern cities in the age of *confessional* struggles period and even later, after the mid-seventeenth century.[31] The same disciplinary goal was present in another set of rituals supposed to provide instruction and to prevent and reduce crime, but these rituals were not socially regarded as a real judicial punishment. For instance, in early modern Castile, this concerned children who had been sodomized and were viewed as having been sexually corrupted by adults. These children were not burnt at the stake, as their corrupters were. Instead, they were made to watch the execution of those burnt at the stake and, afterwards, they were passed through the flames just to feel at first hand the cruel punishment that could await them if they persisted in these kinds of immoral practices.[32]

In Rome, the evolution of the criminals who were quartered to death as a result of a judicial sentence shows a relative chronological persistence in the long run historical perspective. The practice appeared to be clearly declining during the second half of the seventeenth century and in the eighteenth. However, in the final part of this last century and in the beginning of the nineteenth, this punishment was revived in

---

31 Examples quoted by Robert Jütte, *Poverty and deviance;* Mantecón, "Récits de punition". Francesco Calcagno, a priest born in Brescia, was executed in Venice in 1550. He was publicly beheaded after his tongue was cut out. I am grateful to Fabiana Veronese for this information, which comes from her own research on the Secret Vatican Archive, *Sant'Ufficio*, file 8.
32 Mantecon, "La justicia y el castigo".

specific contexts of political upheavals. In this context, the use of quartering expressed a robust and physical response to political dissent and its prevention. Within the context of conflict, political crime was a new modality of penal objective to be fought. Conflict also led to increases in ordinary crime and social convulsions. The Pope fled Rome five days after the urban republic was proclaimed on 15 February 1798. The urban convulsions and agitation in a city that lost 15,000 inhabitants in a so short time and under a political order strongly argued give a general idea of the harshness of this controversial situation.[33]

In 1798, Jacobins of Rome changed the rules of the political game, but the introduction of the new constitution in March failed to put an end to the social unrest. Shortages, decreasing money circulation, increasing fiscal pressure and the tutelage of the French authorities on the young urban republic fed an outburst that even external French military intervention in 1799 could not quell. Within this context, the practice of capital punishment with torture recovered part of its old vigour – largely between 1810 and 1813, when the guillotine and firing squad awaited dissidents of the regime and anachronistic forms of legal punishment were also revitalized. Thus, at the same time as Antonio Canova was involved in city institutions tasked with archaeological and architectonic heritage conservation and urban development planning, the city was still contemplating public execution ceremonies that involved quartering and torture. With the return of Pius VII on 24 May 1814 and the restoration of an enlightened conservative government, the decline in public executions involving dramatic apparatus continued. However, the French left a legacy of more surgical methods of preserving social order, in the forms of the guillotine and the gun.

Some criminals who were found guilty of capital offences had already been shot in some Italian cities since at least the middle of the seventeenth century. Angelo Butturino, who was convicted of illegally

---

33 On this, see Massimo Cattaneo, "L'opposizione popolare al 'gioacobinismo' a Roma e nello Statu pontificio". *Studi Storici* 39 (1998), pp. 533–567.The Roman ghetto (closed since 1555, in the context of intense confessional fever) was reopened on 17 February 1798, recognizing the Jews the right of political participation. Eight days later, riots against the Jews took place in the urban district of Trastevere. This example gives some idea of just how tense social relationships were in this context.

celebrating the Christian liturgy, was shot on 12 November the 1650.[34] As Butturino was not ordained, his celebration of the liturgy was viewed as sacrilegious abuse of the Christians sacraments – a crime worthy of capital punishment. Other prisoners were also shot during this period, although it was clearly not the most common form of execution up to the arrival of the French.

All the examined records that deal with public executions in early modern Rome suggest that the mid-seventeenth century was the dividing point between two distinct periods. The earlier period, from the end of the fifteenth century up to about 1650, was characterized by a great profusion of public executions, with a more intense application of corporal punishments and also diverse forms of torture. These brutal executions took place in very central places within the urban environment. The second period, after 1650, saw a more evident decline in public executions, which were progressively moved away from the city centre and which saw a decline in corporal punishment and torture.

The trend of throat cutting as a method of execution was peculiar in some senses. This was not the most relevant form of penal punishment in early modern Rome. When it was implemented, throat cutting would also be accompanied by further punitive actions taken against the prisoner's body. Such additional punitive actions were particularly in evidence during the second half of the sixteenth century, when throat cutting as a method of execution became more prevalent. Over the course of this period about thirty criminals – less than one per year (about one every two or three years) – were executed in this way. Before the mid-sixteenth century and after 1600 less than half this number of prisoners had their throats cut. Beheading was a more honourable way of being executed and therefore it was issued in the sixteenth and starting seventeenth centuries as one of the papal justice instruments of reducing the urban struggles between patrician families and factions for controlling spheres of power in Rome. The revival of this capital punishment form in new versions, the guillotine, in the end of the eighteenth century was

---

34 ASV (Secret Vatican Archive), *Sant'Ufficio*, file 153. I am once again grateful Fabiana Veronese, who provided this information from her own unpublished research.

related to a more general application of this punitive instrument of social control in an extraordinary context of urban social convulsions and uncertainty about governance models.

After the mid-seventeenth century, official justice in Rome implemented changes in its punitive forms of punishment in ways quite similar to those introduced in other European cities. The public spectacle of blood, corporal suffering and physical punishment lost its old protagonist role. The *culture of suffering* that was produced in a context of baroque spirituality and confessional fever lost some of its disciplinary efficiency at a time when there was a clear increase in social sensitivity and resistance to traditional uses of torture within the penal system or even developed as a result of the implementation of judicial sentences.

Due to all the above-mentioned reasons, the meaning of public and physical torture for condemned prisoners began to change after 1650. Increasingly, this kind of cruel punishment was not seen as a necessary expression of the power of a superior authority and its capacity to protect the *common good*, and an opportunity for the condemned criminal to express his or her penitence and thus earn their eternal glory. Instead, such torture came to be seen as primarily a brutal dramatization of punishment and one that was not required in order to maintain public order. Other developments, such as the evolution of homicide rates, can also help to explain long-term trends and changes in legal punishment.

Throughout the whole period, homicide was the primary reason why prisoners ended up facing the scaffold. In Rome, the proportion of those condemned to death on the grounds of homicide had been historically decreasing since the seventeenth century. During the eighteenth century the rate of murderers who were executed in Rome was equivalent to the level seen in a modern urban society. All the other principal problems of urban criminality had already reduced to tolerable levels and, in effect, nearly only those crimes relating to homicide (also in decline) provoked a judicial sentence of the death penalty. As a consequence, we should note that the disciplinary goal of the repression of the worst expressions of crime was, from a long-term historical perspective, relatively successful, but the drop of the curve of executed homicides was earlier than that of total executions, so the former was not an effect of the punitive system but of the wider changes operated probably in social relationships and cultural values. This issue requires some further comment before we end our discussion of early modern justice and the relationships between crime and punishment in early modern urban European society.

Graph 5: Total executions trend and criminals executed for commission of homicide in Rome 1500–1870

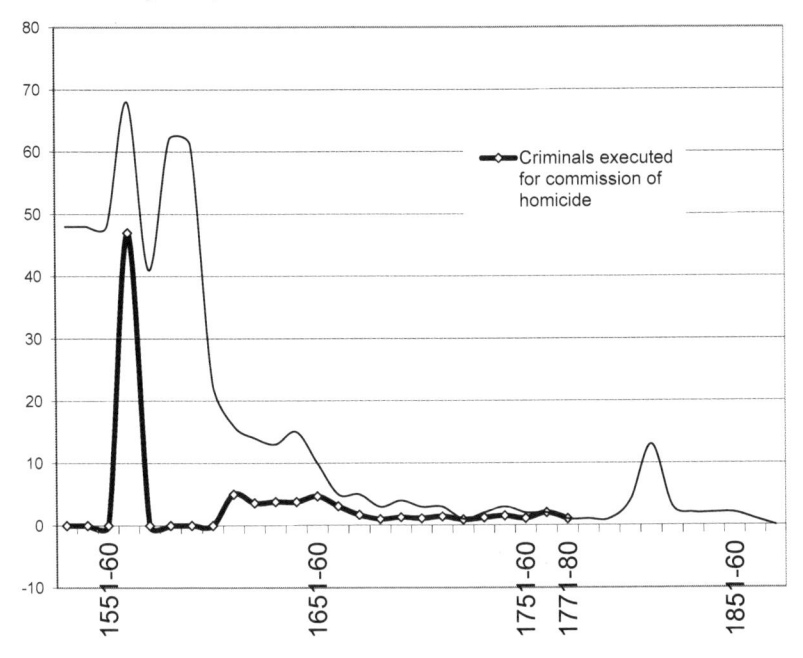

Graph 6: Average (%) of homicides within total executed criminals in Rome 1500–1830

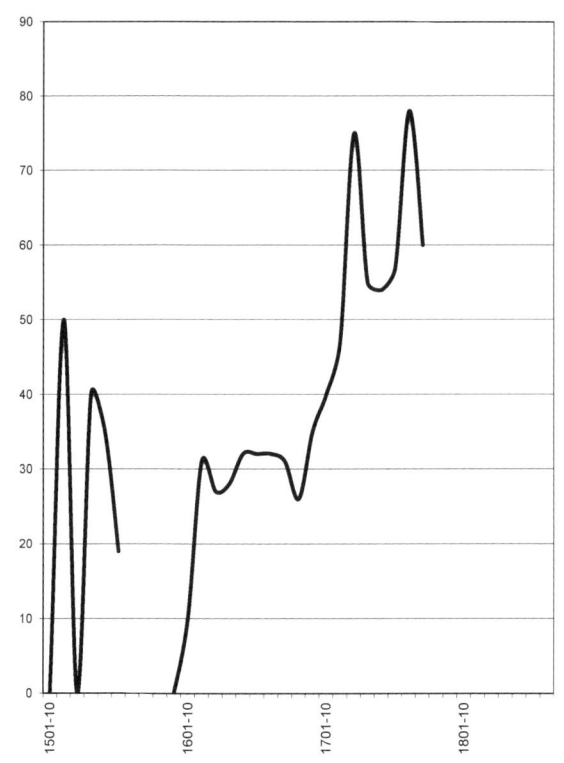

A comparison of the general historical general trends in the rates of all executed criminals with those whose death was the result of a conviction of homicide highlights central issues of the history of crime, criminal justice and social control. Our first impression of these trends is that between 1500 and 1800 capital punishment had lost vigour, its public character and social consent. This was the case not only in Rome, but also in other important Western European cities. In part, this decline was connected to a cultural development: social sensitization against the public spectacle of suffering produced in every execution of death penalty and corporal punishment, particularly since the end of the seventeenth century and increasing the critical intensity in the eighteenth. This was why corporal and torture punishments were effectively abandoned even before they were legally prohibited. Another factor that contributed to the decline of capital punishment was that the commission of homicide (the main reason for receiving a death penalty) had itself been in decline, a trend that both predated and was more apparent than the decline in public torture punishments.

Conclusions

Major early modern Western Europe urban societies experienced a historical transition from a period in which there was a significant presence of legal and illegal violence – licit and illicit *brutality* in everyday behaviours and social relationships – towards another context in which there was a more consolidated *civility*, which affected not only behaviour, but also forms of social control and discipline, from the individual up to the public scope. The Roman example is very clear in this respect: before 1600 Rome executed high numbers of criminals and had a notable rate of registered homicide (about 47 annual perpetrators per 100,000 inhabitants); after 1700, Rome's rates were more moderate (less than 3 annual murderers per 100,000 inhabitants per year). Early modern urban Castile experienced a broadly similar trend, although the main decline there occurred just after 1700.[35] In England and the Netherlands a decline in homicide rates occurred during the seventeenth century.[36]

Before 1600, papal justice in Rome had to contend with other rival forces and spheres of power connected to the local nobility and their various factions. However, during this period Rome also underwent a process of centralization of authority that sought to strengthen the Pope's sovereignty and *domesticate* the urban nobility. The result was a

---

35 Mantecón, "Récits de punition".
36 Manuel Eisner, "Long-Term Historical Trends in Violent Crime". *Crime and Justice; A Review of Research* 30 (2003), pp. 83–142; Manuel Eisner, "Modernization, Self-control and Violence: The Long-term Dynamics of European Homicide Rates in Theoretical Perspective". *British Journal of Criminology* 2001, pp. 618–638; Pieter Spierenburg, Faces of violence: Homicide Trends and Cultural Meanings. Amsterdam, 1431–1816. *Journal of Social History*, 27:4 (1994), pp. 701–716.

suppression of aristocratic violence, the formation of a *court society* with the Pope at its centre and, in the end, the acceptance of the new rules of the game on the parts of members of the urban aristocracy.

This consolidation of the Pope's authority continued until at least 1700, although the great developments in this direction were experienced during the second half of the sixteenth and the first decades of the seventeenth centuries. During the periods of Paulus III, Sixtus V and Clement VIII confessional pressure and the struggle against aristocratic violence and banditry gave the papal office opportunities to advance the construction and consolidation of the Pope's authority in terms of his *superiority*, particularly with regard to his ability to arbitrate between social factions within the urban elite. Perhaps because of this, Sixtus V – who took a hard line against sin and crime – has sometimes been depicted in Rome's urban chronicles as an example of a prudent governor, a good administrator of the public financial resources and someone who was able to maintain the urban peace. However, Sixtus V's period was characterized by great repressive intensity against heresy, aristocratic violence and immorality.

The interlude from 1650 up until the establishment of the urban republic at the end of the eighteenth century saw a contraction of the historical conflict patterns already discussed. It was also was an age characterized by the Pope's authority, the normalization of government and a short of *civilization of violence* (if violence, in any form, could ever have some degree of *civilization*). This means that violence was changing into other versions of social competition, negotiation and struggle. There was also an erosion of the culture of suffering that had been part of the process of public punishment. This can be considered as a factor affecting to the process of *civilization* of legal violence as well. The *civilization of violence* was also expressed in the decline of homicide rates in Rome – similarly to those experienced in other great cities of Western Europe – and in the increased control over struggles between urban social factions.

The main developments in this process were due to a combination of social, cultural and political changes that did not only affect social networks and lead to changes within the urban elite families and their circles of influence, but also influence the culture sphere, including religious beliefs. Particularly, in this last point, with regard to the *culture of suffering* and *culture of penitence* (formalized in the public arena through the criminal's expressions of sorrow) that legitimated many punitive actions against the bodies of those who were publicly executed.

In spite of this, in 1789 the urban republic, and, later, the Napoleonic government, provided scope for the intensification of social and governmental expressions of *brutality*, thus proving that in the history of violence, as well as that of social control, *modernization* was not unquestionably continuous, progressive and irreversible. As is the case in many historical processes, the evolution of public legal and illegal expressions of violence was (and still is) marked by involutions and regressions, factors and contexts that helped or hindered outbursts of social or state violence. The early modern Roman historical experience offers wonderful examples of this complexity. Some of today's great cities – Cairo, Sao Paulo, Cali, New York, Johannesburg, Calicut, Buenos Aires, Mexico City, London, Madrid, Paris, Berlin and Rome – provide opportunities for the expression of diverse forms of urban violence and *cultures of violence*; in some cases with specific territorial identities in urban districts where brutality sometimes dominates everyday rule with its own set of values. In the end, violence – in both its legal and its illegal forms – and its control are still major problems in our own societies. In its struggle against violence, the early modern Roman case seems to prove that capital punishment was a less efficient instrument than social and cultural change. This should provide us with food for thought today.

Sources

ARCHIVAL SOURCES

Secret Vatican Archive (ASV), Sant'Ufficio, files 8, 153.
State Roman Archive (ASR), book 285.

LITERATURE

Amigo, Lourdes 2006: Del patíbulo al cielo. La labor asistencial de la Cofradía de la Pasión en el Valladolid del Antiguo Régimen. *La Iglesia Española y las Instituciones de Caridad. Actas del Simposium 1/4-IX-2006*, Instituto Escurialense de Investigaciones Históricas y Artísticas, San Lorenzo del Escorial, pp. 511–542

Ariès, Philippe 1975: *Essais sur l'histoire de le mort en Occident. Du Moyen-Age à nos jours*, Editions du Seuil, Paris.

Barmas, Pamela 2005: *Homicide and the biblical world*, CUP, Cambridge.

Bergman, Martin 2008: Execution and liturgy. A perspective from Sweden with the 18th and 19th centuries in focus. *Revue d'Histoire Ecclésistique*, 106 (Jan. 1 2008), pp. 97–167.

Boes, Maria R. 1996: Public Appearance and Criminal Judicial Practices in Early Modern Germany. *Social Science History*, 20 (1996), pp. 259–279.

Brown, Keith M. 1986: *Blood feud in Scotland, 1573–1625: violence, justice and politics in an early modern society*. John Donald, Edinburgh.

Cattaneo, Massimo 1998: L'opposizione popolare al "gioacobinismo" a Roma e nello Statu pontificio. *Studi Storici*, 39 (1998), pp. 533–567.

Egmond, Florike 1993: *Underworlds. Organized crime in The Netherlands, 1650–1800*. CUP, Cambridge.

Egmond, Florike 2001: Incestuous Relations and their Punishment in the Dutch Republic. *Eighteenth -Century Life*, 25 (3), Fall 2001, pp. 20–42.

Eisner, Manuel 2003: Long-Term Historical Trends in Violent Crime. *Crime and Justice; A Review of Research*, 30 (2003), pp. 83–142.

Eisner, Manuel 2001: Modernization, Self-control and Violence: The Long-term Dynamics of European Homicide Rates in Theoretical Perspective. *British Journal of Criminology* (2001), pp. 618–638.

Fosi, Irene 2002: Il governo della giustizia. In *Roma moderna*, ed. Giorgio Ciucci. Laterza, Rome-Bari, pp. 115–142.

Fosi, Irene 2007: *La giustizia del papa. Sudditi e tribunali nello Stato Pontificio in età moderna*. Laterza, Roma-Bari.

Foucault, Michel 1975: *Surveiller et punir. Naissance de la prison*. Gallimard, Paris.

Garnot, Benoît 1993: *Un crime conjugal au 18e siècle. L'affaire Boiveau*. Imago, Paris.

Gatrell, V.A.C. 1994: *The hanging tree: execution and the English people, 1770–1868*. OUP, Oxford.

Gómez Urdáñez, José Luis 1981: *La Hermandad de la Sangre de Cristo de Zaragoza: caridad y ritual religioso en la ejecución de la pena de muerte*. Asociación para el Estudio de la Semana Santa, Zaragoza.

Hughes, Steven 1987: Fear and loathing in Bologna and Rome. The Papal police in perspective. *Journal of Social History* 21 (1), Autumn 1987, pp. 97–116.

Iglesias, Raquel 2007: *Crimen, criminales y reos. La delincuencia y su represión en la antigua provincia de Santiago entre 1700 y 1834*. Trea, Gijón.

Jütte, Robert 1995: *Poverty and deviance in early modern Europe*. CUP, Cambridge.

Laqueur, Thomas W. 1989: Crowds, carnival and the state in English executions, 1604–1868. In *The first modern society: essays in honour of Lawrence Stone*, ed. A.L. Beier, David Cannadine and James M. Rosenheim. CUP, Cambridge, pp. 305–356.

Linebaugh, Peter 1992: *The London hanged: crime and civil society in the eighteenth century*. CUP, Cambridge.

Mantecón, Tomás A. 1995: La capacidad del clero secular para apaciguar las disputas entre los campesinos montañeses del siglo XVIII. In *Iglesia y sociedad*. I. *III Reunión Científica de la A.E.H.M*, ed. Enrique Martínez and Vicente Suárez. Univ. Las Palmas de Gran Canaria, Las Palmas, pp. 149–156.

Mantecón, Tomás A. 1997a: Territorio, poderes y actitudes hacia el crimen en la Moderna Cantabria rural. In *Monarquía, Imperio y pueblos en la España Moderna. IV Reunión Científica de la Asociación Española de Historia Moderna*, ed. Pablo Fernández Albaladejo. Univ. Alicante, Alicante, pp. 757–770.

Mantecón, Tomás A. 1997: *Conflictividad y disciplinamiento social en la Cantabria rural del Antiguo Régimen*. Univ. Cantabria, Santander.

Mantecón, Tomás A. 1998: Meaning and social context of crime in Preindustrial Times: rural society in the North of Spain, XVII and XVIII centuries. *Crime, History and Societies* 1 (1998), pp. 49–73.

Mantecón, Tomás A. 1998a: *La muerte de Antonia Isabel Sánchez. Tiranía y escándalo en una comunidad rural del Norte de España*. Centro de Estudios Cervantinos, Alcalá de Henares.

Mantecón, Tomás A. 2002: El peso de la infrajudicialidad en el control del crimen durante la Edad Moderna. *Estudis* (2002), pp. 43–75.

Mantecón, Tomás A. 2002a: El control de la moralidad a través de la fiesta: flagelantes y cencerradas en la España Cantábrica del Antiguo Régimen. *Ludica. Annali di storia e civiltà del gioco*, 8 (2002), pp. 141–159.

Mantecón, Tomás A. 2002b: El mal uso de la justicia en la Castilla del siglo XVII. In *Furor et rabies. Violencia, conflicto y marginación en la Edad Moderna*, ed. José I. Fortea, Juan E. Gelabert and Tomás A. Mantecón. Univ. Cantabria, Santander, pp. 69–98.

Mantecón, Tomás A. 2003: Popular culture and arbitration of disputes in the Northern Spanish 18th century. In *Crimes, punishment and Reform in Europe*, ed. Louis A. Knafla. *Criminal Justice History*, 18 (2003), pp. 39–55.

Mantecón, Tomás A. 2004: Social control from below: popular arbitration of disputes in the Spanish Old Regime. In *History of Social Control*. Vol. 1. *1500–1800*, ed. Pieter Spierenburg and Herman Roodenburg. OUP, Columbus, OUP, pp. 267–287.

Mantecón, Tomás A. 2004a: Les demons de Martin: folie et erreur judiciaire dans la Castille du XVIIe siècle. In *L'erreur judiciaire. De Jeanne d'Arc à Roland Agret*, ed. Benoît Garnot. Imago, París, pp. 61–84.

Mantecón, Tomás A. 2006: Las culturas criminales portuarias en las ciudades atlánticas: Sevilla y Ámsterdam en su edad dorada. In *La ciudad portuaria atlántica en la historia: siglos XVI–XIX*, ed. José I. Fortea and Juan E. Gelabert. Univ. Cantabria, Santander, pp. 159–194.

Mantecón, Tomás A. 2006: La economía del castigo e indulto en la Castilla de Cervantes. *Revista de Historia Económica*, 24 (2006), pp. 69–97.

Mantecón, Tomás A. 2007a: The patterns of violence in early modern Spain. *The Journal of the Historical Society*, VII (2), June 2007, pp. 229–265.

Mantecón, Tomás A. 2007: Récits de punition et de pardon dans la Castille moderne. In *Normes juridiques et pratiques judiciaires du Moyen Âge à l'époque contemporaine*, ed. Benoît Garnot. Éditions Universitaires de Dijon, Dijon, pp. 377–384.

Mantecón, Tomás A. 2008: Homicide et violence dans l'Espagne de l'Ancien Régime. In *Histoire de l'homicide en Europe. De la fin du Moyen Âge à nos jours*, ed. Laurent Mucchielli & Pieter Spierenburg. La Découverte, Paris, pp. 13–52.

Mantecón, Tomás A. 2008a: La justicia y el castigo del cuerpo en la Castilla moderna. In *Las escalas de la historia comparada. Tomo 1: Dinámicas sociales, poderes políticos y sistemas jurídicos*, ed. Marta Bonaudo, Andrea Reguera and Orieta Zeberio. Miño y Dávila Editores, Buenos Aires, pp. 207–228.

Mantecón, Tomás A. 2008b: La "ley de la calle" y la justicia urbana en el Antiguo Régimen. *Manuscrits*, 26 (2008), pp. 165–189.

Matikainen, Olli 2002: *Verenperijät. Väkivalta ja yhteisön murros itäisessä Suomessa 1500–1600-luvulla*. Bibiotheca Historica 78, Helsinki.

McKenzie, Andrea 2007: *Tyburn's Martyrs: execution in England, 1675–1775*. Continuum, London.

Moore, Lucy 1997: *The Thieves' Opera: The Remarkable Lives and Deaths of Jonathan. Wild, Thief-Taker and Jack Shepherd House-Breaker*. Viking, London.

Morin, Edgar 1970: *L'homme et la mort*. Seuil, Paris.

Mucchielli, Laurent & Pieter Spierenburg (ed.) 2008: *Histoire de l'homicide en Europe. De la fin du Moyen Âge à nos jours*. La Découverte, Paris.

Ortelli, Sara 2004: Enemigos internos y súbditos desleales: la infidencia en Nueva Vizcaya en tiempos de los Borbones. *Anuario de estudios americanos*, 61 (2), 2004, pp. 467–489.

Ortelli, Sara 2005: Parientes, compadres y allegados: los abigeos de Nueva Vizcaya en la segunda mitad del siglo XVIII. *Relaciones: Estudios de historia y sociedad*, 26 (102), 2005, pp. 163–199.

Ortelli, Sara 2007: *Trama de una guerra conveniente: Nueva Vizcaya y la sombra de los apaches (1748–1790)*. El Colegio de México, México.

Paglia, Vincenzo 1980: *"La pietà dei carcerati" Confraternite e società a Roma nei secoli XVI–XVIII*, ed. di Storia e Letteratura, Rome.

Paglia, Vincenzo 1982: *La morte confortata. Riti della paura e mentalità religiosa a Roma nell'età moderna*, ed. di Storia e Letteratura, Rome.

Puppi, Lionello 1988: Il mito e la trasgressione liturgia urbana delle esecuzioni capitali a Venezia tra XIV e XVIII secolo. *Studi Veneziani*, XV (1988), pp. 107–130.

Raggio, Osvaldo 1990: *Faide e parentele. Lo Stato genovese visto dalla Fontanabuona*. Einaudi, Torino.

Romeo, Giovanni 1993: *Aspettando il boia. Condannati a morte, confortatori e inquisitori nella Napoli della Controriforma*. Sansoni ed., Rome.

Sharpe, James A. 1985: Last dying speeches: religion, ideology and public execution in seventeenth-century England, *Past and Present*, 107 (1985), pp. 144–167.

Sharpe, James A. 2008: *Review of Tyburn's Martyrs: execution in England, 1675–1775*, Andrea McKenzie (review n° 677), www.history.ac.uk/reviews/paper/sharpe.html (accessed 2 January 2009).

Sbriccoli, Mario 1974: *Crimen laesae maistatis: il problema del reato politico alle soglie della scienza penalistica moderna.* Universidade Nova de Lisboa, Milan.

Spierenburg, Pieter 1984: *The spectacle of suffering. Executions and the evolution of repression: from a preindustrial metropolis to the European experience.* CUP, Cambridge.

Spierenburg, Pieter 1994: Faces of violence: homicide trends and cultural meanings. Amsterdam, 1431–1816. *Journal of Social History*, 27 (4), 1994, pp. 701–716.

Spierenburg, Pieter 1991: *The broken spell: a cultural & anthropological history of preindustrial Europe.* Rutgers, New Brunswick.

Spierenburg, Pieter (ed.) 1998: *Men and violence: gender, honor and rituals in modern Europe and America.* OUP, Columbus.

Spierenburg, Pieter 2008: *A history of murder: personal violence in Europe from the middle ages to the present.* CUP. Cambridge.

Traverso, Chiara 2000: *La scuola di San Fantin o dei "Picai". Caritá e giustizia a Venezia.* Marsilio Editore, Venice.

Veronese, Fabiana 2006: "L'orrore del sacrilegio": abusi di sacramenti, pratiche magiche e condanne a morte a Venezia nel primo ventennio del settecento. *Studi Veneziani*, LII (2006), pp. 265–342.

Vovelle, Michel 1974: *Mourir autrefois: attitudes collectives devant la mort au 17ème et 18ème siècle.* Gallimard, Paris.

Wormald, Jenny 1983: The blood feud in early modern Scotland. In *Disputes and settlements: law and human relations in the West*, ed. John Bossy. CUP, Cambridge, pp. 101–144.

Ylikangas, Heikki 1976: Major fluctuations in crimes of violence in Finland: A historical analysis. *Scandinavian Journal of History*, 1 (1976), pp. 81–103.

Ylikangas, Heikki 2001: What happened to violence? An analysis of the development of violence from medieval times to the early modern era based on Finish source material. In *Five centuries of violence in Finland and the Baltic area*, ed. Petri Karonen, Martti Lehti and Heikki Ylikangas. Hakapaino, Helsinki, pp. 1–84.

Executions in the Eighteenth- and Nineteenth-Century

Messages, Interpretations, and Reactions[1]

Martin Bergman

Although the title of this article opens up a broad field of interpretations, I will restrict the focus to eighteenth- and nineteenth-century north-western Europe, more specifically Sweden and the other Nordic countries except Iceland, Belgium and Germany. When talking about the north-western Europe, many would certainly include and perhaps choose to focus on the British Isles. When executions are added to the equation, Tyburn and Newgate, or possibly the Tower or Smithfield may come to mind, along with Thomas W. Laqueur's influential article *Crowds, Carnival and the State in English Executions, 1604–1868*. Laqueur, whose primary focus is Tyburn, describes executions as generally unruly affairs during which the assembly resembled a rowdy mob:

> The state seemed to show a perverse lack of interest in the solemnity of hangings and in making its presence decently manifest. On the contrary, it perpetrated the shabbiest of rituals with the minimum of authorial control.[2]

---

1 This article was first written as a lecture.
2 Thomas W. Laqueur, "Crowds, carnival and the state in English executions, 1604–1868" in A. L. Beier, David Cannadine and James M. Rosenheim (ed.), *The First Modern Society: Essays in English History*

Views such as Laqueur's are seen by many to describe the typical execution: disorderly and almost lawless. Although this is probably not far off the mark for Tyburn or London and perhaps for the British Isles in general, nevertheless a somewhat different picture emerges if one looks at a more diverse selection of executions. Fights and disruptive behaviour sometimes erupted and so guards were needed, but calmness, solemnity and ritual were generally the dominant traits of such proceedings, as can be seen from the three examples below.

When Jean Corbelet was broken on the wheel in Caen circa 1760, in the sentence his time of suffering was set to one hour. During that hour he prayed and sang with the priest and the crowd. Two hymns, *Veni Creator* and *Ave maris stella*, were sung, with Corbelet and the crowd singing alternate strophes.[3]

In Germany the execution was the grand finale of a ceremonious course of events. The *hochnothpeinliches Halsgericht*, the formal pronouncement of the sentence, was an impressive ceremony that often immediately preceded the execution itself. In such cases, an imposing procession made its way to the site of the execution, displaying the power and glory of the state and the authorities. The *Halsgericht* had been in place since the Middle Ages and continued until the nineteenth century in some states.[4]

On 14 April 1725 four executions took place outside Borås in Sweden. Each delinquent was accompanied by two clergymen. Proceedings at the

---

 in Honour of Lawrence Stone (Cambridge, 1989), p. 309. For views somewhat divergent from and to some extent critical of those expressed by Lacquer, see, for instance, V. A. C. Gatrell, *The Hanging Tree: Execution and the English People 1770–1868* (Oxford, 1994), pp. 32 ff., 56 ff., 90 ff., on the question of state control see especially pp. 97–98.

3   Jacques Mauger, "Journal" in Gabriel Vanel (ed.), *Recueil de Journaux Caennais 1661–1777* (Rouen, 1904), pp. 174–175.

4   See, for instance, *Ausführliche Beschreibung der Hegung des Hochnothpeinlichen Hals-Gerichts, und insonderheit wie es von E E Hochweisen Rathe zu Leipzig nach römischer Sitte, mit allen Umständen und Zeremonien geheget und gehalten wird* (Heilbronn, 1798); Carl August Tittman, "Das gerichtliche Verfahren bei Vollziehung der Todesstrafen" in *Neues Archiv des Criminalrechts VI* (Halle, 1822); Benedictus Carpzov, *Practicæ novæ imperialis saxonicæ rerum criminalum III* (Wittenberg and Frankfurt, 1677), pp. 292 ff.; Karl Grolman, *Grundsätze der Criminalrechtswissenschaft nebst einer systematischen Darstellung des Geistes der Deutschen Criminalgesetze* (Glashütten im Taunus, 1970), pp. 482–483.; and Richard J. Evans *Rituals of Retribution: Capital punishment in Germany 1600–1987* (London, 1997), pp. 65 ff. In 1833 Julius Friedrich Heinrich Abegg reported that a large part of the ceremonies had been abolished, Julius Friedrich Heinrich Abegg, *Lehrbuch des gemeinen Criminal-Prozesses mit besonderer Berücksichtigung des Preussischen Rechts* (Goldbach, 1996), p. 340.

execution site began with a hymn, after which one of the priests read a prayer and St Luke's account of the two criminals who were crucified alongside Jesus. Two more hymns were sung, each followed by a prayer read by a different priest. At this point in the proceedings a sermon and prayer were read by one of the condemned prisoners before the fourth hymn of the day was sung. Events drew to a close with the fifth hymn, during which the four delinquents were executed.[5]

However, the distance between these seemingly contrasting views of executions – disorder and order – is perhaps not as great as it might first appear. Anders Chydenius was a well-known Finnish clergyman, who, in Kronoby in 1786, delivered the earliest known speech after an execution in the country (then Sweden and Finland). In some respects Chydenius may have been closer to the cockney pickpocket than one might imagine.[6] The end of a human life is, for almost anyone, an occasion of some solemnity, and rituals of some kind are needed to handle the situation.

Naturally, the picture is more complicated than hitherto implied. A crowd considered disobedient and unruly by the state could in their own eyes be wise and righteous. Consider a frequently cited execution in Florence in 1830, the first for many years: the road to the site of execution and the site itself were almost deserted; shops were closed and the population gathered at home and in the churches as a protest.[7]

Even leaving Tuscany aside, there is evidence that existing differences were not simply due to national variations. London executions seem to provide the most important evidence to support the "rough crowd and invisible state" theory; there seems to have been greater concerns about "the masses" in cities than in the countryside. During the nineteenth

---

5 Johan Tvet: "Desse 4s Execution" vol 1398 Juridica Straff- och Missgärningsbalken III, Nordinska samlingen, Uppsala universitetsbibliotek, Uppsala, the date confirmed by p. 176 15/4 1725 54:4871 Rådstuvurättens dombok 1724–1727, Rådhusrätten och magistraten i Borås arkiv, Borås Stadsarkiv, Borås.
6 Cf. Anders Chydenius, *Tal, hållit på Afrättsplatsen i Kronoby...då Soldaterna Matts Hjelt, Abraham Frodig och Peter Lindström för begånget mord, rån och mordbränneri uppå Barna-läraren wid Teirijärwi Cappel, Johan Mattson och dess Hustru, til följe af Höglofl Kongl Wasa Hof-Rätts Dom, miste högra handen, halshöggos och steglades den 12 April 1786* (Wasa s a); Peter Linebaugh, "The Ordinary of Newgate and his Account", in J. S. Cockburn (ed.), *Crime in England 1500–1800* (Princeton, 1977), p. 246.
7 See, for instance, Jacques Joseph Haus, *La peine de mort, son passé, son présent, son avenir* (Gand, 1867), p. 157.

century, especially after decades which saw more frequent gatherings of larger crowds of people (some of whom had travelled by train), concerns about crowds became more widespread.[8]

In *De la répression pénale, de ses formes et de ses effets*, Alphonse Bérenger made a substantial case that executions were counterproductive. Some of those present at executions behaved in an unspeakable manner, and their behaviour was also part of the moral torture inflicted on the condemned. Children were hardened by such events and took to recreating executions in their games. For most crowds the execution itself, rather than the crime, was the focus of interest and the defiant delinquent was the most admired. The overall effect was to encourage new instincts in the population, instincts that were contrary to those that the authorities desired.[9] There were, in fact, certain desirable or, at least, desired reactions to executions. Essentially public executions were messages that were supposed to trigger reactions – the condemned also carried the message in his or her body.

When considering the period before the Enlightenment and revolutions spread secularising ideas, it seems possible to describe executions and the co-operation surrounding them in this way. Executions were filled with symbolic actions. If we were to make a distinction, not wholly appropriate for the time, these actions had among their aims both civil and spiritual ends. Although the convict was to be expunged from society, his or her relationship with God had been and continued to be a matter of concern for the clergy. The common interest in the salvation of the condemned was regularly revealed in the execution. The delinquent embodied two roles and served as a double example of punishment and mercy. On this person, on this body, the just punishment for the crime was realised, but in the same person, in the same body, through repent-

---

8 One example of the presence of huge crowds was the execution in Charleroi (29 March 1862) of Auguste Leclercq and Jean-Baptiste Boucher. It was noted that a special train had arrived from France. At least 30, 000 people were said to have lined the route to the site of execution where a crowd of some fifteen to twenty thousand people had gathered, "L'Indépendance belge", Bruxelles 29 March 1862, "Het Handelsblad van Antwerpen", Antwerpen 30–31 March 1862, "Le Précurseur, Journal Politique, Commercial, Maritime et Littéraire", Antwerpen 30 March 1862.
9 Alphonse Bérenger, *De la répression pénale, de ses formes et de ses effets* (volume ix of *Mémoires de l'Académie des sciences morales et politiques de l'Institute de France*, Paris, 1855), pp. 808–861 ff.

ance, the possibility to meet the mercy and forgiveness of God despite all one's crimes was demonstrated.

Those who were executed and the executions themselves also raised questions and opened doors to another world. The condemned embodies Man before God – standing before the eternal judge, what will be the outcome? Under no other circumstances is an individual's death subjected to such planning, preparation and certainty. Under no other circumstances are we faced with the presentation of a human being standing before eternity. Such a sight probably affected most of those who attended executions. The church and state shared a common interest in framing the execution – and, if possible, the person who was executed – in ways that would have an effect upon those who attended; the aim was to create a joint experience that would encourage spiritual growth and strengthen obedience under the law. There was, however, also a worst-case scenario: a dreadful story of an unrepentant sinner's last sacrilege and descent into hell, a day of despair and warning.[10]

Most of us today probably find it hard to accept that officials and rulers were concerned for the salvation of those they condemned to death. Many would be surprised to find words like these in an official letter concerning the salary of the executioner: "*Samme Delinquent gick frimodigt och vackert uti en stor andacht till sin död att man efter Menskelig tanke intet annat kan säij, utan han dödde Sahln*" (The same delinquent went lighthearted and beautiful in great devotion to his death, so that humanly nothing else could be said other than that he died saved). The delinquent in question was Michel Blix and he was executed in Finland in 1733.[11]

This co-operation, this system, has been studied by several other scholars. Of particular note are François Lebrun's pioneering work and Jürgen Martschukat's extensive study, which focuses on Hamburg. Martschukat argues that the system's purpose was to legitimise the political order by connecting it to God; he observes that the authorities emphasised the symbolic content of the execution, in particular power and

---

10 The worst-case scenarios are rarely desribed at length, an exception can be found in Jacob Elisius Gjellebøl, *Spildte Guds Ord paa Balle-Lars* (Næstved, 1861).
11 Letter from Johan Golin to governor Stieerncrantz 25 May 1733 Ea3 Ankomna brev 1733, Nyland länskontors arkiv, Riksarkivet, Helsingfors.

submission, sin, atonement, righteousness and forgiveness. I would argue that there is an evident connection to the sacralisation of the judicial system made possible by the Reformation. Martschukat traces the system to the early sixteenth century and sees its disintegration spreading from the mid-eighteenth century onwards.[12] His results and my own are similar, although my focus has been on the later period and I see the second half of the eighteenth century as a time of transition. During this period the system was still developing – new rituals were introduced, for example – even though dismantling of the system had already begun. One can observe the slow decline and end of a form of co-operation between state and church around the death penalty, the execution and, perhaps most importantly, the executed. The ultimate precondition for the system seems to have been the close relationship between church and state.[13]

One noteworthy example of development was the time allowed for preparing the condemned prisoner. In the Swedish Church ordinance from 1571 archbishop Laurentius Petri recommended that the clergy should strive to secure one or two days for the spiritual preparation of the prisoner. At this time an allowance of three days for preparation was not uncommon in Germany, but in Sweden the archbishop's recommendation would probably have represented an extension of the norm.[14] Preparation times later increased: in the eighteenth century two weeks was perceived as the norm; by the nineteenth century this had become six weeks, although variations were certainly common.[15] A longer period

---

12 François Lebrun, *Les hommes et la mort en Anjou aux 17e et 18e siècles: essai de démographie et de psychologie historiques* (Paris, 1971), for instance p. 417; Jürgen Martschukat, *Inszeniertes Töten, Eine Geschichte der Todesstrafe vom 17. bis zum 19. Jahrhundert* (Köln, 2000), pp. 52–53.

13 Cf. Martin Bergman, *Dödsstraffet, kyrkan och staten i Sverige från 1700-tal till 1900-tal* (Lund, 1996), pp. 193 ff., 196 ff.

14 Sven Kjöllerström (ed.), *Den svenska kyrkoordningen 1571 jämte studier kring tillkomst, innehåll och användning* (Lund, 1971), article 20 p. 133; cf. Sven Kjöllerström, *Guds och Sveriges lag under reformationstiden, en kyrkorättslig studie* (Lund, 1957), p. 51; Lars Levander, *Brottsling och bödel* (Stockholm, 1975), pp. 241, 265; J. Köhler and Willy Scheel (ed.), *Die peinliche Gerichtordnung Kaiser Karls V Constitutio Criminalis Carolina* (vol i. of J. Köhler (ed.), *Die Carolina und Ihre Vorgängerinnen*) (Halle, 1900), p. 45 Constitutio Criminalis Carolina 79.

15 Report by Carl Axel Wachtmeister 23 August 1790 F 521 Bref från H E Riksdrotzet Grefve Carl Axel Wachtmeister, Gustavianska samlingen Uppsala universitetsbibliotek, Uppsala, [Djos Per Andersson], *Testamente från Stupstocken eller strödda anteckningar ur en dödsfånges lefnad*, Upsala 1849 pp. 98 ff., relation by Anders Peter Holmström 3 February 1860 EVI:8 Inkomna religionsberättelser 1859, Styrelsen över fängelser och arbetsinrättningar i riket, Riksarkivet, Stockholm, note 29 March 1887 DId:1 Dagböcker över prästerliga förrättningar 1854–1879, Fångvårdsanstalten i Kristianstads arkiv, landsarkivet i Lund, Lund, "Nya Dagligt Allehanda", Stockholm 18 March 1893.

for spiritual preparation also allowed more elaborate preparations for execution ceremonies and meant that the prisoner could be prepared not only for heaven, but also for his or her forthcoming role as an example. The most important factor was, however, the pastoral care of the condemned prisoner.

Another example of how secular authorities were concerned with the eternal fate of those they executed can be seen in the reasoning behind changes to "the sack" in Saxony during the 1690s. In order to speed up the drowning process and thus reduce the terror and despair endured by the delinquent linen replaced the waxed fabric that had previously been used. Yet condemned were in fact reprieved from the penalty of the sack and instead, because of the possible dangers to their souls, executed by the sword and soon the sack was no longer used in executions.[16]

From the reign of George II (King of Great Britain and Ireland and Duke of Hannover) one can find two examples of how development and dismantling of the system could almost go hand in hand. The *Criminal-Instruction* of Braunschweig-Lüneburg of 1736, approved in London, ruled that prisoners who were condemned to die should not be visited by anyone other than clergy or relatives. This rule was motivated by the perceived need of the prisoner to prepare for death. The state felt an obligation that no prisoner should be executed while in an unrepentant state: if prisoners failed to repent, executions could be postponed for a few days to give the clergy more time to carry out their work.[17]

The British *Murder Act* of 1752 also contained similar restrictions on visits to the condemned. However, it differed from the *Criminal-Instruction* in context. Members of the clergy required an official permit for their visits, and preparation for death and pastoral care were only mentioned in a reference to Holy Communion as an exception to the

---

16 *Neues Archiv für Sächsiche Geschichte und Alterthumskunde* 9 (Dresden, 1888), p. 158; Johann Christian Olearius, *Geistliches Hand-Buch der Kinder Gottes* (Leipzig, 1692), p. 1769; cf. Bruno Preisendörfer, *Staatsbildung als Königskunst, Ästhetik und Herrschaft im preußischen Absolutismus* (Berlin, 2000), pp. 162–163.

17 Criminal-Instruction Cap 13, § 1–3 in: *Chur-Braunschweig-Lüneburgische Landes-Ordnungen und Gesetze II..., Zum Gebrauch Der Fürstenthümer, Graf- und Herrschafften Calenbergischen Theils* (Göttingen, 1740), pp. 880–881; cf. Thomas Krause, *Die Strafrechtspflege im Kurfürstentum und Königreich Hannover, vom Ende des 17. bis zum ersten Drittel des 19. Jahrhunderts* (Aalen, 1991), pp. 30, 178–179.

rule that condemned prisoners could only receive bread and water. In addition, executions were to take place two days after sentencing, unless this was a Sunday in which case the execution would be postponed until Monday.[18] This statute shows how a rule designed to fit into what was then a "classical" system could be used to overturn that same system and its values. Although spiritual preparation was not excluded, the primary motive behind the iteration of the confinement and separation of the prisoner was to inspire terror: the condemned prisoner was not set apart for celebration but as an example of the wrath and might of the state. The impression was clearly given that a murderer was placed outside normal pastoral care. Some eighty years later Edward Gibbon Wakefield wrote of the condemned murderer:

> During the few hours that remain to the murderer after sentence, he is confined in a solitary cell, set apart for that purpose. If visited at all, it is only by a clergyman, and that by stealth, as it were, since it is understood that the offices of religion are denied the murderer. In the same unostentatious way he is taken to the scaffold, and is put to death without any religious ceremonies or other formal observances, – a mode of treatment widely different, it will be seen, from that pursued towards most other persons under sentence of death.[19]

The two laws shared many similarities and were promulgated by the same ruler, but their aims differed. In terms of aims there are, however, German parallels to the British law, not in Hannover but in Prussia.

The relatively well-known Prussian Royal ordinance from 1769 argues that, as the clergy could and should visit and prepare the condemned in prison well in advance of executions, there was no need for priests to accompany Protestants to their executions. This ban was applied to those

---

18 25 Geo. II, cap. 37, § 1, 6–8 in: Danby Pickering (ed.), *The Statues at Large from the 23d to the 26th year of King George II* xx (Cambridge, 1765), pp. 380 ff.
19 Wakefield, Edward Gibbon, *Facts relating to the punishment of death in the metropolis*, London 1831 p. 87.

who had committed murder or crimes that threatened public security.[20] More draconian rules were, however, already in place under Prussian military law. A Royal ordinance from 1765 proscribed all visits of clergymen to certain categories of murderers. They were to be executed without preparation and without any clergymen accompanying them on the road to the execution site. No exceptions were to be made for any confession.[21] In 1768 and 1787 the punishment was extended to those who had been convicted of some other types of murder or attempted murder.[22] This legislation constituted a major change in comparison to earlier Prussian legislation and practice. In the early eighteenth century great care had been given to the preparation of the condemned, and executions were postponed if prisoners had not been sufficiently well prepared, in accordance with the *Criminal-Ordnung vor die Chur- und Renmarck* of 1717.[23] Against this background, how are such laws to be understood?

Their purpose was to challenge the belief that the eternal consequences for those who were executed could be diminished or erased as a result of preparations or the actions of the church and clergy at the execution. First, the implementation of the laws was supposed to inspire terror in those who held this belief. The eventual aim was to weaken and, possibly, exterminate such beliefs. These laws implied that the eternal fate of individuals was of no concern and was subordinate to the present interests of the state. Thus the clergy and religion were seen as irrelevant or wholly immanent. This view seems to presuppose either a clearly atheistic belief or an anthropology and soteriology in which no hope exists for those convicted of grave crimes. According to

---

20 Ordinance nr 48 3/7 1769 *Novum Corpus Constitutionum Prussico-Brandenburgensium Praecipue Marchicarum oder Neue Sammlung Königl. Preuß. und Churfürstl. Brandenburgischer sonderlich in der Chur- und Mark- Brandenburg publicirten und ergangenen Ordnungen, Edicten, Mandaten, Rescripten &c &c von 1766, 1767, 1768, 1769, und 1770,* IV 1766–1770 (Berlin 1771), pp. 6179 ff.
21 Max Lehmann, *Preussen und die katholische Kirche seit 1640, nach den Acten des Geheimen Staatsarchives, IV von 1758 bis 1775* (Leipzig, 1883), p. 236.
22 Georg Friedrich Müller, *Das Krieges- oder Soldatenrecht, so wie solches in älten und neuen Zeiten vornehmlich bey der Königl. Preußl. Armee, und in den Gerichten sämtlicher Preußl. Staaten gesetzlich, üblich und gewöhnlich ist* volume ii (Berlin, 1789), pp. 436–437.
23 Christian Otto Mylius (ed.), *Corpus Constitutionum Marchicarum oder Königl. Preußis. und Churfürstl. Brandenburgischer sonderlich in der Chur- und Mark- Brandenburg, auch incorporirten Landen publicirten und ergangenen Ordnungen, Edicta, Mandata & Rescripta Von Zieten Friedrichs I Churfürsten zu Brandenburg, & bis ietzo unter der Regierung Friedrich Wilhelms König in Preussen & ad annum 1736 inclusive Mit allergn. Bewillung colligiret und ans Licht gegeben* (Berlin s a) II, 3 col 107 chapter XII, § 2 ff.

this view, the judgements made by the worldly court and those made by God harmonise and the condemned have no chance of attaining the ethical standards required for salvation.

Why would such extreme measures be deemed necessary? The first answer is that these laws often primarily and explicitly name a certain kind of murder as their target. Edmond Locard calls them *le crime sans cause* ("crime without cause") and Tyge Krogh *grundløse drab* ("murders without cause").[24] An individual commits murder in order to be executed. In many cases a strong longing for heaven and, often, a deep fear for hell were the fundamental motives for such crimes. Thus, the execution was seen as a gateway to heaven, a shortcut that was also the safest available route to salvation.[25] One may consider that those who harboured and acted on these thoughts were more or less mentally ill, but their interpretations of the services and liturgy that accompanied the execution were reasonable. The executed – forgiven, given communion and blessed – looked like a saint and would sometimes even be dressed fully in white.[26] Even more problematic for the authorities was the model given by the concept of martyrdom in earlier periods of the history of the church.[27] Martyrdom was easy to relate to at many executions – someone professed his or her faith and was then publicly executed – a fellow Christian who shared the pain, humiliation, and expulsion endured by Christ and many martyrs.

---

24 Edmond Locard, "Le crime sans cause", *La Giustizia Penale* 45 (1939); Tyge Krogh, *Oplysningstiden og det magiske, henrettelser og korporlige straffe i 1700-tallets første halvdel* (Copenhagen, 2000), p. 228. Krogh has later in *A Lutheran Plague, Murdering to Die in the Eighteenth Century* (Leiden, 2012) instead written about "suicide murder", a view earlier prominently held by Arne Jansson in *From Swords to Sorrow: Homicide and Suicide in Early Modern Stockholm* (Stockholm, 1988).

25 See, for instance, Karl Ferdinand Hommels, "[Anmerkungen]" in Cesare Bonesana Beccaria, *Des Herren...unsterbliches Werk von Verbrechen und Strafen* (Breslau, 1778), pp. 178 ff.; Johann David Michaëlis, *Moral II* (Göttingen, 1792), p. 44; J. J. Gudenrath, "Mine Skrupler over Selvmords Moralitet, og over dets Straffældighed efter de borgelige Love" *Maanedskriftet Iris* (Copenhagen, 1792), pp. 259–260 note *; Martin Bergman, *Dödsstraffet, kyrkan och staten i Sverige från 1700-tal till 1900-tal*, pp. 108 ff.

26 See for instance Bergman, *Dödsstraffet, kyrkan och staten i Sverige från 1700-tal till 1900-tal*, p. 108 (note 7 contains some twenty references relating to clothing); Krogh, *Oplysningstiden og det magiske*, p. 290; Clodagh Tait, "Adored for Saints: Catholic Martyrdom in Ireland c. 1560–1655" *Journal of Early Modern History* 5 (2001), p. 143.

27 *Neues Hannöverisches Magazin*, Hannover 1800 nr 76 col 1416 ff.; Christel Butterweck, *"Martyriumsucht" in der Alten Kirche? Studien zur Darstellung und Deutung frühchristlicher Martyrier* (Tübingen, 1995), pp. 218 ff., 245–246; cf. Glenn W. Bowersock, *Martyrdom and Rome* (Cambridge, 1995) pp. 1 ff., 41 ff., 48 ff., 55, 59 ff., 71; Geoffrey de Sainte Croix, *Christian Persecution, Martyrdom, and Orthodoxy*, ed. Michael Whitby and Joseph Streeter (Oxford, 2006) pp. 65–66, 153 ff., 164 ff.

However, this answer is not quite adequate. Although some studies suggest that this type of murder was already rather common in the late seventeenth century, the earliest example of legislation that obviously targets such murders is a relatively mild Swedish ordinance from 1741. The ordinance only prohibited pomp and the use of special dress for the condemned prisoner.[28] Thus, an additional explanation is required, one that involves clashes between a more orthodox Christian theology and a theology deeply influenced by the Enlightenment. The central battleground, at least in Germany, was the concept of conversion. Of particular relevance is the extent to which the state had an interest in conversion and the perception of the converted. Was it in the state's interest to produce a joyfully converted person, shining with their eagerness to meet God? Would the state have preferred somebody who had not yet left the earth and was weighed down with sorrow for the sins they had committed? Or would an unconverted heathen, preferably desperate and possibly on the road to hell, have served the interests of the state best? Such scenarios imply different views of the state. Did the state have any religious obligations and identity, or was it solely a secular entity? New answers were emerging at this time. For some who held positions of authority the idea of that a longing for heaven could be a motive for murder probably not only sounded extreme, almost crazy, but was, to an increasing extent, genuinely incomprehensible. This lack of understanding made it easier to act harshly, to increase pain or even to take actions that seemingly endangered salvation. It was not long, however, before the only truly effective cure was implemented: such murderers were not executed and were eventually judged to be insane.[29] These crimes and

---

28 *Kongl. Maj:ts Förordning Angående Dödsfångars och andre Missgierningsmäns klädebonad wid deras afstraffande. Gifwen Stockholm i Rådskammaren then 12 Decembris 1741* (Stockholm, s a). Due to different definitions of subgroups in the category of murder, statistics should be used carefully, but cf. Arne Jansson, "Mörda för att få dö" in Arne Jarrick and Johan Söderberg (ed.) *Människovärdet och makten: Om civiliseringsprocessen i Stockholm 1600–1850* (Stockholm, 1994), pp. 23 ff.; Arne Jansson, *From Swords to Sorrow*, pp. 49–50; Hans Andersson, *"Androm till varnagel...", det tidigmoderna Stockholms folkliga rättskultur i ett komparativt perspektiv* (Stockholm, 1998), p. 103; Maria Kaspersson, *Dödligt våld i Stockholm på 1500-, 1700- och 1900-talen* (Stockholm, 2000), p. 84.

29 Some non-lethal penalties listed in the Danish Royal ordinance of 18 December 1767 in *Chronologisk Register over de Kongelige Forordningar og obne Breve som fra Aar 1670 af ere udkomne, tilligemed et nøiagtigt udtog af de endnu gieldende, for saavidt samme i Almindelighed angaaende Undersaaterne i Danmark og Norge, forsynet med et alphabetisk Register ved Jacob Henric Schou* (Copenhagen, 1795), V:71 ff.; Johan

legislative reactions also demonstrate how the church, pastoral care and liturgy could be seen as a problem. Even though rituals were needed, in a demanding situation they could become a nuisance if their message was perceived to threaten the all-important message of deterrence of the execution.

However, at roughly the same time the co-operation surrounding the delinquents was disintegrating as a result of more general developments. Punishments and rituals were changing. Perhaps the most significant change concerned the way in which the condemned man or woman was perceived. Capital punishment can be said to be the meeting between death and the transgressor, but when delinquents became increasingly invisible only death remained visible. The former "star performer" was increasingly seen as an embarrassment, both in life and in death. Previously those who had been condemned had given speeches of various kinds, sung hymns and made confessions, but now things were changing. The execution of Louis XVI was compared by some to the Passion of Christ: the sacred king became a sacrifice.[30] At the same time the king's attempt to make a speech from the scaffolds was silenced by drums.[31]

Pain was certainly on its way out; now it seemed that executions should be swift and death should come quickly. Over time it seemed that even death should not be visible and ultimately executions were carried out behind prison walls.[32] The liturgical and dramatic character of the execution had been replaced by an attitude of "let's get it done with". One eventually finds a French prison governor waking a prisoner

---

Christian Quistorp, *Ausführliche Entwurf zu einem Gesetzbuch in peinlichen und Strafsachen* (Rostock, 1782), pp. 20–21; A. J. Mannkopff (ed.), *Allgemeinen Landrecht für die Preussischen Staaten* Bd 7 Th II Tit 20 (Berlin, 1838), p. 541, § 831–832; *Förslag till Allmän Criminal-Lag* (Stockholm, 1832), Straffbalken 6:21, motives pp. 29–30. Sentence 6/11 1845 in which Maria Johansdotter was judged as insane in Ala 133 Konga häradsrätts arkiv, Landsarkivet in Vadstena, Vadstena, nr 123 BIIa:294 Huvudarkivet, Göta hovrätts arkiv, Landsarkivet in Vadstena, Vadstena.

30 On the image of Louis XVI, see Preisendörfer, *Staatsbildung als Königskunst, Ästhetik und Herrschaft im preußischen Absolutismus*, p. 78.
31 See, for instance, Jean de Viguerie, *Louis XVI: Le roi bienfaisant* (Monaco, 2003), p. 406.
32 On the present result of this development in the USA see, for instance, Austin Sarat, *When the State Kills: Capital Punishment and the American Condition* (Princeton, 2001), p. 67; Austin Sarat, "Killing Me Softly: Capital Punishment and the Technologies for Taking Life" in id. (ed.), *Pain, Death, and the Law* (Ann Arbor, 2001), p. 46.

with the announcement that he should be brave because a reprieve had been denied, and a British royal commission gathering evidence about how many seconds passed between an executioner entering the cell and the drop.[33] The hundred years between 1750 and 1850 can be seen as the period roughly at the centre of all this change. During the second half of the eighteenth century, the system was being both developed and dismantled; a swifter dismantling of the system was evident by the nineteenth century.

By the end of this period, condemned prisoners had been transformed from subjects into objects, the co-operation between church and state had been demolished, or at least substantially weakened, and the execution itself was increasingly being seen as an embarrassing and repugnant problem.

Let us consider the sad story of two guillotines: the guillotine of Ghent and the guillotine of Antwerp. Things started badly, at least for the Antwerp guillotine. No one would touch or transport the item and so in the end the *département des Deux Nethes* had to send its own staff to fetch it from Ghent, where the *département du Nord* had delivered some of the guillotines made in Lille.[34] The Ghent guillotine could not find any official residence. It was moved between various private storerooms around the city, as nobody wanted to be close to it. The ministry of justice and the governor pressed the city to accommodate the guillotine – making suggestions such as "isn't there any room, in your big city hall, in your new palace of justice?" – but all their efforts were in vain. The city suggested that, had they not been disgusted by it, the military could

---

33 Royal Commission on Capital Punishment 1949–1953, *Report* (London, 1953), pp. 250–251. The traditional ritual at French executions seems to have been both unwavering and flexible. Thus different persons, such as the chaplain or a procureur might have been the first inside the cell, cf., for instance, Robert Badinter, *L'exécution* (s l 1973), p. 215; and Jacques Delarue, *Le métier de bourreau* (Paris, 1979), p. 290. But the unwavering nature is demonstrated by Badinter's quotation: "la phrase rituelle" in Badinter, L'exécution, p. 215.

34 Letter from deputy commissaire J. Chabroud to the *département des Deux Nethes* 7 messidor year IV A 121 9; letter from the city of Lille to the *département des Deux Nethes* 5 thermidor year IV A 121 9° Provinciearchief RAA; letter from the *département du Nord* to the *département des Deux Nethes* 11 floréal year V A 121 10° Provinciearchief Rijksarchief Antwerpen, Antwerpen; letter from the department Escaut to the *département des Deux Nethes* 21 pluviôse year VI A 121 10°, all in A. Franse Tijdvak 1794–1814 121 9°–10° Strafuitvoeringen, Provinciearchief, Rijksarchief Antwerpen, Antwerpen. Cf. Prosper Claeys *Le bourreau de Gand, sa mission, ses fonctions, ses privilèges* (Gand, 1893), pp. 76–77 on the transport of the guillotine of the department Meuse inferieur.

have stored the guillotine. Finally in 1866 the Ghent guillotine found a permanent home: in the prison.[35]

Even though it was housed in the beautiful sixteenth-century city hall, the guillotine of Antwerp seems nevertheless to have fallen victim to the city's attitude towards executions. In 1850 it was so damaged by moisture that it had to be repaired. The city was asked if it could not find a more suitable space in which to store the guillotine, at least while it was being mended. The city could find no better place than the small, dark and dank room in which the device had currently been housed. When the guillotine once again had to be repaired in 1855, the courtyard of the city hall was the only available space in which the work could be carried out. The state's patience with the city's treatment of the guillotine then ran out: since the guillotine of Bruges also was in bad shape, Antwerp's guillotine was moved to Bruges.[36] However, even in Bruges it seems that the Antwerp guillotine was not treated particularly carefully. The guillotine of Brussels was used at an execution in Bruges in 1862; the same guillotine had been used a few days earlier in Charleroi.[37] In the end, this was the only guillotine in use. In July 1847 the Antwerp newspaper *Het Handelsblad* had referred to the guillotine as *het mordtuig* ("the murder implement"), an illustration of how the guillotine had been seen by some.[38]

---

35 See, for instance, draft of letter from the governor of Oost-Vlaanderen to the mayor and council of Ghent 22 August 1839; letter from the mayor and council of Ghent to the governor of Oost-Vlaanderen 2 September 1839; letter from the minister of justice to the governor of Oost-Vlaanderen undated (June 1847); draft of letter from the governor of Oost-Vlaanderen to the mayor and council of Ghent 2 July 1847; letter from the mayor and council of Ghent to the governor of Oost-Vlaanderen 5 July 1847, all in vol 945 (1853/2) Dossier betreffen een opslagsplats voor schavotten 1819–1847, Provincial Archief Oost-Vlaanderen 1830–1850, Rijksarchief Gent, Gent. See also draft of letter from the governor of Oost-Vlaanderen to the mayor and council of Ghent 10 December 1855; letter from the mayor and council of Ghent to the governor of Oost-Vlaanderen 18 December 1855; letter from the Commission administrative des Prisons de Gand to the governor of Oost-Vlaanderen 5 June 1866, all in (1330/4) Stukken en corr. betreffende de huur van een opslagsruimte voor gerechtinstrumenten 1855–56, Provincial Archief Oost-Vlaanderen 1851–1870, Rijksarchief Gent, Gent.
36 Martin Bergman, "The Penalty of Death and Executions: the Tension between National Government, Local Authorities and Population" in Maria Ågren, Åsa Karlsson and Xavier Rousseaux (ed.), *Guises of Power: Integration of Society and Legitimation of Power in Sweden and Southern Low Countries ca 1500–1900* (Uppsala, 2001), p. 103.
37 Het Handelsblad van Antwerpen, Antwerpen 4 April 1862.
38 Het Handelsblad van Antwerpen 14 July 1847.

Stories of this kind could probably be found in other places. As ever-larger crowds gathered to watch the public enactment of justice, attacks on the execution scene grew louder. The actions that took place at executions, the execution sites themselves and those who attended executions were all seen as unsuitable and problematic; actions, sites and persons – three themes mixing and co-operating. As I have already addressed some of the problems relating to actions, let us move on to consider execution sites and those who visited them.

An execution site in the countryside could be moved because local people did not want the smell of decaying bodies near the roads or their fields.[39] The ideal location would be a remote and otherwise useless site that was not owned by anyone. Although corpses were seldom left lying around in cities, the execution site itself was reason enough for complaints. In France and Belgium, at least, the relocation of execution sites was quite a common occurrence. Sometimes several moves took place: the site of execution in Paris, for instance, changed four times. Each time the site was moved further from the city centre and the last move took it inside the prison walls.[40] Three major reasons for changing the sites of executions were put forward. The first reason was complaints: executions lowered property values, disturbed trade and generally disgraced the dignified central square used for festivities. Some residents pressed for relocation, arguing that the population of another location was more in need of the education that proximity to an execution site could provide. The second reason for relocation was that traditional sites could not accommodate the large number of visitors who tended to disturb traffic and commerce. The final reason for changing sites was born out of a desire to control the large crowds. Probably this was why locations near mili-

---

39 See, for instance, the case related in Copy of Ruling by the Governor of Kronoberg 14 November 1839; letter from Johannes Aulander to the governor 5 May 1834; letter from the yeomen of Jät to the governor 5 May 1834, all in bundle "Angående Kinnevalds härads afrättsplats" in Handl. ang. tingshus, tingsplats, häkte och afrättsplats, in volume 120 of Kronofogden i Kinnevalds och Norrvidinge härads fögderi, Landsarkivet i Vadstena, Vadstena.

40 Cyprien Roumieu *Plus d'échafauds! ou de l'abolition immédiate et absolue de la peine de mort* (Paris, 1833) pp. 265–66; Adolphe Chauveau and Faustin Hélie, *Théorie du code pénal, annotée...par Edmond Villey* vol i (Paris, 1887), p 276; Gordon Wright, *Between the Guillotine and Liberty: Two Centuries of the Crime Problem in France* (New York, 1983), pp. 166, 231 note 57.

tary barracks or just outside prison gates were increasingly used as execution sites.[41]

The intramural executions that were introduced in most countries during the nineteenth century answered the demand for control. Those who were admitted to witness executions could be selected. Even when executions were in theory supposed to be public, in practice attendance could be restricted: areas could be sealed off or executions scheduled for the middle of the night.[42]

It would be impossible to ignore class and other social factors when considering the issue of attendance. Newspapers, mainly read by rich burghers, would keep corporal and capital punishment at a distance, often choosing not to mention them at all.[43] In the nineteenth century those in power commonly viewed the crowds as rough, possibly dangerous, mobs that were nevertheless in need of the kind of education that executions could provide. A report from an execution in Bruges in 1851 was typical of the period: it asserted that it was honourable for Bruges that no women other than members of the working class were present.[44]

Children were the first group whose presence at executions was questioned. This had not always been the case. Previously children had been brought, often by schools, to all sorts of executions in order to learn and be warned against transgression. Witnessing hangings, beheadings, burnings or the rack was seen to have instructive value. However, in the first half of the nineteenth century a major change occurred. Rather than being invited to witness executions, children found themselves more or less successfully prohibited from attending public executions. Playing execution, especially using the genuine guillotine, was seen as a nuisance and a problem.[45]

---

41 Bergman, "The Penalty of Death and Executions", pp. 100 ff.; John M. Merriman, The Margins of City Life: Explorations of the French Urban Frontier 1815–1851 (New York, 1991), pp. 18–19.
42 Cf., for instance, John D. Bessler, Death in the Dark: Midnight Executions in America (Boston, 1997).
43 See, for instance, Herman Franke, "Over beschaving en de afschaffing van het schavot" Amsterdam sociologisch Tijdschrift 8 (1981), pp. 213 ff.
44 La Belgique judiciaire, Bruxelles 1851 col 912.
45 Cf. Bergman, "The Penalty of Death and Executions", pp. 98–99 and on playing and jesting, for instance, "Münchener-Intelligenzblatt", München no 36 (28/7) 1780, p. 348 and J. M. J. A. Boisaymé, De la peine de mort, de la probabilité mathematique des jugements de la justice criminelle en Toscane (Marseilles, 1863), pp. 48–49.

The problem was compounded when smaller children sat in the arms of their mothers. The presence of women at executions was also increasingly criticised. In a poem written in 1843 Louis Schoonen expressed his abhorrence at seeing young women with soft faces eagerly awaiting the execution.[46] Was this response because violence could not be reconciled with the ideal of a tender and beautiful woman? Executed prisoners were now a predominantly male group: not least because those women who had killed their own children were increasingly less likely to receive death sentences. Intramural executions often excluded all women from executions. This happened in various German states, where, when intramural executions were introduced, women were no longer allowed to attend executions, other than their own.[47] It seems that this was also the case in Sweden: Anna Månsdotter, executed in 1890, is the only woman known to have attended an intramural execution and there are no indications of others.[48]

The Prussian penal code of 1851 stated that twelve representatives of the local municipality should be present at an intramural execution.[49] A similar provision was included in Swedish legislation from 1877. From the nine executions that took place between 1879 and 1910, one can see changes in how municipalities implemented the law. Rather many witnesses were selected to attend the four executions up to 1890 (10, 10, 12, and 13 respectively). Various professions were represented, although writers, medical professionals, members of the military and policemen seem to have been most frequently selected for the duty. Of the five remaining executions, witnesses were only selected in two cases: Gävle selected two in 1893 and Västerås five in 1900. The state also admitted professionals with some kind of legitimate interest in executions and this might have been one reason why some cities refrained from selecting witnesses. However, such decisions also related to opinions about capital punish-

---

46 Louis Schoonen, "Iambe. Contre l'application de la peine capitale et surtout contre l'application en public" in: *La Belgique judiciaire* col 655–656, Bruxelles, 1843.
47 Evans, *Rituals of Retribution*, pp. 313–14.
48 Bergman, "The Penalty of Death and Executions", p. 99.
49 Albert Friedrich Berner, *Die Strafgesetzgebung in Deutschland vom Jahre 1751 bis zum Gegenwart* (Aalen, 1978), p. 247; cf. Evans, *Rituals of Retribution*, p. 305; Bergman, *Dödsstraffet, kyrkan och staten i Sverige från 1700-tal till 1900-tal*, p. 93.

ment. When, in 1910, the city council of Stockholm decided not to send any representatives to the execution of Alfred Ander, its decision was preceded by a debate on capital punishment in general, during which nobody suggested that municipal witnesses should be required to attend.[50]

Often legislation on intramural executions listed some of those who should or could attend executions in an official capacity. The clergy who prepared the condemned prisoners are among those listed, even in states, such as Prussia and Hamburg, that had previously restricted clerical presence.[51] It seems that many of the clergy would rather have been somewhere else. In Sweden agreements had been in place since at least the mid-eighteenth century, which allowed a prison chaplain to receive an extra salary, paid by his colleagues, if he undertook the responsibility of preparations and executions, thereby relieving others of such duties. There were also instances of priests doing whatever they could to avoid the task.[52]

The presence of officers of the court, the prison and the provincial administration was also mandatory, and in Swedish parliamentary debates such officers raised the issue of executions on several occasions. In 1865 a county secretary proposed that the guillotine be adopted in order to reduce the revolting impression made by the execution. In a bill to abolish capital punishment introduced by a large number of members in 1912, one argument presented in support of the measure concerned the liberation of civil servants from their horrible duties. Three years earlier a county secretary and a prison governor had described how their own experiences had increased their resentment of, and revulsion towards, the death penalty.[53]

Thus, ideally no members of the public, no witnesses, no clergymen and no officials should attend executions. Who then, would be present?

50 Bergman, *Dödsstraffet, kyrkan och staten i Sverige från 1700-tal till 1900-tal*, p. 93; Bergman, "The Penalty of Death and Executions", pp. 103 ff.
51 *Verordnung über die Vollziehung von Todesstrafen Beliebt durch Rath- und Burgerschluß vom 19. October 1854, Auf Befehl Eines Hochedlen Raths der freien und Hansestadt Hamburg publicirt den 20. October 1854* (Hamburg 1854) § 4; *Hinrichtung des Raub- und Doppelmörders Wilhelm Timm, mit der Guilliotine am 10 april 1856*, Morgens 6 Uhr (Hamburg s a); Evans, *Rituals of Retribution*, p. 305.
52 Bergman, *Dödsstraffet, kyrkan och staten i Sverige från 1700-tal till 1900-tal*, pp. 134 ff., 145–146.
53 Bergman, *Dödsstraffet, kyrkan och staten i Sverige från 1700-tal till 1900-tal*, pp. 82, 100–101; Bergman, "The Penalty of Death and Executions", p. 106.

The condemned? Even here one faces problems, at least in Sweden. Johanna Berndtsdotter in 1858 asked to be executed at a different location out of concern for her relatives, who lived near the execution site. Her application was granted.[54] Twenty years earlier, in 1838, Bengta Olsdotter had sought relief for her family. She believed they should be spared from seeing the smoke of her burning body. Her sentence was reduced to simple beheading.[55] Ultimately, in a strange letter, seven relatives of Charlotta Larsdotter, executed in 1861, pled for her pardon. Their main argument and concern was not Charlotta's situation but that her execution would add to their predicament and that they thereby would inherit dishonour and shame.[56]

Many scenarios and interpretations were attached to executions, and thus there are rival or, rather, complementary truths to be presented. The contrast with Laqueur's view at the beginning of this article should thus not be seen as questioning his results, but, rather, as an example of how careful one must be before interpreting any knowledge as a general fact. In this article many "rules" have been broken: examples have been taken from eight countries and across more than 300 years. This is not the kind of rigorous comparison that theory often demands. Sometimes, however, one should attempt to take a sweeping and provocative approach. In doing so, one should exercise care and consider the limitations of this kind of general survey, in which certain common elements and ideas from several countries are presented.

Thus, what is this article all about? It has examined an execution process that conveyed a message of order and deterrence but also hope; an execution process in which part of the message sometimes became counterproductive; an execution process which fell into ruin when it was redefined by the state and the space for ecclesiastical interpreta-

---

54 Bergman, *Dödsstraffet, kyrkan och staten i Sverige från 1700-tal till 1900-tal*, p. 125, Bergman 2001 pp. 106–107.
55 Letter from Bengta Olsdotter to the King in council 30 August 1838, utslagshandlingar 4 December 1838, statsrådsprotokoll i justitieärende 4 December 1838, Nedre Justitierevisionens arkiv, Riksarkivet, Stockholm.
56 Undated letter from Johannes Larsson et al to the King in council (arrived 25 February 1861) utslagshandlingar 5 July 1861, cf. letter from the governor in Jönköping to the King in council 11 July 1861 utslagshandlingar 23 July 1861, Nedre Justitierevisionens arkiv, Riksarkivet, Stockholm.

tions diminished; an execution process that soon lost its meaning after the idea of death as an abstraction became the only remnant of the execution preserved by the state; an execution process soon abhorred by many; an execution process that constructed a foundation for what it called a modern execution process in which the dehumanisation of the condemned was an important characteristic.

Sources

ARCHIVAL SOURCES

Antwerpen
  Rijksarchief Antwerpen, Provinciearchief Antwerpen 1794– c. 1865, A Franse Tijdvak 1794–1814 121 9°–10° Strafuitvoeringen.
Borås
  Borås stadsarkiv, Rådhusrätten och magistraten i Borås arkiv, 54:4871 Rådstuvurättens dombok 1724–1727.
Gent
  Rijksarchief Gent, Provincial Archief Oost-Vlaanderen 1830–1850, vol 945 (1853/2) Dossier betreffen een opslagsplats voor schavotten 1819–1847.
  Provincial Archief Oost-Vlaanderen 1851–1870, (1330/4) Stukken en corr. betreffende de huur van een opslagsruimte voor gerechtinstrumenten 1855–1856.
Helsingfors
  Riksarkivet, Nylands länskontors arkiv, Ea3 Ankomna brev 1733.
Lund
  Landsarkivet i Lund, Fångvårdsanstalten i Kristianstad, DId:1 Dagböcker över prästeliga förrättningar 1875–1891.
Stockholm
  Riksarkivet, Nedre Justitierevisionens arkiv, Statsrådsprotokoll i justitieärende 1838. Utslagshandlingar 1838, 1861.
  Styrelsen över fängelser och arbetsinrättningar i rikets arkiv, EVI 8 Inkomna religionsberättelser 1859.
Uppsala
  Uppsala universitetsbibliotek, Gustavianska samlingen, F 521 Bref från H E Riksdrotzet Grefve Carl Axel Wachtmeister.
  Nordinska samlingen, 1398 Juridica Straff- och Missgärningsbalken III.
Vadstena
  Göta hovrätts arkiv; Huvudarkivet, B IIa:294 Brottmålsutslag Sc divisionen 1845.
  Konga häradsrätts arkiv, AIa:133 Dombok 1845 höstting.
  Kronofogden i Kinnevalds och Norrvidinge härads fögderi, vol 120 Handl. ang. tingshus, tingsplats, häkte och afrättsplats.

LITERATURE

Abegg, Julius Friedrich Heinrich 1996: *Lehrbuch des gemeinen Criminal-Prozesses mit besonderer Berücksichtigung des Preussischen Rechts*. Goldbach.

Andersson, Djos Per 1849: *Testamente från Stupstocken eller strödda anteckningar ur en dödsfånges lefnad*. Upsala.

Andersson, Hans 1998: *"Androm till varnagel...", det tidigmoderna Stockholms folkliga rättskultur i ett komparativt perspektiv*. Stockholm.

Ausführliche Beschreibung der Hegung des Hochnothpeinlichen Hals-Gerichts, und insorderheit wie es von E E Hochweisen Rathe zu Leipzig nach römischer Sitte, mit allen Umständen und Zeremonien geheget und gehalten wird 1798. Heilbronn.

Badinter, Robert 1973: *L'exécution*. S l.

Bérenger, Alphonse 1855: *De la répression pénale, de ses formes et de ses effets*. Paris.

Bergman, Martin 1996: *Dödsstraffet, kyrkan och staten i Sverige från 1700-tal till 1900-tal*. Lund.

Bergman, Martin 2001: The Penalty of Death and Executions: the Tension between National Government, Local Authorities and Population in *Guises of Power: Integration of Society and Legitimation of Power in Sweden and Southern Low Countries ca 1500–1900*, ed. Maria Ågren, Åsa Karlsson and Xavier Rousseaux. Uppsala, pp. 91–108.

Berner, Albert Friedrich 1978: *Die Strafgesetzgebung in Deutschland vom Jahre 1751 bis zum Gegenwart*. Aalen.

Bessler, John D. 1997: *Death in the Dark: Midnight Executions in America*. Boston.

Boisaymé, J. M. J. A. 1863: *De la peine de mort, de la probabilité mathematique des jugements de la justice criminelle en Toscane*. Marseilles.

Bowersock, Glenn W. 1995: *Martyrdom and Rome*. Cambridge.

Butterweck, Christel 1995: *"Martyriumsucht" in der Alten Kirche? Studien zur Darstellung und Deutung frühchristlicher Martyrier*. Tübingen.

Carpzov, Benedictus 1677: *Practicæ novæ imperialis saxonicæ rerum criminalum III*. Wittenberg and Frankfurt.

Chauveau, Adolphe and Hélie, Faustin 1887: *Théorie du code pénal, annotée...par Edmond Villey* vol i. Paris.

Chronologisk Register over de Kongelige Forordningar og obne Breve som fra Aar 1670 af ere udkomne, tilligemed et nøiagtigt udtog af de endnu gieldende, for saavidt samme i Almindelighed angaaende Undersaaterne i Danmark og Norge, forsynet med et alphabetisk Register ved Jacob Henric Schou V 1795. København.

Chydenius, Anders s a: *Tal, hållit på Afrättsplatsen i Kronoby...då Soldaterna Matts Hjelt, Abraham Frodig och Peter Lindström för begånget mord, rån och mordbränneri uppå Barnaläraren wid Teirijärwi Cappel, Johan Mattson och dess Hustru, til följe af Höglofl Kongl Wasa Hof-Rätts Dom, miste högra handen, halshöggos och steglades den 12 April 1786*. Wasa.

Claeys, Prosper 1893: *Le bourreau de Gand, sa mission, ses fonctions, ses privilèges*. Gand.

Chur-Braunschweig-Lüneburgische Landes-Ordnungen und Gesetze II..., Zum Gebrauch Der Fürstenthümer, Graf- und Herrschafften Calenbergischen Theils 1740. Göttingen.

Delarue, Jacques 1979: *Le métier de bourreau*. Paris.

Den svenska kyrkoordningen 1571 jämte studier kring tillkomst, innehåll och användning 1971, ed. Sven Kjöllerström. Lund.

Evans, Richard J. 1997: *Rituals of Retribution: Capital punishment in Germany 1600–1987.* London.
Franke, Herman 1981: Over beschaving en de afschaffing van het schavot. – *Amsterdam sociologisch Tijdschrift* 8 1981, pp. 199–253.
Förslag till Allmän Criminal-Lag 1832. Stockholm.
Gatrell, V. A. C. 1994: *The Hanging Tree: Execution and the English People 1770–1868.* Oxford.
Gjellebøl, Jacob Elisius 1861: *Spildte Guds Ord paa Balle-Lars.* Næstved.
Grolman, Karl 1970: *Grundsätze der Criminalrechtswissenschaft nebst einer systematischen Darstellung des Geistes der Deutschen Criminalgesetze.* Glashütten im Taunus.
Gudenrath, Jacob Just 1792: Mine Skrupler over Selvmords Moralitet, og over dets Straffældighed efter de borgelige Love – *Maanedskriftet Iris* (København), pp.250–266.
Jacques Joseph Haus 1867: *La peine de mort, son passé, son présent, son avenir.* Gand.
Het Handelsblad van Antwerpen 1847, 1862. Antwerpen.
Hinrichtung des Raub- und Doppelmörders Wilhelm Timm, mit der Guilliotine am 10 april 1856, Morgens 6 Uhr s a. Hamburg.
Hommels, Karl Ferdinand 1778: [Anmerkungen]. In Beccaria, Cesare Bonesana: *Des Herren...unsterbliches Werk von Verbrechen und Strafen.* Breslau.
Jansson, Arne 1994: Mörda för att få dö. In *Människovärdet och makten: Om civiliseringsprocessen i Stockholm 1600–1850,* ed. Arne Jarrick and Johan Söderberg. Stockholm, pp. 21–52.
Jansson, Arne 1998: *From Swords to Sorrow: Homicide and Suicide in Early Modern Stockholm.* Stockholm.
Kaspersson, Maria 2000: *Dödligt våld i Stockholm på 1500-, 1700- och 1900-talen.* Stockholm.
Kjöllerström, Sven 1957: *Guds och Sveriges lag under reformationstiden, en kyrkorättslig studie.* Lund.
Kongl. Maj:ts Förordning Angående Dödsfångars och andre Missgierningsmäns klädebonad wid deras afstraffande. Gifwen Stockholm i Rådskammaren then 12 Decembris 1741 s a. Stockholm.
Krause, Thomas 1991: *Die Strafrechtspflege im Kurfürstentum und Königreich Hannover, vom Ende des 17. bis zum ersten Drittel des 19. Jahrhunderts.* Aalen.
Krogh, Tyge 2000: *Oplysningstiden og det magiske, henrettelser og korporlige straffe i 1700-tallets første halvdel.* København.
Krogh, Tyge 2012: *A Lutheran Plague, Murdering to Die in the Eighteenth Century.* Leiden.
Die peinliche Gerichtordnung Kaiser Karls V Constitutio Criminalis Carolina 1900, ed. Josef Köhler and Willy Scheel. Halle.
La Belgique judiciaire 1851. Bruxelles.
Laqueur, Thomas W. 1989: Crowds, carnival and the state in English executions, 1604–1868. In *The First Modern Society: Essays in English History in Honour of Lawrence Stone,* ed. A. L. Beier, David Cannadine and James M. Rosenheim. Cambridge, pp. 305–355.
Lebrun, François 1971: *Les hommes et la mort en Anjou aux 17e et 18e siècles: essai de démographie et de psychologie historiques.* Paris.
Lehmann, Max 1883: *Preussen und die katholische Kirche seit 1640, nach den Acten des Geheimen Staatsarchives, IV von 1758 bis 1775.* Leipzig.

Le Précurseur, Journal Politique, Commercial, Maritime et Littéraire 1862. Antwerpen.

Levander, Lars 1975: *Brottsling och bödel*. Stockholm.

L'Indépendance belge 1862. Bruxelles.

Linebaugh, Peter 1977: The Ordinary of Newgate and his Account. In *Crime in England 1500–1800*, ed. J. S. Cockburn. Princeton, pp. 246–269.

Locard, Edmond 1939: Le crime sans cause. *La Giustizia Penale* 45, I. 1939, pp. 411–422.

Allgemeinen Landrecht für die Preussischen Staaten Bd 7 Th II 1838, ed. Adolph Julius Mannkopff. Berlin.

Martschukat, Jürgen 2000: *Inszeniertes Töten, Eine Geschichte der Todesstrafe vom 17. bis zum 19. Jahrhundert*. Köln.

Mauger, Jacques 1904: Journal. In *Recueil de Journaux Caennais 1661–1777*, ed. Gabriel Vanel. Rouen, pp. 111–294.

Merriman, John M. 1991: The *Margins of City Life: Explorations of the French Urban Frontier 1815–1851*. New York.

Michaëlis, Johann David 1792: *Moral* II. Göttingen.

Müller, Georg Friedrich 1789: *Das Krieges- oder Soldatenrecht, so wie solches in älten und neuen Zeiten vornehmnlich bey der Königl. Preußl. Armee, und in den Gerichten sämtlicher Preußl. Staaten gesetzlich, üblich und gewöhnlich ist* II. Berlin.

Münchener-Intelligenzblatt 1780. München.

Corpus Constitutionum Marchicarum oder Königl. Preußis. und Churfürstl. Brandenburgischer sonderlich in der Chur- und Mark- Brandenburg, auch incorporirten Landen publicirten und ergangenen Ordnungen, Edicta, Mandata & Rescripta Von Zieten Friedrichs I Churfürsten zu Brandenburg, & bis ietzo unter der Regierung Friedrich Wilhelms König in Preussen & ad annum 1736 inclusive Mit allergn. Bewilligung colligiret und ans Licht gegeben II, 3 s a, ed. Christian Otto Mylius. Berlin.

Neues Archiv für Sächsische Geschichte und Alterthumskunde 9 1888. Dresden.

Neues Hannöverisches Magazin 1800. Hannover.

Nya Dagligt Allehanda 1893. Stockholm.

Novum Corpus Constitutionum Prussico-Brandenburgensium Praecipue Marchicarum oder Neue Sammlung Königl. Preuß. und Churfürstl. Brandenburgischer sonderlich in der Chur- und Mark- Brandenburg publicirten und ergangenen Ordnungen, Edicten, Mandaten, Rescripten &c &c von 1766, 1767, 1768, 1769, und 1770, IV 1766–1770 1771. Berlin.

Olearius, Johann Christian 1692: *Geistliches Hand-Buch der Kinder Gottes* 1692. Leipzig.

The Statues at Large from the 23d to the 26th year of King George II xx 1765, ed. Danby Pickering. Cambridge.

Preisendörfer, Bruno 2000: *Staatsbildung als Königskunst, Ästhetik und Herrschaft im preußischen Absolutismus*. Berlin.

Quistorp, Johan Christian 1782 *Ausführliche Entwurf zu einem Gesetzbuch in peinlichen und Strafsachen*. Rostock.

Roumieu, Cyprien 1833: *Plus d'échafauds! ou de l'abolition immédiate et absolue de la peine de mort*. Paris.

Royal Commission on Capital Punishment 1949–1953 1953: *Report*. London.

Sainte Croix, Geoffrey de 2006: *Christian Persecution, Martyrdom, and Orthodoxy*, ed. Michael Whitby and Joseph Streeter. Oxford.

Sarat, Austin 2001: *When the State Kills: Capital Punishment and the American Condition*. Princeton.

Sarat, Austin 2001: Killing Me Softly: Capital Punishment and the Technologies for Taking Life. In *Pain, Death, and the Law*, ed. Austin Sarat. Ann Arbor.

Schoonen, Louis 1843: Iambe. Contre l'application de la peine capitale et surtout contre l'application en public. In *La Belgique judiciaire*. Bruxelles, pp. 655–656.

Tait, Clodagh 2001: Adored for Saints: Catholic Martyrdom in Ireland c. 1560–1655. *Journal of Early Modern History* 5 2001, pp. 128–159.

Tittman, Carl August 1822: Das gerichtliche Verfahren bei Vollziehung der Todesstrafen. In *Neues Archiv des Criminalrechts VI*. Halle.

Verordnung über die Vollziehung von Todesstrafen Beliebt durch Rath- und Burgerschluß vom 19. October 1854, Auf Befehl Eines Hochedlen Raths der freien und Hansestadt Hamburg publicirt den 20. October 1854 1854. Hamburg.

Viguerie, Jean de 2003: *Louis XVI: Le roi bienfaisant*. Monaco.

Wakefield, Edward Gibbon 1831: *Facts relating to the punishment of death in the metropolis*. London.

Wright, Gordon 1983: *Between the Guillotine and Liberty: Two Centuries of the Crime Problem in France*. New York.

Amnesty or Individual Pardons?

Presidential Pardon as a Measure to Control Those Punished as a Result of Disciplinary Proceedings in Finland in 1918

Virpi Anttonen

For years there has been speculation within the Finnish media about whether specific pardons should have been issued by the Finnish president of the day. Pardons have, over the years, been used in many different ways. As a constitutional institution (with a particular form, process and substance), the presidential pardon embodies many moral, political, economic and legal choices and values. Although the procedure has changed over the course of time, pardoning itself can still be understood as a triangular process involving the "king", the convicted party and any potential appellants among the victim's kin.

With its roots in the prerogatives of a sovereign prince, the presidential pardon does not seem to fit well with the idea of the separation of powers or the democratic *Rechtsstaat*, that is, the constitutionally governed state. However, for centuries the power of pardon has been a regular feature of penal justice and a useful way, in exceptional cases, to correct unfairness, error and inequity within different levels of the state. Correspondingly, the power of pardon has also been abused or perverted by personal favour or political expediency. Nevertheless, the regular and continuing use of this power in individual cases – in effect the use of the presidential pardon as a means of determining which offenders should not be (fully) subjected to normal penalties – could function as a substitute for administrative discretion both in judicial decisions and in legislation, whilst at the same time undermining the predictability of punishment.

The pardon, as an essential part of a penal system, cannot easily be detached from the history of crime and control, at least not if we wish to find definitions for different types of homicides or to study the use of capital punishment. In addition to granting mercy to those who had committed serious criminal offences, the power of pardon has been used for political purposes, as well as to strengthen the military (through the recruitment of offenders). For example, when kings campaigned to extend their special protection, the king's firm peace, in England before 1307, the prerogative of pardon was needed in order to provide a safeguard against the resistance of subjects, as their ruler repressed crime by laying down a more severe penalty policy.[1] In thirteenth-century England capital punishment was the penalty for most serious crimes and criminals were pardoned before trial[2] or for military purposes.[3] As a result of this policy, heretics were burnt, poisoners boiled and pirates drowned, although hanging was the punishment chosen for most serious offenders. By the sixteenth century the Tudor monarchs of England exercised their prerogative of, more or less unrestricted, pardon as a tool of state formation. Although the significance of mercy depended on its proper presentation – on a mixture of humility, repentance, submission and reciprocity – pardons could also be invalidated, as they were conditional upon the recipients' continued good behaviour.[4]

---

1. The policy was carried out by reserving pleas of culpable and accidental homicides, homicides carried out in self-defence, sudden deaths from natural causes, suicides and accidental deaths, to the king's hearing only. The recipients of the pardons had to stand to right and to produce their pardons before the itinerant justices. See Naomi D. Hurnard, *The King's Pardon for Homicide Before A.D. 1307* (Oxford, 1969), pp. 13–14, 23, 246.
2. See Hurnard, *The King's Pardon for Homicide Before A.D. 1307*, p. 246. Hunard studied 1,900 pardons recorded in patent rolls from 1226 to mid-1294, of this total 93 percent related to homicides and 7 percent to other felonies.
3. King Edward I of England granted pardons to outlaws, fugitives and prisoners in order that they could undertake for military service from 1294 to 1303; however, this was never intended to be a permanent policy. See Hurnard, *The King's Pardon for Homicide Before A.D. 1307*, pp. 248–49.
4. See K. J. Kesserling, *Mercy and Authority in the Tudor State* (Cambridge University Press 2007), pp. 1–3.

If royal pardons in medieval England were used to lay down more severe penalties, more or less the opposite was true in the Grand Duchy of Finland (under Russian rule) during the nineteenth century. The power of pardon helped to ease the implementation of the new and more lenient Penal Code[5] of 1889. The old Swedish Code of 1734 had formed the harsh basis of criminal legislation within Finland even under Russian rule. Through the first reformation of legislation that took place in the 1860s, sentences of capital punishment for involuntary manslaughter and infanticide were abolished.[6] Two decades later saw a more appropriate time to introduce a second set of reforms: pillory, corporal punishments and capital penalties (except for regicide or high treason) were all abolished under the new Finnish Penal code. Penal scales were introduced at the same time; imprisonment was to be the main form of punishment from now on. Under these circumstances, the pardon played an essential part in the implementation of the new parole system in Finland. It was also regularly used to mitigate existing severe punishments into the more lenient forms of punishment introduced by the new regulations.[7] For many decades in Finland the power of royal pardon also provided a way of increasing settlement in Siberia. Able-bodied vagrants, both male and female, who had been sentenced to years of hard labour in prisons or workhouses would occasionally be pardoned and released so that they could "settle" in Siberia.[8]

Somehow, no matter how harsh these early modern penalty systems were or how much the use of mercy were criticized, the people – subjects – seemed to insist that their ruler, as a just sovereign, had *both a*

---

5 Rikoslaki (Finnish Penal Code) 19 November 1889 came into force in Finland in 1894.
6 See, for example, Toomas Kotkas, "Pardoning in Nineteenth-Century Finland at the Interface of Early Modern and Modern Criminal Law", *Rechtsgeschicte*, 10 (2007), p. 157.
7 See Kotkas, "Pardoning in Nineteenth-Century Finland", pp. 154–156. The Imperial Degree of 1826 (issued by Nicholas I of Russia) made royal pardons more or less automatic in excusable slayings. Additionally, capital punishments were almostalways mitigated to fixed-term or life sentences of hard labour in a fortress in Finland or in a factory or mine in Siberia (ibid., p. 158).
8 For example, in 1841 there were 384 petitions for mercy. Pardon was granted to seventy-four appellants, of whom fifty-nine were vagrants. In 1861 pardon was granted to seventy-four vagrants, who were to receive "a fresh start" as settlers in Siberia. In addition, thirty-six other offenders were also pardoned and sent to Siberia. For more details, see Kotkas, "*Suosiosta ja armosta*": *Tutkimus armahdusoikeuden historiasta autonomian ajan Suomessa* (Helsinki, 2003), pp. 166–171; Kotkas, "Pardoning in Nineteenth-Century Finland at the Interface of Early Modern and Modern Criminal Law", pp. 155–157.

right and a duty to temper justice with mercy, especially during and after periods of rebellion.[9] Kesserling argues that the use of pardons after riots and revolts generally maintained the feudalistic social order. Such a conclusion may have validity in relation to the policy of amnesties and pardons issued during and after the American Civil War (1861–1865), but is it useful in an analysis of the policy carried out after the Finnish Civil War in 1918?[10]

Up until the twentieth century, royal pardons were largely granted to offenders who had committed felonies.[11] So, why in 1919 were pardons granted to scores of state servants who had been dismissed on disciplinary grounds (rather than to traditional offenders)? Were no felonies committed at this time? As a result of the Civil War of 1918 around 2,000 railway officials with permanent appointments were dismissed following disciplinary proceedings. My main argument is that the power of pardon was used as a means of gaining control over those servants of the state whose political loyalty had been called into question either during or after the Civil War. The use of the presidential pardon provided an effective means of controlling the future behaviour of such individuals. An examination of how the presidential pardon took shape – and in particular how the first President of the Republic exercised his

---

9 Negotiations for pardon after riots and revolts were used in early modern England to determine who would live and die. The system was based on traditions of mercy and good lordship, in which this kind of action was taken for granted. As a result of this, mercy became something that could be traded; the sovereign could combine punishment of the leaders with pardons of the rank. See Kesserling, *Mercy and Authority in the Tudor State*, pp. 163–165.

10 The first release of American political prisoners and others held in military custody on parole took place in February 1862. If someone had been indicted for treason, he could *take the oath of allegiance* and receive a pardon. The pardon had to be presented in a court along with a plea in order for the indictment to be dismissed and the defendant discharged. The Proclamation of Amnesty and Reconstruction of December 1863 offered a general pardon with certain exceptions and outlined President Lincoln's plan by which the seceded states could be restored to the Union. For more details, see Jonathan Truman Dorris, *Pardon and Amnesty under Lincoln and Johnson: The Restoration of the Confederates to Their Rights and Privileges, 1861–1898* (Chapel Hill, NC: 1953), pp. 10–12, 34–37.

11 Offences like arson, mayhem, rape, robbery, burglary, larceny, harbouring felons, forest offences, counterfeiting and clipping coins, breaches of the peace and of trading regulations, and breaches of feudal rules such as marriages of heiresses are mentioned by Hurnard in "The King's Pardon for Homicide before A.D. 1307", pp. 245–246. In Finland in 1841 offences like murder, manslaughter, infanticide, larceny, arson, robbery, forgery, coinage offence, smuggling, breaches upon oath or the peace of the church, illegal meeting of devotion and vagrancy were dealt with. For more details, see Kotkas, "Suosiosta ja armosta", pp. 159–170.

power of pardon (as outlined in the Constitution Act[12] of 1919) – allows us to understand this argument more fully. In approaching this subject I have made use of a letter written by a former junior engine driver, in which he petitions for his outstanding claims to be resolved. This letter leads us first to the essence of the disciplinary proceedings and the measures that were taken in Finland after the Civil War; and then to the pardons granted the first Finnish president (and his predecessor, Regent Mannerheim). In addition to this and other letters, I have also consulted contemporary documents produced by the Finnish authorities and other literature. If one agrees with many Finnish legal scholars that each presidential pardon should be granted individually, after the judgements which have gained legal force, the various ways in which the pardoning system operated in practice in 1919 obviously shaped the guidelines of this procedure over the course of decades.

Junior engine driver Arthur's letter

Former junior engine driver Arthur[13], who served at the Finnish Railway Depot in St. Petersburg from 1904 until 1917, forwarded a letter detailing his outstanding claims to a special board at the Ministry of Finance in 1947. In his letter Arthur set out the details of his case as follows:

> I left St. Petersburg and arrived in Finland at the beginning of July 1918. I had to stay at a quarantine camp in Terijoki for two weeks, during which time the Finnish frontier authorities heard my case. It was concluded that I had not taken any part in politics at the time of the Civil War or participated in any other activities that went beyond my official duties. Being back in Finland, I travelled directly to Helsinki, where my first priority was to clarify

---

12 Section 29 of the repealed Constitution Act (Suomen Hallitusmuoto 94/1919) of Finland stated that the President of the Republic could, after obtaining a statement from the Supreme Court, grant full or partial pardon in the case of an individual whose penalty had been imposed by a court.
13 I have chosen to call the engine driver by the English name "Arthur", as one of his Christian names was "Artturi".

my activities as the treasurer of the Provisions Committee of the Railway Employees in St. Petersburg [...] At this time I transferred the means and the accounts that were still in my possession. In recognition of my merits and actions – and because of many cases of disloyalty – I was given a certificate of loyalty and confidence in order to be able to travel without hindrance. (I indeed needed this certificate when I travelled by train: they arrested me once at Riihimäki, but I was released straight away because this document stated that I was loyal to the government.) I then announced myself to the director of the Engine Department. He told me that he would contact me at a later date, and so I travelled to my place of residence and waited for the promised message.

At the beginning of September, without any previous notice, I received a letter from the Disciplinary Board of the [Finnish] Railways. [It stated that] I had already been removed from my office as a result of disciplinary proceedings on 1 March 1918; I had been charged with improper behaviour in office. The decision was a purely biased judgment, as no hearing was conducted and I was offered no opportunity to defend myself. At once I applied for a Presidential Pardon, enclosing in the letter the original decision of the Disciplinary Board and the aforementioned certificate of loyalty. I was granted a pardon on 8 May 1920. Meanwhile I had started work as a filer at the Engineering Works in Pasila Depot, this happened on 4 March 1919. Later, on 1 August 1925, I was appointed sub-foreman. I had been suspended for 7 years and one month. [...] As one can see, my dismissal was an entirely unjustified measure. All the political passions and the discretion of that time are evident in the [disciplinary] measure taken [against me]: all those with dissenting opinions were considered outlaws.[14]

14 Kansallisarkisto, KA (National Archives), Valtiovarainministeriön arkisto, VVM (The Archives of the Ministry of Finance), in Ejc:1 1947–1949, petition E.1196, received on 22 July 1947. Original letter written in Finnish, English translation by the author.

What conditions did Arthur face on his return to Finland? The Civil War in Finland broke out in January 1918, shortly after the declaration of independence in 1917. Fighting between the "Whites" and "Reds" ended in May 1918. Both parties had been guilty of various acts of violence and terror both during and after the conflict. Once it became apparent that they could secure power,[15] the "Whites" began a general purge. The situation was not easy for those with permanent positions who had served the Finnish government and had remained in their official districts during the war, as many railway servants had done. Not all of them lived to see peace.[16] Across Finland there were also shortages of food goods, money, housing and work, all of which compounded ordinary people's suffering. New laws were introduced to punish those who had set themselves against the government during the war.[17] However, the parliament that passed these laws in May 1918 was substantially diminished: 89 of its 200 members were missing.[18] In the meantime thousands of people were detained in temporary prison colonies as political prisoners, and hundreds of people were shot in mass executions. The new state and political life seemed to be in chaos.[19]

Arthur had lived and worked in St. Petersburg for fifteen years.[20] He

---

15 The turning point seems to have been the Battle of Tampere in March and in April 1918. See, for example, Heikki Ylikangas, *Tie Tampereelle: dokumentoitu kuvaus Tampereen antautumiseen johtaneista sotatapahtumista Suomen sisällissodassa 1918* (Porvoo; Helsinki; Juva, 1993).

16 See, example, *Valtionrautatiet 1912–1937* [Official History of the Finnish State Railways] (Helsinki, 1937), pp. 34–40, for information and photographs of sixty-eight railway "servants" who died serving the "legal" government in Finland. Of this total thirty-five were reported to have been "murdered" in 1918.

17 One of the acts, dated 29 May 1918, covered the establishment of the Special Tribunals and a Superior Tribunal for Political Offences in 1918. These tribunals were abolished by the Act 39 on 2 April 1919, but remained in operation until the end of May 1920. Another important act regulated the new system; punishments could be suspended for probational periods.

18 Only 111 members of parliament were present: all except one of the left-wing members had disappeared, died or fled the country, or were being held in custody awaiting trial.

19   Many have estimated that at least 74,000 "Reds" were detained in the prison colonies and that at least 11,000 of them died of hunger or disease in the summer of 1918. Most punishments were pronounced by Special Tribunals for Political Offences, established under the act of 29 May 1918. See, for example, Jukka Kekkonen, *Laillisuuden haaksirikko* (Helsinki: 1991) and Jaakko Paavolainen, *Poliittiset väkivaltaisuudet Suomessa 1918 osa I* [Political Violence in Finland 1918 Part One] and *Poliittiset väkivaltaisuudet Suomessa 1918 osa II* [Political Violence in Finland 1918 Part Two] (Helsinki, 1967).

20 The first railway section Valkeasaari–St. Petersburg was built and governed by the Finnish State; the surrounding area was governed by the Russian revolutionary government. In 1917 around 714 civil servants lived and worked in St. Petersburg. Of these 640 were railway servants who worked either at the depot in St. Petersburg (549) or on the first section (91). For more details about Finnish civil servants in St. Petersburg in the 1910s, see Max Engman, *Pietarinsuomalaiset* (Juva: 2004), pp. 178–180.

and his family had a permanent residence there, but they had to leave their belongings behind when they returned to Finland in July 1918.[21] Unbeknownst to Arthur, the decision to dismiss him – on the grounds of improper behaviour while in office – had already been taken in March 1918, while he was still living in St. Petersburg. Another engine driver also returned to Finland in July 1918. Before his return he had been denounced and was subsequently arrested in Vyborg. After being held in pre-trial custody for five weeks, he was acquitted: the accusation against him was deemed to be unfounded. His case file is a little confusing. It seems that he was in fact dismissed at least three times: in March 1918 by the Board of the State Railways, again in August by a town court and finally by the Disciplinary Board of the State Railways in January 1919.[22]

At the outbreak of the Russian revolution in November 1917, the Finnish state ordered her civil servants in Russia to remain in their official districts and protect the property of the state.[23] Because of the conflict, no one could be sure what Finnish state employees in Russia were doing at this time. This made many Finnish authorities suspicious, especially after the outbreak of the Finnish Civil War. Arthur was one of thirty railway servants who were dismissed in March 1918 because they worked either on the railway section St. Petersburg–Valkeasaari or in the Finnish Railway Station (in St. Petersburg). Since December 1917 both the section and station had been governed by Russian authorities.

When Arthur arrived in Finland in July 1918 the Civil War was over. Instead of returning to work on the railways, he was notified of his dismissal. Arthur's expression that he applied for a presidential pardon "at once" sounds a little vague. In the first place, it seems that the first petitions from civil servants dismissed on disciplinary grounds were received at the registry office of the Finnish Supreme Court on 7 December 1918, but Arthur's name is not in that diary list. Secondly, the first president was not elected until July 1919. Nevertheless, Arthur did find

---

21 After their departure, men from the local Red Guard searched the premises and appropriated all the heavy silverware that Arthur and his family had left behind. See, Valtiovarainministeriön arkisto i (VVM), in Eja:2 1933–1934 , no. 101–225.
22 KA, VVM i, E.1197, received on 22 July 1947.
23 KA, VVM i, Ejc:24; V. 1918 erotettujen rautatieläisten asioita käsittelevän neuvottelukunnan kirjelmät.

a job in March 1919, and he was pardoned in May 1920. To understand the situation in which civil servants found themselves in 1918, we need to examine the role that disciplinary proceedings played in Finland at that time.

Use of disciplinary proceedings to punish civil servants in 1918

Even under Russian rule the majority of Finnish civil servants who lived and worked in St. Petersburg in the 1900s served the Great Grand Duchy of Finland rather than Imperial Russia. Thus their official actions were also governed by the laws of Finland. In the 1910s the main difference between disciplinary proceedings and criminal procedure in Finland lay in the concept of *particular subordination,* which meant that all disciplinary sanctions were exercised by superior authorities. Disciplinary proceedings were based on the old Procedural Code (dating from eighteenth-century Sweden[24]) rather than the new Finnish Criminal Code. However, most of the administrative legislation that regulated disciplinary measures had been passed during the nineteenth-century (under Russian rule). This legislation remained part of the national legal system when Finland achieved full statehood in December 1917.[25]

During disciplinary proceedings the guidelines and principles of the prevailing criminal procedures were often not followed. Formal rules of evidence, for instance, were not applicable; any information or testimony that a superior authority believed to be relevant could be taken into consideration. The regulations concerning disqualification were not followed either, and if votes were evenly split, the president of the disciplinary board or committee had the right to settle the case. As far as the respondent was concerned, the most severe punishment – disci-

---

24 Oikeudenkäymiskaari (Procedural Code), OK 10:26. The provision OK 10:26 was not abrogated until 1997 (690/1997).
25 For example, see K. J. Ståhlberg, *Suomen hallinto-oikeus: Yleinen osa* (Helsinki, 1913), pp. 186–188; Veli-Pekka Viljanen, *Kansalaisen yleiset oikeudet: Tutkimus suomalaisen perusoikeuskäsityksen muotoutumisesta autonomiankaudella ja itsenäisyyden ensi vuosina* (Turku, 1986), pp. 77–78.

plinary dismissal from office – was enforceable irrespective of the fact that the respondent might have a right to appeal.[26] Additionally, the superior would decide whether to impose disciplinary punishments or penal sanctions either as alternative measures or simultaneously.[27] In July 1918 the Finnish Senate (later the Council of State) issued a special decree (82/1918) relating to charges brought against railway servants accused of professional misconduct or violation *during the Civil War*. Under this decree a special (temporary) disciplinary board was established, two of whose five members had to be qualified judges. Respondents did not have the right to appeal against the decisions of this special board. However, a case had to be passed to the Finnish Senate if this was requested by at least two board members.

The documents that I use as source material were all written in 1947, but the events in question took place as early as 1918. Thus, we should bear in mind that memories and descriptions may differ for various reasons. However, all petitioners in 1947 had to provide detailed accounts of the events of 1918 and their consequences. Many petitioners had lost some or all of the documents the authorities now required, and many eyewitnesses were already dead. In order to determine the state's liability for old damages, people were also asked about the disciplinary proceedings that led to their dismissal. Who had taken the final decision that they should be dismissed (was it a superior or a court?), and what grounds for dismissal had been cited? Was the petitioner suspended (either with or without salary) at any time?[28]

From the archives[29] it is possible to draw up a preliminary list of those individuals or institutions that adjudicated in cases of dismissal during and after the Civil War in 1918. I have chosen to examine the information from a sample of 60 applications, although there were more than

---

26 See Ståhlberg, *Suomen hallinto-oikeus*, pp. 191–193.
27 See Ståhlberg, *Suomen hallinto-oikeus*, pp. 194–200; Heikki Kulla, *Hallintolainkäyttö ja hallinto: Tutkimus korkeimman hallinto-oikeuden toimivallan määräytymisen oikeushistoriallisesta taustasta* (SLY no. 148; Helsinki, 1980), pp. 189–90.
28 Suspension with no pay had been common practice in 1918; the alternative was suspension with half pay.
29 There were sixty applications, of these fifty-three were approved and seven rejected. KA, VVM i Ejc:1 (21), Ejc:2 (14), Ejc:6 (5), Ejc:18 (7); V. 1918 erotettujen rautatieläisten asioita käsittelevä neuvottelukunta.

2,000 completed forms available. The following list of active parties and decision makers from different levels enables us to form a general view of the matter. It seems that most of the disciplinary dismissals that took place in 1918 were ruled upon or enforced by the Disciplinary Board of the Finnish State Railway (in twenty-one cases), the Disciplinary Board of the Postal Service (in five cases) and the Special Tribunal for Political Offences (in fourteen cases). In two cases the matter was dealt with by a local tribunal or a public court. A stationmaster, a depot foreman or a corresponding superior official had dismissed their subordinates in ten cases. Three claimants stated that they had been dismissed by "office staff", which could mean a superior or a control group/committee. Both alternatives were possible: one individual verified that Mr AS, an active member of a local "control committee", had forced him to resign from his position.[30] In three cases there was no note of dismissal in the application form at all, and in the final case one person had been shot in a mass execution without receiving any proper hearing.

Obviously the Disciplinary Board of the State Railways was the most active organization in the matter of dismissals. The board (either the ordinary or the special board) used its disciplinary authority to remove hundreds of railway employees from their posts. Many were immediately suspended in January 1918 following the outbreak of the civil war. These employees were generally given suspensions of five to six months.[31] Yet most removals from office seem to have taken place in April or May 1918, when it became more evident which one of the two parties would gain power. Those who had been suspended from work in the winter were dismissed through disciplinary proceedings during the summer and autumn of 1918. What grounds for dismissal were cited in these decisions?

30 "AS" had himself been removed from engine driver's office earlier in the spring. Perhaps as a result of this, "AS" then forced his superiors to dismiss the subject as "red", as he had long been a member of many workers association. See E.17, 9.5.1947.
31 For example, in application E.1306 (29.7.1947) the suspension was for five months and six days; in E.924 (10.7.1947) for five and a half months; and in E.1959 (9.7.1947) for only three and a half months. For example, a former fireman described how he was suspended from his post by one of his superiors in April 1918; he was subsequently arrested but was acquitted in May. His suspension continued until June 1918, when he was asked to return to work by a board of inquiry. Yet his file was "clean": no notes were added to it in 1918 (E.1200 22.7.1947).

The vital importance of the rail network as a means of transporting troops – and especially the need for trained engine drivers – becomes evident in the grounds for dismissal cited in the old personal files. Although the notes are generally brief, they provide valuable details, as can be seen in various annotations: "want of discipline", "political opinions", "participation in rebellion in 1918", "red guardsman", "entered the military service", "entered the red guard on 27 January 1918", "resigned from office himself", "unsuited for office", "promoted the rebellion movement" and "10/10.18 dismissed. Spec. Trib. for Pol. Cr. 10/10.18 for 12 yrs penitentiary and 15 yrs without civil rights"[32]. In April 1918, for example, the retreating "Reds" ordered an engine driver to drive the last train out of the station grounds. Because he followed these orders, the man was later cautioned by the disciplinary board for "collaborating with the rebels".[33] One claimant provided his own account of his dismissal: "I was forced to leave the locality on 5 May 1918, because they were forcing me to enter the White civil guard; otherwise I would have been removed from my office at once"[34]. He chose to hide in the forest rather than be forced into military service.

Interestingly the Postmaster-General in Finland seems to have taken everything very personally: he expressed his firm disapproval and reminded the recipient that he no longer enjoyed the confidence of the Postmaster-General. Only one alternative remained: removal from office.[35]

The aforementioned special tribunal[36] did not always remove a respondent from his post; the tribunal could sentence him to imprisonment and additionally strip him of his civil rights for several years. Individuals found guilty could be dismissed on disciplinary grounds. One of the results of verdicts of this kind was disciplinary dismissal from office. In cases involving pre-trial custody and immediate enforcement

---

32 The subject had first received a life sentence, which was initially mitigated to imprisonment for twelve years in penitentiary and finally to eight years in penitentiary; the subject was released on parole in April 1920. See E.830, 8.7.1947.
33 See E.258 in 1947. The man was later removed from office.
34 See E.922 (11.7.1947).
35 See E.1445 (30.7.1947).
36 For example, see Kekkonen, *Laillisuuden haaksirikko*, p. 117.

of punishment, a convicted individual could also be dismissed immediately. One of the claimants I examined was dismissed in this way,[37] while another was dismissed a week after the judicial proceedings were completed; both dismissals were issued by the Disciplinary Board.[38] Extraordinary brakeman Edward was sentenced to hard labour for six weeks by a few "actives" on a local tribunal; dismissal from office and a fixed-term imprisonment imposed by a Special Tribunal for Political Offences were imposed later the same year.[39]

In summary, Arthur was not the only railway servant who was removed from office at this time. The official history of the Finnish State Railways gives an estimate of the number of railway employees during the 1910s: 23,405 in 1916, down to 19,139 in 1918. Thus there is good reason to assume that because of the Civil War in around 2,000 railway officials with permanent posts were disciplinarily dismissed.[40] Many of the disciplinary dismissals can be criticized: the individual right to proper procedure and hearing was often denied, as was the case for brakeman Edward. In 1918 the number of "suspect" employees under investigation seems to have eventually forced the winning party to turn to summary procedures rather than proper individual hearings.

The uncertain conditions that were characteristic of the time can also be seen in Arthur's life. He had received an official document as evidence of his loyalty to the government; although this helped him to shorten the arrest at Riihimäki in the summer, it did not overturn the decision to dismiss him that had already been taken by the Disciplinary Board in March 1918. He then decided to apply for a pardon "at once", but it seems that his application was only taken up by the authorities in 1919.[41] Did the president really grant Arthur a pardon?

---

37 See E.1401, 30.7.1947, three years in penitentiary and subsequent loss of civil rights for six years.
38 See E.245 5.6.1947. At least 300 railway servants were punished by these special courts and dismissed after proceedings. See Parliamentary Session Protocol of 1923, p. 943 (Mr Kaila, Member of Parliament).
39 See VVM i, Ejc:1 E.618
40 *Valtionrautatiet 1912–1937 I*, pp. 18–20, 415–417. There were also economic reasons: the Finnish State Railway had lost 58 locomotives, and 4,552 coaches and wagons in 1918. Some of these were driven to St. Petersburg by fleeing "red" railway servants.
41 His plea for a pardon was filed as received in 1919 (A.D. 1283/292 O.M. 1919).

The process of pardoning dismissed civil servants

In his letter, Arthur states that he was pardoned by the president (although he does not explicitly name him) in May 1920. Kaarlo Juho Ståhlberg (1865–1952) was elected the first President of the Republic of Finland in July 1919 after the new Constitution Act had been passed by parliament. The Russian tsars had wielded the royal pardon in Finland without restriction – they could pardon all offences both before and after conviction. However, they were also willing to delegate part of their power to the Finnish Senate, to be used only in cases of rejection in the Grand Duchy of Finland. Mannerheim (1867–1951)[42] had exercised this unfettered power of pardon during his brief incarnation as Regent of Finland, but under the new Constitution Act the prerogative was shared between three state organs.[43] Thus, on 8 May 1920, having been advised by the Minister of Justice, President Ståhlberg ruled on Arthur's case and those of twenty-four other applicants:

> On the submission of the Minister of Justice, the President of the Republic finds it appropriate to extend mercy and allow that the rights and privileges incumbent in office should be retained by [Arthur] should he be taken back to serve any employment that the Board of Administration of the Finnish State Railways considers proper.[44]

In the file copy of the statement issued by the Supreme Court, we can see that Arthur had applied for a pardon in order to be able to re-enter the service of the state as a junior or senior engine driver. However, the pardon did not grant Arthur an absolute and positive right to return to his old position. Instead, it restored Arthur's accrued rights and privileg-

---

42 Mannerheim served as Regent of Finland from 12 December 1918 to 25 July 1919.
43 Suomen Hallitusmuoto (94/1919, § 29), stated that the President of the Republic could, after obtaining a statement from the Supreme Court, grant full or partial pardon in an individual case of a penalty imposed by a court of law. An amnesty and the question of abolition came under the jurisdiction of parliament.
44 Oikeusministeriö (The Ministry of Justice, OM), Tasavallan Presidentin esittely (Presentations brought before the President), 8 May 1920. Translated by the author.

es, *if* he ever returned to his previous post or to some other official position within the State Railways. As already mentioned, since March 1919 Arthur had been working as a filer at the Pasila depot in Helsinki, but the filer's job was not an official state post and was not even permanent.

Many state servants who were dismissed on disciplinary grounds during or after the Civil War were not as lucky as Arthur. Notes in a copy of his pension card, included as a supporting document of his application in 1947, may indicate why Arthur chose to apply for compensation. It seems that Arthur "was taken back into employment. According to the president's letter from 8 May 1920 [he] was entitled to rewards and pension as a filer and *ritsaaja*".[45] Additionally Arthur had been on a "leave of absence [from] 1.3.18 [to] 1.4.25" and had been "dismissed for seven years and one month". Arthur's pension entitlement had clearly been reduced as a result of the disciplinary action taken against him in 1918.[46]

However, it had been evident as early as July 1918 that Arthur had not taken any part in the politics of the time. By granting the pardon, the president could restore Arthur's merits to him and thus incidentally provide him with grounds to apply for compensation some years later (compensation was not offered until 1947). But did the pardon really restore accrued merits and privileges to those who had been dismissed?

The individual pardoning of dismissed railway servants was largely accepted as a fair measure in the 1920s, but these pardons were also criticized by some, particularly those on the right. One can argue that a pardon had some effect on state authorities, as it could ease an individual's return to work. One pointsman, for example, was able to resume his work for the state railways as early as October 1919, after he had been pardoned on 29 August 1919.[47] Of course, this pointsman and Arthur were not the only dismissed state employees whom President Ståhlberg

---

45 "Ritsaaja" means the same as "piirrottaja"; its English equivalent might be "draughtsman".
46 KA, VVM i, Ejc:1 1947–49, petition E.1196, received in July 1947. The disciplinary dismissal of Arthur can certainly be criticized. When the Russian revolution broke out, Finnish authorities had ordered state employees to remain and to protect the property owned by the Finnish State in Russia. The letter of recommendation that Arthur received was the evidence of his loyalty in carrying out these orders. KA, VVM i Ejc:24, Committee reports.
47 See E.249, received in June 1947. The president had "allowed B to re-enter to the railways on [the grounds of] mercy" on 29 August 1919. B had "returned to serve the state" on 16 October 1919.

pardoned during his presidency. Of the sixty applications (submitted in 1947) that I examined, seven included some annotations of pardon. In two cases the request for a pardon was rejected in August 1919[48], and in five cases the plea was approved. These pardons were granted in August 1919 (2), in September of the same year; in May 1920; in April 1923; and in April 1924.[49]

There is good reason to argue that in 1918 most disciplinary dismissals of Finnish State Railways employees were part of a political purge. Many of those who had served in the area that was now governed by the Russians did not return to Finland in 1918. If these individuals had begun "to serve the foreign power", there would have been grounds for dismissal. Some of them did not return until three years after the first section (St. Petersburg–Valkeasaari) had been handed over to the Russian authorities.[50] The Finnish authorities had grounds to ask "why now?" in such cases. At the same time, many of these dismissals may have served the purpose of moderating and easing the difficult financial situation faced by the new Finnish state (and the Finnish State Railways). The economic recession of 1917–1918 also exacerbated the hardship and consequences of the Civil War. In such circumstances individual pardons were one of the measures that the president could employ; but was it enough, especially after the establishment of the special tribunals and a superior tribunal to rule on the alleged crimes of tens of thousands of rebels (who in the summer of 1918 had been detained in pre-trial custody)?

Presidential Pardons in 1919

On 1 August 1919, shortly after Ståhlberg was elected the first President of Finland in July, the first pardon applications were forwarded to him

---

48 See E.1015 and E.924, both received in July 1947. There was a short note in the file: "29/8-19 the plea for pardon rejected".
49 See E.249, E.245, E.365, received in June 1947, and E.1400, E.1196, received in July 1947. There were notes such as "27/9-19 pardoned by restoring merits and privileges of office" or "by the letter of 16/4-24 entitled to enter extraordinary employment in the State Railways".
50 VVM i, Eja:2, no. 101–225 in 1933–1934.

by the Ministry of Justice. The *very first plea for a pardon* came from a railway employee who had served in Vyborg. He asked that by *mercy and grace* the president would grant him a pardon and that he would be allowed to re-enter state service, despite the fact that he had been dismissed on disciplinary grounds during the Civil War. Rather than being restored to his former office, he was granted a pardon that restored his right and privileges (merits) if, in the future, he re-entered the service of the state.

In order to find out how the first president exercised the power to pardon, I have examined the first batch of applications for pardons from August 1919 (table 1) and all pleas processed that year (table 2).

Tab. 1: Pardon applications processed by President Ståhlberg in August 1919[51]

Submission from the Minister of Justice received	Pardons granted to railway servants	Rejected pleas from railway servants	Total number of applications from railway servants	Total number of other petitioners (i.e. not railway servants)
1 Aug 1919	13	8	21	0
8 Aug 1919	12	12	24	1
15 Aug 1919	10	13	23	2
22 Aug 1919	3	3	6	7
29 Aug 1919	8	7	15	4
Total	46	43	89	14

As can be seen above, 103 petitions for pardon were processed in August 1919. Eighty-nine dismissed railway workers forwarded pleas and 46 were pardoned by the president; during the same period 14 people applied for their criminal offences to be pardoned (of whom only two were successful[52]). Charges included such offences as manslaughter, forgery, embezzlement, incitement to commit murder, violations of foodstuff regulations and concealment of illegally obtained goods. The number

---

51 Oikeusministeriön arkisto (OM), Tasavallan Presidentin esittelyt, 1919.
52 They were members of parliament and released on parole on the grounds of mercy. For more details, see OM, Tasavallan Presidentin esittelyt, 15 August 1919.

of pleas for pardon from August to December can be seen in table 2. Although the first pardons seem to suggest a clear tendency, we should be wary of assuming that this provides the whole answer to the question of how the first president exercised his power of pardon.

Tab. 2: Pardon applications processed by President Ståhlberg in August–December 1919 (by month)[53]

	Petitioners who were dismissed railway servants	Petitioners who had committed criminal offences
August	89	14
September	42	0
October	89	21 + list
November	63	11 + list
December	16	15
Total number	299	61 + lists*.

The figures in table 2 indicate differences between disciplinary proceedings and criminal procedure, at that time. They also reveal difficulties in the treatment of "Reds". Political crimes (such as high treason; incitement to commit high treason; and aiding and abetting in high treason) and the forfeiture of civil rights as a collateral sanction were matters that fell under the jurisdiction of the special tribunals. Appeals relating to these issues were to be addressed to the Superior Tribunal for Political Offences rather than to the president. If such an appeal were addressed to the president as a plea or application for pardon, the Supreme Court of Finland would inform the president that the Special Superior Tribunal had jurisdiction over the matter and that the appeal was not within the competence of the presidential pardon. The Supreme Court based its interpretation of procedure on the aforementioned parliamentary act of 29 May 1918 that established the special tribunals. Accordingly,

---

53   KA, OM, Tasavallan Presidentin esittelyt, 1919.
*   If a person on the list for a partial pardon had died before the recommendation was brought before the president, another individual took his place and was pardoned instead (the first list was missing, seven persons on the second list). See Tasavallan Presidentin esittelyt, 31 October 1919.

the president dismissed such appeals from 1 August 1919 until 1 June 1920.[54] By the end of December 1919, Ståhlberg had ruled on 299 pleas forwarded by dismissed railway servants (164 were approved and 135 rejected). Sixty-one pleas were received from individuals who had committed criminal offences (of these twenty-two were approved and thirty-nine rejected). Pardons granted by the president were usually mitigations, in other words reduction of fixed-term sentences or release on parole.[55] So was President Ståhlberg the only authority that granted pardons to state servants who had been dismissed on disciplinary grounds?

In order to answer this question one needs to examine how Regent Mannerheim exercised his royal prerogative of pardon. As mentioned earlier, the first pleas from those dismissed on disciplinary grounds were received on 7 December 1918. During the period from 25 January to 10 July 1919, Regent Mannerheim granted sixty-five pardons: of these, thirty-nine were disciplinary dismissals;[56] the rest were criminal offences of various kinds, some of which had been committed whilst serving in the military. During the period of interregnum there was no proper constitution in place and so, as regent, Mannerheim used the imperial prerogative of pardon, which even allowed the mitigation of fixed-term sentences imposed by special tribunals (an incitement to commit high treason)[57] and additionally, the power of abolition.[58] The power of pardon wielded by Ståhlberg under the new Constitution Act was no longer an imperial prerogative, as it was restricted.

---

54 The special tribunals were in operation until 1 June 1920, although they were abolished by Act 39 passed in 1919. For example, see copy files 127–131, 22 January 1920, KKO Da:3 1920.
55 OM, Tasavallan Presidentin esittelyt, 1919.
56 Of these thirty-five were removed from office, three were lowered in rank and one was cautioned. The Supreme Court did not favour pardons in thirteen cases, yet pardons were granted. Korkein oikeus, KKO (The Supreme Court of Finland), Taltiot Dm:2 1919.
57 Mannerheim pardoned four individuals by releasing them on parole. At the same time their collateral sanctions, the forfeiture of civil rights, were also removed. The original penalties were for eight years in penitentiary and subsequent loss of civil rights for five or six years. KKO Taltiot Dm:2 1919.
58 In the case of Mag. Phil. Karl Harald Wiik, the investigation "concerning a complicity in the popular uprising 1918" was abolished in March 1919. KKO Taltiot Dm:2 1919. See also Erkki Tuomioja, *K. H. Wiik Puoluesihteeri ja oppositiososialisti Elämäkerta osa 2 1918–1946* (Helsinki 1982), pp. 23–24, 32.

Individual pardons or amnesty?

The Council of State appointed a special committee in September 1921 to establish the facts behind the disciplinary dismissals of state servants in 1918. I have not yet found the original committee report, but part of its contents can be found in parliamentary documents from 1923. Almost two thousand (1,907) railway officials were subjected to disciplinary proceedings in 1918. Of this total, 881 were dismissed on disciplinary grounds, 24 were demoted, and 802 were cautioned. Less than six hundred (538) individuals were declared not guilty during the proceedings. In the postal service, 186 employees were dismissed (148 of whom were permanent employees and 38 who were "extraordinary" appointments). Within the prison administration, 64 workers lost their jobs as a result of disciplinary procedures. Only three telegraphers were dismissed, while eight were demoted. In addition to the above figures, around thirty railway servants appointed to the St. Petersburg–Valkeasaari district were dismissed by a special ruling of the Board of Administration of the Finnish State Railways. By June 1923, only 180 of the railway servants, and 56 of their counterparts from the postal service, had re-entered state employment. Between 1 August 1919 and December 1923 Ståhlberg had granted 380 pardons to state servants and rejected 287 pleas.[59] My own estimate, based on the documents I have consulted during my research, is that only 240 of those dismissed employees who had been pardoned were able to re-enter the state service by the end of 1923. Thus there was a need for some kind of political action in 1923: either for new individual pardons to be granted or for parliament to grant an amnesty. A third alternative would have been to ignore the whole matter.

Parliament had succeeded in achieving a level of mutual understanding between the different parties and issued an amnesty in January 1920 to mitigate the consequences of the Civil War. Many leading conservatives supported the amnesty as *a fair step*, as did the Supreme Court.[60]

---

59 See Hallituksen esitys, HE 35/1923vp (the Government Bill), p. 1, and Pöytäkirjat 1923 vp (Parliamentary Session Protocol), pp. 896–898.
60 HE 35/1923vp, p. 3–4, the statement from the Supreme Court, dated 13 April 1923.

However, the new amnesty law[61] did not offer any subjective rights to former state servants, only the entitlement to accrued merit after a new position had been offered. Because of this, the amnesty process was a recurrent topic in budget proceedings from 1924 onwards.[62]

The individual pardons granted by President Ståhlberg before the amnesty law came into force were later criticized. In the 1930s Veli Merikoski, a legal scholar, stated that the many pardons granted by Ståhlberg in disciplinary cases between 1919 and 1923 should be regarded as pure letters of recommendation and not *de facto* pardons, because the president had acted like *a referee*.[63] Merikoski made no mention of the pardons granted by the regent. Most of the pardons issued were supported by the Supreme Court, even under the new constitution and after the election of the president. The first supportive statements from the Supreme Court were based on the fact that the St. Petersburg–Valkeasaari railway section and the Finnish Station (in St. Petersburg) were now governed by the Russians, not by the Finns. State servants could not to be blamed for this change of circumstances. In addition, many statements took a pragmatic view: "why not [pardon] if the position is still vacant". In cases of negative statements the Supreme Court might simply point out that the individual "had promoted the rebellious movement by driving an engine". As printed forms replaced the handwritten reports, statements became shorter: either stating "favoured the granting of a pardon" or "no reason to grant any concessions".[64] Were these individual concessions granted by the president actually mere recommendations rather than being *de facto* pardons?

The use of pardons in disciplinary cases can be seen as a measure intended to control both the former actions and the future behaviour of railway servants who had continued to work at stations, in depots and on railway lines during the Civil War in 1918. One way of assessing the various interpretations attached to the use of presidential pardons in disciplinary cases would be to examine the locations in which railway

---

61 See Laki kurinpidollisesti tuomittujen valtion virka- ja palvelusmiesten armahtamisesta 21/1924.
62 See, for example, Pöytäkirjat 1926 vp (Parliamentary Session Protocols in 1926) on budget proceedings.
63 For details, see Veli Merikoski, *Erivapauden käsite* (SLY no. 7; Helsinki, 1936), pp. 68–70, 74.
64 For details, see KKO Taltiot Dm: 2 1919.

servants had served during the war. Unfortunately, some of this information is still missing. However, almost all of the pardons granted by the regent and the president suggest that some official districts were regarded as more suitable or more disloyal than others. Additionally there were also scores of state servants about whom the superior authorities knew nothing, regardless of how they had acted.

Regent Mannerheim did not grant many pardons to railway servants involved in disciplinary cases during his short regency in 1919. Of the thirty-nine pardons Mannerheim issued, six were granted to employees who had worked in St. Petersburg (station or depot); the Supreme Court were in favour in five of these cases. Those who had worked at Galitsina and Kuokkala stations were pardoned (two in each case); however, in these cases the Supreme Court saw no reason to make concessions. All three individuals who had served in Helsinki Station or Pasila Depot were pardoned in spring 1919. The Maaskola Depot in Vyborg seemed to be a "suitable" place, although only one person was pardoned. However, Kyrö and Hyvinkää in the Finnish territory and the twelfth section were not seen as "suitable" by the Supreme Court: the court did not favour any of the five pardons granted by the regent.

In 1919 President Ståhlberg pardoned 164 dismissed railway servants and rejected the applications of 135 others. Of those who had worked in St. Petersburg, fourteen applications were approved and nine rejected; the Supreme Court favoured only nine of these. Twenty-five pleas were also received from those posted in Vyborg (both at the station and at the depot): seventeen were pardoned and eight rejected (the Supreme Court had favoured only ten of them). Significantly, both the station and the depot in Tampere seem to have been regarded as "unsuitable". As discussed earlier, the Battle of Tampere was one of the turning points in the Civil War. Of the twenty-three dismissed employees who had worked in Tampere, only four individuals were pardoned and favoured by the Supreme Court. It seems that the station in Helsinki was less "suitable" than the Pasila Depot. The president had received nineteen pleas for a pardon from Helsinki: he approved thirteen and rejected six of them, but the Supreme Court had favoured only seven. However, all of the ten pleas from former Pasila Depot workers were approved; interestingly, only three of these were favoured by the Supreme Court. Both the president and the Supreme Court clearly regarded Lahti and Seinäjoki as "unsuitable" stations or depots: all applications for pardons (four from each) were rejected.

The above examples can be found in the (ministerial) presentations or recommendations brought before the regent or the president in 1919. They illuminate one aspect of the prevailing policy of the time. Without going into further details here, it seems that many railway stations and depots on the trunk line Helsinki–(Riihimäki)–St. Petersburg were often regarded as unsuitable or later even disloyal. The areas to the east of Vyborg and Valkeasaari were also under suspicion; many railway employees from these districts did not return to Finland until the Peace Treaty of Tartu (between Finland and Soviet Russia) was signed in 1920.

Conclusions

In my introduction I asked why in 1919 pardons had been granted to scores of former state employees, rather than to criminal offenders. I would argue that the power of individual pardons was used as a means of exerting control over those state servants whose political loyalty was deemed questionable during and after the Civil War. In the research I examined sixty letters of outstanding claims submitted to a special board of the Ministry of Finance in 1947, along with the protocols of presentations made to the regent and the president and copied files from the Supreme Court of Finland in 1919.

Presidential pardons can generally serve a number of purposes: to mitigate overly harsh punishments when laws are old fashioned or inelastic; to forgive those who have paid their debt to society; and to unite a nation that has been divided by war. However, individual pardons can also be used as controlling measures. The first two uses of pardons can easily be understood as part of penal policy, but an attempt to unite a nation seems to be a largely political aim – functional rather than legal. However, one can argue that from 1919 one dimension of the presidential pardon was the way it was used to unite and control; the power to pardon was often exercised as a means of political discretion. Since the beginning of 1918, at least 2,750 cases concerning state employees were settled through disciplinary proceedings; of this total around 1,130 individuals were removed from office and 538 cases were acquitted. In majority of cases the cause of dismissal was "disloyalty". One petitioner, for example, described how his superior had told him that although he (the petitioner) had previously been "a person whom both we here and the superiors there have trusted, from now on you do not even enjoy my confidence, because you served the illegal government."[65]

Both engine driver Arthur and his colleague who was held in custody in Vyborg were found to have been loyal; yet it had to be proved through pardoning proceedings that they had "earned" the right to re-enter office. Both men had returned to Finland as soon as it was possible for them to travel (given the violent circumstances of the time), but they had already been dismissed in March 1918. There is good reason to argue that in 1918 most disciplinary dismissals of Finnish State Railways employees were part of the political purge. However, many of those who had served in the area that was now governed by the Russians did not return to Finland in 1918. Thus if these individuals had began "to serve the foreign power", there would have been grounds for dismissal. Some of them did not return until three years after the first section (St. Petersburg–Valkeasaari) had been handed over to the Russian authorities. There was good reason to ask, why did they choose to return now? At the same time, many of these dismissals may have served the purpose of easing the difficult financial situation faced by the new Finnish state (and the Finnish State Railways).

To answer the second question, yes, there was violence and terror on both sides in 1918. However, since the act of 29 May 1918, political crimes (such as high treason; incitement to commit high treason; and aiding and abetting in high treason) and the forfeiture of civil rights as a sanction were matters that fell under the jurisdiction of the special tribunals. Appeals relating to these issues were to be addressed to the Superior Tribunal for Political Offences rather than to the president. If

65 See E.1400 (30.7.1947).

such an appeal were, in error, addressed to the president, the Supreme Court of Finland would inform him that the appeal did not fall within the jurisdiction of the presidential pardon. Ståhlberg dismissed such appeals until the tribunals were abolished in 1 June 1920.

The forfeiture of civil rights was used as an effective collateral sanction after the Civil War. In spite of the general amnesties that were granted from 1918 to 1924, forfeiture of civil rights along with individual pardons for those who had been subjected to disciplinary proceedings provided the means of exerting control over thousands of citizens for years. Although collateral sanction was regulated in the Criminal Code from 1889 until 1969[66] (when it was abrogated), the content of collateral sanction was not to be found in the code itself but in many different parliamentary acts and degrees. This type of sanction could secure public order and at the same time prevent a convicted person from leading a normal life.

The individual pardoning of dismissed railway servants was largely accepted as a fair measure in the 1920s, but these pardons were also widely criticized. These pardons had some effect on state authorities, as in some cases they could ease an individual's return to work. During his regency, Mannerheim granted around sixty-five pardons; thirty-nine of these were disciplinary dismissals and the rest were offences of various kinds (some of which had been committed whilst in military service). In six cases pardons were granted to individuals who had worked in St. Petersburg (either at the station or the depot); the Supreme Court had favoured five of them. The use of the imperial prerogative of pardon was possible because of the interregnum; this enabled the mitigation of fixed-term sentences imposed by Special Tribunals. The pardoning power wielded by president under the new Constitution Act was more restricted. In spite of this, during the first three and a half years of his presidency Ståhlberg granted 380 pardons to dismissed state servants and rejected 287 similar pleas. Of these 164 had already been pardoned and 135 had been rejected by 1919. The president received twenty-five applications from workers who had served in St. Petersburg; fourteen

---

66 For more details, see, for example, HE 51/1945, p. 3, and HE 73/1968 (Government Bills), pp. 1–2.

of these were approved and nine rejected (although the Supreme Court favoured only nine cases).

Although these presidential pardons were later criticized, most were supported by the Supreme Court in 1919. The first supportive statements from the Supreme Court were based on the fact that the St. Petersburg–Valkeasaari railway section and the Finnish Station (in St. Petersburg) were now governed by the Russians, not by the Finns. State servants could not to be blamed for this change of circumstances. In addition, the court often merely stated "why not [pardon] if the position is still vacant". However, in cases of negative statements the Supreme Court might simply point out that the individual "had promoted the rebellious movement by driving an engine". As printed forms replaced the handwritten reports, statements became shorter. They would either state that they "favoured the granting of a pardon" or saw "no reason to grant any concessions".

My own estimate is that only 240 of the dismissed and pardoned individuals were able to re-enter the service of the Finnish State by the end of 1923. Although presidential pardons were largely accepted, by 1923 further political decisions had to be taken. Either new individual pardons had to be issued or parliament would have to grant an amnesty (the third alternative would have been to ignore the whole matter). The already numerous applications for pardons of disciplinary cases increased significantly as those who were convicted by the special tribunals began to appeal to the president for mercy. In the end, a general amnesty of disciplinary cases was issued in 1924. However, the new amnesty law did not give former railway servants any subjective rights: only entitlement to old merit after a new position was offered. Therefore, this amnesty process remained a recurrent topic in budget proceedings in parliament from 1924 onwards.

Sources

ARCHIVAL SOURCES

The National Archives of Finland
Oikeusministeriön arkisto (OM, Ministry of Justice), Pöytäkirjat, Esittelyt Valtionhoitajalle ja Tasavallan Presidentin esittelyt, 1919.
Korkein oikeus (Supreme Court of Finland), Taltiot Dm, 1919–1920.
Valtiovarainministeriön arkisto I (Ministry of Finance), Erinäiset korvaushakemukset / Vuonna 1918 kurinpidollisesti erotetut rautatieläiset, korvaushakemukset, 1947–49.
University of Eastern Finland Library
Valtiopäiväasiakirjat (Parliament of Finland Acts), 1923 vp & 1926 vp.

LITERATURE

Dorris, Jonathan Truman 1953: *Pardon and Amnesty under Lincoln and Johnson: The Restoration of the Confederates to Their Rights and Privileges, 1861–1898.* The University of North Carolina Press.
Engman, Max 2004: *Pietarin-suomalaiset.* WSOY, Helsinki.
Hurnard, Naomi D. 1969: *The King's Pardon for Homicide before A.D. 1307.* Clarendon Press, Oxford.
Kekkonen, Jukka 1991: *Laillisuuden haaksirikko Rikosoikeudenkäyttö Suomessa vuonna 1918.* Lakimiesliiton Kustannus, Helsinki.
Kesserling, K. J. 2007: *Mercy and Authority in the Tudor State.* Cambridge University Press.
Kotkas, Toomas 2003: *"Suosiosta ja armosta" Tutkimus armahdusoikeuden historiasta autonomian ajan Suomessa.* Finnish Lawyers' Society, Helsinki.
Kotkas, Toomas 2007: Pardoning in Nineteenth-Century Finland At the Interface of Early Modern and Modern Criminal Law – *Rechtsgeschicte*, 10 / 2007, pp.152–168.
Kulla, Heikki 1980: *Hallintolainkäyttö ja hallinto Tutkimus korkeimman hallinto-oikeuden toimivallan määräytymisen oikeushistoriallisesta taustasta.* Finnish Lawyers' Society, Helsinki.
Merikoski, Veli 1936: *Erivapauden käsite.* Otava, Helsinki.
Paavolainen, Jaakko 1967: *Poliittiset väkivaltaisuudet Suomessa 1918, osa I.* Tammi, Helsinki.
Paavolainen, Jaakko 1967: *Poliittiset väkivaltaisuudet Suomessa 1918, osa II.* Tammi, Helsinki.
Ståhlberg, Kaarlo Juho 1913: *Suomen hallinto-oikeus. Yleinen osa.* Otava, Helsinki.
Tuomioja, Erkki 1982: *K. H. Wiik Puoluesihteeri ja oppositiososialisti Elämäkerta, osa 2 1918–1946.* Tammi, Helsinki.
Valtionrautatiet 1912–1937. Suomen rautateiden 75-vuotispäiväksi julkaissut Rautatiehallitus, osa I, Yleisesitys valtionrautateiden kehityksestä; Valtioneuvoston kirjapaino, Helsinki 1937.
Viljanen, Veli-Pekka 1986: *Kansalaisen yleiset oikeudet Tutkimus suomalaisen perusoikeuskäsityksen muotoutumisesta autonomiankaudella ja itsenäisyyden ensi vuosina.* [University of Turku] Åbo Academi, Turku.
Ylikangas, Heikki 1993: *Tie Tampereelle: dokumentoitu kuvaus Tampereen antautumiseen johtaneista sotatapahtumista Suomen sisällissodassa 1918.* WSOY, Helsinki.

Abstract

Satu Lidman & Olli Matikainen (eds.)

Morality, Crime and Social Control in Europe 1500–1900

A wide range of regulated practices and institutions that mediate action between humans can be treated as manifestations or forces of social control. In this volume, family, local courts, parish meetings, prisons, the army and the gallows are discussed, to name a few. A common feature of all these institutions is the way in which they develop a set of practices and rituals, some of which are enduring and seemingly unchanging, some in a state of transition or subjected to challenges, and others "new" and in the process of formation.

On the one hand, narrower definition of social control reserves the concept primarily for analysing planned responses to crime and deviance, which in practice emphasizes the role of state organizations. On the other hand, all members of society and all institutions serve social control functions. In the history research, analysing forms of social control as a means of dealing with conflicts has become a central idea. In this volume, both perspectives – the efforts of authorities and the "social control from below" – are present. The authors of the collection offer a close reading of a wide variety of primary sources including court records, jurisprudence and legislation as well as newspapers, administrative sources and folklore.

Combined with morality and crime, social control is one of the key terms assisting in understanding the shared European past. Therefore, the articles span a long time from the beginning of the early modern period up to the twentieth century, and a wide geographical spread from various places in Finland and other Nordic countries to continental Europe and the British Isles.

List of contributors

Virpi Anttonen, Licenciate of Administrative Sciences (Const. Law), University of Eastern Finland, is finishing her doctoral theses on power of pardon as an elemental part of historic constitutions. Her research focuses particularly on Finland in the time period of 1917–1921.

Martin Bergman, Dr. Th. and ordained in the Church of Sweden, works as a parish priest in Vimmerby, Sweden. His doctoral thesis in ecclesiastical history, *Dödsstraffet, kyrkan och staten i Sverige från 1700-tal till 1900-tal* (Capital punishment, church and state in Sweden between the 1700's and the 1900's), was presented in 1996 at the University of Lund. In his articles he has emphasized international perspectives and comparisons in the history of capital punishment.

Clive Emsley is Professor Emeritus of History at the Open University, UK. Among his most recent publications are: *Crime, Police and Penal Policy: European Experiences 1750–1940* (Oxford 2007), *The Great British Bobby: A History of British Policing from the 18th Century to the Present* (London 2009), and *Soldier, Sailor, Beggarman, Thief: Crime and the British Armed Services since 1914* (Oxford 2013).

Suki Haider, Dr. Soc. Sc., is an Associate Lecturer at the Open University, UK. She completed her doctoral thesis *Female Petty Crime in Dundee, 1865–1925: Alcohol, Prostitution and Recidivism in a Scottish City* at the University of St Andrews in 2013. After that she has published an article: *A Notable Absence of Hostility?: Attitudes Towards the Irish in Dundee 1865–1925* (History Studies 2007).

Teemu Keskisarja, Dr. Phil., is Adjunct Professor (History of Finland and Nordic Countries) at the University of Helsinki, Finland. He has published several books about criminal history and military history in Finnish.

Sofia Kotilainen, Dr. Phil, M. Soc. Sci and Adjunct Professor (Finnish History), is a Senior Researcher and Academy of Finland post-doctoral researcher in the Department of History and Ethnology at the University of Jyväskylä, Finland. She has studied the long-term cultural, family and gender history of Finnish naming practices, intangible capital in social relations and the history of literacy and education (c. 1800–1950). Her publications include *An early spokesman for a vernacular literature: Matti Taipale, farmer, librarian and a promoter of Finnish culture in nineteenth-century Finland* (Scandinavica 2012) and *The Genealogy of Personal Names: towards a more productive method in historical onomastics* (Scandinavian Journal of History 2011). She is also a member of the board in the Genealogical Society of Finland.

Satu Lidman, Dr. Phil. and Adjunct Professor (History of Criminal Law), has been teaching legal history at the University of Turku since 2010. Her doctoral theses *Zum Spektakel und Abscheu. Schand- und Ehrenstrafen als Mittel öffentlicher Disziplinierung in München um 1600* (Frankfurt a. M. 2008) focused on the analyses of shaming punishments in the early modern Duchy of Bavaria. She has published several articles and, in 2011, a history of shame entitled *Häpeä! Nöyryyttämisen ja häpeämisen jäljillä* (Shame! On the Tracks of Humiliation and Embarrassment). Her research interests include history of sexuality and crime as well as historical continuities in issues related to gender and violence. She is a member of the editorial board of the series Crossing Boundaries (Turku Centre for Medieval and Early Modern Studies & Amsterdam University Press).

Jonas Liliequist is Professor of History at the Umeå University, Sweden. He has published widely on history of sexuality, violence, gender and emotions, most recently: *From Honour to Virtue: The Shifting Social Log-*

ics of Masculinity and Honour in Early Modern Sweden (in *Honour, Violence and Emotion* edit. Carolyn Strange, Bloomsbury 2014). He is also the editor of *A History of Emotions 1200–1800* (Pickering & Chatto 2012) and affiliated to the Centre of Excellence for The History of Emotions at the University of Western Australia.

Tomás Mantecón is Professor of Early Modern History (Social and Cultural History) at the University of Cantabria, Spain. His research fields include history of violence, (infra)justice and social control in the 17th and 18th centuries. He has published several books in Spanish on social discipline, popular religion, conflicts, rural communities and counter-Reformation. His articles include *Pardon in Anthropology and History* (Limoges 1999), *Crimes, Punishment and Reform in Europe* (Westport 2003), *History of Social Control* (Ohio UP 2004), *L'erreur judiciaire. De Jeanne d'Arc à Roland Agret* (París 2004), and *Histoire de l'homicide en Europe. De la fin du Moyen Âge à nous jours* (Paris 2009).

Olli Matikainen, Dr. Phil. and Adjunct Professor (Finnish History), is a Senior Researcher in Finnish History in the Department of History and Ethnology at the University of Jyväskylä, Finland. In addition to articles on various themes in Finnish social history, he has published a doctoral theses *Verenperijät* (Recovering Blood: Violence and Community in the Age of Transition, Finnish Literature Society 2002) and a monograph *Akateemisia kansalaisia ja maakunnan toivoja* (Academic Citizen and Transition of Society in Finland 1945–1970) in 2005. Matikainen is co-author in Anssi Halmesvirta (edit.): *Land unter dem Nordlicht. Eine Kulturgeschichte Finnlands* (Primus Verlag 2013).

Päivi Pukero, Dr. Phil., works as a Career Counsellor in the City of Tornio (Putaa comprehensive school), Finland. Since 2003 she has also been a teacher in basic studies of history at the University of Eastern Finland. Her doctoral theses *"Epämääräisestä elämästä Kruunun haltuun". Irtolaisuuden ja huono-osaisuuden kontrolli Itä-Suomessa 1860–1885* (Policing of Vagrants and the Poor in Eastern Finland from 1860 to 1885) was published in 2009.

Päivi Räisänen-Schröder, Dr. Phil., received her PhD in Medieval and Early Modern History at the University of Göttingen, Germany. She is currently a post-doctoral fellow at the University of Helsinki, Department for Church history. Her research interests include social and cultural history of religion, religious nonconformity, and everyday life as well as history of gender, medicine and healing. In addition to many articles she has published the monograph *Ketzer im Dorf. Visitationsverfahren, Täuferbekämpfung und lokale Handlungsmuster im frühneuzeitlichen Württemberg* (Konstanz 2011).

Pasi Saarimäki, Dr. Phil., is post-doctoral researcher in Finnish history, Department of History and ethnology at the University of Jyväskylä, Finland. His research interests include illegitimacy, marriage and divorce in Finland in the late 19th and early 20th centuries. His doctoral theses *Naimisen normit, käytännöt ja konfliktit. Esiaviollinen ja aviollinen seksuaalisuus 1800-luvun lopun keskisuomalaisella maaseudulla* (The norms, practices and conflicts of sex and marriage. Premarital and marital sexual activity in rural Central Finland in the late nineteenth century) was published in 2010. He has also co-edited an anthology *Lapsi matkalla maailmaan. Historiallisia ja kulttuurisia näkökulmia syntymään* (A child's journey into the world. Historical and cultural perspectives of the birth), published in 2012.

Ella Viitaniemi, M. A., is a doctoral student at the School of Social Sciences and Humanities (History) at the University of Tampere, Finland. Her doctoral thesis on the church building project of Kokemäki parish focuses on the relations between the local parish and the central authorities and the change of the political culture in the late 18th century Finland. Additionally, she has published articles of the development of the parish administration and legislation for public buildings in the Swedish realm.

Index

A
Abuse 12, 20– 22, 24–28, 30–31, 36, 41, 91–92, 201, 287, 323
Adamsson (Johan) 12, 75–84
Adultery, adulterous 13, 107–109, 115, 118–123
Alms-house 208–209, 211–215, 217, 219, 221–222
Amnesty 326, 336, 342–343, 348
Amsterdam 266–270
Anabaptism, Anabaptist 127, 140–142, 144–145, 147
Apology, apologize 19, 22, 27, 39 (see also public apology)
Aristocracy, aristocratic 8, 87–88, 91, 95–96, 101, 292
Assault (assault and abuse, verbal assault, physical assault etc.) 11, 19, 21, 25, 28, 33, 40, 78, 199, 202, 204, 233–235, 245, 276 (see also parental abuse)

B
Banish 95, 98, 102, 133
Bavaria (Dutchy of), Bavarian 10, 87–89, 92, 94, 97–98, 100, 103
Beccaria (Cesare) 79, 209
Belgium 190, 196, 299, 313
Belin (Thure) 162–163, 167, 169–170, 173–175, 177
Berndtsdotter (Johanna) 317
Betrothal, betroth 109, 113, 116–117
Bishop 130–131, 150, 164, 304
Brenz (Johannes) 134
Britain, British 10, 185–186, 188, 190, 192, 194–196, 200–201, 218, 226, 229, 236–239, 248, 260, 282, 299–300, 305–306, 311

C
Capital punishment 19, 21–22, 35, 75–76, 79–81, 83, 266, 268–269, 273, 278, 284, 286–287, 290–291, 293, 310, 314, 316, 324–325 (see also death penalty)

Castigation, castigate 31, 38
Catholic 88, 90–91, 93, 96, 260–262, 282
Ceremony 77, 80, 300
Ceremonial, ceremonious 140, 142, 261–262, 272, 278–279, 283, 286, 300, 305–306
Chaste, chastity 91, 96, 101, 110–111, 250
Chastise, chastisement 22, 31–32, 38, 69
Christian name(s) 44–46, 56, 327
Christie (Nils) 209
Christoph (Duke of Württemberg) 127
Church building 13, 131, 158, 166–167, 172
Church pew 157–158, 163–170
Church visitations 13, 127–130, 142, 146, 150
Civil servant(s) 160, 165–166, 169, 316, 329–331, 336
Civil War (American) 186, 326
Civil War (Finnish) 326–327, 329–330, 332–333, 335, 337–339, 342–345, 347
Closed institution(s) 14, 208–210, 212–213, 216–218, 220–222
Cohen (Stanley) 8–9, 209
Collective biography, collective biographical data 49–50, 54
Concubinage, concubine(s) 88, 93–94, 98, 103
Confession(s) 116–117, 119, 141–142, 231, 282, 307, 310
Confessional, confessionalization 88–89, 95, 97, 100, 279, 283–286, 288, 292
Correction(al) 208–209, 212, 215, 218, 221
Crime rate(s), homicide rate(s) 14, 81–82, 186, 239, 269, 288, 291–292
Crime record(s), criminal record(s) 191, 227, 235, 247
Criminal law 11, 22, 24, 76, 81, 108, 113, 118, 315, 325, 331, 347
Criminal justice 12, 14, 87–88, 190, 196, 198, 201, 226–227, 248, 250, 290
Criminality 13–14, 79, 82, 89, 103, 194, 196, 200, 222, 225–226, 229, 252, 288

Criminalize, criminalization 21–22, 32, 88, 101, 103, 188, 259, 284
Culture(s) of suffering 260, 278–279, 282, 288, 292–293

D

Death penalty 14, 21–22, 40–41, 76, 79–81, 118, 209, 276, 279, 281, 288, 290–291, 304, 316 (see also capital punishment)
Decalogue, ten commandments 21, 23, 37, 145
Deterrent, deterrence 36, 93, 310, 317
Deviance, deviancy, deviant 8, 11, 63, 70, 131, 140, 146, 208–213, 214–216, 218, 220–222
Disciplinary dismissal 333–335, 337–337, 341–342, 346–347
Disciplinary proceedings 326–328, 331–333, 340, 342, 346–347
Discipline 8, 13, 22, 69, 87, 89, 100, 127, 134, 159, 172, 188, 193–194, 196, 221, 259, 262, 284, 291, 334
Dishonour, dishonouring, dishonourable 35, 93–95, 98, 101–102, 272, 317
Divorce 107–109, 115, 118–123
Drunken(ness) 118, 129, 136, 162, 193–195, 207, 211, 227, 231, 241, 244
Dundee 14, 225–247, 249–251

E

Ecclesiastic(al) 94, 107–110, 113, 116–117, 122, 127, 131–132, 134, 138, 142, 317
Elias (Norbert) 209
Engaged, engagement(s) 107–123
England 186, 190–191, 198–199, 201, 204, 207, 212, 214, 218–219, 235, 239, 279, 282, 292, 324–326
Eucharist, Lord's Supper 134, 142, 144
Execution(s), execute 8, 12, 14–15, 22, 76–77, 79–81, 83, 97, 194, 260–262, 266–274, 276, 278, 280–281, 283–293, 299–318, 329, 333
Execution site 260, 262, 266, 272–273, 280, 307, 313–314, 317
Executioner 12, 77, 80, 303, 311
Extramarital 107, 122

F

Family (background, identity, member) 12, 32, 44, 55–57, 63–64, 67, 70, 200
Father (godfather, step-father, grandfather, father-in-law etc.) 19–21, 22, 29–31, 33–41, 44, 50, 57, 66, 68, 78, 89, 93, 108, 112, 116, 138, 160–163, 177, 189–190, 213, 274
Female, femininity 14, 28–31, 65, 90, 94, 98–100, 204, 215, 225–229, 231, 233–237, 239, 242, 245–249, 252, 325
Finland 10, 12–14, 19, 23, 25, 28, 31, 37, 44, 47–48, 53, 58, 75–77, 79–83, 107–108, 117–118, 121–123, 158, 168, 207–208, 210–211, 213–221, 265, 301, 303, 325, 327, 329–331, 334, 336, 338, 340, 345–347
First World War 188, 190–191, 194–196, 198–199, 236
Forced labour 76, 213, 215
Forenames 44, 46, 55, 57–58
Fornication 13, 78, 109, 120, 122–123, 141, 147
Foucault (Michel) 9, 209, 261–262
France, French 56, 149–150, 186–187, 195–196, 201, 207, 260, 271, 274, 286–287, 302, 310–311, 313

G

Gender, gendered 14, 26–29, 40, 45, 54, 57, 97, 163, 215
Germany, German 8, 13, 93, 127–129, 134, 186, 190, 201, 217, 299–300, 304, 306, 309, 315
God's law 21, 279
God's wrath, God's punishment 89, 96, 101, 132, 135
Gränzingerin (Maria) 101–102
Gulf War 185
Gustav III (King of Sweden) 77
Gypsies 208, 215
Göta (royal court) 26, 28

H

Habitual (offenders, thieves, prostitutes) 191, 231, 235

358 INDEX

Hanging 272–273, 280, 283, 299, 314, 324
Harjula alms-house 211–214, 216–217, 219–222
Homicide 41, 75, 80–83, 189, 198, 203, 269, 272, 288–292, 324
Honour 21, 23, 47, 52, 63, 70, 90, 93, 95, 101, 114, 143, 169, 171, 188
Honourable(ness) 51–52, 62, 69, 91, 119, 287, 314
Household(s) 25–26, 30–33, 36, 38, 48, 58, 61, 64, 68, 93–95, 165, 172, 174
Household authority, head of the household, master of the household 31–34, 133
Household work 213, 217, 219
Husband 31–32, 34, 44, 57, 68, 118–120, 163, 200, 274

I
Immoral, immorality 87–89, 92–98, 103, 215, 217, 240, 285, 292
Imprisonment 82, 109, 118, 142, 191, 208, 213, 250, 325, 334–335
Italy, Italian 201, 209, 260, 265, 268, 281–282, 285–286

J
Jurisdiction 35, 87, 100, 103, 193, 336, 340, 346–347

K
Kokemäki (manor house, parish, district court etc.) 157–164, 166–175, 177
Kuopio (province, parish) 210–211, 213, 215–216, 219, 221–222
Kylliälä children's home 211, 213, 220–222

L
Label, labelling 12, 14, 91, 95, 140, 143, 215, 235, 260 (see also stigma)
Larsdotter (Charlotta) 317
Legislation 10, 13, 15, 21, 76, 80–81, 88, 100–101, 107–108, 113, 116–117, 120–122, 307, 309, 315–316, 324–325, 331
Liturgy, liturgical 287, 308, 310

London 79, 193, 196, 230, 244, 248, 260, 267–268, 270, 293, 300–301, 305
Luostanlinna (penal colony) 211, 213, 215, 217–218, 220–222
Luther (Martin) 131
Lutheran (church, reformers, catechism etc.) 21–23, 37, 129, 131, 133, 140, 146

M
Male 28–31, 57, 64–65, 190, 195, 226, 248, 315, 325
Marriage 31, 33, 38, 44, 49, 90–91, 95, 107–110, 112–123, 140, 163, 200, 214, 228
Masculine, masculinity 45, 188
Maximilian (Duke of Bavaria) 94–95, 98
Melanchthon (Philipp) 131
Modernization, modernized, modernity 12, 45, 48, 51, 53, 64, 67, 70, 81, 293
Moral offence(s), moral offender(s) 88–90, 92, 97–98, 101, 103, 129, 134–135, 141, 146
Morality 10, 13, 50, 70, 89, 100, 132, 207, 284
Moral (values, attitudes, standards, control etc.), morals 25, 37, 45, 49–50, 69, 78, 88–90, 93–96, 99–103, 127–135, 146–148, 150, 220, 279, 302, 323
Mother (godmother, stepmother, mother-in-law, grandmother) 12, 19–21, 23, 29–31, 35–36, 40, 78, 108, 115–116, 117, 138, 160–161, 189, 213–214, 315
Motherhood 90, 99
Munich 13, 88–89, 92–94, 96, 99, 101–103
Murder, murderer 12, 21, 41, 76–79, 83, 190, 276–277, 288, 291, 306–309, 312, 326, 329, 339
Månsdotter (Anna) 315

N
Name-calling 43, 45, 47, 51, 61, 63, 69–70
Naming (practices, processes) 43, 45–46, 49–50, 52–54, 57–58, 63–70
Netherlands 291
Newspaper report(s) 212, 214, 238, 241
Nicknames, nicknaming 9, 12, 43–47, 49–50, 52–61, 63–70, 161

Nilsson (Rikus Anders) 19, 28–30, 34–41

P

Pardon, pardoning 15, 103, 149, 265, 317, 323–328, 330–331, 335–348
Parental abuse, abuse of parents 12, 20–22, 24, 26, 28 (see also assault)
Paris 186, 246, 266, 293, 313
Particular subordination 331
Pastoral care 305–306, 310
Peasant, peasantry 29–30, 33, 37, 44–47, 50, 60, 70, 129, 144, 159, 163, 169–170, 173–175, 219
Personal names 43, 46, 49
Pillory 90, 99–100, 102, 325
Pinker (Steven) 11
Police (police chief, policemen, station, reports etc.) 61–62, 172, 185, 191–197, 207, 211, 231, 233–237, 239–240, 242–251, 315
Political culture 158–159, 167–168, 174–176
Political (crime, offence, prisoner) 273–274, 286, 326, 329, 333, 335, 340, 346
Political purge 338, 346
Politics 88, 100–101, 167, 176, 327, 337
Polviander (Anders) 161–163, 177
Poor 14, 81–82, 91, 96, 145, 148, 165, 170, 172, 207, 210–214, 217, 219, 221–222, 230
Poor relief 212–213, 219–222
Pope (pope's justice, authority, sovereignty) 265, 272, 277, 283, 286, 291–292
Porvoo 109–110
Power of pardon 265, 323–327, 336, 340–341
Pregnancy, pregnant 97, 99, 111–112
Premarital 88, 91–92, 95, 97, 99
Preparation (of prisoners, for death, spiritual) 304–307, 316
President, presidential pardon 323, 326–328, 330–331, 335–341, 343–348
Prevention, prevent (crime, immorality, God's wrath etc.) 83, 93, 98, 100, 259, 266, 271, 277, 285–286
Prison(s) 7, 77, 81–82, 102, 185, 208–209, 211–213, 217–218, 221–222, 236, 249, 272, 306, 310, 312–314, 316, 325, 329, 342

Property crime 78, 189, 196–197, 202, 227, 232–233, 250–251
Prostitute, prostitution 14, 88, 91–92, 99–100, 189, 215, 226–251, 284–285
Protestant 90, 96, 127–128, 130, 133, 140, 306
Prussia(n) 186, 306–307, 315–316
Public apology 19, 22
Public execution(s), to publicly execute 8, 15, 79–80, 267–272, 283–284, 286–287, 293, 302, 308, 314
Public punishment 102, 261–262, 270, 272, 292

R

Rape 190, 199–200, 204, 326
Recidivism, recidivist 92, 95, 101, 103, 118, 222, 230, 234, 237, 241, 249–250
Reformation, post-Reformation 13, 21, 35, 88, 127, 129, 131–132, 137, 304
Regulate, regulation(s) 7, 21, 32, 43, 50, 89, 101, 103, 107, 122–123, 136, 139, 146, 158, 168, 210–211, 222, 248, 261, 266, 325–326, 329, 331, 339, 347
Reputation 12, 47, 51–52, 57, 62–63, 68, 70, 96, 99, 101–102, 137, 143, 214, 230
Ritual 7, 15, 27, 94, 100, 262, 274, 285, 299–301, 304, 310
Roma people 213, 215, 222
Rome 265, 267, 270–274, 278, 280–281, 283–293
Russia(n) 76–77, 80–81, 167, 241, 243, 325, 329–331, 336–338, 343, 345–346, 348

S

Salvation 132, 261–262, 279, 302–303, 308–309
Saxony (Electorate of) 131, 305
Schilling (Heinz) 8, 92
Schorndorf (district of) 127, 135–136, 140, 144, 148
Schwenckfeld (Caspar von) 140
Scotland, Scottish 226–227, 235, 237, 246–247, 249, 251, 265
Second World War 192–193, 195–196, 199

Serial killer, serial murderer, serial killings 12, 77–78, 80–81, 83
Sexual behaviour 92, 97–98, 100, 107, 110, 120–122
Sexuality 13, 89–90, 107, 109, 113, 117, 120–123
Shame, shameful 27, 93, 101–102, 317
Shaming 87, 90, 93–94, 97, 100–101, 103, 268
Sibelius (nickname) 61–62
Siberia 76, 80, 218, 325
Soldier(s) 34, 163, 186–188, 190–191, 193–196, 200, 201–202, 230, 242–243
Spierenburg (Pieter) 8–9, 87, 92, 172, 259
Spiritual, spirituality, spiritualization, spiritualist 91, 131, 140, 279, 282, 288, 302–306
Statistic(s), statistical 23–25, 31, 49, 64, 81–82, 186, 194, 198–199, 204, 232–233, 235, 247, 251, 259, 267, 309
Stengrund (Simon) 157–163, 165–167, 169–171, 173–177
Stigma, stigmatize, stigmatization 51, 60, 63, 69, 93, 97, 103, 188 (see also label)
Stockholm 167, 247, 316
St. Petersburg 76, 177, 327–331, 335, 338, 342–348
Stuttgart 127, 132, 134, 148–149
Ståhlberg (Kaarlo Juho, President of Finland) 336–344, 347
Surname(s) 44, 46–47, 58, 61, 66, 160–161
Suspension 332–333
Svea (royal court) 26, 28, 41
Sveaborg (fortress) 77, 81
Sweden, Swedish 12, 19–21, 23–25, 28, 31, 37, 44, 46, 77, 79, 81–83, 107–108, 117, 122, 157, 168, 175, 212, 217, 299–301, 304, 309, 315–317, 325, 331
Switzerland 129, 134

T
Theft 14, 192, 194–197, 226–227, 230, 232–237, 241–247, 250–251, 285
Thieves 227, 229, 231–232, 234, 237, 239, 241–247, 250–251

Tolpo (Nicolaus) 157–158, 162, 164–165, 167, 169–172, 175
Torture 76–77, 81–82, 98, 261–262, 265, 273–274, 276, 278–281, 284, 286–288, 291, 302
Turku 109–110, 159, 161, 164, 167, 169, 172, 216
Tübingen 128, 138

U
Unchaste, unchastity 91, 98, 215

V
Vagrancy, vagrant(s) 14, 110, 121, 146, 207–208, 210–215, 217–218, 221–222, 247, 325–326
Vasa (Gustav, King of Sweden) 21
Veteran(s) 185–186, 189–190, 192, 200
Violence 13, 15, 20, 25, 27–28, 30–31, 36, 39–41, 68, 80, 82–84, 186, 188–190, 195, 197, 200, 202, 239, 263, 266, 269, 277, 292–293, 315, 329, 346
Violence (legal) 263, 266, 278, 291, 292
Violence (against parents, elderly people, in-laws, within family) 11–12, 21–22, 34, 36
Violent crime 82, 185, 197–198
Virgin, virginity 91, 95, 99
Visitation (church visitation, visitation commission) 13, 127–150
Vyborg 211, 213, 219, 222, 330, 339, 344–346

W
War, wartime 13–14, 76, 89, 166–167, 185–201, 218, 236, 247–248, 326–327, 329–330, 332–333, 335, 337–339, 342–345, 347
Whip, whipping 19, 22, 95, 99–100, 102, 259–260, 269, 278
Wife, wives 30–34, 36, 38, 44, 58, 96, 114–115, 118–120, 138–139, 163, 177, 190
Württemberg (Duchy of) 13, 127–138, 142, 146, 149–150

Y
York 237–238, 251

Z
Zwinglian 134.

Å
Åbo (royal court) 23, 26, 28